Certain Sermons or Homilies (1547)
and
*A Homily against Disobedience and
Wilful Rebellion* (1570)

Along with the Book of Common Prayer and the Articles of Religion, the
first book of homilies (1547) is the major legacy of the Edwardian Reformation. Its twelve sermons articulated a doctrinal standard, assisted the
parochial clergy in their preaching, and served the religious establishment
as a means of propaganda. The sermons are plain but sophisticated expressions of the interests of the early protestants in England. They are concerned with not only the primacy of the Bible and the relationship of faith
to good works, but also matters of Christian conduct such as sexual
morality, swearing, the attitude to death, charity, and obedience. Since
they were required reading from most English pulpits these homilies were
probably heard by writers as different as Shakespeare, Spenser, and Donne
and eventually influenced John Wesley in the eighteenth century, and
Samuel Taylor Coleridge and Cardinal Newman in the nineteenth.

The first book of homilies was joined by a second in 1563 and by the
long, polemical homily against rebellion in 1570. The last is at once an
occasional piece, written in the aftermath of the Northern Rebellion of
1569, and a classic apologia for passive nonresistance to appointed authority.

This edition brings together the first book of homilies and the sermon
against rebellion. The introduction traces the development and decline
of interest in the homilies both as aids for preachers and as statements of
reformed doctrine. In addition it analyses the themes, organization, and
styles of the homilies presented. The text preserves the original spelling and
is accompanied by brief explanatory notes and a critical apparatus.

RONALD B. BOND is Associate Professor and Head of the Department
of English, University of Calgary.

Certain Sermons or Homilies (1547)

AND

A Homily against Disobedience and Wilful Rebellion (1570)

A CRITICAL EDITION

RONALD B. BOND

UNIVERSITY OF TORONTO PRESS

Toronto Buffalo London

© University of Toronto Press 1987
Toronto Buffalo London
Printed in Canada

ISBN 0-8020-5719-5

Printed on acid-free paper

Canadian Cataloguing in Publication Data

Main entry under title:

Certain sermons or homilies (1547); and, A homily against disobedience and wilful rebellion (1570)

Includes bibliographical references
ISBN 0-8020-5719-5

1. Church of England – Sermons. 2. Sermons, English – 16th century. 3. England – Church history – 16th century – Sources. 4. Anglican Communion – Sermons. I. Bond, Ronald B., 1946–   . II. Title: A homily against disobedience and wilful rebellion (1570).

BX5133.A1A3 1987   252'.0342   C87-093599-2

55, 233

Publication of this book is made possible by a grant from the Canadian Federation for the Humanities, using funds provided by the Social Sciences and Humanities Research Council of Canada.

To Shirley,

wife and companion in love and charity

Contents

Preface

The purpose of this edition is to make available some important texts of the English Reformation. The first book of homilies (1547) deserves consideration along with the Book of Common Prayer and the Thirty-nine Articles as one of the earliest statements of that Reformation. In fact, because it antedates both of these well-known expressions of the reforming impulse in England, it may claim special attention among the formularies of the Tudor church. I have yoked the first book of homilies with the long *Homily against Disobedience and Wilful Rebellion* (1570) chiefly because the latter's polemical edge throws into relief the less shrill protestantism of the homilies of 1547. One has only to compare the homily occasioned by the Northern Rebellion (1569) with its counterpart from the first book of homilies, 'An Exhortation to Obedience,' to see how rapidly the official Reformation in England advanced.

The first book of homilies consists of twelve sermons that address some of the main concerns of the Reformation. The first homily treats the primacy of the Bible, and it is followed quickly by sermons that treat the relationship of faith to good works. Perhaps because the homilies are aimed, ultimately, at ordinary parishioners, other sermons deal with Christian conduct, discouraging swearing, sexual promiscuity, and the fear of dying, and encouraging charity, obedience, and toleration. The homilies of 1547 do not discuss overtly the truly complex theological problems we associate with the Reformation: they are silent on the subjects of predestination and the mystery of the Eucharist. Since the homilies were to be read regularly, Sunday by Sunday, through the whole country, they can be regarded as attempts to achieve a grass-roots Reformation among humble people essentially indifferent to doctrinal niceties. In a way, then, the homilies published in 1547 are prime examples of English Christian humanism, the goal of which was to spread the best that learning had to offer to the people at large.

But like the later homily that inveighs stridently against rebellion, the homilies of 1547 are also propaganda. One of the aims of my introduction is to reveal how the homilies were pressed into service by authorities in church and state intent upon controlling public opinion. These authorities recognized that the pulpit, if controlled, could be an instrument of public persuasion and a vehicle for moving England toward conformity. Much as modern governments see the press, Tudor and Jacobean governments saw the homilies. As set sermons, which all but a few licensed ministers were compelled to read to their people, the homilies belong to the domain of the 'mass media.' Sociologists might be justified in calling their use 'hegemonic,' for the homilies stood in the way of a 'free pulpit,' as puritans were quick to point out.

I first became interested in the homilies because critics of English Renaissance literature were once particularly fond of referring to them when discussing the 'intellectual climate' surrounding Shakespeare and his contemporaries. This edition does not cast the homilies as background to the literature of the age, though I hope in a companion volume to this edition to address that topic, among others. What should be said, here, however, is that my study indicates that the imposition of the homilies met with dissent and that many of the ideas in them won resistance rather than approval. The hostile reaction to these texts must be considered, if the texts themselves are to function properly in discussions of the 'intellectual climate' of Renaissance England.

For good reason this edition does not capitalize 'protestant,' 'puritan,' 'anglican,' or even 'anabaptist,' a generic rather than a specific term in the sixteenth century. Influenced by Patrick Collinson and other revisionist ecclesiastical historians, I wish to avoid anachronistic labels. I do find evidence to suggest that the first book of homilies attempts to negotiate between extremes, but puritans took their place beside more moderate protestants within the English church. We do well to remember that the anglican church of the sixteenth century preferred Edmund Grindal, a man with puritan proclivities, to the position of archbishop of Canterbury.

It remains for me to express my gratitude to those who have supported my work on the homilies. Professor Denton Fox of the University of Toronto suggested to me long ago that an edition of the sort I have attempted to produce would be worth while. Since then I have received encouragement, in various ways, from Professors William Blissett, Jerry Dees, A.C. Hamilton, William Haugaard, and Arthur Kinney. I wish also to record my thanks to librarians at the British Library, Oxford, Cambridge, the Newberry Library, and, last but by no means least, the University of Calgary, where I have used the 1623 edition of the homilies held by the Special Collections division. My research in these and other libraries has been assisted by grants from the Social Sciences and Humanities Research Council of Canada, which awarded me a leave fellowship to prepare this edition. Publication has been made possible, in part, by a grant from the Endowment Fund of the University of Calgary. I have also benefited from the wisdom and good sense of Mary Baldwin and Prudence Tracy, who have skilfully and tactfully transformed my work from script to disk to print. Were it not for the extraordinary patience and efficiency of Valerie Matwick, friend and typist, that transformation would have been impossible.

Last I thank my family: my parents, my children, Geoffrey and Jennifer, and my wife, Shirley. They have sustained me in what has sometimes seemed a lonely labour.

Abbreviations

AV	*The Holy Bible Containing the Old and New Testaments* (1611; repr Cambridge n d)
CSPD	*Calendar of State Papers, Domestic* ed Robert Lemon and M.A.E. Green, 12 vols (London 1856–72)
DNB	*The Dictionary of National Biography* ed Leslie Stephen and Sidney Lee, 22 vols (1885–1901; repr London 1921–2)
EHR	*English Historical Review*
ELR	*English Literary Renaissance*
HLQ	*Huntington Library Quarterly*
JEH	*Journal of Ecclesiastical History*
L&P	*Letters and Papers (Foreign and Domestic) of the Reign of King Henry VIII* ed J.S. Brewer and J. Gairdner, 21 vols (London 1862–1910)
ME	Middle English
NCE	*The New Catholic Encyclopedia* ed M.R.P. McGuire et al, 16 vols (New York 1967)
OE	Old English
OED	*The Oxford English Dictionary* ed J.A.H. Murray et al, 13 vols (Oxford 1933)
PG	*Patrologiae cursus completus, series Graeca* ed J.-P. Migne, 166 vols (Paris 1857–66)
PL	*Patrologiae cursus completus, series Latina* ed J.-P. Migne, 221 vols (Paris 1844–64)
TRHS	*Transactions of the Royal Historical Society*
Vg	*Biblia Sacra iuxta Vulgatam Clementinam* (Madrid 1965)

INTRODUCTION

1   A Two-Edged Sword: The History of the Tudor Homilies

The Tudor homilies are set sermons that were designed to help ignorant parish priests discharge the duty of regular preaching to those for whom they had cure of souls. Yet they are also incisive formulations of a new and relatively uncompromising protestantism, dissent from which the royal supremacy would not tolerate. On the one hand they resemble the medieval homiliaries, the books of model sermons on which the inadequately trained curate could rely when instructing the flock in the rudiments of the faith;[1] on the other, they reflect a 'Cromwellian' desire to use the pulpit as an agent of religious change and an instrument for promoting the 'new learning.'[2] If they were a response to the church's recognition that priests turned ministers could hardly meet the demands of a new economy of salvation in which sermons, *ex opere operato*, played the central part,[3] they were also a response to the state's conviction that a popular conversion to the religious policies it adopted might require coercion. *Cujus regio ejus religio*: the maxim applies well to the Tudor homilies and the means by which they were enforced.

The ancient homily of the primitive church was a simple dilation, chiefly expository, on a scriptural text that it evaluated and glossed in a variety of straightforward ways. Often the homily, as its synonym 'postil' (*post illa*) implies, was wedded to the appropriate pericope of the liturgical year.[4] Relaxed in tone and devoid of both scholastic and rhetorical pretensions, the homily as a form persisted, essentially unchanged, beside the more varied, but formal, genre of the sermon. Luther's *Kirchenpostillen*, published between 1522 and 1543, are Reformation examples of the type, as are Erasmus Sarcerius' *Postillen*, the model for Taverner's English postils of 1539–40.[5] But *Certain Sermons or Homilies* deserves to be known as a book of homilies only in a carefully restricted sense. While like patristic, medieval, and protestant precursors it is an aid to preaching meant for use throughout the church year, the discourses it contains are not, by definition, homilies. They do not expound or comment upon selected scriptural texts; instead they enlarge on topics deemed significant, using Scripture along with patristic authorities, homely similitudes, and a range of very basic argumentative techniques to develop their themes. In function the book is a homiliary, but its contents are not homilies, but simple sermons.

The first book of homilies, which has the distinction of preceding the first Book of Common Prayer, consists of twelve sermons published on 31 July 1547, shortly after Edward VI had come to the throne. They bring to fruition the efforts of Archbishop Cranmer to make a book of sermons that could be propagated throughout the realm – efforts that had begun in 1539 and were renewed, unsuccessfully, during the Convocation of 1542–3.[6] The Henrician antecedents of the first book of homilies are of several kinds. The sermons Cromwell and Cranmer required of their bishops and clergy during the campaign to enforce the royal supremacy (1535–7) are earlier instances of a government's attempt to tune the pulpits to official policy.[7] Formularies such as the Ten Articles (1536) and the Bishops' Book (1537), clear examples of incipient protestantism, were both meant to be preached, and they serve as reminders that the reformers were adept at manipulating the pulpit as well as the press in their attempt to mould public opinion.[8] Finally, Richard Taverner's *Postils* (1540), simple expositions of Scripture based on the liturgical year and meant for dissemination to untutored priests, provides the first protestant example in English of a rota of sermons framed for an avowedly educational or humanistic purpose.[9] The official Edwardian homilies, topical rather than expository articulations of the faith, but destined none the less to be delivered seriatim, Sunday by Sunday, in a revised liturgy, combine features inherited from these parents and originals.

The first book of homilies derives its authority from a preface issued in the name of the king and alleging for the book the support of both the Privy Council and, by the advice of the duke of Somerset, the king himself. The authority claimed in the book itself is less important, however, than that claimed for it by the royal injunctions which were published in 1547 in connection with the visitation that served as harbinger for the coming religious changes. The thirty-second injunction stated that

because through lack of preachers in many places of the king's realms and dominions, the people continue in ignorance and blindness, all persons, vicars, and curates shall read in their churches every Sunday one of the homilies, which are and shall be set forth for the same purpose by the king's authority, in such sort as they shall be appointed to do in the preface of the same.[10]

As prototype for a succession of episcopal articles of enquiry that were enforceable in the normal way through the church courts, this injunction made reading of the homilies for all but the few licensed preachers a binding responsibility. Throughout the rest of the century and well into the seventeenth century, churchwardens were compelled to furnish pulpits with copies of the book of homilies, and the clergy were required to read them in the prescribed fashion. The inevitable lapses on both counts appear among the *detecta* and *comperta* entered in the records of the consistory and archidiaconal courts.

The leaders of the young king's church took care to situate the homilies in both the liturgical and doctrinal reformations then under way. The creation of homilies meant the curtailment of the Sunday morning service, since an injunction stipulated that when a homily was read 'Prime and Hours shall be omitted.'[11] Abandoning the Hours meant abandoning the three services of Terce, Sext, and None: only Lauds and Mattins remained.[12] The first Book of Common Prayer (1549) included as part of its description of the communion service a rubric that further refined the position of the homily: 'After the Crede ended, shall folowe the Sermon or Homely, or some porcion of one of the Homelyes, as thei shalbe herafter devided.'[13] The homily, therefore, or one of its parts (each was divided in 1549 'according as is mencioned in the boke of common prayer') was to serve as a propaedeutic to reception of the sacrament and was accorded a regular position in the service in lieu of a sermon.

Liturgical function aside, the book of homilies came to be regarded as a benchmark of reformed belief in England. When the Forty-two Articles were written in 1552, the thirty-fourth item asserted that the homilies 'be godly and wholesom, containing doctrine to be received of all men.' The eleventh article, moreover – the crucial one on justification – defers completely to the teaching of the homilies: 'Justification by only faith in Jesus Christ, in that sense as it is declared in the homily of Justification, is a most certain and wholesome doctrine for Christian men.'[14] We misconstrue the nature of the homilies and the motives that lay behind their use if we see them only as surrogates for sermons in parishes unfortunate enough not to have established a true preaching ministry. As Peter Heylyn insists, in a statement unusually candid in its acknowledgement that the Church of England had from the outset placed much stock in the 'Doctrinals of the Book of Homilies,' the book was composed 'not only for the help of unpreaching Ministers, but for the regulating, and instructing even of Learned Preachers.'[15] Soon after they were introduced, in fact, it became apparent that they could be used as a standard for measuring conformity and a means of controlling maverick preachers of whatever persuasion. An awareness of how the homilies might serve as a vehicle for controlling the pulpit emerges, for example, in a set of injunctions issued to the bishops in the very year the homilies were published. One item of these injunctions dispels the view that the homilies were intended to cater just to the needs of Sir John Lacklatin:

You shall not at any time or place preach or set forth unto the people any doctrine contrary or repugnant to the effect and intent contained and set forth in the King's Highness' Homilies, neither admit or give licence to preach to any other within your diocese but to such as you shall know or at the least assuredly trust will do the same. And if at any time by hearing or by report proved you shall perceive the contrary, you shall incontinent inhibit that person so offending and punish him and revoke your licence.[16]

In the second year of the reign, on 24 April, all preaching licences, except those signed by the king, Somerset, or Cranmer, were revoked; an explanatory letter advises those stripped of their licences to fall back on the book of homilies that the sermons therein 'might the better in the meanwhile sink into his subjects' hearts, and be learned the sooner, the people not being tossed to and fro with seditious and contentious preaching, while every man according to his zeal, some better, some worse, goeth about to set out his own fantasy, and to draw the people to his opinion.'[17] Despite this restriction, 'certain controversious and seditious preachers' continued to gain a hearing during the following summer, and so the authorities struck a decisive blow in a proclamation of 23 September 1548: sermons by licensed and unlicensed preachers alike were forbidden and, in the interim, the king's loving subjects were enjoined to occupy themselves with the 'godly homilies ... that they may be the more ready with thankful obedience to receive a most quiet, godly and uniform order to be had throughout all his said realms and dominions.'[18]

If the government's treatment of Bonner, bishop of London, and Gardiner, bishop of Winchester, is any indication, resistance to the imposition of the homilies in these first few years was not regarded as a trifling matter or a mere eccentricity. In lengthy letters to Cranmer, Somerset, and the Privy Council, Gardiner raised a series of objections to Cranmer's book, the anthology to which even he had been asked to contribute. He maintained that homilies were rendered illegal and redundant by the King's Book, the throwback to conservatism given statutory cachet in 1543: 'God gave our late soverayne lorde the gyfte of pacificacion in those matters, which, establyshed by his Hyghnes authoryty in the Convocation, extynquished our devises [the homilies projected in 1542], and remayneth

of force with your Grace.' He claimed that the common people would
be no more attentive to new sermons than to old, and that in eradicating
the *Golden Legend* and Mirk's *Festial* the homilies might pull up the wheat
with the cockle. He argued, moreover, that the teaching of the homilies
was at several points incompatible not just with the King's Book, but also
with Erasmus' *Paraphrases*, which, in a new English translation, the royal
injunctions had also urged upon the parochial clergy.[19] For all his pains,
Gardiner, deprived by Henry's will of a seat on the council, succeeded
only in removing himself further from a position of influence. He was
imprisoned in the Fleet in September of 1547, just as the king's visitors
began their rounds. When he refused to concur with the homilies' teaching
on justification later in the fall, he was again incarcerated.[20] Throughout
the rest of the 1540s, in fact, Gardiner's refusal to accept the homilies kept
him in prison, or under close house arrest. At his trial in 1550 he balked
at an article worded much as the thirty-fourth of the Forty-two Articles
was to be worded: he withheld his assent from the proposition that the
homilies are 'godly and holsomme, and do teache suche doctrine as ought
to be embraced of all men.'[21]

Bonner's resistance to the homilies was short-lived compared to Gardiner's. On receiving the injunctions and the book of homilies from the
king's visitors, Bonner said, 'I do receive thies Injunctions and Homelies
with this protestacion; that I will observe them if they be not contrary and
repugnant to Goddes Lawe and the Statutes and Ordinances of this
Churche.'[22] The remarkable thing about Bonner's protest and, after a term
in the Fleet, his subsequent retraction of it as 'neyther resonabill nor
siche as might well stand with the dutye of an humble subject' is simply
that he had himself written the sermon on love and charity, the sixth of the
sermons in the collection Cranmer had put together.[23] There is no evidence
to explain Bonner's rejection of a book to which he was a contributor. It
is likely, however, that he resented either the purposes to which he saw
the volume now being put or the rather militantly protestant company with
which his own offering had been forced to keep.

The homilies on justification, which more than any others exercised
Gardiner and Bonner, continued to excite interest and controversy. In 1548
Martin Bucer, who had long been both a friend of Cranmer and one of
Gardiner's principal adversaries, lauded the homilies' exposition of that
doctrine in his *Gratulatio Martini Buceri ad ecclesiam Anglicanum*, subsequently translated into English by Sir Thomas Hoby.[24] Later, after moving
to England at Cranmer's invitation and becoming Regius Professor of
Divinity at Cambridge, Bucer appealed to the views expressed in the homilies when defending himself against an attack launched by Dr John

Young, soon to become master of Pembroke Hall.[25] When Bucer had recourse to the homily on good works in support of the thesis that 'the good works which any seem to do before justification have the nature of sin,' Young, much to the scornful delight of his opponent, conceded that he was 'pressed hard' with the homilies even though he had previously subscribed to them.[26] Like Young, Dr John Redman, master of Trinity College, Cambridge and dean of Westminster, was reluctant to accept the unalloyed Lutheranism of the homilies' attitude to good works: so afraid was he that the doctrine propounded in the homilies would encourage 'carnal liberty' that he embraced it only on his deathbed.[27] Yet for many of the more conspicuous members of the Edwardian reformation, the homilies constituted a norm applicable to many of the important theological issues of the day. In 1554 Hooper, Ferrar, Taylor, Bradford, Philpot, Rogers, Saunders, and some other reformers who were being detained in prison wrote 'A Supplication Unto the King and Queen's Most Excellent Majesties, and to their Most Honourable and High Court of Parliament,' in which they promised willingly to die if unable to prove the doctrinal propriety of the prayer book and the homilies.[28] The homely homilies, to use Latimer's pun, had become one of the cornerstones of the temple built by the young Josias.[29] As Jewell was to point out in 1563 when describing 'the manner how the Church of England is administered and governed' in the appendix to his *Apology*: 'there be prescribed unto the curates of meaner understanding certain homilies devised by learned men which do comprehend the principal points of Christian doctrine; as of original sin, of justification, of faith, of charity, and suchlike ...'[30] In response to the problem created by the ineffectual clergy, the church had articulated some of the most important doctrinal and ethical positions for which it craved national support.

It had apparently been Cranmer's intention from the start to supplement the twelve sermons found in the first book, since at its close appears a list of topics for future consideration. In Edward's *Journal*, moreover, two items allude to the homilies: the first merely records the setting forth of the injunctions and homilies in 1547; the second, endorsed in Cecil's hand, is a memorandum for the council, dated 13 October 1552: 'the making of more homilies.'[31] It is likely that Edward is here reacting to Bucer's comments in *Omnia censura*, his observations on the Book of Common Prayer written in 1551. Bucer felt that 'the list of homilies is too short and covers too few aspects of our religion in its teaching. And so, since the Lord has endowed this kingdom with a number of distinguished preachers, they should be required to compile more homilies on the most necessary matters ...' Bucer did not hesitate to supply a table of contents for the supplemental volume he envisaged.[32]

When Elizabeth came to the throne, she was undoubtedly aware of these unfulfilled plans. In 1559 she reissued the first book, having first supervised revisions designed to simplify the text 'for the better understandyng of the simple people.'[33] Then, in 'The Interpretations of the Bishops' (1560), which elaborate on the queen's injunctions of the preceding year, we learn that 'homilies [are] to be made of those arguments which be showed in the book of homilies, or others of some convenient arguments, as of the sacrifice of the Mass, of the Common Prayers to be in English, that every particular church may alter and change their public rites and ceremonies of their church, keeping the substance of the faith inviolably, with such like. And that these be divided to be made by the bishops, every bishop two and the Bishop of London to have four.'[34] In 1563, after a draft preface by Cox had been spurned and after Elizabeth herself had delayed final publication by insisting on making some changes in the copy delivered to her for approval, a second tome of homilies joined the first.[35] As a set, this collection is far less impressive than the first. Although it deals with some important topics neglected in the original homilies, such as images, matrimony, and the sacraments, it is on the whole much more diffuse and derivative than its forerunner.

Throughout her reign Elizabeth demonstrated such extraordinary confidence in homilies that we can only conclude that she saw their use as a complement to the control she wielded over Paul's Cross, the principal pulpit in the land.[36] In the aftermath of the Admonition controversy, the debate between puritans and those of the established church who were essentially content with the achievements of the Elizabethan settlement, the issue of a preaching versus a reading ministry became contentious.[37] For her part, Elizabeth refused to acknowledge that an original purpose of publishing homilies in her brother's time had been to combat clerical ignorance. She insisted on the durability of the homilies as a means of keeping potentially wayward clergy in check. Thus she would not tolerate the 'prophesying' exercises, the educational value of which was extolled by the puritans, of course, but also by most of her own bishops. In 1576 Edmund Grindal, who had just been translated from the province of York to the primacy at Canterbury and who for years had been requiring the reading of homilies by visitation articles circulated in his name, challenged the queen's recalcitrance.[38] As Ambrose *redivivus* to her Theodosius, he pointed out that homilies merely supplied the room of sermons and that homilies would become superfluous if a duly educated preaching ministry were ever mustered.[39] Elizabeth, however, thought that 'it was good for the Church to have few preachers, and that three or four might suffice for a county; and that the reading of the homilies to the people was enough.'[40] Grindal deemed the homilies incapable of answering to 'the diversity of times, places, and hearers' and insisted that the church had resorted to homilies only as a *pis aller*, according to an 'old and a true proverb, Better half a loaf than no bread.'[41] In this dramatic and, for Grindal, tragic confrontation, neither party seemed to recognize that from the beginning the homilies had been a two-edged sword, a weapon keen on one side to the problems of providing regular preaching, a weapon keen on the other side to the problems of assuring uniformity of belief.

In 1585 Elizabeth conducted an irascible interview with Archbishop Whitgift, who had succeeded Grindal in 1583. This colloquy affords another glimpse of the queen's eagerness to promote the homilies. In the presence of three bishops, some representatives of the Lower House of Convocation, and members of her Privy Council, she unburdened herself on the subject of a reformed ministry:

Again you suffer many ministers to preach what they list and to minister the sacraments according to their own fancies, some one way, some another, to the breach of unity: yea, and some of them so curious in searching matters above their capacity as they preach they wot not what – that there is no Hell but a torment of conscience. Nay, I have heard there be six preachers in one diocese the which do preach in six sundry ways. I wish such men to be brought to conformity and unity: that they minister the sacraments according to the order of this Realm and preach all one truth; and that such as be found not worthy to preach, be compelled to read homilies ... for there is more learning in one of those than in twenty of some of their sermons. And we require you that you do not favour such men ... for they will be hanged before they will be reformed.[42]

At this point, Whitgift had the temerity to remark that it was impossible to license learned men for all of England's thirteen thousand parishes. Elizabeth retorted that he had not caught her drift: 'Jesus! thirteen thousand! It is not to be looked for ... My meaning is not (that) you should make choice of learned ministers only, for they are not to be found, but of honest, sober and wise men and such as can read the scriptures and homilies well unto the people.'[43] For Elizabeth, then, a minister who did not deviate from the text of the homilies was a minister who could not lapse into theological error and would not provoke controversy. Such a minister was truly conformable, truly attuned to the exigencies of the religious settlement so precariously established and maintained. Elizabeth

regarded the enforced reading of the homilies as a crucial component
of ecclesiastical polity, though Richard Hooker, sometimes taken as an
apologist for the Elizabethan settlement, could manage only faint praise for
homilies, admitting that they were a 'most commendable institution' that
supplied 'the necessarie defect of sermons,' but allowing too that 'aptnes to
followe particular occasions presentlie growinge, to put life into wordes
by countenance voice and gesture, to prevaile mightelie in the suddaine
affections of men, this sermons may challenge.'[44] Hooker implies that
he prefers an animated sermon, composed for a particular occasion and
responsive to the particular needs of its audience, to the inert reading of a
set sermon, or homily, however expedient.

The most committed and enthusiastic patron of homilies in Elizabethan
England, then, was the queen herself, and the Tudor church owed its
continued use of the two books to the impetus she provided. In 1570,
unnerved by the Northern Rebellion, the queen commissioned a whole
host of measures to reinforce her sense of power and her subjects' allegiance. Among these devices was the *Homily against Disobedience and Wilful
Rebellion* Its sheer length and its range of documentation and argument
betray an unabashedly polemical purpose. It was quickly appended to the
second tome and was heard habitually, therefore, by loyal subjects who
had never contemplated the possibility of rebellion. To include it among
the other sermons was to concede more or less openly that the government
conceived of homilies, first and foremost, as political measures.

During the latter part of Elizabeth's reign the puritans increasingly
contended that the use of set sermons was an impediment to the creation
of a preaching ministry, that homilies, apocryphal accretions to Scripture,
did not just replace but actually competed with the sermons that promoted
a lively faith.[45] At the Hampton Court Conference in 1604, James must
have surprised most of the participants by acknowledging the force of this
puritan complaint. James agreed with the bishops that 'a homily read
by a man who was unable to write a sermon might inculcate very excellent
lessons,' but he refused to accede to Bishop Bancroft's request that 'his
Majesty would appoynt more homilies to be made in the churche.' Instead
of homilies, said James, 'we meane to plante preachers.'[46] But James, for
all his enlightened liberalism at Hampton Court, came eventually to realize
that the freedom extended the preachers and lecturers under his reign
could get out of hand. When he discerned aberrations from an 'acceptable
standard' of preaching in the early 1620s he issued directions that decreed

that no preacher of what title or denomination soever, shall presume from hence-
forth in any auditory within this kingdom to declare, limit, or bound out, by

way of positive doctrine, in any lecture or sermon, the power, prerogative, jurisdiction, authority, or duty of sovereign princes, or otherwise meddle with these matters of state, and the references betwixt princes and the people, than as they are instructed and presidented in the homily of obedience, and in the rest of the homilies and articles of religion, set forth ... by public authority; but rather confine themselves wholly to those two heads of faith and good life, which are all the subject of the ancient sermons and homilies.[47]

As an adjunct to these directions, Archbishop Abbot wrote a letter to the bishops; he explained that James, in adducing the authority of the homilies and in reducing all preaching to the scope they set, had called to mind the saying of Tertullian, 'Id verum quod primum.'[48] Another attempt to justify the king's decision appeared in a sermon John Donne preached at St Paul's.[49] Donne rehearsed the usual arguments about the primitive church's reliance on homilies, but preached, as John Chamberlain tells us, with an unaccustomed lack of enthusiasm.[50] In these circumstances there appeared in 1623 the large folio edition of the two books of homilies, again with the imprimatur of public authority.

During the seventeenth century, as the educational attainments of the parochial clergy improved and the goal of filling every pulpit with a preacher came closer to realization, the church's dependence on the homilies waned.[51] After 1660, of course, monarchs meddled less with things ecclesiastical, and had fewer occasions to use the homilies as either carrots or sticks. Then too, as styles in preaching changed, the venerable homilies seemed more and more antiquated. Yet despite the development of a 'more sophisticated, "professional" and formalistic approach to public persuasion,' the collection, according to Millar MacLure, was 'the greatest single influence' in forming the characteristic temper of Jacobean and Caroline divines.[52] Moreover, in the debates over extempore preaching that so beguiled Restoration churchmen, the homilies seemed to some to be superior to other compositions read from the pulpit. In his Oxford visitation sermon of 1660, for example, Robert South noted that there was 'in the Esteem of many, but little difference between Sermons read, and Homilies, save only this, that Homilies are much better.'[53] About 1708, Bishop George Bull advised his clergy

not to trust at first to their own compositions, but to furnish themselves with a provision of the best sermons, which the learned divines of our church have published; that by reading them often, and by endeavouring to imitate them, they may acquire a habit of good preaching themselves. And where through poverty, or any other impediment, ministers are incapable of discharging this duty as they ought, he directed them to use the Homilies of the church.[54]

Bull relegates the homilies to their traditional role as a boon to those who, in South's metaphor, were pieces of lead bearing the royal stamp. But that traditional role was almost played out by the end of the century. In 1687 there had appeared an edition of the homilies for the use of private families,[55] and this shift from a public audience to a private one is a tell-tale sign that the homilies had virtually outlived their usefulness as aids for unskilful preachers.

The most serious attempt to supplant the Tudor homilies was represented by its originators as an attempt merely to supplement them. In 1690, when John Tillotson, future archbishop of Canterbury, was still dean of St Paul's, he broached with Gilbert Burnet and several other bishops the possibility of preparing a completely new set of homilies. Burnet, whose *An Essay towards a New Book of Homilies* was published in 1713 as an addendum to *Some Sermons Preached on Several Occasions*, recalled that Tillotson did not intend 'to lay aside the Book of Homilies already Established, but to add a New one to that we have had now for above an hundred and fifty Years.'[56] But Tillotson was clearly disaffected with a book he considered dated:

> He thought that [it] was not full enough and that it was according to the state of things at the time in which it was composed; fitted chiefly to settle People's Minds right with relation to the Reformation, and in opposition to Papacy.
>
> He thought that such a Work had been of great use to the Nation, but that another Book of Homilies, that should contain a full and plain account both of the Doctrinal and Practical Parts of the Christian Religion; such as should give a clear Explanation of every thing related to our Holy Faith, or to the conduct of our Lives, was necessary chiefly for the Instruction of the Clergy, and it might be also a Family-Book for the general use of the whole Nation.[57]

Tillotson projected a total of sixty-two homilies, one for each Sunday and ten more for certain specified holy days. In his detailed comments on the contents so arranged, Burnet reveals that Tillotson and the other projectors chafed under the stringent solifidianism of the original book: 'In the Six Sundays to Whitsontide, the Doctrine of Justification was to be explained; and some Expressions in the first Book, that seem'd to carry Justification by Faith only, to a heighth that wanted some mitigation, were to be well-examined; and all that St. Paul had writ on that Head, both to the Romans, and the Galatians, was to be explained and reconciled to what James wrote on the same subject.'[58] In light of this unauthorized challenge to the very core of the 1547 book, it is not surprising that the plan had to be abandoned: 'We found a Spirit of Opposition and Contradiction grew so strong, and it was so much animated and supported, that we saw it was to no purpose to struggle against it at that time.'[59] When the seven sermons Burnet assayed surfaced some twenty-three years later, even they encountered resistance. George Sewell complained that Burnet's revival of Tillotson's scheme lacked sufficient authority, Convocation having been ignored in the initial stages and there being no plan for submitting the finished sermons to it for approval. He impugned the credentials of those involved, even though Tillotson was then dead and Burnet was over seventy. In like vein, he declared the results a failure: 'In what your Lordship (unwilling that any thing of yours should be quite lost) has offer'd to the Public, I must freely confess that I can't perceive any thing like the old Compositions of your excellent Predecessors on the same Occasion. I can't see that primitive Vein of Plainness and Simplicity, that Spirit, and Strength of Reasoning, that due Application of Scripture argument, and pathetical Recommendation of Truth, which is the distinguishing Character of the ancient Homilies.'[60] If Burnet and Tillotson had executed the plan they envisioned, eighteenth-century clergymen would have had a panoply of homilies from which to choose, and the original homilies might in time have been disestablished. In fact, however, these ancient homilies continued to hold uneasy sway.

Rather than add to the Tudor homilies, Peter Nourse, chaplain to Queen Anne, tried to renew and refurbish them. His 'improvement,' *Practical Discourses on Several Subjects: Being Some Select Homilies of the Church of England, Put into a New Method and Modern Stile and fitted to Common Use*, had appeared in four editions by 1731. In the preface to the first part of the book, Nourse remarks that 'it is no wonder the People should be so generally prejudiced, as we find they are, against the original books of homilies' and explains that he has 'endeavoured in the following Discourses to recover those Homilies that are upon the most useful and most practical Subjects, from such Defects and Imperfections as are incidental to their Antiquity.'[61] Apparently using the criterion of usefulness and practicality, Nourse rejects from his book the homily on the misery of man and the three on the process of justification. As for defects in the others, he maintains that

the Cause of this general Aversion to them is to be ascribed in a great measure to the Alteration, which has been made in our Language since the Times they

were writ in; not only the Words, but the Manner of Expression, and all the Way
and Method of Preaching, is very different now from what it was in that Age;
and there having been a new Translation of the Bible since those Times, the Scriptures themselves, which in the Homilies are quoted from the former version
must needs sound harsh and uncouth to those who are accustomed only to the
new one.[62]

Nourse, whose prefatory material is valuable in revealing some eighteenth-
century attitudes to the works he would alter, is himself adamant about
the necessity for homilies, even though he concedes that the common
opinion will be that he has laboured in vain, 'the End being now ceased
for which they were at first composed and published.'[63]
     A second device for renovating the homilies came in an elaborate edition
intended for the use of private families; the book was sufficiently popular
to have been reprinted three times by 1758. Although the 'Advertisement'
disclaims any desire to alter such 'truly Evangelical compositions,'[64] the
effect of the 'pious reflections and spiritual observations' offered by an
anonymous divine is to deck the text with modern devotional trappings.
Bishop Beveridge's *Private Thoughts*, for instance, and a number of hymns
appear in the annotations. Watts' 'Oh if my soul is form'd for woe' is
quoted in all five verses as a gloss on or a devotional counterpart to the
second homily on the passion.[65] In a note on the homily that treats good
works, the commentator remarks ruefully on the desuetude of the homilies
in public services and even gives a Low Church reason why they have
fallen out of fashion: 'Not many years ago these Homilies were wont to
be publickly read in churches, but as they savour so strongly of the gospel,
it was thought prudent to lay them aside, as not fit to the present time,
because the current doctrine is clean contrary to them. The doctrines
of Grace, on which our excellent church is entirely established, are almost
extinct, forgotten or misunderstood, and the contrary doctrines of free-
will, salvation by moral works etc. are substituted in their stead.'[66]
     It was John Wesley who gave the homilies, themselves almost extinct,
forgotten, and misunderstood, a new lease on life. In 1738, he published his
first manifesto, which was in fact an abridgement of Cranmer's three
homilies on justification. Proceeding through some nineteen editions in
Wesley's lifetime, this redaction became a 'staple item in Methodist instruction.'[67] When Wesley returned from a tour of Methodist societies
throughout England and Ireland in 1788, he reported that

The book which next to the Holy Scripture was of the greatest use to them in
settling their judgment as to the grand point of justification by faith is the book of

Homilies. They were never clearly convinced that we are justified by faith alone till they carefully consulted these and compared them with the sacred writings [the Bible]. And no minister of the Church, can, with any decency, oppose these, seeing that at his ordination he subscribes to them in subscribing the thirty-sixth [*sic*] article of the Church.[68]

Wesley's final sentence is a slur on established churchmen such as Tillotson and Bull who, while supporting the reading of the homilies, regretted their demotion of good works.[69] But it was the issue of clerical subscription to the homilies that was increasingly receiving attention.

An indication of this attention occurs among the works of Dr John Disney, who along with Bishop Hoadley was one of the most vociferous opponents of the Corporation and Test Acts. In 1773 he wrote a series of open letters on the subject, subsequently published as *Observations on the Homilies of the Church of England* (1790), in which he questions the propriety of requiring assent to a book that is 'now never read in our churches, and very seldom even in the studies of the clergy.' He alleges, moreover, that the homilies 'are frequently subscribed without having been seen' and suggests that with his help a discerning reader will readily see that there is much in them that fails to qualify as 'godly and wholesome doctrine.'[70] Among the more interesting of Disney's observations are those on the homilies' exhortations to obedience. Disney derides the 'unreasonable degree of absurdity' to which the doctrines of passive obedience and nonresistance are carried in the homilies and says that these doctrines 'would have effectually prevented the glorious revolution of 1688, and have excluded the house of Brunswick from the throne of these kingdoms, had not more just and rational notions prevailed.'[71] For Disney, the thinking of Somers, Sidney, and John Locke has superseded the crude and immature principles which all ministers were, quite unreasonably, expected to espouse. (It is worth noting in this regard that George Hickes and the later nonjurors had found in these homilies on obedience texts to support their position, as a work such as *Causa dei et reipublica contra novatores* [1748] demonstrates.)[72] In most other respects, Disney's criticisms of the homilies are the common ones voiced by their eighteenth-century detractors. Following a passage in the *Free and Candid Disquisitions* (1750), he carps at textual errors, archaisms, 'coarse applications,' the use of an unauthorized translation of the Bible, and quotations from the apocrypha.[73] When, some years later, Bishop John Jebb argued against the use of the homilies in catechetical examinations administered by the 'Association for Discountenancing Vice,' he repeated most of the same reservations and added that the antipapal invective was indecorous and especially harmful to girls.[74]

In the middle of the nineteenth century, the first scholarly editions of the homilies appeared. G.E. Corrie's text was published by Cambridge University Press in 1850 and nine years later came the magisterial edition of John Griffiths, published by the press at Oxford. The information contained in these editions might have saved many an earlier commentator from embarrassment: had Disney, for example, realized that the deeply conservative John Harpesfield had written the piece on the misery of mankind, he would not perhaps have complained that the homily was imbued with the 'calvinistic principle.'[75] But the most interesting events concerning the history of the homilies in the nineteenth century precede these editions. Coleridge read the homilies in a humble, uncluttered edition issued by the newly formed Prayer Book and Homily Society, and was moved by the one on prayer to write an impassioned three-page note on the book's endpapers.[76] Newman also discovered the homilies and became one of their most thoughtful students during his tractarian years. In Newman's view, the homilies 'in no respect have greater claims upon us than as comments upon the Articles.'[77] But for a man trying to reconcile his Anglican loyalties to his incipient Catholic convictions, these very claims, limited though they were, assumed great importance. First in Tract 82 and then in Tract 90 (1841), Newman's last irenic utterance before his conversion in 1845, he deliberated on the homilies and attempted to explicate the Articles with the commentary they provided.[78] He elucidates the purpose of his appeal to the homilies in the notice written for the tract when it was reprinted in *The Via Media of the Anglican Church* (1877); the appeal

determined the *animus* and drift of the Articles to be Catholic. It was evidence of this in two ways, positively and negatively: – positively, in asmuch as the Homilies, though hitherto claimed by the Evangelical party as one of their special weapons against the High Church ... were found on a closer inspection to take a view more or less favourable to Rome as regards the number of the Sacraments, the Canon of Scripture, the efficacy of penance, and other points; and negatively, because the Homilies for the most part struck, not at certain Roman doctrines and practices, but at their abuse, and therefore, when once these Homilies were taken as a legitimate comment on the Articles, they suggested that the repudiations of Roman teaching in the Articles were repudiations of it so far as it was abused, not as it was in itself.[79]

Newman resorted to what he took to be the Catholicity of the homilies, then, in order to prove that behind the contrived ambiguities of the Articles stood reformers, not revolutionaries.

In coupling the homilies with the Articles, even in this decidedly idiosyncratic way, Newman conferred on them a status they had long since lost and have never recovered.[80] Yet they still deserve to be read: they are fine examples of sixteenth-century popular preaching and major specimens of the early protestants' pastoral mission; they are documents crucial to the history of English propaganda; they are texts that exerted considerable influence, over several centuries, on those who heard them, or who chose or were forced to read them.

NOTES

1   For information on the medieval homiliary, see Milton McC. Gatch *Preaching and Theology in Anglo-Saxon England: Aelfric and Wulfstan* (Toronto: University of Toronto Press 1977) 27–39 and Henri Barré *Les Homéliaires carolingiens de l'Ecole d'Auxerre* Studi e Testi 225 (Vaticani: Biblioteca Apostolica Vaticana 1962). D.W. Robertson, Jr ('Frequency of Preaching in Thirteenth-Century England' *Speculum* 24 [1949] 376) points out that 'it was an established principle of canon law that every priest should have, among other books, "*omelie per circulum anni dominicis diebus et singulis festituiatibus [sic] apte*," ' but it was not canon law but rather the tenth decree of the Fourth Lateran Council (1215) that resulted in a proliferation of preachers' handbooks (see R.H. and M.A. Rouse *Preachers, Florilegia and Sermons: Studies on the 'Manipulus florum' of Thomas of Ireland* [Toronto: Pontifical Institute of Mediaeval Studies 1979] 57–64). In late medieval England one of the most popular homiliaries was John Mirk's *Liber festialis*; twenty-six manuscripts contain the work in whole or in part, and nearly twenty printed texts were published in the period from 1483 to 1532. See M.F. Wakelin 'The Manuscripts of John Mirk's *Festial*' *Leeds Studies in English* n s 1 (1967) 93–118.

2   See G.R. Elton *Policy and Police: The Enforcement of the Reformation in the Age of Thomas Cromwell* (Cambridge: Cambridge University Press 1972) and Joseph Block 'Thomas Cromwell's Patronage of Preaching' *The Sixteenth Century Journal* 8 (1977) 37–50.

3   See Heiko Obermann 'Preaching and the Word in the Reformation' *Theology Today* 18 (1961) 16–29.

4   In 'Praedicare-Tractare-Sermo: Essai sur la terminologie de la prédication paléochrétienne' *Le Maison-Dieu* 39 (1954) 97–107 Christine Mohrmann adduces passages from St Augustine to confirm that *sermones populares* are *quod Graeci homilias vocant* (106). It remains to be said, however, that in the Middle Ages a sermon tended to be a piece of moral exhortation, whereas

a homily was a piece of expository exegesis: see Henri Barré *Les Homéliaires carolingiens de l'Ecole d'Auxerre* 7–10, 24 for this distinction. Barré points out that *Homiliae Venerabilis Bedae*, for instance, were 'explicationes Lectionum seu Epistolarum Dominicis diebus, festivitatibus, ac feriis' (7).

5 Gerald Strauss notes that the library of a Thuringian pastor in 1570 included more books of homilies than works in any other form: 'he owned twelve, altogether, including the archetype, Luther's *Kirchenpostillen* and Sarcerius' *Postillen*' ('The Mental World of a Saxon Pastor,' in *Reformation Principle and Practice* ed P.N. Brooks [London: Scolar Press 1980] 162). On Taverner's translation of Sarcerius, see below, 19 n 9.

6 On 8 March 1539 John Butler and other English churchmen informed Pellican and the Helvetian church that Cranmer 'is now wholly employed in instructing the people and in composing discourses in English, which our clergy are to use instead of those Latin ones which they have hitherto prated in their churches like so many parrots' (*Original Letters Relative to the English Reformation* ed Hastings Robinson, Parker Society 42 [Cambridge: Cambridge University Press 1847] 626). For the discussion of homilies in the Convocation of 1542–3, see David Wilkins *Concilia Magnae Britanniae et Hiberniae* 4 vols (1737; facs repr Brussels 1964) III 863 and *The Letters of Stephen Gardiner* ed James A. Muller (Cambridge: Cambridge University Press 1933) 296 and 310.

7 Block and Elton supply the details.

8 The Ten Articles, adopted by Convocation in 1536, were the first formularies in England to reflect reformed doctrine; these articles were superseded by those in the Bishops' Book, so called because a group of bishops composed them. Reaction against the reformed views expressed in these articles appears both in the Six Articles (1539) and in the King's Book, published in 1543 with a preface by Henry himself. Each of the Ten Articles contains the formula 'we will that all bishops and preachers shall instruct and teach ...,' and each article in the Bishops' Book (*The Institution of a Christian Man*) asserts 'we think it convenient that all bishops and preachers shall instruct and teach the people committed unto their spiritual charge ...' In contrast, the articles in the King's Book (*A Necessary Doctrine and Erudition for Any Christian Man*) usually begin with 'it is to be noted that ...' or 'it is to be considered that ...' For texts of all three of these, see *Formularies of Faith Put Forth By Authority During the Reign of Henry VIII* ed Charles Lloyd (Oxford: Oxford University Press 1856).

9 Published in two parts, the postils, as the title-pages declare, were 'drawn forth by diuerse learned men for the singuler commoditie of al good christen persons and namely of Prestes and Curates.' For a modern edition, see Richard Taverner *Postils on the Epistles and Gospels* ed Edward Cardwell (Oxford: Oxford University Press 1841) and the excerpts in *English Reformers* ed T.H.L. Parker, The Library of Christian Classics 26 (Philadelphia: The Westminster Press 1966). On Taverner's protestantism, see John K. Yost

'Taverner's Use of Erasmus and the Protestantization of English Humanism' *Renaissance Quarterly* 23 (1970) 266–76 and 'German Protestant Humanism and the Early English Reformation: Richard Taverner and Official Translation' *Bibliothèque d'humanisme et renaissance* 32 (1970) 613–25.

10 Cardwell *Documentary Annals of the Reformed Church of England* 2 vols (Oxford: Oxford University Press 1839) I 19. The homilies and injunctions of 1547 were often bound together. R.W. Heinze terms the item on reading homilies 'the most controversial section' of the injunctions. See *The Proclamations of the Tudor Kings* (Cambridge: Cambridge University Press 1976) 205.

11 *Documentary Annals* I 55. At Winchester Cathedral, the reading of both Scripture and homily resulted in an order that the sequences customarily chanted after the gradual 'shall utterly surcease and be no more used.' See *Documents Relating to the Foundation of the Chapter of Winchester 1541–1547*, ed G.W. Kitchin and F.T. Madge (London: Hampshire Record Society 1889) 180. At Canterbury Cathedral, the homily superseded the Lady mass. See W.H. Frere and W.P.M. Kennedy *Visitation Articles and Injunctions of the Period of the Reformation 1536–1575* (Alcuin Club Collections XIV-XVI) XV 142.

12 See *Statutes of Lincoln Cathedral* ed H. Bradshaw and Christopher Wordsworth, 2 vols in 3 (Cambridge: Cambridge University Press 1892–7) II 583–96 and R.W. Dixon *History of the Church of England* 6 vols (London: George Routledge and Sons 1878–1902) II 432.

13 *The [First] Book of Common Prayer* (1549; repr London: William Pickering 1844) f cii[r].

14 *The Two Liturgies ... Set Forth By Authority in the Reign of King Edward* VI ed Joseph Ketley, Parker Society 29 (Cambridge: Cambridge University Press 1844) 535 and 528. Cf the thirty-fifth and the eleventh of the Thirtynine Articles. The reference to the homily of justification perhaps alludes to the homilies on salvation, faith, and good works; there is no homily of justification.

15 *Ecclesia restaurata* (London 1661) sig A4[r] and page 34.

16 Kennedy and Frere XV 132.

17 *Tudor Royal Proclamations* ed P.L. Hughes and J.F. Larkin, 3 vols (New Haven: Yale University Press 1964–9) I 422 (#303); Cardwell *Documentary Annals* I 32.

18 *Tudor Royal Proclamations* I 432–3 (#313).

19 *The Letters of Stephen Gardiner* 296, 312, 381–8.

20 On the harassment of Gardiner, see J.A. Muller *Stephen Gardiner and the Tudor Reaction* (New York: Macmillan 1926) 166ff.

21 *Acts of the Privy Council of England* n s, ed J.R. Dasent, 32 vols (London 1890–1938) III 76.

22 *Acts of the Privy Council* II 126.

23 *Acts of the Privy Council* II 127.

24 The original Latin work was published in Basle in 1548. Thomas Hoby, then a member of Bucer's entourage, translated the work under the title *The Gratulation of the mooste famous Clerke M. Martin Bucer ... vnto the churche of Englande for the restitution of Christes religion* and sent it to his brother Philip, who was a privy councillor and ambassador to the court of the emperor; the English version appeared in 1549. See 'A Book of the Travaile and Lief of Me, Thomas Hoby' ed Edgar Powell, in *Camden Miscellany* 10 (1902) 5–6. Constantin Hopf (*Martin Bucer and the English Reformation* [Oxford: Basil Blackwell 1946] 187 n 2) notes that in copies now in the Bodleian Library and the Bibliothèque Nationale the *Gratulatio* is bound with Bucer's *Disputata Ratisbonae* (1548), a book on justification meant as a reply to Gardiner's *Epistola* (1546). Hopf remarks that 'the general trend of the Homilies as regards justification and faith was almost equal to that of Bucer in his arguments against Gardiner and the Roman Catholics' (185) and cites parallel passages between them (193).

25 This intense and bitter controversy is amply documented from both Young's and Bucer's perspectives in *Martini Buceri scripta Anglicana* (Basle 1577) 711–862. The material has never been adequately studied, though short accounts based on it appear in C.H. Smyth *Cranmer and the Reformation Under Edward VI* (Cambridge: Cambridge University Press 1926) 164–6 and in Hopf 83–5. G.C. Gorham provides a translation of Bucer's letter to Grindal (31 August 1550), with excellent explanatory notes, in *Gleanings of a Few Scattered Ears During the Period of the Reformation in England* 1533–88 (London: Bell and Daldy 1857) 163–7. See also John Strype *Ecclesiastical Memorials* 3 vols (Oxford: Clarendon Press 1822) II 327–8.

26 *Scripta Anglicana* 803.

27 See John Foxe *The Acts and Monuments* ed George Townshend, 8 vols (1843–9; repr New York: AMS Press 1965) VI 268–74.

28 *The Writings of John Bradford*, ed Aubrey Townshend, 2 vols, Parker Society 6 and 7 (Cambridge: Cambridge University Press 1848) I 403–5. The same interest in being allowed to prove the doctrinal authority of the homilies is expressed in two other communications written by the imprisoned reformers. See 'A Prayer for Deliverance from Trouble' and 'The Prisoners for the Gospel, their Declaration Concerning King Edward His Reformation' in *The Writings of John Bradford* I 276–7 and 400.

29 Hugh Latimer *Sermons* ed G.E. Corrie, Parker Society 31 (Cambridge: Cambridge University Press 1844) 121. A comparison between Edward VI and the boy-reformer Josias (2 Kings 22–3; 2 Chron 34–5) was made by Cranmer in his coronation address and by Nicholas Udall in his preface to Erasmus' *Paraphrases*; it soon became a cliché among protestants. See *The Literary Remains of King Edward the Sixth* ed J.G. Nicols, 2 vols (1857; facs repr New York: Burt Franklin n d) I ccv note a.

30 John Jewell *An Apology for the Church of England* ed J.E. Booty, Folger Documents of Tudor and Stuart Civilization (Ithaca, NY: Cornell University

Press 1963) 140–1. Cf a remarkably similar passage in William Harrison *The Description of England* [1577] ed Georges Edelen (Ithaca, NY: Cornell University Press 1968) 33. Edelen conjectures that Harrison might have been the author of the appendix to the *Apology* (23 n 17).

31 *The Chronicle and Political Papers of King Edward* VI ed W.K. Jordan (Ithaca, NY: Cornell University Press 1966) 6 and 179.

32 *Martin Bucer and the Book of Common Prayer* ed E.C. Whitaker, Alcuin Club Collections 55 (Essex: The Alcuin Club 1974) 46–9.

33 On these changes, see my 'The 1559 Revisions in *Certayne Sermons or Homilies*: "For the Better Understandyng of the Simple People" ' ELR 8 (1978) 239–55.

34 Kennedy and Frere XVI 60.

35 See William P. Haugaard *Elizabeth and the English Reformation* (Cambridge: Cambridge University Press 1968) 273–6 and *The Two Books of Homilies* ed John Griffiths (Oxford: Oxford University Press 1859) xviii–xxii. Griffiths is correct, I think, in assuming that BL C.25.h.3 is a presentation copy delivered to Elizabeth and that textual differences between it and other copies reflect the last-minute interference of the queen.

36 See Miller MacLure *The Paul's Cross Sermons, 1534–1642* (Toronto: University of Toronto Press 1958).

37 The controversy began in 1572, when John Field and Thomas Wilcox attempted to present their puritan 'Admonition' to parliament. The controversy soon involved John Whitgift, as spokesman of the bishops, and Thomas Cartwright, as his puritan adversary.

38 See the recent studies by Patrick Collinson: 'If Constantine, then also Theodosius: St. Ambrose and the Integrity of the Elizabethan *Ecclesia Anglicana*' JEH 30 (1979) 205–29 and *Archbishop Grindal, 1519–1583: The Struggle for a Reformed Church* (London: Jonathan Cape 1979).

39 Grindal *Remains* ed William Nicholson, Parker Society 33 (Cambridge: Cambridge University Press 1843) 376–90.

40 Grindal *Remains* 375.

41 Grindal *Remains* 382–3.

42 J.E. Neale *Elizabeth I and Her Parliaments* 1584–1601 (London: Jonathan Cape 1957) 70.

43 Neale 71.

44 *Of the Laws of Ecclesiastical Polity, Book* V ed W. Speed Hill (Cambridge: The Belknap Press 1977) 78 and 100.

45 See, for example, *A Parte of a Register* (1593; facs repr New York: Da Capo Press 1973) 82–4, 454, 553–4. Cf Horton Davies *The Worship of the English Puritans* (Westminster: Dacre Press 1948) 64–6 and 182–9, and Paul S. Seaver *The Puritan Lectureships* (Stanford: Stanford University Press 1970) 17–18.

46 R.G. Usher *The Reconstruction of the English Church* 2 vols (New York: D. Appleton and Co 1910) I 325 and II 347. For an account that takes more

seriously than Usher's the strength of the puritans' arguments, see M.H. Curtis 'The Hampton Court Conference and Its Aftermath' *History* 46 (1961) 1-16. Curtis (9 n 29) supplements Usher's sources – William Barlow's *The Summe and Substance of the Conference* (1604) and Harleian MS 828 – with an account of James' comments found in BL Add MS 38492, f 83ᵛ.

47 Cardwell *Documentary Annals* II 202. For the crisis in preaching that precipitated this direction, see Godfrey Davies 'English Political Sermons, 1603–1640' HLQ 3 (1939) 1-22 and M.H. Curtis 'The Alienated Intellectuals of Early Stuart England' *Past and Present* 23 (1962) 26. Note that James' order was taken over by Charles II in a letter to Archbishop Juxon in 1662 (Cardwell *Documentary Annals* II 306–7).

48 Cardwell *Documentary Annals* II 203–6.

49 *The Sermons of John Donne* ed E.M. Simpson and G.R. Potter, 10 vols (Berkeley: University of California Press 1953–62) IV 206–7. Donne's attitude to the homilies is ambivalent: although he disparages them as 'cold meat' (*Sermons* III 338), he praises them in other contexts (*Sermons* X 93–4).

50 *The Letters of John Chamberlain* ed N.E. McClure, 2 vols (Philadelphia: American Philosophical Society 1939) II #413.

51 See Rosemary O'Day *The English Clergy: The Emergence and Consolidation of a Profession* 1558–1642 (Leicester: Leicester University Press 1979) and Rosemary O'Day and Felicity Heal eds *Continuity and Change: Personnel and Administration of the Church in England* 1500–1642 (Leicester: Leicester University Press 1976).

52 *The Paul's Cross Sermons* 170. MacLure goes on to call the homilies 'a trusted guide and ready inspiration for the preachers, an index to most of their commonplaces.'

53 Quoted in Irène Simon *Three Restoration Divines* 2 vols (Paris: Société d'Edition 'Les Belles Lettres' 1967–76) II 231.

54 Quoted in James Downey *The Eighteenth Century Pulpit* (Oxford: Clarendon Press 1969) 6.

55 Noted by Griffiths lxxvi.

56 *Some Sermons Preached on Several Occasions; and an Essay towards a New Book of Homilies* (London 1713) sig oiʳ. Burnet's account of the scheme appears verbatim in Thomas Birch *The Life of the Most Reverend Dr. John Tillotson* (London 1752) 385–90.

57 Burnet sig o1ʳ–o1ᵛ.

58 Burnet sig o2ᵛ.

59 Burnet sig o4ᵛ.

60 *A Second Letter to the Bishop of Salisbury* (London 1713) 32–3.

61 I quote the 1731 edition i and x.

62 Nourse *Practical Discourses* i–ii.

63 Nourse v.

64 *Certain Sermons or Homilies* (London 1758) sig Aiᵛ.

65 *Certain Sermons* (1758) 362.

66 *Certain Sermons* (1758) 60.
67 *John Wesley* ed A.C. Outler (New York: Oxford University Press 1964) 121. Outler prints Wesley's abridgement 122–33.
68 Quoted by Outler *John Wesley* 107.
69 See W.R. Cannon *The Theology of John Wesley with Special Reference to the Doctrine of Justification* (New York: Abingdon Press 1946) 85–8.
70 John Disney *Observations on the Homilies of the Church of England* (London 1790) viii.
71 Disney 16.
72 W.H. Greenleaf *Order, Empiricism and Politics* (Oxford: Oxford University Press 1964) 52 n 73.
73 Disney iv.
74 John Jebb *The Homilies Considered* (London 1826). Jebb was answered by R.H. Graves in *The Homilies Re-Considered* (Dublin 1826). Graves maintained that 'the language of the Homilies is still perfectly intelligible to all ranks, and to the lower order, I believe, (and I speak from experience) much more so than any modern publications. To those that seek for information without display, reverence for antiquity without superstition, zeal without innovation, close reasoning without subtilty, doctrine without metaphysics, morality without methodism, in short the Gospel without human inventions; the nervous condensation, and bold simplicity of the Homilies will supply an almost inexhaustible treasure' (51).
75 Disney 15.
76 Coleridge's annotation appears in *Sermons or Homilies of the United Church of England and Ireland* (London 1815) held in the British Library (c. 43.a.21) The first published transcription appeared in *Critical Annotations ... Being Marginal Notes Inscribed in Volumes Formerly in the Possession of Coleridge* ed W.F. Taylor (Harrow 1889) 47.
77 *The Via Media of the Anglican Church* 2 vols (3rd ed London: Longmans, Green and Co 1885) II 285.
78 On the significance of Tract 90, see A.O.J. Cockshut ed *Religious Controversies of the Nineteenth Century: Selected Documents* (London: Methuen and Co 1966) 60.
79 *The Via Media* 263–4.
80 This generalization stands, despite several attempts to revive interest in the homilies during the twentieth century. At the turn of the century, for example, W.E. Collins, Professor of Ecclesiastical History at King's College, London, published *The Witness of the Homilies* (London: SPCK 1900), a book that accurately sketches the early history of the homilies and asserts their importance in the face of his own concession that they do not bear synodal authority (13 n 1). Sir E.C. Hoskyns, one of the century's most notable biblical scholars, based a series of sermons on the homilies when he was dean of chapel of Corpus Christi College, Cambridge: see *Cambridge Sermons* ed Charles Smyth (London: SPCK 1938). See also Marcus Donovan

and A.R. Vidler 'The Homilies' *Theology* 43 (1941) 284–95. Donovan, who reports that the only time he had ever heard a homily read 'was on a liner, the captain of which conducted the morning service ... and read the Homily against Adultery,' suggests 'it is time that official action should be taken to disown them; if printed at all, they should be put forward, not by the Tract Committee of SPCK, but as documents illustrative of the depth to which religion had sunk as the result of the Reformation' (288).

2 "Lean and Flashy Songs": The Themes, Organization, and Style of the First Book of Homilies

The original book of Tudor homilies owes its existence and its characteristic features to Thomas Cranmer, as Bale recognized in 1557 when he attributed the 'Homelias Christianos Lib. 1' to him.[1] Like another Cranmerian legacy, the Book of Common Prayer, the book of homilies reveals a 'mingled and mixed religion,' a mean between radical protestantism and residual Catholicism that appealed to the temper of the times, despite the worries of some zealots that such 'mediocrity' was leaden, not golden.[2] Although the homilies denounce 'popish' practices and decry the tenets of what was loosely called 'anabaptism,' and although they explain an uncompromising theory of justification, Cranmer evidently hoped that they would win support from those on both the 'right' and 'left' sides of the religious question. His aim was to forge from the extremes a viable anglican way. To this end he commissioned contributions to his project from both 'reforming' and 'conservative' churchmen and then, as editor, reduced anomalies to a minimum. The object was to produce a book with the integrity of Erasmus' *Paraphrases* in English, where there is 'some diversitee of style and endictyng: yet is there in the whole worke no contrarietee of doctrine.'[3]

Although the homilies were always anonymously published, several sixteenth-century witnesses testify to Cranmer's authorship of the homilies on salvation (3), faith (4), and good works (5). Supplementing Bale's attribution is Gardiner's correspondence, which refers to the archbishop as their author.[4] Finally, when John Woolton, an Elizabethan bishop of Exeter, wrote *The Christian Manual* in 1576, he dealt with a justifying faith in much the same way as do the homilies, 'unto whom I remit the reader desirous of an absolute discourse in this matter ... What we teach and think of good works, those homilies written in our English tongue of salvation, faith and works, by that light and martyr of Christ's church,

Cranmer, archbishop of Canterbury, do plain testify and declare; which
are built upon so sure a foundation, that no sycophant can deface them,
nor sophister confute them, while the world shall endure.'⁵ To these
witnesses, we may add the testimony of Cranmer's 'Notes on Justification,'
a catena of quotations he compiled from his reading in the Fathers.⁶
Among the patristic citations found there are several found also in the
three sermons on the topic. For one or more of these reasons, all com-
mentators since the nineteenth century have assigned the crucial portion of
the book to Cranmer.

As if to indicate that traditional doctrine could lead both to and from
advanced protestant thought, Cranmer flanked his own section of the
book with John Harpesfield's 'Of the Misery of All Mankind' (2) and
Edmund Bonner's 'Of Christian Love and Charity' (6). Bonner (1500?-69)
had been enthroned as bishop of London since 1540, and Harpesfield
(1516–78) was his chaplain. Both men later gained notoriety for their part
in the Marian persecution of protestants, and both contributed significantly
to the set of homilies brought out during Mary's reign in an effort to replace Cranmer's collection with what, for Catholics, was a more palatable
gathering of *sermones ad populum*. Yet the homilies written for Cranmer
did double duty: with only minor alterations, such as the translation of
scriptural quotations from English into Latin, the sermons on man's misery
and Christian love reappeared, signed with Harpesfield's name and Bonner's initials, respectively, in the Marian homily book of 1555.⁷ Bonner's
rejection of the Edwardian book in 1547 suggests that these two conservative homilies had been written earlier, perhaps in 1542, before either
author knew fully the degree to which Cranmer would push doctrinal
innovation. If that is the case, Cranmer was able, none the less, to integrate
the unexceptional doctrine expressed by Bonner and Harpesfield with
the distinctly more inflammatory views that he himself put forward at
the later, more propitious time.

Thomas Becon, the author of the homily 'Against Whoredom and
Adultery' (11), had courted reforming opinions so objectionable to the
Henrician authorities that he had twice been required to recant his 'heresies.'⁸ Forced to seek asylum in Kent during the early 1540s, he is responsible for a series of books, written under the pseudonym of 'Theodore
Basille,' that were arraigned by the leaders of the conservative element then
dominant in Henry's church.⁹ Becon found favour with Cranmer in 1547.
Not only was he welcomed into Cranmer's household as chaplain, but
he was made one of the six prebendary preachers at Canterbury cathedral
and through Cranmer was introduced to Somerset, whom he later served as
chaplain. His disquisition on whoredom and adultery probably dates

from 1547, as his biographer D.S. Bailey suggests,[10] since Becon acknowledged the sermon as belonging to his Edwardian phase by placing it in the
second of the three-volume collected works, published in folio in 1563–
4.[11] Becon also wrote an 'Invective Against Swearing,' a tract that may have
influenced the homily 'Against Swearing and Perjury' (7).[12] The homily
departs sufficiently from the 'Invective,' however, that we cannot confi-
dently attach his name to it.

Cranmer and Becon, Bonner and Harpesfield: to these quite different
pairs of men the evidence for authorship leads us. We can only conjecture
who wrote the others. It is likely that Cranmer is responsible for the
'Exhortation to the Reading of Holy Scripture' (1), the collection's exor-
dium. The approach taken by the homily recalls Cranmer's approach to the
topic in his preface to the Great Bible (1540), and five patristic excerpts
corroborating the argument appear too in Cranmer's commonplace book
under the rubric 'Sacrae Scripturae intellectus et utilitas.'[13] Cranmer has
also been linked with the homily 'An Exhortation against the Fear of Death'
(9) by virtue of 'there being among the fragments of his composition,'
according to his seventeenth-century biographer Richard Todd, 'part of a
discourse on this subject';[14] more recent scholarship has been unable to
confirm Todd's claim. Nor has any evidence appeared to support a tradition
that Latimer, who refers to the homilies both in his 'Sermon of the
Plough' and his 'Second [Lenten] Sermon Before Edward VI,' composed
the homily 'Against Strife and Contention' (12).[15] And no one has even
conjectured who wrote the homily 'Of the Declining from God' (8) and
the famous 'Exhortation to Obedience' (10). Cranmer's 'Notes for a
Homily Against Rebellion' are germane to the theme of the latter, but they
stem specifically from the troubles of 1549.[16]

The first book of homilies is more than an anthology of randomly
ordered sermons: Cranmer shaped the whole into two parts, the first of
which treats various matters that pertain to Christian belief, or faith,
the second of which treats several aspects of Christian conduct, or 'works.'
In the first part occur the discourses on original sin and salvation; in the
second we find admonitions on obedience and the need to avoid contention, together with diatribes against swearing and adultery. The book
presents both the principles and practice of Christianity, then, and by so
doing endeavoured to 'cut off antinomianism at the root.'[17]

The deft hand of an editor intent on achieving a larger design and eager
to mould the material he had collected into a logically consistent and
theologically persuasive entity is particularly evident in the first six homilies.
The first sermon extols the primacy of a Christian's reliance on Scripture;
the Word is the source from which all else flows and the foundation on

which edification rests. We hear that Scripture alone is the bedrock of both belief and conduct, an encyclopaedia of the 'most necessary poinctes of our duetie towardes God and our neighebours' (64). The focus of the next sermon, Harpesfield's 'Of the Misery of All Mankind,' is at first resolutely upon man: 'what we be, wherof we be, from whence we came, and whether we shal' (70). Consigned there by original sin, man seems to be in a state of irrevocable misery. But God, we learn near the end of this sermon, intervenes 'of his meere mercie, frely' (75), and Christ's sacrifice atones for man's sinfulness. An overt reference to the 'next homelie' (76), that is, Cranmer's piece on salvation, displays the logic of the sequence thus far: sin evokes grace; *miseria* calls forth *misericordia*. Cranmer's sermons on salvation, faith, and good works carry the twin burden of demonstrating that justification is utterly gratuitous, the effect of faith rather than conduct, and of insisting, only seemingly to the contrary, that such thoroughly Lutheran dogma does not, as a marginal note says, 'teach carnall libertie, or that we should do no good workes.' This, a well-worn crux of Reformation theology, Cranmer attempts to solve by appealing to the scriptural distinction between a lively faith, the consequence of which is a life fruitful with good works, and a dead faith, rooted in intellectual assent but refusing to flower into a life transformed. Cranmer's advocacy of a committed faith emerges most clearly in his assertion that three things are to be noted of a lively faith: it does not lie dead in the heart, but emanates in good deeds; without it no good works can be done; it issues in particular kinds of works – not the veneration bestowed on images by Gentiles and Pharisaical Jews in times past, nor the devotion practised by 'papistical' believers in times present, but rather pursuit of and adherence to the 'moral commandments.' Although Cranmer 'annexed' to his homily on faith the homily on works, this proleptic passage, found near the beginning of the former (92), discloses his determination not to sever two phases of a single impulse. Indeed, since the homily on *works* merely enlarges on the second and third things noted of *faith*, we may infer that Cranmer may originally have intended to write but one sermon on the subject.

The final sermon in the progression we have been tracing is a consideration of Christian love and charity. The sixth homily harks back to the opening of the exhortation to the reading of Scripture by defining charity as love of God, a subsidiary theme of the sermons on faith and works; by defining charity as love of neighbours as well, it hints at a motif that recurs in the remaining six sermons. Bonner's homily, then occurs at an important juncture: it serves both as coda to the book's emphasis on a faith that leads to virtuous living and as prelude to its emphasis on 'civil

conversation' grounded in Christian faith. The sermons that follow –
on swearing, apostasy, the fear of death, obedience, adultery, and contention – display nothing comparable to the internal logic of the first six.

Although the second half of the book is less tightly knit than the first,
we can discern in the design of the whole a hierarchical arrangement
that differentiates important from less important matters and deliberately
and systematically introduces us first to the things essential to salvation.
Such a format is related to the common understanding of the Ten Commandments as having two tables, one treating duties to God and the other,
duties to man, and it has affinities, too, with the priority taken by the
Gospel over the Law. Largely because of Erasmus' and Melanchthon's
influence, this 'Pauline distinction between the *kerygma* and *didache*, and
between the "milk" and "meat" of Christ's message' came to involve a
theological distinction between the things indifferent to salvation (*adiaphora*) and the things essential to it.[18] C.L. Manschreck has observed, *vis-a-
vis* protestant assimilation of the theory, that 'if one insists that justification
is by faith alone, everything else is adiaphoristic.'[19] While Manschreck's
logic flirts with antinomianism, it does explain a tendency visible among
English reformers. Whereas the usual application of the theory separated
the substance or kernel of belief from the adiaphoristic integuments of
rite and ceremony, the 'English reformers would seem to have been the
first to have made any extensive use of the term *adiaphoron* in relation
to doctrine.'[20] An example of the conventional application is the division
of the Ten Articles (1536) into two sorts, the first based on things 'necessary
to salvation' (1–5), the second, on 'such things as have been of a long
continuance for a decent order and honest policy ... although they be not
expressly commanded of God, nor necessary to our salvation' (6–10).[21]
An example of adiaphorism applied to doctrine is the first book of homilies,
with its handful of sermons assigned to the principal concerns of the
Reformation (1–6) and its handful devoted to lesser matters (7–12). Obedience is undoubtedly a virtue, but in this discriminating scheme, it is a
virtue that subsists on faith.

Woven into this scheme is a purposeful 'mediocrity' first fully noted by
Gilbert Burnet in a statement that nicely delineates the controversial
contexts of the first book of homilies.

The chief design in them was, to acquaint the people with the method of salvation
according to the gospel; in which there were two dangerous extremes at that
time that had divided the world. The greatest part of the ignorant commons seemed
to consider their priests as a sort of people who had such a secret trick of saving
their souls, as mountebanks pretend in the curing of diseases; and that there

was nothing to be done but to leave themselves in their hands and the business would not miscarry. This was the chief basis and support of all that superstition which was so prevalent over the nation. The other extreme was, of some corrupt gospellers, who thought, if they magnified Christ much, and depended on his merits and intercession, they could not perish, which way soever they led their lives. In these homilies therefore special care was taken to rectify these errors. And the salvation of mankind was on the one hand wholly ascribed to the death and sufferings of Christ, to which sinners were taught to fly, and to trust to it only, and to no other devices for the pardon of sin. They were at the same time taught that there was no salvation through Christ but to such as truly repented, and lived according to the rules of the gospel. The whole matter was so ordered, to teach them, that, avoiding the hurtful errors on both hands they might all know the true and certain way of attaining eternal happiness.[22]

The design or order of the homilies, then, subverts the 'carnal' practices and doctrinal errors of the 'gospellers' and so-called anabaptists, while asserting salvation *ex sola scriptura* and *ex sola fide* in the face of Roman doctrine. Since this aspect of the homilies has of late been ignored,[23] it is perhaps timely to emphasize that the homilists reveal a bias against corrupt gospellers every bit as pronounced as the prejudice against popish superstition. The homily on swearing makes a case for lawful oath taking before magistrates just because anabaptists objected to the practice. The homily on obedience is not merely an apologia for royal supremacy or a vindication of the schism with Rome; it also takes aim at the anabaptists' unwillingness to submit to temporal authority of any kind on the grounds that secular rulers could not be Christians. The homily on the misery of mankind refutes a denial of the doctrine of original sin, while the homily on declining from God disproves the notion 'that a man who has been reconciled to God is without sin and cannot sin' and tries to eradicate the desperate view that a sinful man cannot regain redemption after baptism.[24] If, as Hardwick claimed, eighteen of the Forty-two Articles (1552) are directed specifically against anabaptists,[25] the homilists' concern for sectarian as well as Roman error is a herald of the things to come. Despite the disclaimer of the final sermon, the homilies are contentious. They testify to divisions within the Church and by confronting extremes discover the seams of Christ's coat. 'He is a Pharisei, he is a gospeler, he is of the new sorte, he is of the olde faythe, he is a new broched brother, he is a good catholique father, he is a papist, he is an heretique' (191): the finger is often in the margins.

The controversial and catechetical purposes of the book give rise to the simplicity of utterance found in the individual sermons. John N. Wall has seen in all the homilies but the second the seven-part format of the classical oration as described by Thomas Wilson and other rhetoricians.[26] But the book follows no such prescriptions for form, and none of the sermons is as elaborately structured as Wall argues. The homilies achieve what W.F. Mitchell terms 'a form of plain consecutive statement' without relying on any of the rhetorical structures recommended by the *artes praedicandi* or the books on construction of orations.[27] Cumulative and reiterative, the homilies in the book envelop their topics with accretions. Unlike Latimer's sermons, they seldom digress from the main thrust of argument or persuasion, since detours could conceivably distract the catholic and popular audiences they had to reach.[28] But the structure of the individual homilies is organic, and is not imposed from without. The first sermon is bipartite: the beginning shows why knowledge of Scripture is necessary and profitable and what that knowledge comprises; the second part exposes the rationalizations of those who refuse to read the Bible and thus clears the way for the exhortation that justifies the full title. Such a simple but effective plan corresponds to Latimer's description of a preacher's functions: *exhortari per sanam doctrinam* and *contradicentes convincere*.[29] These functions underlie too the finely ironic structure of the sermon on the fear of death, which proceeds from a Baconian opening – 'It is not to be marveyled that worldly men do feare to dye' (147) – to an analysis of the three reasons death inspires fear. The sermon belittles the first two of these as fallacies that delude the natural man and admits the reality of the third only for the unfaithful. As in the other homilies, the structure of the sermon and the strategy behind its argument evolve from features inherent in the theme.

The style of the homilies deliberately conforms to the reformers' ideal of plain yet forceful syntax and language, contrived to miss the colloquially undignified register at one extreme and the ornately artificial mode at the other. The major premise leading to cultivation of this style is that 'plainness and simplicity [are] the natural vesture of truth.'[30] Protestants held the Bible itself as the supreme exemplar of such a style and consciously tried to imitate what they regarded as biblical plainness. Although this style admitted metaphors, it did not recruit the devices used by the friars in their sermons – secular tales, elaborately fanciful exegeses, vivid details from saints' lives, and rhetorical embellishments – nor did it enlist the distinctions or etymological and logical subtleties of scholastic and university preaching. An important exponent of this 'low' level of expression was Augustine, who argued its compatibility with the essence of Christianity. Throughout the later Middle Ages, as Auerbach has pointed out, a number of writers shaped the theory and practice of *sermo humilis*, patterning stylistic accommodation of high matter to lowly art after the Incarnation.[31] In England, Wycliffe's writings extol the virtues of *sermo simplex* and, as Peter Auksi has shown, denigrate ornament and superfluity.[32] By the 1540s, Lancelot Ridley's desire to spread 'Goddes worde symply and playnely / more regardynge the truethe / then the eloquence of wordes' was a commonplace in protestant circles.[33]

The homilies, then, opt deliberately for a sober, lucid style, well described by Janton as 'égal et pondéré.'[34] The measured cadences, casually mixed metaphors, and relaxed perspicuity of diction, coupled with unobtrusive alliterative effects, make the following passage typical of the 'not inelegant' plainness evident in them.[35] The homilist is describing God's forsaking us; he dwells, anthropomorphically, on 'significacions ... taken of the properties of mens maners':

So when God doeth shew hys dreadfull countenaunce towardes us, that is to say, doeth send dreadful plagues of sword, famyne or pestilence upon us, it appereth that he is greatly wroth with us. But when he withdraweth from us hys Woorde, the righte doctryne of Christe, hys gracious assistence and ayde, which is ever joyned to hys Worde, and leaveth us to our awne wit, our awne wyll and strength, he declareth then that he beginneth to forsake us. For where as God hath shewed to all them that truely beleve his Gospel his face of mercy in Jesus Christ, whiche doeth so lighten theyr hartes that they, if they beholde it as they ought to do, be transformed to hys image, bee made partakers of the heavenly light and of hys Holy Spirite, and bee fashioned to him in all goodnes requisite to the children of God: so, if they after do neglecte thesame, if they bee unthankefull unto hym, if they ordre not their lyfes accordynge to hys example and doctryne and to the settyng furth of hys glory, he wyll take awaye from them hys kyngdom, his Holy Word wherby he should reigne in them, because they bryng not furth the fruit therof that he loketh for. (139)

From this trim, muscular, and – in the nineteenth-century sense – "nervous' prose, we can move equally easily to the Olympian detachment of the familiar opening of the exhortation to obedience or to the emphatically affective hectoring of the sermon against whoredom and adultery. The cerebral, analytical mode of the one –

Almightie God hath created and appointed all thinges in heaven, yearth and waters in a moste excellent and perfect ordre. In heaven, he hath appoynted distinct orders and states of archangelles and angels. In yearth, he hath assigned kynges, princes, with other governors under them, all in good and necessary ordre. The water above is kept and rayneth doune in due time and ceason. The sunne, mone, sterres, rainbow, thunder, lightning, cloudes and al birdes of the aire do kepe their ordre (161) –

contrasts markedly with the frankly emotional pitch of the other:

What shal I speake of other incommodities which issue and flowe out of this stinkynge puddell of whoredome? Is not that treasure which before all other is most regarded of honest persons, the good fame and name of man and woman, loste through whoredome? What patrimony, what substaunce, what goodes, what riches doth whoredome shortly consume and brynge to naughte! What val-iauntnes and strengthe is many times made weake and destroyed with whoredome! What wyt is so fyne that is not doted and defaced throughe whoredome? (180)

At their most magisterial, the homilies never anticipate the Ciceronianism of Hooker; at their most mundane they never match the colloquialism of Latimer or Lever. At times the limpid merely limps, but on the whole they achieve success with a style that is notoriously difficult to sustain.

An illustration of the problems faced by a writer trying to create a plain style comes in the form of the emendations wrought in the text of the first book of homilies when it was reissued by Elizabeth in 1559.[36] The title-page declares that these revisions were undertaken for stylistic not theolog-ical reasons, since the volume was 'by her Graces advyse perused and oversene, for the better understandying of the simple people.' Greater intelligibility, then, was the goal. The principal effect of these changes was to purge the text of Latinate forms and possibly obscure terms. As 'workes of supererogacion' (1547) becomes 'workes of overflowinge aboundance' (1559), 'delectation' becomes 'delight,' and 'theyr benefactors' becomes 'them that doe good unto them,' we see Latinate deferring to vernacular vocabulary. But this pursuit of plainness can sometimes grate against the original homilist's sense of style. In preferring 'fleshely' (1559) to 'carnall' (1547), for example, the revision loses one component of a resonant alliterative and assonantal sequence: 'Therfore forsakyng the corrupt judge-ment of carnall men, whiche care not, but for their carcasse' (61). Rhythm and cadence sometimes collapse under the stress of the doubling that occurs in 1559. We become 'stuck in the stile,' for instance, of 'matri-monye or wedlock,' 'mitigate and asswage less,' 'consequently or folow-yngly.' In general, the 1559 version of the homilies caters generously to the parishioner (or even the priest) who did not understand or was uncom-fortable with the language's assimilation of Latinate diction, but it also divests the text of a few flourishes. One sentence singled out by Blench as an example of uncommon colloquial vigour simply disappears, perhaps because it was thought too vivid or too beholden to the medieval bestiary tradition: 'Let us loke upon our fete, and then doune pecockes fethers, doune proude harte, doune vile clay, frayle and britle vessels' (73).[37] Since the sentence serves to cap the 'pulling down' motif of the second sermon, its absence in all but the early editions is regrettable. But it was a vexed question for the homilists how to fashion a style reserved enough to clothe the new theology with dignity and popular enough to make that reformed learning accessible to a largely unlearned auditory.

By cleaving mainly to the Bible, the homilists narrowed many of the choices they had to make and furthered knowledge of Scripture among the illiterate who could only hear the Word. The imagery of the homilies, for example, tends to come from biblical sources quoted in the course of the sermons themselves. Gustatory imagery, based on the double understanding of *sapere* as 'taste' and 'know,' percolates through the first sermon and releases the complex of meanings the Bible attaches to partaking of the Word. In as fine an example of *sermo humilis* as any, the final paragraph of the sermon domesticates this imagery and exhorts us to 'ruminate and, as it wer, chewe the cudde, that we maie have the swete jeuse, spirituall effecte, mary, hony, kirnell, tast, comfort, and consolacion' (67) of the Bible. In other places, the homilies develop, as one might expect, the biblical images of trees and fruit. These passages occur not just in the sermons on faith and works, but also in 'Of the Declining from God' (141) and 'Of the Misery of All Mankind' (73). But the imagery of the homilies offers few surprises: the homilies eschew metaphysical wit in favour of what a marginal note calls the 'apt similitude.'

A chaste decorum, a concern for what is apt, governs other considerations too. The homilies rarely testify to there having been a 'Renaissance' as well as a 'Reformation.' A passing reference to Caesar's *Commentaries*, a few exempla culled from Plutarch's *Lives*, a survey of the legal sanctions taken by some heathen nations against whoredom – only in instances such as these do the homilies allude to profane learning. In these cases, moreover, the allusions are part of an 'outdoing' topos for which *quanto magis* is the appropriate formula: the Christian appears beside his pagan counterpart so that it can be revealed 'by how much the more' he should surpass him.[38] Decorum governs as well use of the patristic material, to which Cranmer, especially, is drawn. Virtually all the invocations of patristic authority call on Fathers who belong to the 'primitive' church, defined in 1559 by Jewell's Challenge Sermon as lasting only six hundred years beyond Christ's death.[39] Finally, we may note that for all their simplicity, the homilies do not want rhetorical devices, the figures of thought and speech that equipped much of the poetry and prose of the time with a kind of secret language.[40] Anaphora, the piling up of sentences that begin with the same or similar words, appears frequently, for example, as does antiphora, the anticipation and answering of objections. Rhetorical questioning forms the substance of Becon's sermon on whoredom and adultery and enlivens 'Against Strife and Contention': 'If I be evil reviled, shal I stand stil like a goose, or a foole, with my finger in my mouth? Shall I be such an ydiot and diserde to suffre every man to speake upon me what thei list, to rayle what they liste, to spewe out al their venyme agaynst me at their pleasures?' (195) Alliteration, assonance, anthithesis, and antithesis mixed with parison, or verbal symmetry, occur too. But in comparison with many other works of the period, the homilies rely little on the schemes and tropes, and elevate matter over art. Though not, obviously, what Dr Johnson would call a 'considerable branch of literature,' they are sermons 'wherein was most of God, least of man, when vain flourishes of wit, and words were declined, and the demonstration of Gods power and spirit studied ...' In them we encounter assured simplicity – not 'negligent rudenesse,' but 'studied plainnesse.'[41]

NOTES

1 *Scriptorum illustrium Maioris Brytanniae catalogus* 2 vols (1557; facs repr Farnborough: Gregg International Publishers 1971).

2 John Hooper *Early Writings* ed Samuel Carr, Parker Society 24 (Cambridge: Cambridge University Press 1843): 'The which mingled and mixed religion is so much the more dangerous, as it is accompted for pure and good ... Christ cannot abide to have the leaven of the Pharisees mingled with his sweet flour. He would have us either hot or cold; the lukewarm he vomiteth up, and not without cause' (436); John Jewell to Peter Martyr (1559?): 'Others are seeking after a *golden*, or as it rather seems to me, a *leaden* mediocrity; and are crying out, that the half is better than the whole' (*Zurich Letters* ed Hastings Robinson, 2 vols, Parker Society 43–4 [Cambridge: Cambridge University Press 1842–5] 1 23).

3 Nicholas Udall's preface to Desiderius Erasmus *The first (second) tome or volume of the paraphrase of Erasmus upon the newe testament* (London 1548–9) sig i^r.

4 *The Letters* ed Muller 397, 403, 406, 408, 413.

5 Parker Society 49 (London 1851; facs repr New York: Johnson Reprint 1968) 31.

6 *Miscellaneous Writings and Letters* ed J.E. Cox, Parker Society 18 (Cambridge: Cambridge University Press 1846) 203–11. Much work remains

to be done on the relation of Cranmer's reading to his writing; The Courtenay Library of Reformation Classics series has announced a volume entitled *Cranmer's Library*. In 1892, Edward Burbidge compiled a census of Cranmer's books for Bernard Quaritch's *Contributions toward a Dictionary of English Book Collectors*: see *The Work of Thomas Cranmer* ed G.E. Duffield, intro J.I. Parker (Appleford, Berks: Sutton Courtenay Press 1964) 341–65. Burbidge believed that the 'Notes on Justification ... formed the basis of the Homilies published in 1547, on Salvation, Faith and Works' (346).

7   'The Table,' in Edmund Bonner *A profitable and necessarye doctryne, with certayne homelies adioyned therunto set forth by the reverende father in God, Edmonde byshop of London* (London 1555) f i[v]. The homilies total thirteen.

8   D.S. Bailey *Thomas Becon and the Reformation of the Church in England* (Edinburgh: Oliver and Boyd 1952) 16 and 30–45, referring to recantations in 1541 and 1543.

9   Charles Wriothesley reports that in 1543 Becon cut in pieces eleven of his books during his recantation at Paul's Cross; see *A Chronicle of England During the Reigns of the Tudors* ed W.D. Hamilton, Camden Society n s 11 (London 1875) 142–3. Cf L&P XVII, i, 314. 'Basille's' books are among those specifically proscribed in the proclamation 'Prohibiting Heretical Books' (1546): Hughes and Larkin 1 373–5.

10   *Thomas Becon* 142.

11   *The Workes* 3 vols (London 1560–4) 1 sig CV[v]. The homily itself, introduced by three scriptural admonitions, appears at 11 sig FClvii[r]; it is reproduced in *The Catechism* ed John Ayre, Parker Society 3 (Cambridge: Cambridge University Press 1844) 642–50.

12   *The Early Works* ed John Ayre, Parker Society 2 (Cambridge: Cambridge University Press 1843) 350–92.

13   First noted by Griffiths xxvii.

14   Noted by Cox 128 n 1.

15   *Sermons* ed G.E. Corrie, Parker Society 31 (Cambridge: Cambridge University Press 1844) 61 and 121–2.

16   *Miscellaneous Writings* ed Cox 188–9.

17   The phrase is Parker's in the introduction to *The Work of Thomas Cranmer* xxv.

18   See Bernard J. Verkamp *The Indifferent Mean: Adiaphorism in the English Reformation to 1554* (Ohio: Ohio University Press 1977) 94 and passim.

19   'The Role of Melanchthon in the Adiaphora Controversy' *Archiv für Reformationsgeschichte* 48 (1957) 165.

20   Verkamp 94. He goes on to say that the doctrine of justification became a 'formal principle ... which to almost all the reformers represented the sum and substance of Christian belief to such an extent that its connection with other doctrines was considered a decisive factor in the determination of their fundamentality or lack thereof' (96).

21 Lloyd *Formularies* xvi. The royal injunctions of 1536 also adhere to this
format.

22 *The History of the Reformation of the Church of England* ed Nicholas Pocock,
7 vols (Oxford: Clarendon Press 1865) II 73.

23 Neither I.B. Horst *The Radical Brethren: Anabaptism and the English
Reformation to* 1558 (Nieuwkoop: B. de Graaf 1972) nor D.M. Loades 'Anabaptism and English Sectarianism in the Mid-Sixteenth Century,' in
Reform and Reformation: England and the Continent ed Derek Baker (Oxford: Basil Blackwell 1979) 59–70 notices the homilies' bias against anabaptist
beliefs.

24 See *Certain Sermons* ed G.E. Corrie (Cambridge: Cambridge University
Press 1850) viii–ix.

25 C.H. Hardwick *A History of the Articles of Religion* (Cambridge: Cambridge
University Press 1859).

26 'The "Book of Homilies" of 1547 and the Continuity of English Humanism
in the Sixteenth Century' *Anglican Theological Review* 58 (1976) 83–5.

27 *English Pulpit Oratory from Andrewes to Tillotson* (London 1932; repr New
York: Russell and Russell 1962) 63.

28 On the form and style of Latimer's sermons, see Pierre Janton, *L'Eloquence
et la rhétorique dans les sermons de Hugh Latimer* (Paris: Presses Universi-
taires de France 1968).

29 *Sermons* 129.

30 R.F. Jones *The Triumph of the English Language* (Stanford: Stanford
University Press 1953) 31.

31 *Literary Language and Its Public in Late Latin Antiquity and in the Middle
Ages* tr Ralph Mannheim, Bollingen Series 74 (New York: Pantheon Books
1965) 58–9.

32 'Wyclif's Sermons and the Plain Style' *Archiv für Reformationsgeschichte* 66
(1975) 5–23.

33 Quoted by Auksi 21.

34 Janton 164.

35 The phrase is J.W. Blench's in *Preaching in England in the Late Fifteenth
and Sixteenth Centuries* (Oxford: Basil Blackwell 1964) 153.

36 See my 'The 1559 Revisions in *Certayne Sermons or Homilies*: "For the Better
Understandyng of the Simple People" ' ELR 8 (1978) 239–55.

37 Blench 155.

38 On the *quanto magis* formula in Renaissance preaching, see John O'Malley
*Praise and Blame in Renaissance Rome: Rhetoric, Doctrine, and Reform in
the Sacred Orators of the Papal Court* (Durham, NC: Duke University Press
1979) 57.

39 On the reformers' use of the Fathers, see Hughes Oliphant Old *The
Patristic Roots of Reformed Worship* (Zürich: Theologischen Verlag Zürich
1975) and S.L. Greenslade *The English Reformers and the Fathers of the*

Church (Oxford: Clarendon Press 1960). Greenslade discusses Jewell's famous sermon.

40 See Blench 153–5.

41 I take this description of 'perspicuitie' from John Geree, as quoted in Irène Simon of *Three Restoration Divines* (Paris: Société d'Edition 'Les Belles Lettres' 1967–76) I 27.

The Northern Rising
and *Against Rebellion*

In the northern reaches of England the Reformation had made little
headway when, ten years after Elizabeth's accession, Mary crossed the
border seeking refuge from her Scottish troubles. In these 'dark corners of
the land,' recusants surfaced with disturbing regularity for, as Sir Ralph
Sadler reported to Cecil, 'the ancient faith still lay like lees at the bottom of
men's hearts and if the vessel was ever so little stirred came to the top.'[1]
It was Mary's arrival that stirred the earls of Westmorland and Northumberland, along with Leonard Dacres in Cumberland, into open revolt
against the queen in the winter of 1569. The rebellion brought in its wake
the papal bull *Regnans in excelsis*, an unprecedented governmentally controlled propaganda campaign, and a stiffening of protestant resolve that
resulted in legislative redefinition of treason and a less tolerant policy
on religious nonconformity.[2] The lengthy *Homily against Disobedience and
Wilful Rebellion*, published in the spring of 1570, testifies eloquently to
this renewed protestant zeal. It is one of the most formidable pieces of
verbal artillery rushed to guard an old front.

Although 'seditious bruits' and rumours of war had been rife throughout
the autumn, the rebel forces did not gather until 14 November.[3] Besides
the two earls, the chief instigators were Richard Norton, who had partici-
pated in the Pilgrimage of Grace in 1536, and, in the government's view,
Dr Nicholas Morton. Both men had ties with the continent, but the
apparent involvement of Morton must have been particularly disconcerting
to the protestant regime. Named by Cardinal Pole as one of the six
Canterbury preachers in 1556, Morton had gone to Rome after Elizabeth's
accession and had been appointed apostolical emissary to England. In
1562–3 he had been one of the witnesses during the hearings held to consider the excommunication of Elizabeth. The government's assessment
of Morton's influence, and its awareness that the rebels had been commu-

nicating with the Spanish ambassador about possible military assistance from Philip tended to reinforce the view that 'the coals were kindled here; but the bellows which gave the wind lay at Rome, and there sat he which made the fire.'[4]

As the rebels proceeded south from Durham to Darlington and York, with the aim of eventually freeing Mary at Tutbury, they left no doubt that their cause was religious. At Ripon, they attended mass at the collegiate church and processed behind a banner decorated with the five wounds.[5] The proclamation issued at Darlington on 16 November stressed the patriotism of the insurgents even as it spoke of the need to restore the 'ancyent customes and usages' lest foreign powers intervene.[6] At his trial in 1572 Northumberland, who had been reconciled to Rome in 1567 by an itinerant priest named Copley, testified that 'our first object in assembling was the reformation of religion and preservation of the person of the Queen of Scots, as next heir, failing issue of Her Majesty, which causes I believed were greatly favoured by most of the noblemen of the realm.'[7] Only Westmorland refused to 'colour' the latter cause with religion, 'for such quarrels were accounted rebellion in other countries, and he would not blot his long stainless house.'[8]

The government suppressed the rising easily. On 24 November the queen issued a proclamation declaring the treason of the earls, and within forty days, as Grindal wrote to Bullinger, Sussex had proved victorious in the field.[9] Executions occurred in Durham and elsewhere in the new year,[10] but then the queen, with a proclamation dated 18 February, extended pardon to those followers of the earls who had been 'seduced' into rebellion.[11] Meanwhile, the Dacres rebellion in Cumberland had come to a head. Dacres was proclaimed a traitor on 19 February and was defeated by Lord Hunsdon the next day. With the failure of Dacres, who had been particularly fervent in his hopes for Mary, the northern upstarts had been disarmed, disgraced, and dismayed.

On 25 February 1570, the same day, ironically, on which Edward Dering presumed to prescribe to the queen a puritan's view of her duties, Pope Pius V issued the bull which excommunicated and deposed her.[12] The rebels had written to the pope on 8 November and had been offered money to be sent through Ridolphi, a Florentine banker living in London who was even then a papal agent.[13] By 18 January the southern Catholics, Southampton and Montague, had expressed to Don Guerau, the Spanish ambassador, the hope that the pope would promulgate a bull that would absolve them of allegiance to Elizabeth and thus pave the way for a more successful rebellion than the one in which the northerners had engaged.[14] But the pope's help came too late. By releasing subjects from the obligation of fidelity to the queen the bull merely posed a dilemma for loyal Catholics and exacerbated anti-Catholic sentiments within the protestant establishment.[15] Forced to acknowledge the existence of the bull when John Felton posted a copy on the gate of the bishop's palace on 15 May, the queen proclaimed the arrest of those circulating seditious books and bulls on 1 July.[16]

The perceived gravity of this blow to Elizabethan sovereignty emerges in the literature evoked by it. Even before the rebellion had been crushed, pamphleteers such as John Awdelay, Thomas Norton, William Seres, Edmond Elviden, and William Elderton composed polemical tracts bearing such titles as Norton's *To the Quenes Maiesties Poor Deceived Subiects in the North Countrey*. J.K. Lowers' study of this activity leaves little doubt that it was planned by the government and executed at the government's behest. At a more exalted level was the defence of regal policy in church and state entitled *A Declaration of the Queen's Proceedings since her Reign*.[17] Issued in February 1570, this stern document was deemed suitable for dissemination through the pulpit: 'Considering the multitude of our good people are unlearned, and thereby not able by reading hereof to conceive our mind ... We will that, beside the ordinary publication hereof in all the accustomed places of our Realm, all curates in their parish churches shall at sundry times as the Bishops and ordinaries shall appoint, read this our admonition to their parishioners.'[18] To deal with the pope's claim to have released English subjects from loyalty to Elizabeth, Bishop Cox of Ely asked for Heinrich Bullinger's help. From Zürich, the reliable ally of the English church responded with *Bullae papisticae* (1571), a solemn diatribe translated and published by Arthur Golding in 1572 under the title *A Confutation of the Pope's Bull*. Bullinger's treatise is tripartite: it analyses the fragility of the papal pretensions to absolute authority; it surveys the scriptural, historical, and legal bases for Elizabethan policy; it narrates some of the conflicts fomented by previous popes.[19] Coming from one of the elder statesmen of continental protestants, the tract must have provided reassurance to nervous protestants in England. It is among works such as these that the homily occasioned by the rebellion takes a place.

According to W.E. Collins, the original segments of the lengthy and ambitious homily against rebellion are the prayer and the thanksgiving.[20] The prayer, which in the finished text was to be repeated after each of the homily's sections, certainly does ask for deliverance from the rebels as if the outcome were still in the balance: it is thus reasonable to conjecture that it was written and perhaps used separately during December 1569. The thanksgiving, therefore, might have been composed and offered as a separate prayer in January of 1570, before being attached to the end of the homily as we now have it. The complete work consisting of five parts, divided by the repeated prayer and concluded by the thanksgiving, is difficult to date with precision. It is likely, however, that it was published in April or May, since its strenuous attack on papal interference in regal affairs suggests that it was written after the promulgation of the papal bull on 25 February. That the homily refers neither directly nor obliquely to Pius v and *Regnans in excelsis* need not deter us from using 25 February – and perhaps an even later date, given the time news took to reach England from Rome – as a terminus before which the sermon was not likely to have been written. As T.H. Clancy has observed, the government was content to bury the bull, since it was not eager 'to publicize such a vigorous indictment.'[21] A similar if more complicated desire dictated the silence accorded Mary's role as magnet for the rebels. In this respect, the homily conforms to what seems to be deliberate policy. So delicate was Elizabeth's situation *vis-a-vis* a sovereign ousted from the Scottish throne by 'rebels' that official publications could not risk attacking her, no matter how threatened Elizabeth might have felt by Mary's pretensions to the English throne. J.E. Phillips points out that 'a contemporary reader whose sole information came from authorized accounts of the Northern Rebellion would probably never have been aware of the Queen of Scot's implication in the plot.'[22] The contemporary reader or hearer of the homily would hear plenty about the usurped power of various bishops of Rome and would learn much of past incidents in which popes had excommunicated and deposed rulers, but from the homily he would receive not even a whisper of the news that such history had recently repeated itself in a way that involved the Queen's half-sister.

Sandys and Grindal, in reflecting on the rebellion several years after the fact, ascribed the insurgence to the ignorance of the people involved, ignorance which they attributed directly to the lack of preaching.[23] The homily was originally intended as a pedagogical instrument for use in the northern province exclusively and it was not until 1571 that it was added to the second book of homilies, thus to become a fixture of preaching throughout the realm. It was probably conceived during the hurly-burly days of December when a minute found in the 'Memorial of Proceeding to Be Taken in the North' notes that 'the vulgar people wold be tought, how this rebellion was prnicious [pernicious] to the Realme, and ageynst the honor of God.'[24] It may also be related, as Collins suggests, to some instructions issued by the queen to Sussex and his fellow commissioners for dealing with the supporters of Leonard Dacres:

You shall cawse their repentance to be manifestly seen by their submission and

confession of their horrible crymes, and to thintent they may be the redier to ac-
knowledg the same, It shall do well, that at certan days mete for the purpose
there may be Instructions given them by some discrete prechers in open sermons,
to the which they may be directed to resort before they shall appear before you,
and there be tought to know their synes against Almighty God, and their offences
agaynst us.[25]

In any case, the homily, as its protracted and rhetorical insistence on rebels'
ignorance tends to confirm, had the practical and immediate purpose of
repairing the gap left in parishioners' knowledge by deficiencies in reformed
preaching. That such an aim should have resulted in a work that distils
what is sometimes called the Tudor myth is not surprising, for the rebellion
itself quickly gained a mythical status, as is seen in a comment found in
one of Sandys' sermons: 'The red bloody dragon doth still vex the woman
with her child, Christ with his Church. The practice hereof all nations
have felt, and England cannot forget. The late rebellion in this realm, raised
for no other cause but by force to subvert religion, by no other man than
the father of these foxes, is fresh in memory.'[26]

NOTES

1 Quoted by Anthony Fletcher *Tudor Rebellions* (London: Longmans 1968)
   105.
2 On the rebellion and various aspects of its aftermath, see Fletcher 91–106;
   Wallace T. MacCaffrey *The Shaping of the Elizabethan Regime* (London:
   Jonathan Cape 1969) 221–46; J. Neale 'Parliament and the Articles of Reli-
   gion 1571' EHR 67 (1952) 510–21; J.K. Lowers *Mirrors for Rebels: A Study
   of Polemical Literature Relating to the Northern Rebellion in 1569* (Berkeley:
   University of California Press 1953); M.E. James 'The Concept of Order and
   the Northern Rising 1569' *Past and Present* 60 (1973) 49–83; John Bellamy
   The Tudor Law of Treason (Toronto: University of Toronto Press 1979).
   Primary material is found in *Memorials of the Rebellion of 1569* ed Cuthbert
   Sharpe (London: John Bowyer Nichols and Sons 1840) and *Calendar
   of State Papers, Domestic: Addenda 1566–1579* ed M.A.E. Green, 2 vols (London 1867–72).
3 For the 'seditious bruits,' see CSPD, *Addenda 1566–79* 99.
4 John Jewell *A View of a Seditious Bull*; quoted by W.E. Collins *Queen
   Elizabeth's Defence of Her Proceedings in Church and State* (1899; repr London: SPCK 1958) 12.
5 R.R. Reid 'The Rebellion of the Earls, 1569' TRHS n s 20 (1906) 198.
6 Text in Fletcher 150.

7 Fletcher 153.
8 CSPD, *Addenda* 1566–1579 404.
9 Hughes and Larkin II 323–5 (#567); *Zurich Letters* 332.
10 The extent of the executions has been studied by H.B. McCall 'The Rising in the North: A New Light upon One Aspect of It' *Yorkshire Archaeological Journal* 18 (1905) 74–87.
11 Hughes and Larkin II 326–8 (#568).
12 Text in G.R. Elton ed *The Tudor Constitution* (Cambridge: Cambridge University Press 1960) 414–18.
13 McCaffrey 232.
14 J.A. Froude *History of England from the Fall of Wolsey to the Death of Elizabeth* 12 vols (New York: Scribner, Armstrong and Co 1873) IX 561.
15 Patrick McGrath asserts that the bull 'was issued in ignorance of the fact that a rebellion had already taken place and had ended in disaster': see *Papists and Puritans Under Elizabeth I* (New York: Walker and Co 1967) 70.
16 Hughes and Larkin II 341–3 (#577).
17 This is the subject of Collins' *Queen Elizabeth's Defence.*
18 Collins 51.
19 For discussion of the work and its structure, see David J. Keep 'Bullinger's Defence of Queen Elizabeth,' in *Heinrich Bullinger 1504–1575: Gesammelte Aufsatze zum 400. Todestag* Band II ed Ulrich Gabler and Erland Herkenrath (Zürich: Theologischen Verlag Zürich 1975) 231–41.
20 Collins 20 n 8.
21 *Papist Pamphleteers: The Allen-Persons Party and the Political Thought of the Counter-Reformation in England, 1572–1615* (Chicago: Loyola University Press 1964) 47.
22 *Images of a Queen: Mary Stuart in Sixteenth-Century Literature* (Berkeley: University of California Press 1964) 58.
23 Edwin Sandys *Sermons* ed John Ayre, Parker Society 46 (Cambridge: Cambridge University Press 1841) 154; Grindal *Remains* 380.
24 Collins 30.
25 Collins 31.
26 *Sermons* 65.

4 The Texts

The Text of the First Book of Homilies

This edition aims to make available the text of the homilies in a form close to that in which they were read and heard in mid-sixteenth-century England. I have by no means attempted to produce a 'definitive' edition, since that task would have required exhaustive examination and collation of all the issues of some thirty-four editions of the first book that appeared between 1547 and 1687. But I have attempted, while keeping in mind the needs of readers unfamiliar with the language and idiom of Tudor English, to present an old-spelling text that is, substantially, Edwardian. In this respect, the version of the first book of homilies that appears here differs significantly from that found in the monumental edition of John Griffiths (based on an Elizabethan copy-text and modernized) or that found in M.E. Rickey and T.B. Stroup's black-letter facsimile (reproduced from the 1623 folio edition). The principle, now well established, that early editions yield purer texts than later ones was acknowledged even during the sixteenth century: Francis Thynne in his *Animadversions* on Speght's Chaucer said that a text 'must needs gather corruptione, passyng through so manye handes, as the water dothe, the further it runneth from the pure founteyne.' For this fundamental reason priority is given here to the 1547 edition of the homilies.

Deviations from the 1547 edition are of several kinds. Substantive errors have been corrected almost invariably on the authority of one or more of three later editions (1549, 1559, and 1623) which have been collated in their entirety. Each of these editions is significant in a different way. The 1549 edition is the first of the early ones to divide the homilies into parts. The lections thus created involved the interpolation into the original sermons of summary and transitional passages, which are here printed within square brackets. The 1559 edition, the first of Elizabeth's reign, is important because in it many words and phrases are altered 'for the better understandyng of the simple people.' I have not admitted these revisions into the text, but the critical apparatus that accompanies each homily makes it possible for those interested in studying them to ascertain the nature and extent of the changes, which, together with the division of the homilies into parts, were incorporated into all subsequent editions. The last edition I have collated bears the date 1623: it is the first collected edition of the homilies from both books, and copies of it abound in North American and British libraries.

Although the text I have prepared is conservative in substance, its accidentals have been modernized to some extent. The conventional practice of normalizing *i* and *j*, and *u* and *v*, and of expanding such abbreviations as ampersands and tildes (the abbreviation for an omitted *n*) has been followed. The loosely rhetorical punctuation, moreover, has sometimes been modified in the interest of intelligibility; paragraphing and capitalization, often highly irregular in the 1547 edition, have also been subjected to editorial intervention. The result, I trust, is a practical text that none the less preserves the essence of the original for the contemporary student of sixteenth-century thought and literature.

Among the chief problems to be faced by any editor of the homilies is how to indicate their dependence on Scripture. Strict quotation from the Bible mixes with paraphrase and allusion in the text, so that often we encounter a collage of exact and inexact references to Scripture – an assemblage of verses, phrases, and even individual words that have been run together to form a new whole. The marginal glosses found in the early editions acknowledge the heavy reliance of the homilists on Scripture, but nowhere in the first book do the glosses specify the verses adduced: only book and chapter references appear. In some sermons, especially Harpesfield's 'Of the Misery of All Mankind,' it is clear that the Vulgate rendering is the version invoked, yet in other instances, as one might expect, the Coverdale or 'Great' Bible seems to be recollected. In the text found here, I resort to the following procedures:

1 As in the sixteenth-century editions, biblical material is not differentiated from the surrounding text either by italics or quotation marks (which are, therefore, reserved for the marking of patristic and historical quotations).
2 The notes signal the homilists' indebtedness to the Bible and expand on the marginal glosses by adding verse numbers. The brief marginal passages that merely abstract the text have not been reproduced.
3 These notes refer to the Authorized Version, its names for biblical

books, and its numbering of the Psalms. For the apocryphal books, I
have used *The Oxford Annotated Bible with the Apocrypha* ed H.G. May
and B.M. Metzger (New York: Oxford University Press 1965).
4 When the Vulgate rendering is especially pertinent, the notes so indicate.

Readers who wish a more detailed bibliographical account of the various editions in which the homilies appeared should consult volume 1 of
the revised STC (forthcoming) or John Griffiths' 'A Descriptive Catalogue
of Editions of the Homilies to the End of the Seventeenth Century,' in
The Two Books of Homilies Appointed to be Read in Churches (Oxford: Oxford
University Press 1859) xlix–lxxvi.

EDITIONS USED IN PREPARING THE TEXT

1547 (British Library)
Title: CERTAYNE / Sermons, or Home- / lies, appoynted by the Kyn- / ges
Maiestie, to be decla- / red and redde, by all per- / sones, Uicars, or
Cu- / rates, euery Son- / daye in their / churches, / where / they haue /
Cure. / Anno. 1547.
Collation: A⁴–Z⁴
Colophon: IMPRINTED AT LONDON, THE / LASTE DAIE OF IVLII, IN THE /
FIRST YERE OF THE REIGNE / OF OVR SOVEREIGNE LORD / KYNG EDVVARD
THE. VI. / BY RICHARD GRAFTON / PRINTER TO HIS / MOSTE ROYALL /
MAIESTIE. / ANNO. 1547. /
Cum priuilegio ad impri- / mendum solum.

1549 (British Library)
Title: CERTAYNE / Sermons, or Home- / lies, appointed by the Kyn- / ges
Maiestie, to be decla- / red and redde, by all per- / sones, Uicars, or Cu- /
rates, euery Son- / daye in their / churches, / wher / they haue / Cure /
Newly imprinted and by / the Kynges highnes / aucthorite deuided. / ANNO
M.D.XLIX.
Collation: A⁴–Z⁴, Aa⁴
Colophon: Excusum Londini, in aedibus Richardi Graftoni / Regij Impressoris. / Mense Augustij. M.D.xlix. / Cum priuilegio ad imprimendum
solum.

1559 (Bodleian Library, Oxford)
Title: Certayne Sermons appoynted by / The Quenes Maiestie, / to be
declared and read, / by all Persones, Uycars, and / Curates, euery Sonday
and / holy daye, in theyr Churches: / And by her Graces aduyse / perused
and ouersene, for / the better vnderstan- / dyng of the simple / people. /

Newly Imprynted in partes, / accordyng as is menci- / oned in the booke /
of Commune prayers. / (:) / Anno. M.D.L.ix. / Cum priuilegio Regiae /
Maiestatis.
Collation: A⁴–Z⁴, Aa⁺
Colophon: Imprynted at London in Powles / Churchyarde by Richarde
Iugge and / Iohn Cavvood printers to the / Quenes Maiestie. / Cum
priuilegio Regiae Maiestatis.

1623 (The University of Calgary Library, Special Collections Division)
Title: CERTAINE SERMONS OR HOMILIES / appointed to be read in /
CHVRCHES, / In the time of the late Queene Elizabeth / of famous memory.
/ And now thought fit to bee reprinted by / Authority from the KINGS
most / Excellent Maiestie. / LONDON, / Printed by IOHN BILL, Printer to /
the Kings most Excellent / Majestie. 1623.
Collation: a⁺, A⁶–I³, Aa⁶–Ddd⁶
Colophon: LONDON / Printed by John Bill, Printer to the Kings most /
Excellent Maiestie. 1623.

The Text of the Homily against Rebellion

In editing *An Homelie against Disobedience and Wylfull Rebellion*, I have
used essentially the same principles as were explained in the note on the
text of the first book of homilies. The text is based on the version in
five parts published, one can reasonably conjecture, in early 1570, although
the book was printed with neither title-page nor date. It is collated with
an edition printed in six parts later in 1570 and with the folio edition
of 1623.

The reader will note that for this homily alone scriptural quotations
appear within quotation marks. This is not an inconsistency, but rather a
style dictated by the practice of the 1570 editions, which mark with inverted
commas found in the extreme margins the biblical material actually quoted.
In other instances, the marginal glosses direct the reader to clusters of
biblical verses that support the argument or supplement it with further
information. For the convenience of the modern reader I have expanded in
the notes the marginal glosses that allude to historical figures and events.

EDITIONS USED IN PREPARING THE TEXT

A (Cambridge University Library)
Heading [No Title]: An Homelie against / disobedience and wylfull
rebellion.

Collation: A⁴–K⁴. The following lacunae have been filled from the Huntington Library copy: Aiiii^{r–v}, Diiii^v–Diiii^r, Hiiii^v–Ii^r.

Colophon: Imprinted at Lon- / don in Powles Churchyarde by / Richard Iugge and Iohn Cawood, / printers to the Queenes Ma- / iestie. / Cum priuilegio Regiae Maiestatis.

B (British Library)

Heading [No Title]: An Homilie a / gaynst disobedience and wyl / ful rebellion.

Collation: A⁴–K⁴

Colophon: Imprinted at Lon- / don in Powles Churchyarde, by Ri- / charde Iugge and Iohn Cawood, / Printers to the Queenes / Maiestie. / Cum priuilegio Regiae Maiestatis.

1623

See 49 above.

CERTAYNE SERMONS OR HOMELIES, Appoynted by the Kynges Majestie to Be Declared and Redde by All Persones, Vicars, or Curates, Every Sondaye in Their Churches Where They Have Cure.

Anno. *1547.*

A Table of the Sermones or Homelies Conteined in This Presente Volume

Finis.

The Preface [1547]

The Kynges moste excellent Majestie, by the prudente advyse of hys moste deere beloved uncle, Edwarde Duke of Somersett, governor of hys Majesties persone and protector of all hys Hyghnes realmes, dominions and subjectes, with the reste of hys moste honorable counsayll, moste graciously considerynge the manifolde enormities whiche heretofore have crept into hys Graces realme throughe the false usurped power of the Bishoppe of Rome and the ungodly doctryne of hys adherentes, not onelye unto the greate decaye of Christian religion, but also, if Gods mercy were not, unto the utter destruction of innumerable soules whiche, through hypocrysy and pernicious doctrine, were seduced and brought from honoryng of the alone, true, livynge and eternall God unto the worshippyng of creatures, yea, of stockes and stones, from doyng the commaundementes of God unto voluntary workes and phantasyes invented of men, from true religion unto popishe supersticion; considerynge also the earnest and fervent desire of his derely beloved subjectes to bee delivered from all errors and supersticions, and to be truely and faythefully instructed in the verye Worde of God, that lively foode of mannes soule, wherby they may learne unfainedly and accordyng to the mynd of the Holy Ghoste, expressed in the Scriptures, to honor God and to serve their Kyng with all humilitie and subjeccion, and godly and honestly to behave theim selfes toward all men; agayn callynge to remembraunce that the next and moste ready waie to expell and avoide, aswell all corrupte, vicious and ungodly livynge, as also erronious doctrine tendyng to supersticion and idolatrie, and clerely to put away all contencion whiche hath heretofore rysen through diversitie of preachyng, is the true settyng furthe and pure declarynge of Gods Woorde, whiche is the principall guyde and leader unto all godlinesse and vertue; finally, that all curates, of what learnyng soever they be, may have some godly and fruitfull lessons in a readines to reade and declare unto their parishioners, for their edifiyng, instruction and comfort: hath caused a booke of homelies to bee made and set furthe, wherein is conteined certain wholsome and godly exhortacions to move the people to honor and worshippe almighty God and diligently to serve hym, every one accordynge to their degre, state and vocacion. The whiche homelies, his Majestie commaundeth and streightely chargeth all persones, vicares, curates and all other havyng spirituall cure, every Sondaye in the yere, at hygh masse when the people be moste gathered together, to reade and declare to their parishioners, playnly and distinctely, in suche ordre as they stande in the boke – excepte any sermon bee preached, and then for that cause onely, and for none other, the reading of the sayde homelie to be differred unto the nexte Sondaye folowyng. And when the foresayde boke of homelies is redde over, the Kynges Majesties pleasure is that thesame be repeted and redde agayn, in suche lyke sorte as was before prescribed, unto suche tyme as his Graces pleasure shall further be knowen in thys behalfe.

Also, hys Majestie commaundeth that the sayde ecclesiasticall persones, upon the firste holy daye fallyng in the weke tyme of every quarter of the yere, shall reade his Injunccions openly and distinctely to the people, in maner and fourme in thesame expressed. And upon every other holy and festival daye through the yere, likewise fallyng in the weke tyme, they shal recite the Pater Noster, the Articles of our Fayth and the Tenne Commaundementes in Englishe, openly before all the people, as in the sayd Injunccions is specified: that all degrees and al ages may learne to know God and to serve him, accordynge to hys Holy Woorde.

Amen.

The Preface [1559]

Considering howe necessary it is that the Worde of God, which is the onely foode of the soule and that mooste excellent lyght that wee muste walke by in this our most daungerous pylgrymage, shoulde at all convenient times be preached unto the people, that thereby they may both learne theyr duetie towardes God, theyr Prince and theyr neyghbours, accordyng to the mynd of the Holy Ghoste expressed in the Scriptures; and also to avoyde the manyfolde enormities which hearetofore by false doctrine have crept into the churche of God, and howe that all they whiche are appoynted ministers have not the gyft of preachyng sufficiently to instruct the people which is commytted unto them, whereof great inconvenyences myght ryse and ignoraunce styll be mayntayned, yf some honeste remedye be not speedely founde and provyded: the Quenes moste excellent Majestie, tenderynge the soule health of her lovyng subjectes and the quietyng of theyr consciences in the chiefe and principall poyntes of Christian religion, and wyllyng also by the true settyng foorth and pure declaryng of Gods Word, which is the principall guyde and leader unto all godlynesse and vertue, to expell and dryve awaye as well all corrupt, vicious and ungodly lyvynge, as also erronious and poysoned doctrines tendyng to supersticion and idolatrye, hath, by thadvyse of her moste honourable counsayloures for her discharge in this behalfe, caused a boke of homelies, which hearetofore was sette foorth by her moste lovynge brother, a Prince of moste worthy memory, Edwarde the Syxte, to be prynted a newe. Wherein are conteyned certayne wholsome and godly exhortacions to move the people to honour and worshyppe almyghty God and diligently to serve hym, every one accordynge to theyr degree, state and vocacion. All whiche homelies her Majestie commaundeth and strayghtly chargeth all persons, vycars, curates and all other havyng spirituall cure, every Sonday and holy day in the yere, at the ministryng of the Holy Communion,

or if there be no Communion ministered that day, yet after the Gospell
and Crede, in suche order and place as is appoyncted in the Booke of
Common Prayers, to reade and declare to theyr paryshyoners playnely and
distynctlye one of the sayde homelies in suche order as they stande in
the booke – except there be a sermon, according as it is injoyned in the
booke of her Hyghnesse Injunctions, and then for that cause onely, and for
none other, the readyng of the sayde homelye to be dyfferred unto the
next Sonday or holy day folowyng. And when the foresayde boke of
homelyes is read over, her Majesties pleasure is that the same bee repeated
and read agayne, in such lyke sorte as was before prescrybed. Furthermore,
her Hyghnesse commaundeth that notwithstandyng this order the sayde
ecclesiasticall personnes shal reade her Majesties Injunctions at such tymes
and in suche order as is in the booke thereof appoynted. And that the
Lordes Prayer, the Articles of the Fayth and the Ten Commaundementes
be openly readd unto the people, as in the sayde Injunctions is specifyed,
that all her people of what degree or condicion so ever they be maye
learne howe to invocate and call upon the name of Godde and knowe what
dutie they owe both to God and man: so that they maye pray, believe
and worke accordynge to knowledge whyle they shall lyve heare, and after
this lyfe be with hym that with his bloud hath bought us all. To whom
with the Father and the Holy Ghost, be all honor and glory for ever.
   Amen.

NOTES

55   *The Preface [1547]*: superseded in 1559 and in all subsequent editions by the
       Elizabethan preface that follows.
     Somersett ... honorable counsayll: On Seymour's advanced protestantism, see
       M.L. Bush *The Government Policy of Protector Somerset* (London: Edward
       Arnold 1975) esp 106–12. On Henry VIII's will, which influenced the
       membership of the Edwardian Privy Council and pointedly excluded the
       conservative Stephen Gardiner, see W.K. Jordan *Edward VI: The Young
       King* (London: George Allen and Unwin 1968) 128–9 and D.E. Hoak *The
       King's Council in the Reign of Edward VI* (Cambridge: Cambridge Uni-
       versity Press 1976).
     stockes and stones: used to justify iconoclasm, the belief that images are idols
       was widespread among protestants. It appears, for instance, in 'The
       Homily against Peril of Idolatry' in the second book of homilies. The
       phrase *stockes and stones* dates, according to the OED, from at least the time
       of Aelfric, c 1000.

voluntary workes: penitential deeds undertaken, without prompting, by the forgiven sinner in order to recompense the temporal punishment due to sin and to relieve the suffering of the soul in purgatory. Protestants objected that Christ's merit alone achieved satisfaction. Cf Article 14 of the Thirty-nine Articles.

unfainedly: without pretence.

56 *streightely*: straightway.

persones, vicares, curates: Although the terms used to describe members of the secular clergy were sometimes applied loosely, a parson was the rector, or the incumbent of an ecclesiastical living who was paid the greater or rectorial tithes; a vicar was the rector's duly appointed substitute, recipient of the minor tithes; a curate was a chaplain invested with cure of souls. By naming all three, the preface and the title-page take pains to ensure that all the classes of the clergy will be required to read the homilies.

differred: deferred.

Injunccions: the royal injunctions issued during the 1547 visitation and frequently bound with the homilies. Similar sets of injunctions were issued in 1536 and 1558 as means of declaring royal jurisdiction over matters ecclesiastical. Although their constitutional status is uncertain, they were generally regarded as having the force of law. For the pertinent injunctions, see Cardwell *Documentary Annals* 12, 30–5.

TEXTUAL APPARATUS

Title-Page

52 Certayne ... Cure] Newly imprinted and by the / Kynges highnes aucthorite / devided *added 1549*; Certayne Sermons, appoynted by / the Quenes Majestie, / to be declared and read, / by all Persones, Vycars, and Curates, / every Sonday and / holy daye, in theyr Churches: / And by her Graces advyse / perused and oversene, for / the better understan / dyng of the simple / people. / Newly Imprynted in partes, / accordyng as is mencioned, / in the booke / of Commune prayers. / Anno. M.D.L.ix. / Cum privilegio Regiae Majestatis. *1559*; Certaine / Sermons / or / Homilies / appointed to be read in / Churches, / In the time of the late Queene Elizabeth / of famous memory. / And now thought fit to bee reprinted by / Authority from the Kings most / Excellent Majestie. / London / Printed by John Bill, Printer to / the Kings most Excellent Majestie. *1623*.

A Table

54 A Table] *after Preface 1623*. or Homelies] *not in 1559*. i–xii] *wrongly numbered 1549; paginated in right margin 1623.*

Preface [1547]
55–6 hygh masse] the communion *1549.* festival] *1549*; fevall *1547*.

Preface [1559]
57–8 The Preface] as it was published in the yeere 1562 *added* 1623. Godde and
      knowe] *1623*; Godde, Knowe *1559*.

1   A Fruitfull Exhortation to the Readyng and Knowledge of Holy Scripture

Unto a Christian man there can be nothynge either more necessarie or profitable then the knowledge of Holy Scripture: forasmuche as in it is conteyned Gods true Word, settyngefurth his glorie and also mannes duetie. And there is no truth, nor doctrine, necessary for our justificacion and everlastyng salvacion, but that is, or may be, drawen out of that fountain and welle of truth. Therfore, as many as be desirous to entre into the right and perfect way unto God must applie their myndes to knowe Holy Scripture, without the which they can neyther sufficiently knowe God and his will, neither their office and duetie. And as drynke is pleasaunt to them that be drie, and meat to them that be hungery, so is the readyng, hearyng, searchyng and studiyng of Holy Scripture to theim that be desirous to knowe God or them selfes, and to do his will. And their stomackes only do lothe and abhorre the heavenly knowledge and foode of Gods Word that be so drouned in worldly vanities that they neither savor God, nor any godlines: for that is the cause why they desire suche vanities rather then the true knowledge of God. As they that are sicke of an ague, whatsoever they eate or drinke, though it bee never so pleas-aunt, yet it is as bitter to theim as wormewoode, not for the bitternesse of the meat, but for the corrupt and bitter humor that is in their awne toungue and mouth: even so is the swetenesse of Gods Woorde bitter, not of it self, but onely unto them that have their myndes corrupted with long custome of synne and love of this world. Therfore, forsakyng the corrupt judgement of carnall men whiche care not, but for their carcasse, let us reverently heare and reade Holy Scriptures, whiche is the foode of the soule. Let us diligently searche for the welle of life in the bokes of the New and Old Testament, and not ronne to the stinkyng podelles of mennes tradicions, devised by mannes imaginacion for our justificacion and salvacion.

For in Holy Scripture is fully conteined what we ought to do and what
to eschewe, what to beleve, what to love and what to loke for at Gods
handes at length. In those bokes we shall finde the Father, from whome,
the Sonne, by whome, and the Holy Ghoste, in whome, all thynges have
their beyng and conservacion, and these thre persones to be but one
God and one substaunce. In these bokes we may learne to know our selfes,
how vile and miserable we be, and also to know God, how good he is of
hymself and how he communicateth his goodnes unto us and to al creatures. We may learne also in these bokes to know Gods wil and pleasure,
asmuche as, for this present tyme, is convenient for us to knowe. And,
as the greate clerke and godly preacher Sainct Jhon Chrisostome saieth,
'whatsoever is required to salvacion of man is fully conteyned in the
Scripture of God. He that is ignoraunte maye there learne and have
knowledge. He that is harde harted and an obstinate synner shall there
finde eternall tormentes, prepared of Gods justice to make him afraied and
to mollifye him. He that is oppressed with misery in this world shal there
find relief in the promises of eternal life, to his great consolacion and
comfort. He that is wounded by the devil unto death shall find there
medecine, wherby he may be restored agayn unto health.' 'If it shal require
to teach any truth or reprove false doctrine, to rebuke any vice, to com-
mend any vertue, to geve good counsail, to comfort, or to exhort, or to do
any other thyng requisite for our salvacion, all those thinges,' saieth S.
Chrisostome, 'we maye learne plentifully of the Scripture.' 'There is,' saith
Fulgentius, 'abundantly enough, both for men to eate and children to
sucke. There is whatsoever is convevient for all ages, and for all degrees
and sortes of men.'

These bokes, therfore, ought to be much in our handes, in our eyes, in
our eares, in oure mouthes, but moste of all, in our hartes. For the
Scripture of God is the heavenly meate of our soules; the hearing and
kepyng of it maketh us blessed, sanctifieth us and maketh us holy. It
converteth our soules; it is a light lanterne to oure fete; it is a sure, a
constant and a perpetuall instrument of salvacion. It geveth wisedom
to the humble and lowly hartes; it comforteth, maketh glad, chereth and
cherisheth our consciences. It is a more excellent jewell or treasure then
any golde or precious stone; it is more sweter then hony or hony combe;
it is called the best parte whiche Marie did chose, for it hath in it everlastynge comforte. The wordes of Holy Scripture be called wordes of everlastyng life: for they be Gods instrument, ordeyned for thesame purpose.
They have power to converte through Gods promise and thei be effectuall
through Gods assistence; and, beyng received in a faithfull harte, thei
have ever an heavenly spirituall woorkyng in them. Thei are lively, quicke,

and mightie in operacion, and sharper then any two edged sworde, and
entereth through even unto the dividyng a sonder of the soule and the
spirit, of the joyntes and the mary. Christ calleth hym a wise buylder
that buyldeth upon his Worde, upon his sure and substanciall foundacion.
By this Woorde of God we shalbee judged, for the Worde that I speake,
saieth Christ, is it that shall judge in the last daie. He that kepeth the
Worde of Christ is promised the love and favor of God, and that he shalbe
the mansion-place or temple of the blessed Trinitie. This Woorde whosoever is diligent to reade and in his harte to printe that he readeth, the
great affeccion to the transitory thynges of this worlde shalbe minished
in hym, and the greate desire of heavenly thynges that bee therein promised
of God shall increase in hym. And there is nothyng that so muche estab-
lisheth our faithe and trust in God, that so much conserveth innocencie
and purenesse of the harte, and also of outwarde godly life and conversacion, as continual readyng and meditacion of Gods Woorde. For that
thyng whiche by perpetuall use of readyng of Holy Scripture and diligent
searchyng of thesame is depely printed and graven in the harte at length
turneth almoste into nature. And moreover, the effecte and vertue of Gods
Worde is to illuminate the ignorant and to geve more light unto theim
that faithefully and diligently reade it, to comfort their hartes, and to in-
corage theim to performe that whiche of God is commaunded. It teacheth
pacience in all adversitie; in prosperitie, humblenes; what honour is due
unto God, what mercie and charitie to our neighbor. It geveth good
counsaill in al doubtfull thynges. It sheweth of whom we shall loke for
aide and helpe in all perils, and that God is the onely gever of victory in all
battailes and temptacions of our enemies, bodily and ghostely. And in
readyng of Gods Woorde, he moste proffiteth not alwaies that is most
ready in turnyng of the boke, or in saiyng of it without the boke, but
he that is moste turned into it, that is most inspired with the Holy Ghost,
moste in his harte and life altered and transformed into that thyng whiche
he readeth: he that is daily lesse and lesse proude, lesse irefull, lesse
covetous and lesse desirous of worldely and vayne pleasures; he that daily,
forsakyng his olde vicious life, increaseth in vertue, more and more. And
to be short, there is nothyng that more mainteineth godlines of the mynd
and expelleth ungodlines then doth the continuall readyng or hearyng
of Gods Worde, if it be joyned with a godly mynde and a good affeccion
to knowe and folowe Gods wil. For without a single iye, pure intent
and good mynde, nothyng is allowed for good before God. And on the
otherside, nothyng more obscureth Christ and the glory of God, nor
induceth more blindnesse and all kyndes of vices then doth the ignoraunce
of Gods Word.

[The Second Parte of the Sermon of the Holie Scripture

In the first part of this homilie which exhorteth to the knowledge of Holie
Scriptur was declared wherefore the knowledge of thesame is necessarie
and profitable to al men, and that by the true knowledge and understandyng of Scripture, the most necessary poinctes of our duetie towardes God
and our neighebours are also knowen. Now as concerning thesame matter,
yow shal heare wat foloweth.]

If we professe Christe, why be we not ashamed to be ignoraunt in his
doctryne, seyng that every man is ashamed to be ignoraunt in that learning
whiche he professeth? That man is ashamed to be called a philosophier
whiche readeth not the bookes of philosophie, and to be called a lawyer,
and astronomier or a phisicion, that is ignoraunt in the bokes of law,
astronomie and phisicke. Howe can any man then saie that he professeth
Christ and his religion, if he will not applye hymself, as farfurthe as he
can or maie conveniently, to reade and hear, and so to knowe the bokes of
Christes Gospell and doctrine? Although other sciences be good and to
be learned, yet no man can deny but this is the chiefe, and passeth all other
incomparably. What excuse shal we therfore make, at the last daie before
Christ, that delight to reade or heare mennes phantasies and invencions
more then his moste Holy Gospell, and will fynd no tyme to doo that
whiche chiefly above all thynges wee should do, and wil rather reade other
thynges then that for the whiche wee ought rather to leave readyng of
all other thynges? Lette us, therefore, apply our selfes, as farforth as we can
have tyme and leasure, to knowe Gods Worde by diligent hearyng and
readyng therof, as many as professe God and have faithe and trust in hym.

But thei that have no good affeccion to Gods Word, to colour this
their faulte, alledge commonly twoo vaine and fained excuses: some go
about to excuse them by their awne frailnesse and fearfulnes, saiyng that
thei dare not read Holy Scripture, leaste through their ignoraunce thei
should fall into any error; other pretende that the difficultie to understande
it and the hardnes thereof is so great that it is meete to bee reade onely
of clearkes and learned men.

As touchyng the firste: ignoraunce of Gods Worde is the cause of al
error, as Christ hymself affirmed to the Sadduces, saiyng that thei erred
because thei knewe not the Scripture. How should thei then escheue error
that will be still ignoraunt? And how should thei come out of ignoraunce
that wil not read, nor heare that thyng whiche should geve them knowledge? He that now hath moste knowledge was at the first ignoraunt,
yet he forbare not to reade for feare he should fall into error; but he
diligently redde, lest he should remain in ignoraunce, and through igno-

raunce, in error. And if you will not knowe the truthe of God – a thyng
moste necessary for you – least you fall into error, by thesame reason
you maie then lye still and never go, leaste, if you goo, you fall in the
mire; nor eate any good meate, least you take a surfet; nor sow your corne,
nor labour in your occupacion, nor use your marchaundise, for feare you
lose your sede, your labor, your stocke: and so by that reason, it should be
beste for you to live idlely, and never to take in hande to do any maner
of good thyng, least peradventure some evill thyng maie chaunce therof.
And if you be afraied to fal into error by readyng of Holy Scripture, I
shall shewe you how you maie reade it without daunger of error. Reade it
humbly, with a meke and a lowly harte, to thintent you maie glorifie
God, and not your self, with the knowledge of it; and reade it not without
daily praiyng to God that he would directe your readyng to good effecte;
and take upon you to expounde it no further then you can plainly understande it. For, as Sainct Augustine saieth, the knowledge of Holy Scripture is a great, large and a high palace, but the doore is verie lowe so that
the high and arrogant man cannot runne in, but he must stoupe lowe
and humble hym self that shall entre into it. Presumpcion and arrogancie
is the mother of all error, and humilitie nedeth to feare no error. For
humilitie will onely searche to knowe the truthe; it will searche, and will
conferre one place with another: and where it cannot fynde the sense,
it will praie, it will inquire of other that knowe, and will not presump-
teously and rasshely define any thyng whiche it knoweth not. Therfore, the
humble man maie searche any truthe boldely in the Scripture without
any daunger of error. And if he bee ignoraunt, he ought the more to read
and to search Holy Scripture to bryng hym out of ignoraunce. I saie
not naie, but a man maie prospere with onely hearyng, but he maie muche
more prospere with bothe hearyng and readyng. This have I said, as
touchyng the feare to read through ignoraunce of the person.

    And concernyng the difficultie of Scripture, he that is so weake that he
is not hable to brooke strong meate, yet he maie sucke the swete and
tender milke, and differre the rest untill he waxe stronger and come to
more knowledge. For God receiveth the learned and unlearned, and casteth
awaie none, but is indifferent unto al. And the Scripture is full, aswel of
lowe valleis, plain waies and easie for every man to use and to walke in, as
also of high hilles and mountaines, which few men can ascende unto.
'And whosoever geveth his mynd to Holy Scriptures with diligent studie
and fervent desire, it cannot be,' saieth Sainct Jhon Chrisostom, 'that
he should be destitute of helpe. For either God almightie will sende hym
some godly doctor to instruct hym, as he did to instruct Eunuchus, a
noble man of Ethiope and threasorer unto Quene Candace, who havyng a

great affeccion to read the Scripture, although he understode it not, yet
for the desire that he had unto Gods Worde, God sent his apostle Phillip
to declare unto hym the true sense of the Scripture that he redde; or
els, if we lacke a learned man to instruct and teache us, yet God hymself
from above will geve light unto our myndes, and teach us those thynges
whiche are necessary for us and wherin we be ignoraunt.' And in another
place, Chrisostom saith that 'mannes humain and worldly wisedom, or
science, nedeth not to the understandyng of Scripture, but the revelacion
of the Holy Ghoste, who inspireth the true sense unto theim that with
humilitie and diligence do search therfore.' He that asketh shall have, and
he that seketh shal find, and he that knocketh shall have the doore open.
If we reade once, twise or thrise, and understande not, let us not cease so,
but still continue readyng, praiyng, askyng of other and so by still knock-
yng, at the laste the doore shalbe opened, as Saint Augustyne saieth.
Although many thynges in the Scripture bee spoken in obscure misteries,
yet there is no thyng spoken under darke misteries in one place, but
the selfe same thyng in other places is spoken more familiarly and plainly,
to the capacitie bothe of learned and unlearned. And those thynges in
the Scripture that be plain to understande and necessarie for salvacion,
every mannes duetie is to learne theim, to print theim in memorye,
and effectually to exercise theim; and as for the obscure misteries, to be
contented to bee ignoraunt in theim, untill suche tyme as it shall please
God to open those thynges unto hym. In the meane ceason, if he lacke
either aptnesse or opportunitie, God will not impute it to his foly: but yet
it behoveth not that suche as bee apt should set aside readyng, because
some other be unapte to reade; neverthelesse, for the difficultie of suche
places, the readyng of the whole ought not to be set a part. And briefly
to conclude, as Saint Augustine saieth, by the Scripture, all men be
amended: weake men be strengthened and strong men be comforted. So
that surely none bee enemies to the readyng of Gods Worde, but such
as either be so ignoraunt that thei knowe not how wholsome a thyng it is,
or els be so sicke that thei hate the moste comfortable medicine that
should heale them, or so ungodly that thei would wishe the people still to
continue in blindnesse and ignoraunce of God.

   Thus we have briefly touched some part of the commodities of Gods
Holy Worde, whiche is one of Gods chief and principall benefites, geven
and declared to mankynde here in yearth. Let us thanke God hartely
for this his greate and speciall gyfte, beneficiall favor and fatherly providence. Lette us be glad to revive this precious gyft of our heavenly father.
Let us heare, reade and knowe these holy rules, injunccions and statutes
of our Christian religion, and upon that we have made profession to God

at our baptisme. Lette us with feare and reverence laie up in the cheste
of our hartes these necessarie and fruitfull lessons. Lette us night and daie
muse, and have meditacion and contemplacion in theim. Lette us ruminate
and, as it wer, chewe the cudde, that we maie have the swete jeuse,
spirituall effecte, mary, hony, kirnell, tast, comfort and consolacion of
theim. Let us staie, quiet and certifie our consciences with the moste
infallible certaintie, truthe and perpetual assuraunce of them. Let us praie
to God, the onely aucthor of these heavenly meditacions, that we maie
speake, thynke, beleve, live and depart hence, accordyng to the wholesome
doctrine and verities of theim. And by that meanes, in this worlde wee
shall have Gods proteccion, favor and grace, with the unspeakeable solace
of peace and quietnes of conscience; and after this miserable life, we
shall enjoy the endlesse blisse and glorie of heaven, whiche he graunt us all
that died for us all, Jesus Christ: to whom, with the Father and Holy
Ghost bee all honor and glorie, both now and everlastyngly.
   Amen.

NOTES

61   *office*: duty, as the doubling explains.
    ague: acute fever.
    wormewoode: the plant *Artemisia absinthium*, cited by Coverdale in the Great
       Bible as a type of what the soul finds bitter.
    humor: one of the four fluids that, according to Galenic physiology,
       determined a person's physical and mental health.
    carnall ... care ... carcasse: a punning alliterative phrase in which the Latinate
       words (*caro*, 'flesh') play against the English 'care.'
    foode of the soule: Matt 4:4.
62   *communicateth*: give to another as partaker, from Latin *communicare* (to
       make common to many).
    convenient: appropriate.
    '*whatsoever is required ... health*': Pseudo-Chrysostom *In Evangelium Mat-
       thaei, Hom* 41 (PG 56: 862). Cf Cranmer *Commonplace Book* (BL Royal MS
       7B XI) f 10.
    '*If it shal require ... Scripture*': Chrysostom *In Epistolam 2 ad Timotheum* 4, 9
       (PG 62: 650). Cf Cranmer *Commonplace Book* f 9.
    '*There is ... sortes of men*': Fulgentius *Sermo 1: 'De dispensatoribus Domini'*
       (PL 65: 721). Cf Cranmer *Commonplace Book* f 12.
    Scripture ... comforte: The passage is typical of the homilies in conflating bits
       and pieces of the Bible: Matt 4:4; Luke 11:28; John 17:17; Pss 19:7–10
       and 119:105, 130; Luke 10:42. The phrases *precious stone* and *best parte*, not
       found in the AV, translate the Vg wording.

wordes ... life: John 6:68.

effectual ... woorkyng: Col 1:6, 29.

lively ... mary: Heb 4:12.

63 *mary*: marrow.

buylder: Matt 7:24.

Woorde ... daie: John 12:48.

kepeth ... Trinitie: John 14:23.

mansion-place: dwelling-place.

conversacion: behaviour.

gever of victory: 1 Sam 14:4–23; 2 Chron 20:7, 17, 29; 1 Cor 15:57; 1 John 5:4.

single iye: simple or honest eye, as used in Luke 11:34.

obscureth ... Word: Isa 5:13, 24; Matt 22:29; 1 Cor 14:20, 37–8.

64 *farfurthe*: to such an extent.

colour: disguise.

saiyng ... Scripture: Matt 22:29.

65 *take in hande*: attempt.

Augustine saieth: *Confessiones* 3, 5 (PL 32: 686).

conferre: compare.

brooke ... knowledge: 1 Cor 3:2.

indifferent: impartial.

'*And whosoever ... ignoraunt*': Chrysostom *In Genesim, Hom* 35 (PG 53: 321). Cf Cranmer *Commonplace Book* f 10.

66 '*mannes humain ... search therfore*': Chrysostom *In Genesim, Hom* 21 (PG 53: 175).

He that asketh ... open: Matt 7:8.

If we reade ... Augustyne saieth: Augustine *Sermo 270: 'In die Pentacostes'* 1 (PL 38: 1237–8); *Enarratio in Ps 33* 1 (PL 36: 300).

misteries ... plainly: Augustine *De doctrina christiana* 2, 6 (PL 34: 39).

aptnesse: ability.

by the Scripture ... heale them: Augustine *Epistola 137* 5, 18 (PL 33: 524). Cf Cranmer *Commonplace Book* f 11.

67 *night ... in theim*: Ps 1:2.

TEXTUAL APPARATUS

61 neyther sufficiently] neycher *1559*. savor] favor *1549, 1559, 1623*. eate or drinke] eat and drinke *1623*. carnall] fleshely *1559*. mannes imaginacion]

62 mens *1623*. those bokes] these Books *1623*. conservacion] kepyng uppe *1559, 1623*. communicateth ... creatures] maketh us and all creatures partakers of his goodnes *1559, 1623*. whatsoever] *1549, 1559, 1623*; whatsoevr *1547*. eternall] everlastyng *1559, 1623*. mollifye] or soften *added 1559, 1623*. eternal] everlastyng *1559, 1623*. convenient] meete *1559, 1623*. converteth] turneth *1559, 1623*. a constant and a perpetuall] a stedfast and everlastyng *1559, 1623*.

consciences] conscience *1549, 1559, 1623*. sweter] swete *1559, 1623*. converte]
63 tourne *1559, 1623*. mary] marrow *1623*. for the Worde] woords *1559*. Worde
of Christ] Worde or Christ *1559*. mansion] dwellyng *1559, 1623*. establisheth]
strengtheneth *1559, 1623*. conserveth] keepeth up *1559, 1623*. meditacion]
recordyng *1559, 1623*. perpetuall] continuall *1559, 1623*. alwaies that] alwaies
that that *1547*. transformed] changed *1559, 1623*. irefull] wrathfull *1559,
1623*. expelleth] dryveth away *1559, 1623*. obscureth Christ] *1549*; obscureth
Chrste *1547*; darkeneth Christe *1559, 1623*. induceth] bryngeth in *1559,
64 1623*. The Second Parte of the Sermon of the Holie Scripture] The Second
Part of the Sermon of the Knowledge of Holy Scripture *1623*. homilie]
Sermon *1559, 1623*. wat] what *1559, 1623*. ignoraunt] ignorauut *1547*. farforth]
65 farfuth *1547*. alledge] alleage *1559*. hardnes] h dnesse *1623*. palace] place *1623*.
nedeth] endeth *1623*. conferre] bryng together *1559, 1623*. fynde the sense]
fynde out the meaning *1559, 1623*. inquire] aske *1559, 1623*. difficultie]
hardenesse *1559, 1623*. ascende] clymbe *1559, 1623*. fervent] burninge *1559,
1623*. destitute] left without *1559, 1623*. instruct] teache *1559, 1623*. Eunuchus]
66 Ennuchus *1547*. havyng a great affeccion] havyng affeccion *1623*. sense]
meaning *1559, 1623*. obscure] darke *1559, 1623*. difficultie] hardenes *1559, 1623*.
67 people] poeple *1547*. meditacions] studies *1559, 1623*. proteccion] defence
1559, 1623. and Holy Ghost] and the Holy Ghost *1559, 1623*.

2 An Homelie of the Miserie of Al Mankynd, and of Hys Condempnacion to Death Everlastyng, by Hys Awne Synne

The Holy Ghost in writing the Holy Scripture is in nothinge more diligent then to pulle doune mannes vainglory and pride, whiche, of all vices, is most universally grafted in al mankynd, even from the first infection of our first father Adam. And therfore, we reade in many places of Scripture many notable lessons against this old rooted vice, to teache us the moste commendable vertue of humilitie, how to knowe our selfes, and to remembre what we be of our selfes. In the boke of Genesis, almighty God geveth us al a title we be of our selfes. In the boke of Genesis, almighty God geveth us al a title and name in our great graund father Adam, which ought to admonish us al to considre what we be, wherof we be, from whence we came and whether we shal, saiyng thus: in the sweat of thy face shalt thou eate thy bread, til thou be turned again into the ground; for out of it wast thou taken, in asmuch as thou art dust, and into dust shalte thou be turned again. Here, as it wer in a glasse, we may learne to know our selfes to be but grounde, earth and asshes, and that to earth and asshes we shall returne. Also, the holy patriarche Abraham did well remembre this name and title, dust, earth and asshes, appoynted and assigned by God to all mankynde, and therfore he calleth hymself by that name, when he maketh his earnest praier for Sodome and Gomore. And we read that Judith, Hester, Job, Hieremie, with other holy men and women in the Old Testament, did use sacke cloth and to cast dust and asshes upon their heddes, when they bewailed their synfull livyng. They called and cried to God for help and mercye with suche a ceremonie of sacke clothe, duste and asshes that thereby thei might declare to the whole worlde what an humble and lowly estimacion thei had of themselfes, and how well thei remembred their name and title aforesayd, their vile, corrupt, fraile nature – dust, earth, and asshes. The boke of Wisedom also, willing to pul doune our proude stomackes, moveth us diligently to

remembre our mortall and earthly generacion whiche we have all of hym
that was firste made, and that all men, aswell kynges as subjectes, come
into this worlde and go out of thesame in lyke sorte, that is, as of our selfes
full miserable, as we may dayly see. And almightye God commaunded
hys prophet Esaie to make a proclamacion and crie to the whole worlde.
And Esaie askinge, what shall I crie?, the Lorde aunswered, crie, that
all fleshe is grasse and that al the glory of man therof is but as the floure
of the felde: when the grasse is withered, the floure falleth away, when the
wynd of the Lord bloweth upon it; the people surely is grasse, the which
drieth up, and the floure fadeth awaye. And the holy prophete Job, havyng
in himself great experience of the miserable and sinful estate of man,
doth open thesame to the world in these wordes: Man, saith he, that is
borne of a woman, livyng but a short tyme, is ful of manifold miseries: he
spryngeth up like a floure, and fadeth again, vanishyng awaye, as it wer
a shadowe, and never continueth in one state. And doest thou judge
it mete, O Lorde, to open thyne eyes upon suche a one and to bring hym
to judgement with the? Who can make hym cleane that is conceived of
an uncleane seede? And all men of their evilnesse and natural pronesse wer
so universally geven to synne that, as the Scripture saith, God repented
that ever he made man. And by synne, hys indignacion was so muche provoked against the worlde that he drouned all the worlde with Noes
floud, except Noe hymself, and hys litle housholde.

It is not without greate cause that the Scripture of God doeth so many
tymes call all men here in this worlde by this woorde: yearth. O thou
yearth, yearth, yearth, sayth Jeremie: heare the Worde of the Lord. This
our right name, vocacion and title, yearth, yearth, yearth, pronounced
by the prophete, sheweth what wee bee in deede, by whatsoever other
stile, title or dignitie men do call us. Thus he plainly named us who
knoweth best both what we be and what we ought of right to be called.
And thus he describeth us, speakyng by hys faithfull apostle S. Paule:
all men, Jewes and Gentiles, are under syn; ther is none righteous, no, not
one; ther is none that understandeth, there is none that seketh after God:
thei are al gone out of the way, thei are all unprofitable; ther is none
that doth good, no, not one: their throte is an open sepulchre; with their
tongues they have used craft and deceipt; the poyson of serpentes is
under their lippes; their mouth is full of cursing and bitternes; their fete
are swift to shed bloud; destruccion and wretchednes are in their waies,
and the way of peace have thei not knowen: there is no feare of God
before their eyes. And in another place S. Paule writeth thus: God hath
wrapped all nacions in unbelefe that he might have mercy on all. The
Scripture concludeth all under synne, that the promyse by the faith of Jesus

Christ should be geven unto theim that beleve. S. Paule in many places
painteth us out in our colours, callyng us the children of the wrath of God
when we be borne, saiyng also that we cannot thinke a good thought of
our selfes, muche lesse we can saye wel, or do wel of our selfes. And
the Wiseman saieth in the boke of Proverbes: the just man falleth seven
times a day. The most tried and approved man, Job, feared all hys workes.
S. Jhon the Baptist, beynge sanctified in his mothers wombe and praised
before he was borne, called an aungell and great before the Lord, replenished even from his birthe with the Holy Ghost, the preparer of the
way for our savior Christ, and commended of our savior Christ to be more
then a prophet and the greatest that ever was borne of a woman, yet he
plainly graunteth that he had nede to be wasshed of Christ; he worthely
extolleth and glorifieth his Lorde and master Christ, and humbleth hymself, as unworthy to unbuckle his showes, and geveth all honor and glory
to God. So doth S. Paule bothe oft and evidently confesse himself, what
he was of himself, ever gevyng, as a moste faithfull servaunt, all praise to
his master and savior. So doth blessed S. Jhon the Evangelist, in the
name of hymself and of all other holy men, be they never so just, make
this open confession: if we saye we have no synne, we deceyve oure selfes,
and the truthe is not in us; if we knowledge our synnes, God is faithful
and just to forgeve us our synnes and to clense us from al unrighteousnes;
if we saye we have not sinned, we make hym a liar, and hys Worde is
not in us. Wherfore the Wiseman, in the boke called Ecclesiastes, maketh
this true and generall confession: there is not one just man upon the earth
that doeth good, and synneth not. And S. David is ashamed of hys
synne, but not to confesse his synne. How oft, how earnestly and lamenta-
bly doth he desire Gods great mercy for his great offences, and that God
should not entre into judgement with him! And agayn, how well weigheth
thys holy man his synnes, when he confesseth that they bee so many in
numbre, and so hid, and hard to understande that it is in maner unpossible
to knowe, utter or numbre them! Wherfore, he having a true, earnest and
depe contemplacion and consideracion of his sinnes, and yet not commyng
to the botome of them, he maketh supplicacion to God to forgeve him
his privy, secret, hid sinnes, to the knowledge of the which, he can not
attein unto. He weigheth rightly his sinnes from the original roote and
spring hed, perceiving inclinacions, provocacions, stirrynges, stingynges,
buddes, braunches, dregges, infeccions, tastes, felinges and sentes of them
to continue in hym still. Wherfore he saith: marke and behold, I was
conceived in synnes: he saith not, sinne, but in the plural numbre, sinnes,
forasmuch as out of one, as fountayn, spryngeth all the reste.

And our savior Christ saieth: there is none good but God, and that we

can do nothyng that is good without hym; nor no man can come to
the Father, but by hym. He commaundeth us all to saye that we be unprofitable servauntes, when we have done al that we can do. He preferreth
the penitent Publicane before the proude, holy and glorious Pharisey.
He calleth hymself a phisicion, but not to them that be whole, but to them
that be sicke and have nede of his salve for their sore. He teacheth us in
oure prayers to reknowledge our selfes sinners and to aske forgevenes
and deliveraunce from all evilles at our heavenly Fathers hande. He declareth that the synnes of oure awne hartes do defile our awne selfes. He
teacheth that an evill worde or thought deserveth condempnacion, affirmyng that we shall geve an accompte for every idle worde. He saith he
came not to save, but the shepe that were utterly lost and cast away.
Therfore fewe of the proude, just, learned, wise, perfect and holy Phariseis
were saved by him, because thei justified themselfes by their counterfeit
holynes before men. Wherefore, good people, let us beware of suche
hypocrisy, vainglory and justifiyng of our selfe. Let us loke upon our fete,
and then, doune pecockes fethers, doune proude harte, doune vile clay,
frayle and britle vessels.

[The Second Parte of the Sermon of the Miserie of Man

For asmuche as the true knowlege of our selves is very necessarye to come
to the right knowlege of God, ye have heard in the last readyng howe
humblie all godlie men alwaies have thought of them selves, and so to
thinke and judge of them selves are taught of God, their creator, by
his Holy Worde. For] of our selfes, we be crabbe trees that can bryng
furth no apples. We be of our selfes of suche yearth as can brynge furthe
but wedes, netles, brambles, briers, cocle and darnell. Oure fruites be
declared in the v. chap. to the Gala. We have neither faith, charitie, hope,
pacience, chastitie, nor any thyng els that good is, but of God, and
therfore, these vertues be called there the fruites of the Holy Ghost, and
not the fruites of man.

Let us, therfore, acknowledge our selfes before God, as we be in dede,
miserable and wretched synners. And let us earnestly repent and humble
our selfes hartely, and crie to God for mercye. Let us all confesse with
mouthe and harte that we be full of imperfeccions. Let us know our awn
workes, of what imperfeccion they be, and then we shall not stande
foolishly and arrogantly in our awne conceiptes, nor chalenge any part of
justificacion by our merites or workes. For truly there be imperfeccions
in our best workes: we do not love God so much as we are bounde to do,
with all our hart, mynd and power; we do not feare God so muche as

we ought to do; we do not praye to God, but with greate and many imperfeccions; we geve, forgeve, beleve, live and hope unperfectly; we speke, thinke and do unperfectly; we fight agaynst the devill, the worlde, and the fleashe unperfectly. Let us, therfore, not be ashamed to confesse plainly our state of imperfeccion, yea, let us not be ashamed to confesse imperfeccion, even in all our awne beste workes. Let none of us be ashamed to say with holy S. Peter, I am a sinfull man. Let us al saye with the holy prophet David, we have synned with our fathers, we have doen amisse, and dealt wickedly. Let us all make open confession with the prodigal sonne to our Father, and saye with hym, we have synned agaynst heaven, and before the, O Father; we are not worthy to be called thy sonnes. Let us al saye with holy Baruch, O Lorde our God, to us is worthily ascribed shame and confusion, and to the, righteousnes: we have synned, we have doen wickedly, we have behaved our selfes ungodly in all thy righteousnes. Let us al saie with the holy prophet Daniell, O Lorde, right-eousnes belongeth to the; unto us belongeth confusion. We have synned, we have bene naughtie, we have offended, we have fled from the, we have gone backe from al thy preceptes and judgementes. So we learne of all good men in Holy Scripture to humble our selfes, and to exalt, extoll, prayse, magnifie and glorifie God.

Thus we have heard how evill we be of our selfes; how of our selfes, and by our selfes, we have no goodnes, helpe, nor salvacion, but contrari-wise, synne, dampnacion and death everlastynge: whiche, if we depely weigh and consider, we shall the better understande the great mercy of God and how our salvacion commeth onely by Christ. For in our selfes, as of our selfes, we find nothing wherby we may be delivered from this miserable captivitie, into the which we were caste throughe the envie of the devill by transgressing of Gods commaundement in our first parent Adam. We are all become uncleane, but we all are not able to clense our selfes, nor to make one another of us cleane. We are by nature the children of Gods wrathe, but we are not able to make oure selfes the children and inheritors of Gods glorye. We are sheepe that ronne astraie, but we cannot of our awn power come agayn to the shepefold, so great is our imperfeccion and weakenes. In our selfes, therfore, maye not we glorie, which of our selfes are nothyng but synfull. Neither we maye rejoyse in any woorkes that we do, which al be so unperfect and unpure that thei are not able to stande before the righteous throne of God. As the holy prophete David saieth, entre not into judgement with thy servaunt, O Lorde, for no man that liveth shalbe found righteous in thy sight.

To God, therfore, muste we flee, or els shall we never finde peace, rest and quietnesse of conscience in our hartes. For he is the Father of mercies and God of all consolacion. He is the Lorde, with whom is plenteous redempcion. He is that God which of his awne mercie saveth us, and setteth out his charitie and exceding love towardes us, in that of his awne voluntary goodnesse, when we wer perished, he saved us and provided an everlastyng kyngdom for us. And all these heavenly treasures are geven us not for our awne desertes, merites, or good deedes (whiche of our selfes wee have none), but of his meere mercie, frely. And for whose sake? Truely, for Jesus Christes sake, that pure and undefiled lambe of God. He is that dearely beloved Sonne, for whose sake God is fully pacified, satisfied and sette at one with man. He is the lambe of God, whiche taketh awaie the synnes of the worlde, of whom onely it maie be truely spoken that he did al thynges well, and in his mouthe was founde no craft nor subtilitie. None but he alone maie saie, the Prince of the worlde came, and in me he hath nothyng. And he alone maie saie also, whiche of you shall reprove me of any faulte? He is that high and everlastyng priest whiche hath offered hymself once for all upon the aulter of the Crosse, and with that one oblacion hath made perfect for evermore them that are sanctified. He is the alone mediator betwene God and man, whiche paied our raunsome to God with his awne bloud, and with that hath he clensed us all from synne. He is the phisicion whiche healeth al our diseases. He is that savior whiche saveth his people from all their synnes. To be shorte, he is that flowyng and moste plenteous fountain, of whose fulnesse all we have received. For in hym alone are all the treasures of the wisedom and knowledge of God hidden. And in hym, and by hym, have wee from God the Father all good thynges perteinyng either to the body or to the soule. O howe muche are wee bounde to this our heavenly Father for his greate mercies, whiche he hath so plenteously declared unto us in Christe Jesu our Lorde and Savior! What thankes worthy and sufficient can we geve to him? Let us all with one accorde burste out with joyfull voyces, ever praisyng and magnifiyng this Lorde of mercy for his tendre kyndnesse shewed to us in his derely beloved Sonne, Jesus Christ our Lord.

Hetherto have we heard what wee are of our selfes: verely, synfull, wretched and dampnable. Again we have heard how that of oure selfes, and by oure selfes, wee are not hable either to thynke a good thought or worke a good deede, so that we can fynd in our selfes no hope of salvacion, but rather whatsoever maketh unto our destruccion. Again we have heard the tendre kyndenesse and greate mercie of God the Father towardes us, and how beneficial he is to us for Christes sake, without our merites or desertes, even of his awne meere mercie and tendre goodnesse.

Now, how these excedyng great mercies of God set abrode in Christe Jesu for us bee obteined, and how we be delivered from the captivitie

of synne, deathe and helle, it shall more at large, with Gods helpe, be
declared in the next homelie. In the meane season, yea, and at all tymes, let
us learne to knowe our selfes, our frailtie and weakenesse, without any
ostentacion or boostyng of our awne good dedes and merites. Let us also
knowledge the excedyng mercie of God towardes us, and confesse that
as of our selfes commeth all evill and dampnacion, so likewise of hym
commeth all goodnesse and salvacion, as God hymself saieth, by the
prophet Oze: O Israell, thy destruccion commeth of thy self, but in me
onely is thy helpe and comforte. If wee thus humbly submit our selfes in
the sight of God, wee maie bee sure that in the tyme of his visitacion
he will lifte us up unto the kyngdome of his derely beloved Sonne, Christe
Jesu our Lorde: to whom with the Father and the Holy Ghoste, bee all
honour, and glory for ever.
    Amen.

NOTES

70   *whether*: a form of 'whither.'
    in the sweat ... again: Gen 3:19.
    Abraham ... Gomore: Gen 18:27.
    Judith ... Hieremie: Jdt 4:10–11 and 9:1; Esther 14:2; Job 42:6; Jer 6:26 and
      25:34.
    proude stomackes: haughtiness; OED *stomach* 7b cites Coverdale: 'After a
      proud stomake there foloweth a fall.'
    boke of Wisedom ... dayly see: Wisd 7:1–6.
71   *Esaie ... fadeth awaye*: Isa 40:6–8.
    Job ... uncleane seede: Job 14:1–4.
    Scripture saith ... housholde: Gen 6:6 and 7:11–24.
    O thou yearth ... Lord: Jer 22:29.
    S. Paule ... eyes: Rom 3:9–18.
    in another place: Rom 11:32.
    The Scripture ... beleve: Gal 3:22.
72   *S. Paule ... thought of our selfes*: Eph 2:3; 2 Cor 3:5.
    Wiseman saieth: Prov 24:16 (Vg 'Septies enim cadet justus').
    Job ... workes: Job 9:28 (Vg 'Verebar omnia opera mea, Sciens quod non
      parceres deliquenti').
    S. Jhon ... glory to God: Luke 1:15, 76; Matt 11:9–11 (Vg 11:10 ' "Ecce ego
      mitto angelum meum ante faciem tuam," 'quoting Mal 3:1); Matt 3:11, 14;
      Mark 1:7.
    replenished: filled.
    showes: shoes.
    S. Paule ... savior: 1 Cor 15:8–10; 1 Tim 1:11–17.

S. Jhon ... not in us: 1 John 1:8–10.

knowledge: acknowledge.

Wiseman ... synneth not: Eccles 7:20.

S. David: Ps 51.

not entre into judgement: Ps 143:2.

confesseth ... numbre them: Ps 19:12 and 40:12.

privy ... sinnes: Ps 19:12

marke ... synnes: Ps 51:5 (AV 'Behold, I was shapen in iniquity, and in sin did my mother conceive me'; Vg Ps 50:7 'Ecce enim in iniquitatibus conceptus sum').

Christ ... but by hym: Matt 19:17; Mark 10:18; Luke 18:19; John 15:5 and 14:6.

73 *commaundeth ... we can do*: Luke 17:10.

preferreth: Luke 18:14.

calleth ... sicke: Matt 9:12.

teacheth ... Fathers hande: Matt 6:12–13; Luke 11:4.

reknowledge: acknowledge.

declareth ... awne selfes: Matt 15:19–20.

accompte ... worde: Matt 12:36.

He saieth ... cast away: Matt 15:24.

cocle: a corn-weed, frequently used to render *zizania*, found in Vg Matt 13:25.

darnell: another corn-weed, English for Vg *lolium*.

Gala. ... man: Gal 5:19–23.

chalenge: claim falsely.

love God ... power: Matt 22:37; Deut 6:5.

74 *I am a sinfull man*: Luke 5:8.

we have synned ... wickedly: Ps 106:6.

we have synned ... sonnes: Luke 15:18–19.

O Lorde ... thy righteousnes: Bar 2:6, 12.

O Lorde ... judgementes: Dan 9:7, 5.

in our selfes ... nothing: 2 Cor 3:5.

uncleane ... cleane: Ps 51:1–10.

by nature ... wrathe: Eph 2:3.

sheepe: Isa 53:6; cf 1 Pet 2:25.

entre ... sight: Ps 143:2.

Father ... consolacion: 2 Cor 1:3.

75 *plenteous redempcion*: Ps 130:7.

awne mercie saveth us: Titus 3:5; Rom 5:8.

pure ... lambe: 1 Pet 1:19.

lambe ... worlde: John 1:29.

spoken ... subtilitie: Mark 7:37; 1 Pet 2:22.

the Prince ... nothyng: John 14:30.

whiche of you ... faulte: John 8:46.

high ... sanctified: Heb 7:24–7 and 10:14.

alone mediator ... synne: 1 John 1:7.

phisicion ... diseases: Ps 103:3.
saveth ... synnes: Matt 1:21.
of whose fulnesse ... received: John 1:16.
in hym alone ... hidden: Col 2:3.
all good thynges: Rom 8:32.
meere: sole, with legal connotations.
76 *O Israell ... helpe*: Hos 13:9.
tyme of his visitacion: ie the day of judgment.

TEXTUAL APPARATUS

70 An Homelie] A Sermon *1559, 1623*. admonish] warne *1559, 1623*. dust and
71 asshes] dust an asshes *1549*. help and mercye] help ad mercy *1559*. glory of
man therof] glory therof *1559, 1623*. prophete Job] man Job *1623*. vanishyng]
vanisheth *1623*. wer so] be so *1549, 1559, 1623*. vocacion] callyng *1559, 1623*.
describeth us] setteth us forth *1559, 1623*. concludeth] shutteth up *1559, 1623*.
72 called] beyng called *1559, 1623*. replenished] fylled *1559, 1623*. what] that *1623*.
forgeve us our synnes] forgeve our synnes *1623*. secret, hid] secret his
1547. he] we *1623*. as fountayn] as a fountayn *1623*. And our] Our *1559,*
73 *1623*. foregevenes] ryghteousnes *1549, 1559, 1623*. Let us loke upon our fete,
and then, doune pecockes fethers, doune proude harte, doune vile clay,
frayle and britle vessels] *not in 1559, 1623*. vile] wyle *1549*. is very] if very
74 *1549*. God, as] God ss *1549*. For truly] For trule *1549*. speke] seake *1549*.
unperfectly] imperfectly *1623*. our awne beste] our beste *1623*. transgressing]
breakyng *1559, 1623*. not we glorie] we not glorie *1623*. we maye rejoyse]
may we rejoyse *1623*. in any woorkes] in any woiks *1623*. throne] judgement
75 seat *1559, 1623*. that God] the God *1559, 1623*. maie saie also] maie also say
1623. that high] the high *1623*. once for all] ons for all *1559*. sufficient]
suffient *1549*. voyces] voyce *1623*. shewed to us] shewed unto us *1623*. verely]
very *1623*. heard the tendre] heard thee tendre *1549*; harde the tendre *1559*.
76 homelie] sermon *1559, 1623*. ostentacion] crakyng *1559, 1623*. Let us also
knowledge the excedying] Let us also knowledge. The exce dyng *1547*.

3 An Homelie of the Salvacion of Mankynd, by Onely Christ Our Savior, from Synne and Death Everlastyng

Because all men be synners and offendors against God, and breakers of his law and commaundementes, therfore can no manne by his awne actes, woorkes and deedes – seme thei never so good – be justified and made righteous before God; but every man of necessitie is constrayned to seke for another righteousnesse, or justificacion, to be received at Gods awne handes, that is to saie, the remission, pardon and forgevenesse of his synnes and trespasses in suche thynges as he hath offended. And this justificacion or righteousnesse whiche we so receive by Gods mercie and Christes merites, embraced by faithe, is taken, accepted and allowed of God for our perfect and full justificacion. For the more ful understandyng hereof, it is our partes and duetie ever to remembre the greate mercie of God, how that, al the worlde beyng wrapped in synne by breakyng of the lawe, God sent his onely Sonne, our savior Christe into this worlde to fulfill the lawe for us, and by shedyng of his moste precious bloud, to make a sacrifice and satisfaccion or, as it maie bee called, amendes to his Father for our synnes, to asswage his wrathe and indignacion conceived against us for thesame. In so much that infantes, beyng baptised and diyng in their infancie, are by this sacrifice wasshed from their synnes, brought to Gods favor, and made his children and inheritors of his kyngdome of heaven. And thei whiche actually do synne after their baptisme, when thei converte and turne again to God unfainedly, thei are likewise washed by this sacrifice from their synnes, in suche sorte that there remaineth not any spotte of synne that shalbe imputed to their dampnacion. This is that justificacion, or righteousnes, whiche Sainct Paule speaketh of when he saieth: no man is justified by the workes of the law, but frely by faith in Jesus Christ. And again he saieth, we beleve in Christ Jesu that we be justified frely by the faith of Christe, and not by the workes of the lawe, because that no man shalbe justified by the workes of the law.

And although this justification be fre unto us, yet it commeth not so frely unto us that there is no raunsome paied therfore at all. But here maie mannes reason be astonied, reasonyng after this fashion: if a raunsome be paied for our redempcion, then is it not geven us freely, for a prisoner that paieth his raunsome is not let go frely, for if he go frely, then he goeth without raunsome. For what is it els to go freely then to bee set at libertie without paiment of raunsome?

This reason is satisfied by the greate wisedome of God in this mistery of our redempcion, who hath so tempered his justice and mercie together that he would neither by his justice condempne us unto the perpetuall captivitie of the devill and his prison of hel, remediles for ever without mercie, nor by his mercy deliver us clerely, without justice, or paiment of a just raunsome: but with his endlesse mercie, he joyned his moste upright and equall justice. His greate mercy he shewed unto us in deliveryng us from our former captivitie, without requiryng of any raunsom to be paied, or amendes to be made upon our partes: whiche thyng by us had been impossible to bee doen. And where as it laie not in us that to do, he provided a raunsome for us that was the moste precious body and bloud of his awne moste dere and best beloved Sonne, Jesu Christe, who besides his raunsom, fulfilled the lawe for us perfectly. And so the justice of God and his mercie did embrace together and fulfilled the mistery of our redempcion. And of this justice and mercie of God knit together, speaketh Saincte Paule in the .iii. chapiter to the Romans: al have offended and have nede of the glory of God, but are justified frely by his grace, by redempcion whiche is in Jesu Christ, whom God hath set furth to us for a reconciler and peace maker, through faith in his bloud, to shewe his righteousnesse. And in the .x. chapiter: Christ is the ende of the law unto righteousnes to every man that beleveth. And in the .viii. chapi: that whiche was impossible by the lawe, in asmuche as it was weake by the flesh, God sendyng his awne Sonne, in the similitude of synfull fleshe, by synne dampned synne in the fleshe, that the righteousnesse of the lawe might be fulfilled in us which walke not after the flesh, but after the spirite.

In these foresaied places, the apostle toucheth specially three thynges whiche muste concurre and go together in our justificacion. Upon Gods part, his greate mercie and grace; upon Christes parte, justice, that is, the satisfaccion of Gods justice, or the price of our redempcion, by the offryng of his body and shedyng of his bloud with fulfillyng of the law perfectly and throughly; and upon our part, true and lively faithe in the merites of Jesu Christe, whiche yet is not oures, but by Gods workyng in us. So that in our justificacion is not onely Gods mercie and grace, but also his justice, whiche the apostle calleth the justice of God, and it

consisteth in paiyng our raunsome and fulfillyng of the lawe: and so the
grace of God doth not exclude the justice of God in oure justificacion,
but onely excludeth the justice of man, that is to saie, the justice of our
woorkes as to be merites of deservyng our justificacion. And therefore
Sainct Paule declareth here nothyng upon the behalf of man concernyng
his justificacion, but onely a true and lively faith, whiche nevertheles is the
gift of God and not mannes onely worke without God. And yet that
faithe dooth not exclude repentaunce, hope, love, dread and the feare of
God to be joyned with faithe in every man that is justified, but it excludeth
them from the office of justifiyng. So that although thei be all present
together in hym that is justified, yet thei justifie not all together. Nor that
faithe also doth not exclude the justice of oure good workes necessarily
to bee doen afterward of duetie towardes God (for wee are moste bounden
to serve God in doyng good deedes, commaunded by hym in his Holy
Scripture, all the daies of oure life), but it excludeth theim so that we maie
not doo theim to this intent: to be made good by doyng of them. For
all the good workes that we can do bee unperfecte, and therfore not able
to deserve our justificacion, but our justificacion dooth come frely by
the mere mercie of God, and of so greate and free mercie that whereas all
the worlde was not able of their selfes to paye any parte towardes their
raunsome, it pleased our heavenly Father, of his infinite mercie, without
any our deserte or deservyng, to prepare for us the mooste precious
jewelles of Christes body and bloud, wherby our raunsome might be fully
paied, the lawe fulfilled, and his justice fully satisfied. So that Christe is
nowe the righteousnesse of all them that truely doo beleve in hym. He for
theim paied their raunsome by his death. He for theim fulfilled the lawe
in his life. So that nowe, in hym and by hym, every true Christian man
maie be called a fulfiller of the lawe, forasmuche as that whiche their infirmitie lacketh Christes justice hath supplied.

[The Second Parte of the Sermon of Salvacion

Ye have hearde of whome all men ought to seke their justificacion and
righteousnesse, and howe also this righteousnesse commeth unto men by
Christes death and merites. Ye hearde also how that three thinges are
required to the obtainyng of our righteousnes: that is, Gods mercy, Christes
justice, and a true and a lively faithe, out of the whiche faithe spryngeth
good woorkes. Also] before was declared at large that no manne can
be justified by his awne good workes, because that no manne fulfilleth the
lawe accordyng to the full request of the lawe. And Saincte Paule, in his
Epistle to the Galathians, proveth thesame, saiyng thus: If there had been

any lawe geven whiche coulde have justified, verely, righteousnesse should have been by the lawe. And again he saieth, if righteousnesse bee by the lawe, then Christe died in vain. And again he saieth, you that are justified by the lawe are fallen awaie from grace. And furthermore, he writeth to the Ephesians on this wise: by grace are ye saved through faithe, and that not of your selfes, for it is the gift of God, and not of workes, lest any man should glorie. And to bee shorte, the summe of all Paules disputacion is this: that if justice come of woorkes, then it commeth not of grace; and if it come of grace, then it commeth not of woorkes. And to this ende tendeth al the prophetes, as Saincte Peter saieth in the tenthe of the Actes: of Christe, all the prophetes, saieth Saincte Peter, do witnes, that through his name al they that beleve in him shal receive the remission of synnes.

And after this wyse to be justifyed, onely by this true and lively faithe in Christ, speaketh all the olde and auncient aucthors, bothe Grekes and Latyns. Of whom I will specially reherse thre: Hillary, Basill and Ambrose. Sainct Hillary sayeth these wordes plainly in the ninth Canon upon Matthewe: 'Faithe onely justifyeth.' And Saincte Basill, a Greke aucthor, writeth thus: 'This is a perfect and a whole rejoysyng in God, when a man avaunteth not hymselfe for hys awne righteousnes, but knowledgeth hymself to lacke true justice and righteousnes, and to be justifyed by the onely faithe in Christ. And Paul,' saieth he, 'doeth glory in the contempte of hys awne righteousnes, and that he loketh for his righteousnes of God by faythe.' These be the verye woordes of Saint Basill. And Saint Ambrose, a Latyn aucthor, sayeth these wordes: 'This is the ordinaunce of God, that he whiche beleveth in Christ should be saved without workes, by faithe onely, freely receivyng remission of his synnes.' Consyder diligently these woordes: without woorkes, by faythe onely, freely we receyve remissyon of oure synnes. What can be spoken more plainlye then to saye that freely, withoute woorkes, by fayth onely, we obteyne remission of oure synnes?

These and other lyke sentences that we be justifyed by fayth onelye, frelye, and without workes, we do reade oftymes in the moste best and auncient writers. As beside Hillarye, Basill and Saint Ambrose, before rehersed, we read thesame in Origene, Saincte Chrisostome, Saincte Cypriane, Saincte Augustine, Prosper, Oecomenius, Phocius, Bernardus, Anselme, and many other aucthors, Greke and Latine. Nevertheles, this sentence – that we be justified by fayth onely – is not so meant of them that the sayed justifiyng fayth is alone in man, without true repentaunce, hope, charitie, dread and feare of God, at any tyme or ceason. Nor when they say that we be justified frely, they meane not that we should or

might afterwarde be idle, and that nothyng should be required on oure
partes afterward. Neither thei meane not so to be justified without our
good workes that we shoulde do no good workes at all, lyke as shalbe
more expressed at large hereafter. But this proposicion – that we be justifyed by faith onely, frely, and without workes – is spoken for to take
away clerely all merite of oure workes, as beyng insufficient to deserve our
justificacion at Gods handes, and thereby moste plainly to expresse the
weakenes of man and the goodnes of God, the great infirmitie of oure
selfes and the myght and power of God, the imperfectnes of oure awne
workes and the moste aboundaunt grace of our savior Christe: and thereby
wholy to ascribe the meryte and deserving of our justificacion unto Christe
onely, and his moste precious bludshedyng. This faythe the Holy Scripture
teacheth; this is the strong rocke and foundacion of Christian religion;
this doctryne all olde and auncient aucthors of Christes churche do ap-
prove; this doctrine advaunceth and setteth furthe the true glory of Christ,
and suppresseth the vayne glory of man; this, whosoever denieth, is not
to be reputed for a true Christian man, not for a setter furth of Christes
glory, but for an adversarye of Christe and his Gospell, and for a setter
furth of mennes vainglory.

And although this doctrine be never so true (as it is most true in dede)
that we be justified freely, without al merite of our awne good workes,
as S. Paule doth expresse it, and freely, by this lively and perfect fayth in
Christe onely, as the auncient aucthors use to speke it, yet this true doctrine
must be also truely understande and moste plainly declared, lest carnall
men should take unjustly occasyon thereby to lyve carnally after the appetite
and will of the world, the flesh and the devil. And because no man
should erre by mistakyng of this doctrine, I shall plainely and shortely so
declare the right understandyng of the same that no man shall justly thinke
that he maye therby take any occasion of carnall libertie to folowe the
desires of the flesh, or that therby any kind of synne shalbe committed, or
any ungodly livyng the more used.

First, you shall understande that in our justificacion by Christ it is not
all one thinge, the office of God unto man and the office of man unto
God. Justificacion is not the offyce of man, but of God: for man cannot
justifye himselfe by his awne workes, neither in parte nor in the whole, for
that were the greatest arrogancie and presumpcion of man that Antechrist
could erect agaynst God, to affirme that a man might, by his awne workes,
take awaye and purge his awne synnes, and so justifie himself. But justificacion is the office of God onely, and is not a thyng whiche we rendre
unto hym, but whiche we receive of him, not whiche we geve to him, but
whiche we take of him by his free mercie and by the onely merites of

his moste derely beloved Sonne, our onely redemer, saviour and justifier, Jesus Christ. So that the true understandyng of this doctrine – we be justified freely by faith, without workes, or that we be justified by faithe in Christ onely – is not that this our awne acte to beleve in Christe, or this oure faithe in Christe, which is within us, dooth justifie us and merite oure justificacion unto us (for that were to compte our selfes to be justified by some acte or vertue that is within oure selfes), but the true understand-ynge and meanynge thereof is that although we heare Gods Woorde and beleve it, although we have faith, hope, charitie, repentaunce, dread and feare of God within us, and do never so many good woorkes thereunto, yet we must renounce the merite of all our saied vertues of faith, hope, charitie, and all our other vertues and good dedes, which we either have doen, shal do or can do, as thynges that be farre to weake, and insufficient, and unperfecte to deserve remission of our synnes and oure justification. And therefore we must trust onely in Gods mercie, and in that sacrifyce whiche our high prieste, and savior Christ Jesus, the Sonne of God, once offered for us upon the crosse, to obtein therby Gods grace and remission, aswel of our originall synne in baptisme, as of all actuall synne committed by us after oure baptisme, if we truely repente and converte unfainedly to hym agayn. So that as Sainct Jhon Baptiste, although he were never so vertuous and godly a man, yet in this matter of forgevyng of synne, he did put the people from hym and appoynted them unto Christ, saiyng thus unto them, Behold, yonder is the lambe of God, whiche taketh awaye the synnes of the world: even so, as greate and as godly a vertue as the lively fayth is, yet it putteth us from it self and remitteth or appointeth us unto Christ, for to have only by him remission of oure synnes, or justification. So that our fayth in Christ, as it were, saieth unto us thus: It is not I that take awaye your synnes, but it is Christ onely, and to him onely I send you for that purpose, renouncyng therein all your good vertues, woordes, thoughtes and woorkes, and onely puttyng your trust in Christe.

[The Thirde Parte of the Sermon of Salvacion

It hathe been manifestlye declared unto you that no man can fulfill the lawe of God, and therfore by the lawe all men are condempned: where upon it folowed necessarilye that some other thyng should be required for our salvacion than the lawe, and that is a true and a livelye faithe in Christ, bringing forth good workes and a life accordyng to Godes com-maundementes. And also you heard the auncient aucthours mynde of this proposicion – faithe in Christ only justifyeth man – so playnlye declared that you see] the very true sense of thys proposicion – we be justifyed by faythe in Christe onely – accordyng to the meanyng of the old auncient aucthors, is this: we put oure faithe in Christe that we be justifyed by hym onely, that we be justified by Gods free mercie and the merites of our savior Christe onely, and by no vertue or good worke of our awne that is in us, or that we can be able to have or to do for to deserve thesame, Christ hymself onely beyng the cause meritorious thereof.

Here you perceive many woordes to be used to avoyd contencion in wordes with them that delighte to braule aboute woordes, and also to shewe the true meaning to avoyde evill talking and misunderstandyng. And yet peradventure all wyll not serve with theim that be contencious, but contenders will ever forge matter of contencion, even when thei have none occasion thereto. Notwithstandyng, such be the lesse to be passed upon so that the rest maye profite which wil be more desirous to know the truth then, when it is playn enough, to contende aboute it, and with contencious and capcious cavillacions, to obscure and darken it. Truthe it is, that our awne woorkes doo not justifye us, to speake properly of our justificacion – that is to saie, our workes do not merite or deserve remission of our synnes, and make us of unjust, juste before God – but God of his mere mercie, through the onely merites and deservynges of his Sonne, Jesus Christ, doth justifie us. Neverthelesse, because fayth doth directely sende us to Christe for remission of our synnes, and that by faithe geven us of God, we embrace the promise of Gods mercie and of the remission of oure synnes, whiche thyng none other of oure vertues or woorkes properly doth, therfore Scripture useth to say that faith without workes doth justifie. And for asmuch that it is al one sentence in effecte to saye, faithe without woorkes, and onely fayth doth justifie us, therfore the olde auncient fathers of the churche from tyme to tyme have uttered our justificacion with this speach, onelye faythe justifieth us, meanyng none other thing then Sainct Paule meant, when he sayd, faith without workes justifieth us. And because al this is brought to passe through the onely merites and deservinges of our savior Christ, and not through our merites, or through the merite of any vertue that we have within us, or of any worke that commeth from us, therfore, in that respecte of merite and deservyng, we renounce, as it wer, altogether agayn, faith, workes and all other vertues. For our awne imperfeccion is so greate through the corrupcion of original synne that al is imperfect that is within us: faithe, charitie, hope, dreade, thoughtes, wordes and workes, and therefore, not apte to meryte and deserve any parte of our justificacion for us. And this forme of speakyng we use in the humblyng of oure selfes to God, and to geve all the glory to our savior Christ, whiche is best worthy to have it.

Here you have heard the office of God in oure justificacion, and how
we receyve it of him, frely, by his mercie, without our desertes, through
true and lyvely faythe. Now you shall heare the offyce and duetie of a
Christian man unto God, what we ought on oure parte to rendre unto
God agayne for his greate mercye and goodnes. Oure offyce is not to
passe the tyme of this present lyfe unfruictfully and idlely after that we are
baptised or justified, not caryng howe fewe good workes we do to the
glory of God and proffite of our neighbors; much lesse it is oure office,
after that we be once made Christes membres, to lyve contrary to thesame,
makyng our selfes membres of the devil, walking after his inticementes
and after the suggestions of the world and the fleshe, wherby we know
that we do serve the world and the deuill, and not God. For that faythe
which bryngeth furth, without repentaunce, either evyll workes or no
good workes, is not a right, pure and lively faithe, but a ded, devilishe,
counterfeit and feyned fayth, as Sainct Paul and Sainct James cal it. For
even the devilles know and beleve that Christ was borne of a virgyn,
that he fasted forty dayes and fortye nightes without meate and drynke,
that he wroughte all kynde of myracles, declaryng hymself very God. They
beleve also that Christe for oure sakes suffered moste paynfull death to
redeme us from eternal death, and that he rose agayn from death the thyrde
daye. They beleve that he ascended into heaven, and that he sitteth on
the right hand of the Father, and at the laste ende of this world shal come
agayne, and judge bothe the quicke and the deade. These articles of our
faith the devilles beleve, and so they beleve all thinges that be written
in the New and Old Testament to be true, and yet for all this faith they be
but devilles, remainyng styll in their dampnable estate, lackyng the very
true Christian fayth. For the right and true Christian faith is not onely to
beleve that Holy Scripture and all the forsaied articles of our fayth are
true, but also to have a sure trust and confidence in Gods mercifull promises
to be saved from everlastynge dampnacion by Christe, wherof doeth
folowe a lovyng harte to obey his commaundementes. And this true Christian faythe neyther any devyll hath, nor yet any man which in the outwarde profession of his mouth and in his outward receivyng of the
sacraments, in commyng to the churche, and in all other outward appar-
aunces, semeth to be a Christian man, and yet in his livyng and deedes
sheweth the contrary. For how can a man have this true faith, this sure
truste and confidence in God, that by the merites of Christe his synnes
be remitted, and he reconciled to the favor of God, and to be partaker of
the kyngdom of heaven by Christ, when he liveth ungodly and denieth
Christe in his dedes? Surely no suche ungodly man can have this faith and

trust in God. For as they know Christe to bee the onely savior of the
worlde, so they knowe also that wicked men shall not possesse the kyngdom of God. Thei know that God hateth unrighteousnes, that he will
destroye all those that speake untruly, that those that have doen good
workes (whiche can not be doen without a lively faythe in Christe) shall
come forth into the resurrection of lyfe, and those that have doen evill
shall come unto resurrection of judgement. And very well they know also
that to them that be contencious, and to them that will not be obedient
unto the truth, but will obey unrighteousnes, shall come indignacion,
wrathe, and affliccion. &c. Therfore, to conclude, considerynge the infinite
benefites of God, shewed and exhibited unto us mercifully withoute oure
desertes, who hath not onely created us of nothyng, and from a pece
of vile clay of his infinite goodnes hath exalted us (as touchyng our soule)
unto hys awne similitude and lykenesse, but also, wheras we were condempned to hel and death eternall, hath geven his awne natural Sonne,
beyng God eternall, immortall and equal unto himselfe in power and glory,
to bee incarnated, and to take our mortall nature upon him with the
infirmities of the same, and in thesame nature, to suffre moste shamefull
and paynful death for our offences, to thintent to justifye us and to restore
us to lyfe everlastyng, so makyng us also his dere beloved chyldren,
brethren unto his only Sonne, our savior Christ, and inheritors for ever
with him of his eternall kyngdom of heaven.

These greate and mercifull benefites of God, if they be well considered,
do neither minister unto us occasion to be idle and to live without doyng
any good workes, neither yet stirreth us by any meanes to do evill thinges;
but contrarywise, if we be not desperate persones and oure hartes harder
then stones, they move us to rendre our selfes unto God wholy, with
all our wil, hartes, might and power, to serve him in all good dedes,
obeyng his commaundementes during our lifes, to seke in al thinges
his glory and honor, not our sensuall pleasures and vaynglory, evermore
dreadynge willingly to offende suche a merciful God and lovyng redemer
in worde, thought or dede. And thesayde benefites of God, depely considered, do move us for his sake also to be ever redy to geve our selfes to
our neighbours, and asmuch as lyeth in us, to study with all oure indevour
to doo good to every man. These be the fruites of the true faythe: to do
good, asmuche as lieth in us, to every man, and above all thynges and
in all thinges, to avaunce the glory of God, of whom only we have our
sanctificacion, justificacion, salvacion, and redempcion: To whome be ever
glory, prayse, and honor, worlde without ende.

Amen.

NOTES

79 [Title]: the repetition of 'Mankynd,' 'Synne,' and 'Death Everlastyng' from
    the title of the previous sermon reinforces the link between *miseria*
    and *misericordia*.
    actually: actively, with deeds (as opposed to original sin).
    no man is justified ... Jesus Christ: Rom 3:19–28.
    we beleve ... workes of the law: Gal 2:16.
80 *clerely*: unreservedly.
    equall: equitable.
    al have offended ... righteousnesse: Rom 3:23–5 (AV 3:23 all sinners 'come short
    of the glory of God'; Vg 'Egent gloria Dei').
    Christ ... beleveth: Rom 10:4.
    that whiche was impossible ... spirite: Rom 8:3–4.
    apostle calleth the justice of God: Rom 3:21–6 (AV has 'righteousness'; Vg
    'iustitia').
81 *gift of God*: Eph 2:8.
    office: function.
    If there had ... lawe: Gal 3:21.
82 *if righteousnesse ... in vain*: Gal 2:21.
    you that are justified ... grace: Gal 5:4.
    by grace ... glorie: Eph 2:8–9.
    if justice ... not of woorkes: Rom 11:6.
    of Christe ... synnes: Acts 10:43.
    'Faithe onely justifyeth': Hilary *In Evangelium Matthaei* 8, 6 (PL 9: 961).
    'This is a perfect ... by faythe': Basil *Homilia 20: De humilitate* 3 (PG 31: 529–
    30). Basil quotes Phil 3:9.
    avaunteth: speak proudly of.
    'This is the ordinaunce ... synnes': Ambrosiaster *In Epistolam ad Corinthios* 1, 1
    (PL 17: 185). 'Ambrosiaster' is the term coined by Erasmus to attach to
    works doubtfully ascribed during the Middle Ages to Ambrose.
    Origene ... and many other aucthors: For extracts on solifidianism from
    almost all of these commentators, see Cranmer's 'Notes on Justification,'
    printed in *Miscellaneous Writings and Letters* ed J.E. Cox, Parker Society 18
    (Cambridge: Cambridge University Press 1846) 203–11.
83 *understande*: a common sixteenth-century form of the past participle.
    carnall men: Cranmer warns against antinomianism, the libertine exaggera-
    tion that claims God's grace relieves Christians of the need to comply
    with moral laws. John Agricola fell out with Luther over this issue. It
    was associated with the early Gnostic sects and, during the sixteenth
    and seventeenth centuries, with 'anabaptists.'
84 *Behold ... world*: John 1:29.
85 *cavillacions*: frivolous objections.
86 *Sainct Paul and Sainct James*: 2 Tim 3:5; Titus 1:10; James 2:17–26.

hateth ... untruly: Ps 5:5–6.
doen good workes ... judgement: John 5:29.
to them that be contencious ... &c: Rom 2:8.
similitude and lykenesse: Gen 1:26; (AV 'image'; Vg 'ad imaginem et
  similitudinem').
minister ... occasion: provide opportunity.

TEXTUAL APPARATUS

79 An Homelie] A Sermon *1559, 1623*. remission, pardon and] *not in 1559, 1623*.
    receive by Gods] receive of Gods *1623*. duetie] duties *1623*. savior Christe]
    savior Chrste *1547*. heaven] heavev *1549*. actually do] in act or deed do *1559*,
80 *1623*. converte and] *not in 1559, 1623*. paieth] paied *1623*. paiment] paying
    1623. perpetuall] everlasting *1559, 1623*. his mercy] this mercy *1549*. his
    raunsom] this raunsom *1623*. God, but are justified] *1559, 1623*; God, justified
    1547, 1549. by redempcion] by the redempcion *1549*. concurre and] *not in*
81 *1559, 1623*. part, his] part, hiz *1549*. exclude] shut out *1559, 1623*. excludeth]
    shutteth out *1559, 1623*. exclude] shut out *1559, 1623*. excludeth them] shutteth
    them out *1559, 1623*. office of justifiyng] office or justifiyng *1623*. that
    faithe] the faithe *1623*. exclude] shut out *1559, 1623*. frely by] freel, yby *1549*.
    lacketh] lacked *1623*. to seke] the seeke *1559*. workes, because that]
82 workes, that *1559, 1623*. avaunteth] avaunceth *1549, 1559, 1623*. saieth he]
    saiethhe *1549*. his righteousnes] the righteousnes *1549, 1559, 1623*. that he
    whiche] that they which *1623*. his synnes] their synnes *1623*. Phocius]
    Procius *1623*. and feare] and the feare *1549, 1559, 1623*. tyme or ceason] time
83 and ceason *1549, 1559, 1623*. our good workes] good workes *1623*. proposi-
    cion] sayinge *1559, 1623*. insufficient] unable *1559, 1623*. thereby wholy]
    thereby whoey *1547*; therefore wholy *1549, 1559, 1623*. teacheth;] teacheth us
    1623. suppresseth] beateth downe *1559, 1623*. to be reputed] to be coumpted
    1559; bee accounted *1623*. true Christian] Christian *1549, 1559, 1623*. not
    for] nor for *1623*. adversarye of] adversary to *1549, 1559, 1623*. God: for]
    God, or *1623*. justifye himselfe] making him selfe righteous *1559*; make him-
    selfe righteous *1623*. erect] set up *1559, 1623*. But justificacion] But in
84 justificacion *1559*. by faithe] by faist *1549*. merite] deserve *1559, 1623*. merite]
    mertte *1547*. all our other] all other *1623*. in that sacrifyce] that sacrifyce
    1559, 1623. oure baptisme] oure bptisme *1549*. converte] tourne *1559, 1623*.
    Baptiste] Babtist *1549*. send you] send your *1547*. renouncyng] forsakyng
    1559, 1623. folowed] followeth *1623*. mynde] myndes *1559, 1623*. proposicion]
85 saying *1559, 1623*. you see the ... sense] *1549*; Thus you do see that ... sense
    1547; you see that ... meanynge *1559, 1623*. proposicion] or saying *added*
    1559, 1623. worke] workes *1623*. talking] taking *1559, 1623*. matter] matters
    1623. be more] be the more *1623*. mere mercie] owne mercie *1623*. this
    is brought] this brought *1623*. renounce] forsake *1559, 1623*. imperfect] un-

86 perfect *1623*. deserve] discerne *1623*. we use] use wee *1549, 1559, 1623*. heard]
harde *1549*. this present] his present *1547*. proffite of] profite to *1549*.
lesse it is] lesse is it *1559, 1623*. James cal] James calleth *1549*. redeme us from
eternal] redeme us from everlastyng *1559*; redeme from everlasting *1623*.

87 remitted, and he] forgeven, and he *1559*; forgeven and be *1623*. possesse]
enjoye *1559, 1623*. forth into] forth in *1549*. unto resurrection] unto the
resurrection *1623*. judgement. And very] judgement: very *1559, 1623*. exhib-
ited] geven *1559, 1623*. as touchyng] touchyng *1549*. death eternall] death
everlastyng *1559, 1623*. upon him] upon oim *1547*. dere beloved chyldren]
dere chyldren *1559, 1623*. stirreth us] stirreth us up *1623*. do move us]
move us *1549, 1559, 1623*.

4 A Short Declaration of the True, Lively and Christian Faithe

The firste entrie unto God, good Christian people, is through faith, whereby, as it is declared in the laste sermon, we be justifyed before God. And least any man should be deceyved for lacke of right understanding thereof, it is diligently to be noted that faythe is taken in the Scripture two maner of wayes.

There is one fayth, whiche in Scripture is called a dead faythe, whiche bryngeth furth no good workes, but is idle, barrain and unfruitefull. And this faith by the holy apostle Sainct James is compared to the fayth of devilles, which beleve God to be true and juste, and tremble for feare, yet they do nothynge well, but al evill. And suche a maner of fayth have the wicked and naughtie Christian people, whiche confesse God, as Saincte Paule sayeth, in their mouthe, but denye hym in their deedes, beynge abhominable, and withoute the righte fayth, and to all good workes reproveable. And this faith is a persuasion and belief in mannes harte, wherby he knoweth that there is a God, and assenteth unto all trueth of Gods most Holye Worde conteyned in Holy Scripture. So that it consisteth onely in beleving of the Woorde of God that it is true. And thys is not properlye called faythe. But as he that readeth Cesars Commentaries, belevyng thesame to be true, hath thereby a knowledge of Cesars lyfe and noble actes, because he beleveth the history of Cesar, yet it is not properly saied that he beleveth in Cesar, of whome he loketh for no helpe, nor benefite: even so, he that beleveth that all that is spoken of God in the Bible is true, and yet liveth so ungodly that he cannot loke to enjoy the promises and benefites of God, although it maye be saide that such a man hath a faith and belief to the wordes of God, yet it is not properly saied that he beleveth in God, or hath suche a fayth and truste in God, wherby he may surely loke for grace, mercy and eternall lyfe at Gods hand, but rather for indignacion and punishment, according to the merites of hys wicked life. For as it is written in a boke entituled to be of Didimus Alexandrinus, 'forasmuch as faith without workes is ded, it is not now faith, as a ded man is not a man.' This ded faith, therfore, is not the sure and substancial faith which saveth synners.

Another fayth there is in Scripture whiche is not, as the foresayde faith, idle, unfruitfull and dead, but worketh by charitie, as S. Paule declareth (Gal. v). Whiche, as the other vayn faith is called a ded faithe, so maye thys be called a quicke or lively faith. And this is not onely the common belefe of the articles of our faith, but it is also a sure truste and confidence of the mercy of God, through our lorde Jesus Christ, and a stedfast hope of all good thynges to be received at Gods hande; and that although we, through infirmitie, or temptacion of our ghostly enemie, do fall from him by synne, yet if we returne agayn unto hym by true repentaunce, that he wyll forgeve and forget oure offences for hys Sonnes sake, our savior Jesus Christ, and will make us inheritors with him of hys everlastyng kyngdom; and that in the meane tyme, untyll that kyngdom come, he will be our protector and defendor in all perils and daungers, whatsoever do chaunce; and that, though som tyme he doth sende us sharpe adversitie, yet that evermore he wilbe a lovyng Father unto us, correctyng us for our synne, but not withdrawyng hys mercy finally from us, if we trust in hym, and commit our selfes wholy unto hym, hang onely upon hym, and call upon hym, ready to obey and serve hym. Thys is the true, lively and unfayned Christian faith, and is not in the mouthe and outward profession onely, but it liveth and stirreth inwardly in the hart. And this faythe is not without hope and truste in God, nor without the love of God and of our neyghbors, nor without the feare of God, nor without the desyre to heare Gods Worde, and to folowe thesame in eschewyng evill and doyng gladly all good workes.

Thys faith, as Sainct Paule describeth it, is the sure ground and foundacion of the benefites whiche we ought to loke for and trust to receyve of God: a certificat and sure expectacion of them, although they yet sensiblie appere not unto us. And after he saith: he that commeth to God must beleve both that he is, and that he is a mercifull rewarder of wel doers. And nothyng commendeth good men unto God so muche as this assured faith and trust in him. Of this faithe iii. thinges are specially to be noted. First, that this faithe doth not lye ded in the hart, but is lively and fruitful in bringing furth good workes. Second, that without it can no good workes be doen that shalbe acceptable and pleasaunt to God. Thirde, what maner of good workes thei be that this faith doth bryng furth.

For the first, as the light cannot be hid, but will shewe furthe it self at one place or other, so a true faith cannot be kept secret, but when occasion

is offered it will breake out and shew it self by good workes. And as the
livyng body of a man ever exerciseth suche thinges as belongeth to a
naturall and livyng body for nourishement and preservacion of thesame, as
it hath nede, opportunitie and occasion, even so the soule that hath a
lively faith in it wyl be doyng alwaye some good worke, whiche shall
declare that it is livyng, and will not be unoccupied. Therfore, when men
heare in the Scriptures so high commendacions of faythe, that it maketh
us to please God, to live with God, and to be the children of God, if then
they phantasie that thei be set at libertie from doyng all good workes,
and may live as thei liste, thei trifle with God and deceyve themselfes. And
it is a manifest token that thei be farre from having the true and lively
faith, and also farre from knowledge what true faith meaneth. For the very
sure and livelye Christian faith is not only to beleve al thinges of God
whiche are conteyned in Holy Scripture, but also is an earnest trust and
confidence in God: that he doth regarde us and hath cure of us, as the
father of the child whom he doth love; and that he will be mercifull unto
us for his onely Sonnes sake; and that we have our savior Christ, oure
perpetuall advocate and priest, in whose onely merites, oblacion and sufferyng we do trust that oure offences be continually wasshed and purged,
whensoever we, repentyng truly, do returne to hym with our whole
harte, stedfastly determinyng with our selfes, through his grace, to obey
and serve him in kepyng his commaundementes, and never to turne backe
again to synne. Such is the true faythe that the Scripture doeth somuche
commende, the whiche, when it seeth and considereth what God hath
doen for us, is also moved through continual assistence of the spirite of
God to serve and please hym, to kepe hys favor, to feare hys displeasure, to
continue his obedient children, shewing thankefulnes agayn by observyng
his commaundementes, and that frely, for true love chiefly, and not for
dread of punishement or love of temporall reward, consideryng how clerely,
without our deservynges, we have receyved his mercy and pardon frely.

Thys true faythe will shewe furthe it selfe and cannot longe be idle. For
as it is written, The juste man doth live by his fayth. He neither sleapeth,
nor is idle, when he should wake and be well occupyed. And God by
his prophete Hieremie sayeth that he is a happy and blessed man whiche
hath fayth and confidence in God. For he is lyke a tree sette by the water
syde, that spreedeth hys rootes abroode towarde the moysture, and feareth
not heate when it commeth; his leafe will be grene, and will not cease
to brynge furth his fruite: even so faithefull men, puttyng awaye all feare
of adversitie, wyll shewe furthe the fruite of their good workes, as occasion
is offered to do them.

[**The Second Parte of the Sermon of Faythe**

Ye have hearde in the fyrste parte of thys sermon that ther be two kyndes of fayth: a dead and an unfruitfull fayth and a faythe lyvely that worketh by charitie, the fyrst to be unprofitable, the seconde necessarie for the obtaynynge of our salvacion, the whych fayth hath charitye alwayes joyned unto it, and is fruitful, bringyng forth al good woorkes. Now as concern-ynge the same matter you shall heare what foloweth.]

The Wiseman saieth, he that beleveth in God wil harken unto his commaundementes. For if we doo not shewe our selfes faithfull in oure conversacion, the faith which we pretend to have is but a fayned faith, because the true Christian faith is manifestly shewed by good livyng, and not by woordes onely: as Sainct Augustine saith, 'good livyng cannot be separated from true faith, which worketh by love.' And S. Chrisostome saith, 'faith of it self is full of good workes: as sone as a man doth beleve, he shalbe garnished with them.'

How plentifull this faith is of good workes, and how it maketh the woorke of one man more acceptable to God then of another, S. Paule teacheth at large in the .xi. chap. to the Hebr., saiyng that faith made the oblacion of Abell better then the oblacion of Cain. This made Noe to buyld the arcke. This made Abraham to forsake his countrey and all his frendes, and to go unto a far countrey, there to dwel emong straungers. So did also Isaac and Jacob, dependyng onely of the helpe and trust that they had in God. And when they came to the countrey which God prom-ysed them, they would buylde no cities, townes, nor houses, but lived like straungers in tentes that might every daye be removed. Their trust was so muche in God that they set but litle by any worldly thyng, for that God had prepared for them better dwelling places in heaven of hys awne foundacion and buylding. This faithe made Abraham ready at Gods commaundement to offre hys awne sonne and heire Isaac, whom he loved so well, and by whom he was promysed to have innumerable issue, emong the whiche one should be borne in whom all nacions should be blessed; trustynge so muche in God that, though he were slain, yet that God was able by his omnipotent power to raise him from death, and perfourme his promyse. He mistrusted not the promise of God, although unto hys reason every thyng semed contrary. He beleved verely that God woulde not forsake hym in dearthe and famyne that was in the coun-trey. And in al other daungers that he was brought unto, he trusted ever that God would be hys God and his protector, whatsoever he sawe to the contrary. Thys faithe wrought so in the hart of Moses that he refused to be taken for Kyng Pharao hys daughters sonne, and to have great inheritaunce in Egypt, thinkyng it better with the people of God to have affliction and sorowe then with naughtie men in synne to lyve pleasauntly for a tyme. By faith, he cared not for the threatenynge of Kyng Pharao, for his trust was so in God that he passed not of the felicitie of this worlde, but loked for the rewarde to come in heaven, settyng hys hart upon the invisible God, as if he had seen hym ever present before hys eyes. By faith, the children of Israel passed through the Redde Sea. By fayth, the walles of Hiericho fell doune without stroke, and many other wonderfull miracles have been wrought. In al good men that heretofore have been, faithe hath brought furth their good woorkes, and obteyned the promises of God. Faith hath stopped the lions mouthes; faithe hath quenched the force of fire; faith hath escaped the swordes edges; faithe hath geven weake men strength, victorie in battaill, overthrowen the armies of infidels, raised the dedde to lyfe. Faith hath made good men to take adversitie in good parte: some have been mocked and whipped, bounde and caste in prison; some have loste all their goodes and lived in great povertye; some have wandered in mountaines, hilles and wildernesse: some have been racked, some slayn, some stoned, some sawen, some rent in peces, some hedded, some brent without mercy, and would not be delivered because they loked to rise agayne to a better state.

All these fathers, martyrs and other holy men, whom Sainct Paul spake of, had theyr fayth surely fixed in God, when all the worlde was agaynst them. They did not onely knowe God to be the Lord, maker and governor of all men in the worlde, but also they had a special confidence and trust that he was, and would be their God, their comfortor, aider, helper, mainteyner and defendor. This is the Christian faythe whiche these holy men had, and we also ought to have. And although thei were not named Christian men, yet was it a Christian faithe that they had, for they looked for all benefites of God the Father, throughe the merites of hys Sonne, Jesu Christe, as we now do. This difference is betwene them and us: for they looked when Christ should come, and we be in the tyme when he is come. Therfore saieth Sainct Augustyne: 'the tyme is altered, but not the faythe. For we have both one fayth in one Christ.' Thesame Holy Ghost also that we have, had they, saieth Sainct Paule. For as the Holy Ghoste doeth teache us to trust in God and to call upon hym as our Father, so did he teache them to saye, as it is wrytten: Thou, Lord, arte our Father and redemer, and thy name is without beginnyng and everlastyng. God gave them then grace to be hys chyldren, as he doeth us now. But now by the comming of our savior Christ we have receyved more abundantly the spirite of God in our hartes, wherby we maye conceyve a greater faithe and a surer truste then many of them had. But in effect they and we be al one: we have thesame faith that they had in God, and thei thesame that we have. And S. Paul so muche extolleth their faith because we should no lesse, but rather more geve oure selfes wholy unto Christ, both in profession and living, now when Christ is come then the olde fathers did before his commyng. And by all the declaracion of .S. Paule, it is evident that the true, lively and Christian fayth is no dead, vain or unfruictfull thyng, but a thyng of perfecte vertue, of wonderful operacion and strength, bryngyng furth all good mocions and good workes.

All Holye Scripture agreably beareth witnesse that a true lively faith in Christ doeth bryng furth good workes, and therfore every man must examine himself diligently, to know whether he have thesame true lively faythe in hys harte unfaynedly or not, whiche he shall know by the fruictes therof. Many that professed the faith of Christ were in this error, that they thoughte they knewe God and beleved in hym, when in their lyfe they declared the contrarye: whiche error, Sainct Jhon in his first Epistle confutynge, writeth in this wyse, Hereby we are certified that we know God, if we observe his commaundementes; he that saieth he knoweth God, and observeth not his commaundementes, is a liar, and the trueth is not in him. And again he saieth, whosoever synneth doeth not se God, nor knowe him: let no man deceive you, welbeloved children. And moreover he saieth, hereby we know that we be of the truth, and so we shal perswade our hartes before hym, for if our awne hartes reprove us, God is above our hartes and knoweth al thinges. Welbeloved, if our hartes reprove us not, then have we confidence in God, and shall have of hym whatsoever we aske, because we kepe hys commaundementes and do those thynges that please hym. And yet further he saieth, every man that beleveth that Jesus is Christe is borne of God, and we knowe that whosoever is borne of God doeth not synne, but the generacion of God purgeth him, and the devill doth not touche hym. And finally he concludeth and shewing the cause why he wrote this Epistle sayth, For this cause have I thus written unto you: that you maye knowe that you have everlastyng lyfe whiche do beleve in the Sonne of God. And in hys thirde Epistle he confirmeth the whole matter of faith and workes in fewe wordes, saiyng, he that doth well is of God, and he that doeth evill knoweth not God. And as S. Jhon saieth that as the lively knowledge and faith of God bryngeth furth good workes, so saieth he likewise of hope and charitie, that they cannot stande with evill livynge. Of hope, he writeth thus: we knowe that when God shall appere, we shalbe lyke unto hym, for we shall se hym even as he is. And who soever hath this hope in him doth purifie himself, like as God is pure. And of charitie he saieth these woordes: He that doeth kepe Gods Woorde or commaundemente, in hym is truely the per-

fecte love of God. And agayne he saieth: this is the love of God, that
we should kepe hys commaundementes. And S. Jhon wrote not this as a
subtile proposicion, devised of hys awne phantasie, but as a moste certain
and necessarie truth, taught unto him by Christ himself, the eternall and
infallible veritie, who in many places doth moste clerely affirme that fayth,
hope and charitie cannot consist without good and godly workes. Of
faith, he saith: He that beleveth in the Sonne hath everlastyng life, but he
that beleveth not in the Sonne shal not se that life, but the wrath of
God remayneth upon him. And thesame he confirmeth with a double othe,
saiyng: Forsothe and forsothe, I saye unto you, he that beleveth in me
hath everlastyng lyfe. Now, for asmuch as he that beleveth in Christ hath
everlasting lyfe, it must nedes consequently folow that he that hath this
faith must have also good workes, and be studious to observe Gods commaundementes obediently. For to them that have evill workes, and leade
their lyfe in disobedience and transgression of Gods commaundementes,
without repentaunce, perteineth not everlasting life, but everlastyng death,
as Christ himself saieth: they that do wel shal go into life eternal, but
thei that do evill shal go into the eternal fire. And again he saith: I am the
first lettre and the last, the beginnyng and the endyng: to him that is a
thirste I wil geve of the welle of the water of lyfe frely; he that hath the
victorye shal have all thynges, and I will be his God and he shalbe my
sonne, but thei that be fearfull, mistrusting God and lacking faith, thei that
be cursed people, and murderers, and fornicators, and sorserers, and
idolaters, and all liars, shall have their porcion in the lake that burneth with
fire and brimstone, which is the second death. And as Christe undoubtedly
affirmeth that true faythe bringeth furth good workes, so doth he say
likewyse of charitie: Whosoever hath my commaundementes and kepeth
them, that is he that loveth me. And after he saieth: he that loveth me will
kepe my Worde, and he that loveth me not kepeth not my woordes.
And as the love of God is tried by good workes, so is the feare of God
also, as the Wiseman saieth: the dread of God putteth awaye synne. And
also he saieth: he that feareth God wil do good workes.

[The Thyrde Part of the Sermon of Faithe

Yow have heard in the second parte of this sermon that no man shoulde
thynke that he hath that lyvely fayth whiche Scripture commaundeth,
when he liveth not obedientlie to Godes lawes, for all good workes spryng
out of that faith. And also it hath been declared unto yow by examples
that faith maketh men constant, quiet and pacient in all afliccions. Now as
concernyng thesame matter yow shall heare what foloweth.]

A man may sone deceive hym self and thinke in hys awne phantasie that he by fayth knoweth God, loveth him, feareth him, and belongeth to him, when in very dede he doth nothyng lesse. For the triall of all these thinges is a very godly and Christian lyfe. He that feleth hys harte set to seke Gods honor and studieth to know the wil and commaundementes of God, and to conforme himself therunto, and leadeth not hys life after the desire of hys awne fleshe, to serve the devill by synne, but setteth hys minde to serve God for Gods awn sake, and for his sake also to love al hys neighbors, whether they be frendes or adversaryes, doyng good to every man, as opportunitie serveth, and willingly hurtyng no man: such a man maye wel rejoyce in God, perceivinge by the trade of his life that he unfainedly hath the right knowledge of God, a lively fayth, a constant hope, a true and unfeined love and feare of God. But he that casteth awaie the yoke of Gods commaundementes from hys necke, and geveth hymself to live without true repentaunce after hys awne sensual mynde and pleasure, not regardynge to know Gods Worde, and much lesse to live according therunto: such a man clerely deceiveth himself, and seeth not hys awn harte, if he thinketh that he either knoweth God, loveth him, feareth him, or trusteth in him. Some peradventure phantasie in themselfes that thei belong to God, althouh they lyve in synne, and so they come to the church and shewe themselfes as Godes dere children. But .S. Jhon sayth plainly: if we saie that we have any company with God, and walke in darkenesse, we do lye. Other doo vainly thinke that thei know and love God, although they passe not of his commaundementes. But S. Jhon saieth clerely: he that saieth I know God, and kepeth not hys commaundementes, he is a liar. Some falsly perswade themselfes that thei love God, when they hate their neighbors. But S. Jhon saieth manifestly: if any man say, I love God, and yet hateth his brother, he is a liar. He that saieth that he is in the light, and hateth his brother, he is stil in darkenesse. He that loveth his brother dwelleth in the light, but he that hateth hys brother is in darkenesse, and walketh in darkenesse, and knoweth not whether he goeth, for darkenesse hath blynded hys eyes. And moreover he saieth: hereby we manifestly knowe the children of God, from the children of the devill: he that doeth not righteously is not the childe of God, nor he that hateth hys brother.

Deceive not your selfes, therfore, thinkynge that you have faith in God, or that you love God, or do truste in hym, or do feare hym, when you lyve in sinne, for then your ungodly and sinfull life declareth the contrary, whatsoever ye saye or thinke. It perteineth to a Christian man to have this true Christian fayth, and to trye himself whether he hath it or no, and to knowe what belongeth to it, and how it doeth worke in hym. It is not the worlde that we can trust to: the world and all that is therin is but vanitie. It is God that muste be oure defence and protection against all temptacion of wickednesse, and sinne, errors, supersticion, ydolatrie, and al evill. If al the world were on our side and God against us, what could the worlde availe us? Therfore let us set our whole fayth and trust in God, and neither the worlde, the devil, nor al the power of them shal prevayle against us. Let us, therfore, good Christian people, trie and examyne our faith what it is: let us not flatter our selfes, but loke upon our woorkes, and so judge of our fayth what it is. Christe himself speaketh of this matter and saieth: The tree is knowen by the fruicte. Therefore let us doo good workes and therby declare our faythe to be the lively Christian faith. Let us by suche vertues as ought to spryng out of fayth shew our eleccion to be sure and stable, as S. Peter teacheth: Endevor your selfs to make your calling and election certain by good workes. And also he saieth: minister, or declare, in youre faith, vertue; in vertue, knowledge; in knowledge, temperaunce; in temperaunce, pacience; again in pacience, godlinesse; in godlinesse, brotherly charitie; in brotherly charitie, love. So shall we shew in dede that we have the very lively Christian faith, and may so both certefie our conscience the better that we be in the righte faith and also by these meanes confirme other men. If these fruictes do not folowe, we do but mocke with God, deceive our selfes, and also other men. Wel maye we beare the name of Christian men, but we do lacke the true faith that doeth belonge thereunto. For true faithe doeth ever brynge furthe good workes, as S. James saieth: shewe me thy faythe by thy deedes. Thy deedes and workes must be an open testimonial of thy fayth; otherwise, thy fayth, beyng without good workes, is but the devils faith, the faith of the wicked, a phantasy of faith, and not a true Christian faith. And like as the devils and evil people be nothyng the better for their counterfet faith, but it is unto them the more cause of dampnacion, so thei that be christened and have received knowledge of God, and of Christes merites, and yet of a set purpose do live idlely, without good workes, thinkyng the name of a naked faith to be either sufficient for them, or els settyng their mindes upon vain pleasures of this world, do live in syn without repentaunce, not utteryng the fruites that do belong to suche an high profession: upon suche presumpteous persons and wilful synners must nedes remain the great vengeaunce of God, and eternal punishment in hel prepared for the devil and wicked livers. Therfore, as you professe the name of Christ, good Christian people, let no suche phantasy and imaginacion of faith at any time beguile you, but be sure of your faith, trie it by your livyng, loke upon the fruites that commeth of it, marke the increase of love and charitie by it towardes God and your neighbor, and so shal you perceive it to be a true lively faith. If you fele and perceive suche a faith in you, rejoyce in it, and be diligent to maintein it, and kepe it stil in you. Let it be daily increasing, and more and more by wel workyng, and so shal ye be sure that you shal pleace God by this faith: and at the length, as other faithful men have doen before, so shal you, when his wil is, come to him and receive thende and final reward of your faith – as S. Peter nameth it, the salvacion of your soules: the which, God graunt us, that hath promised thesame unto his faithfull. To whom, be al honor and glory, worlde without ende. Amen.

NOTES

91 *dead faythe*: James 2:17, 19.
    confesse ... reproveable: Titus 1:16.
    reproveable: reprehensible.
92 *'forasmuch as faith ... is not a man'*: Didymus Alexandrinus *2 Enarratio in Epistolam B. Iacobi* 2, 26 (PG 39: 1752).
    worketh by charitie: Gal 5:6.
    ground and foundacion ... appere not unto us: Heb 11:1.
93 *he that commeth ... wel doers*: Heb 11:6.
    phantasie: fantasize.
    hath cure of: takes spiritual care of; cf 'cure of souls.'
    The juste man ... fayth: Hab 2:4.
    he is a happy ... his fruite: Jer 17:7–8.
94 *he that beleveth ... his commaundementes*: Sir 32:24.
    'good livyng ... by love': Augustine *De fide et operibus* 23, 42 (PL 40: 224).
    'faith of it self ... with them': Pseudo-Chrysostom *De fide et lege naturae* 1 (PG 48: 1081).
    garnished: furnished.
    .xi. chap. to the Hebr.: Marginal notes in the homily direct attention to the Old Testament sources used by Paul in Heb 11:4–38.
    oblacion of Abell ... emong straungers: Gen 4:4–5 and 6:22; Sir 44:17; Gen 11:31 and 12:1–5.
    Abraham ... to the contrary: Gen 22:1–18 and 26:1–35; Sir 44:20.
    Moses ... Redde Sea: Exod 2:11 and 14:22.
95 *passed not of*: heeded not.
    walles of Hiericho: Josh 6:20.
    stopped the lions ... dedde to lyfe: Dan 6:16–23 and 3:13–28.
    in good parte: without offence.
    been mocked ... some sawen: Heb 11:36–8.
    brent: a common form of the past participle, from ME 'brennen,' to burn.

'the tyme is altered ... one Christ': Augustine *In Ioannis Evangelium Tr 45*
10, 9 (PL 35: 1722).
Thesame ... Sainct Paule: 2 Cor 4:13.
Thou, Lord ... everlastyng: Isa 63:10.
96 *mocions*: motives.
Hereby we are certified ... not in him: 1 John 2:3–4.
whosoever synneth ... children: 1 John 3:6–7.
hereby we know ... that please hym: 1 John 3:19–22.
every man ... touche hym: 1 John 5:1, 18 (Vg 5:18 'sed generatio Dei conservat
eum').
For this cause ... Sonne of God: 1 John 5:13.
he that doth well ... knoweth not God: 3 John:11.
we knowe that when ... God is pure: 1 John 3:2–3.
He that doeth kepe ... perfecte love of God: 1 John 2:5.
97 *this is the love ... hys commaundementes*: 1 John 5:3.
consist: stand firm.
He that beleveth ... remayneth upon him: John 6:47.
Forsothe ... everlastyng lyfe: John 6:47.
they that do wel ... fire: Matt 25:46; John 5:29.
I am the first ... second death: Rev 21:6–8.
porcion: allotted destiny.
Whosoever hath my commaundementes ... my woordes: John 14:21–4.
the dread of God ... good workes: Sir 1:21 and 15:1.
98 *trade*: course.
althouh: an old form of 'although.'
if we saie ... do lye: 1 John 1:6.
he that saieth ... liar: 1 John 2:4.
if any man say ... hys eyes: 1 John 4:20 and 2:9–11.
whether: whither.
hereby we manifestly ... hys brother: 1 John 3:10.
99 *The tree ... fruicte*: Matt 12:33.
Endevor ... good workes: 2 Pet 1:lo.
endevor your selfs: exert yourselves.
minister ... charitie, love: 2 Pet 1:5–7.
shewe me ... thy deedes: James 2:18.
100 *salvacion of your soules*: 1 Pet 1:9.

TEXTUAL APPARATUS

91 entrie] comming *1559, 1623*. assenteth] agreeth *1559, 1623*. beleving of]
beleving in *1549, 1559, 1623*. noble] notable *1559, 1623*. eternall] everlastyng
92 *1559, 1623*. Alexandrinus] Alexandrius *1623*. and will make] and believe
93 that he will make *1549*. expectacion of] lokyng for *1559, 1623*. breake out and

shew] breake out, shew *1549*. body] bod e *1623*. belongeth] belong *1623*. hath cure of us] that he is careful over us *1559, 1623*. of the child] is over the child *1559, 1623*. observyng] or kepyng *added 1559, 1623*. love of] love or *1549*. our deservynges] deservynges *1623*. neither ... should wake] never ...

94 would wake *1623*. syde, that] syde, and *1623*. bringyng] brnginge *1547*; and bringeth *1623*. Augustine] Agustine *1623*. go unto] go into *1623*. dependyng] or hanging *added 1559, 1623*. worldly] wordly *1559*. Isaac, whom] Isaac, woome *1559*. dearthe] death *1623*. God would be] God should be *1623*.

95 protector] and defendour *added 1559, 1623*. Redde] reede *1549*. some hedded] some beheaded *1623*. difference ... for] difference ... that *1623*. altered]

96 and chaunged *added 1559, 1623*. operacion] or working *added 1559, 1623*. examine] and trye *added 1559, 1623*. professed] professe *1549*. his commaundementes] is commaundementes *1549*. whosoever] whatsoever *1559*. but the generacion ... purgeth him] but he that is begotten of God purgeth himselfe *1623*. shewing ... sayth] sheweth ... saying *1623*. Woorde or com-

97 maundemente] Woorde and commaundement *1623*. proposicion] sayinge *1559, 1623*. consist] or stande *added 1559, 1623*. Forsothe and forsothe] Verily, Verily *1623*. commaundementes] commaundemetes *1547*. transgression] or breakyng *added 1559, 1623*. the eternal] the everlasting *1559*; everlasting

98 *1623*. and idolaters] *not in 1623*. constant] stedfaste *1559, 1623*. conforme] frame *1559, 1623*. constant] stedfast *1559, 1623*. his commaundementes]

99 the commaundementes *1549, 1559, 1623*. election] chosyng *1559*. again in pacience] in pacience *1623*. christened] Christians *1623*. devil] unjust *1623*. towardes God] towades God *1547*.

5 An Homelie, or Sermon, of Good Woorkes Annexed unto Faithe

In the last sermon was declared unto you what the lively and true faithe of a Christian man is: that it causeth not a man to be idle, but to be occupied in bringyng furthe good workes, as occasion serveth.

Now by Gods grace shalbe declared the seconde thyng that before was noted of faith: that without it can no good worke be doen acceptable and pleasaunt unto God. For as a braunche cannot beare fruit of it self, saith our savior Christ, except it abide in the vine, so cannot you, except you abide in me: I am the vine and you be the braunches; he that abydeth in me, and I in hym, he bringeth furthe muche fruit, for without me, you can do nothyng. And S. Paule proveth that Enoche had faithe, because he pleased God. For without faithe, saieth he, it is not possible to please God. And again to the Roma. he saith: whatsoever worke is doen without faith, it is sinne. Faith geveth life to the soule, and thei bee asmuche ded to God that lacke faith as thei be to the world whose bodies lacke soules. Without faith al that is doen of us is but ded before God, although the woorke seme never so gaie and glorious before man. Even as the picture graven or painted is but a ded representacion of the thyng it self, and is with out life, or any maner of movyng, so be the workes of all unfaithfull persones before God. Thei do appere to be lively workes, and in deede thei be but ded, not availyng to the eternall life. Thei bee but shadowes and shewes of lively and good thynges, and not good and lively thynges in dede. For true faith doth geve life to the workes, and out of suche faith come good woorkes that be very good woorkes in dede, and without it no worke is good before God: as saieth Saincte Augustine, 'wee muste set not good workes before faithe, nor thynke that before faithe, a man maie do any good worke, for suche workes, although thei seme unto men to bee praise worthy, yet in deede thei bee but vain,' and not allowed before God. Thei bee as the course of a horse that runneth out of the waie,

whiche taketh great labor, but to no purpose. Let no man, therefore,' saieth
he, 'recken upon his good workes before his faithe. Whereas faithe was
not, good woorkes were not; the intent,' saieth he, 'maketh the good
workes, but faith must guide and order thintent of man.' And Christ saith:
if thine iye be naught, thy whole body is ful of darkenesse. 'The iye doth
signifie the intent,' saith Sainct Augustine, 'wherwith a man doth a thyng.
So that he whiche doth not his good workes with a godly intent and a
true faithe that woorketh by love, the whole body beside – that is to saie,
all the whole numbre of his workes – is darke, and there is no light in
it.' For good deedes bee not measured by the factes theimselfes, and so
dissevered from vices, but by the endes and intentes for the whiche thei bee
doen. If a heathen man clothe the naked, fede the hongerie, and do suche
other like workes, yet because he doth theim not in faithe for the honor
and love of God, thei be but ded, vain and fruitles workes to hym.

Faithe is it that dooth commende the woorke to God, for as S. Augustine
saith, 'whether thou wilt or no, that worke that commeth not of faithe is
naught': where the faith of Christ is not the foundacion, there is no good
worke, what buildyng soever we make. There is one worke in the which
be al good workes, that is, 'faithe, whiche worketh by charitie': if thou
have it, thou hast the ground of all good woorkes. For the vertues of
strength, wisedom, temperaunce and justice be al referred unto this same
faith. Without this faith we have not them, but onely the names and
shadowes of them, as S. Augustine saieth: 'All the life of them that lacke
the true faithe is syn, and nothyng is good without hym that is the aucthor
of goodnes: where he is not, there is but feined vertue, although it be in
the best workes.' And S. Augu. declaryng this verse of the psalme, the
turtle hath found a nest where she may kepe her young birdes, saith that
Jewes, heretiques and pagans do good workes – thei clothe the naked,
fede the poore, and do other workes of mercy – but because thei be not
doen in the true faithe, therfore the birdes be loste. But if thei remain
in faith, then faith is the nest and savegard of their birdes, that is to say,
safegard of their good workes, that the reward of them be not utterly lost.

And this matter, whiche S. Augustin at large in many bokes disputeth,
S. Ambrose concludeth in fewe wordes, saiyng: 'he that by nature would
withstand vice, either by naturall will or reason, he doth in vain garnishe
the tyme of this life, and atteineth not the very true vertues, for without the
worshippyng of the true God, that whiche semeth to be vertue is vice.'
And yet moste plainly to this purpose writeth S. Jhon Chriso. in this wise:
'you shall finde many which have not the true faith, and be not of the
flocke of Christ, and yet, as it appereth, thei florishe in good workes of
mercy. You shall finde them full of pitie, compassion, and geven to justice,

and yet for all that, thei have no fruite of their workes, because the chief
worke lacketh. For when the Jewes asked of Christ what thei should do to
worke good workes, he aunswered: this is the worke of God, to beleve
in hym whom he sente: so that he called faithe the worke of God. And
assone as a man hath faith, anone he shall florish in good workes, for
faith of it self is full of good workes, and nothyng is good without faith.'
And for a similitude he saith that 'thei whiche glister and shine in good
workes without faithe in God be like dead men whiche have goodly and
precious tombes, and yet it availeth them nothyng. Faith may not be
naked without good workes, for then it is no true faith, and when it is
adjoyned to workes, yet is it above the workes. For as men that be very
men in dede first have life, and after be norished, so must our faithe in
Christe go before, and after be norished with good woorkes. And life maie
be without norishment, but norishment cannot be without life. A man
must nedes be norished by good workes, but first he must have faithe: he
that doth good deedes, yet without faith, he hath no life. I can shew a
man that by faith without workes lived and cam to heaven, but without
faithe, never man had life. The thiefe that was hanged when Christe
suffered did beleve onely, and the moste mercifull God did justify hym.
And because no manne shall objecte that he lacked tyme to doo good
woorkes, for els he would have doen them, truthe it is, and I will not
contend therin; but this I will surely affirme: that faithe onely saved hym.
If he had lived, and not regarded faith and the workes thereof, he should
have lost his salvacion again. But this is the effecte that I saie: that faithe
by it self saved hym, but workes by theim selfes never justified any man.'
Here ye have heard the minde of Sainct Chrisostome, wherby you maie
perceive that neither faith is without workes, havyng opportunitie therto,
nor workes can availe to eternall life without faithe.

[The Second Parte of the Sermon of Good Workes

Of the three thynges whiche were in the former sermon specially noted of
lively faithe, two be declared unto you: the first was that faithe is never
ydle without good woorkes when occasion serveth; the second, that good
workes acceptable to God can not be done wythout faythe.]

Now to procede to the third parte, whiche in the former sermon was
noted of faithe, that is to say, what maner of workes thei be whiche spring
out of true faithe and leade faithfull menne unto eternall life. This cannot
bee knowen so well, as by our savior Christe hymself, who was asked
of a certain greate man thesame question. What woorkes shall I do, said a
prince, to come to everlastyng life? To whom Jesus aunswered: If thou

wilte come to the eternall life, kepe the commaundementes. But the prince
not satisfied herewith, asked farther, whiche commaundementes? The
Scribes and Phariseis had made so many of their awne lawes and tradicions
to bryng men to heaven, besides Gods commaundementes, that this man
was in doubte whether he should come to heaven by those lawes and
tradicions or by the lawes of God, and therfore he asked Christe whiche
commaundementes he meante. Whereunto Christe made hym a plain
aunswere, rehersyng the commaundementes of God, saiyng: Thou shalte
not kill; thou shalt not commit adultery; thou shalt not steale; thou shalte
not beare false witnesse; honor thy father and mother; and love thy
neighboure as thy self. By whiche woordes Christe declared that the lawes
of God bee the very waie that do lead to eternall life, and not the tradicions and lawes of men. So that this is to bee taken for a moste true lesson
taught by Christes awne mouth, that the workes of the moral commaundementes of God be the very true workes of faithe, whiche leade to the
blessed life to come.

But the blyndenesse and malice of man, even from the beginnyng, hath
ever been redy to fal from Gods commaundementes. As Adam the firste
man, havyng but one commaundement, that he should not eate of the
fruite forbidden, notwithstandyng Gods commaundement he gave credite
unto the woman, seduced by the subtile perswasion of the serpent, and
so folowed his awne will, and lefte Gods commaundement. And ever synce
that tyme, al his succession hath been so blinded through original sinne
that thei have been ever ready to decline from God and his lawe, and
to invent a new waie unto salvacion by workes of their awne devise: so
muche, that almoste all the worlde forsakyng the true honor of the onely
eternall, livyng God wandered aboute their awne phantasies, worshyppyng
some the sunne, the moone, the sterres; some Jupiter, Juno, Diana,
Saturnus, Apollo, Neptunus, Ceres, Bacchus and other dedde men and
women; some, therewith not satisfied, worshipped diverse kyndes of
beastes, birdes, fishe, foule and serpentes, every region, toune and house in
maner beyng divided, and settyng up images of suche thynges as thei
liked and worshippyng thesame. Suche was the rudenes of the people after
thei fell to their awne phantasies, and left the eternall livyng God and
his commaundementes, that thei devised innumerable images and gods. In
whiche error and blindnes thei did remain, untill suche time as almighty
God, pitiyng the blindnesse of man, sent his true prophet Moses into
the worlde to reprehende this extreme madnes, and to teache the people to
knowe the onely livyng God and his true honor and worshippe.

But the corrupt inclinacion of man was so muche geven to folowe his
awne phantasies, and, as you would saie, to favoure his awne birde, that he

brought up hymself, that al the admonicions, exhortacions, benefites and threatnynges of God could not kepe hym from suche his invencions.

For notwithstandyng al the benefites of God shewed unto the people of Israell, yet when Moses went up into the mountain to speake with almighty God, he had taried there but a few daies, when the people began to invent new gods. And as it cam in their heddes, thei made a calfe of golde and kneled doune and worshipped it. And after that, thei folowed the Moabites, and worshipped Beelphegor, the Moabites god. Read the boke of Judges, the bokes of the Kynges and the Prophetes, and there shal you find how inconstant the people wer, how ful of invencions, and more ready to runne after their awne phantasies then Gods moste holy commaundementes. Ther shal you reade of Baall, Moloche, Chamos, Mechom, Baalpeor, Astaroth, Beel the dragon, Priapus, the brasen serpente, the twelve signes and many other unto whose images the people with greate devocion invented pilgrimages, preciously deckyng and censyng them, kneling doune and offering to them, thinking that an high merite before God, and to be estemed above the preceptes and commaundementes of God. And where at that tyme God commaunded no sacrifyce to be made but in Jerusalem onely, they did cleane contrary, makyng aulters and sacrifyces every where, in hylles, in wooddes, and in houses, not regardyng Gods commaundementes, but estemynge theyr awne phantasyes and devocion to be better then theim. And the error hereof was so spred abrode that not onely the unlearned people, but also the priestes and teachers of the people, partly by glory and avarice were corrupted, and partly by ignoraunce blindly seduced wyth thesame abhominacions: so muche that Kyng Achab, havyng but onely Helyas, a true teacher and minister of God, there were eight hundred and fiftie priestes that perswaded hym to honor Baal, and to do sacrifyce in the woddes or groves. And so continued that horrible error, untyll the three noble kynges, as Josaphat, Ezechias and Josias, Gods elect ministers, destroyed the same clerely, and reduced the people from suche theyr fayned invencions unto the very commaundementes of God, for the whiche thyng their immortall rewarde and glory doeth, and shall remayn with God for ever.

And beside the foresayed invencions, the inclinacion of man to have hys awne holy devocions devised newe sectes and religions, called Phariseis, Sadduces and Scribes, with many holy and godly tradicions and ordinaunces, as it semed by the outward apparaunce and goodly glisteryng of the workes, but in very deede, all tendynge to idolatrye, supersticion and hipocrisye, theyr hartes within beynge full of malice, pride, coveteousnesse and all iniquitie. Against which sectes and their pretensed holynes, Christe cryed out more vehemently then he did against any other persones,

saiyng and often repetyng these wordes: Wo be to you, Scribes and
Phariseis, ye hypocrites, for you make cleane the vessell without, but within
you be full of ravyn and fylthinesse; thou blynd Pharisei and hypocrite,
firste make the inwarde parte cleane. For notwithstanding all the goodly
tradicions and outward shewes of good workes, devised of their awne
imaginacion, whereby they appered to the world moste religious and holy
of all men, yet Christ, who sawe their hartes, knewe that they were
inwardly in the sight of God moste unholy, moste abhominable, and farthest from God of all men. Therefore sayed he unto theim: Hypocrites,
the prophete Esaie spake full truely of you when he sayed, This people
honor me with their lippes, but their harte is farre from me; they worshyppe me in vayne that teache doctrines and commaundementes of men,
for you leave the commaundementes of God to kepe your awne tradicions.

And though Christe sayed they worship God in vain that teache doctrines and commaundementes of men, yet he meant not therby to overthrowe all mennes commaundements, for he himself was ever obedient to
the princes and their lawes made for good ordre and governaunce of
the people, but he reproved the lawes and tradicions made by the Scribes
and Phariseis, whiche were not made onely for good ordre of the people,
as the civil lawes were, but they wer so highly extolled that they were
made to be a ryght and syncere worshippinge of God, as they had been
equall with Gods lawes or above them, for many of Gods lawes could not
be kept, but were fayn to geve place unto them. This arrogancie God
detested, that man shoulde so advaunce his lawes to make theim equall
with Gods lawes, wherein the true honoryng and ryght worshippyng
of God standeth, and to make his lawes for theim to be omitted. God hath
appoynted his lawes, whereby hys pleasure is to be honored. His pleasure
is also that all mannes lawes, beyng not contrary to his lawes, shalbe
obeied and kepte, as good and necessarye for every common weale, but
not as thynges wherein principally his honor resteth. And all civil and
mannes lawes either be, or shulde be made to induce men the better to
observe Gods lawes, that, consequently, God shoulde be the better honored
by them. Howbeit, the Scribes and Phariseis were not content that theyr
lawes should be no higher estemed then other positive and civil lawes,
nor would not have them called by the name of other temporall lawes, but
called them holy and godly tradicions, and would have them estemed
not onely for a right and true worshippyng of God, as Gods lawes be in
deede, but also to be the moste high honoryng of God, to the which
the commaundementes of God should geve place. And for this cause did
Christ so vehemently speake against them, saiyng: your tradicions, which

men esteme so highe, be abhominacion before God. For commonly of
suche tradicions foloweth the transgression of Gods commaundementes,
and a more devocion in the observyng of suche thynges, and a greater
conscience in breakyng of them then of the commaundementes of God. As
the Scribes and Phariseis so supersticiously and scrupulously kepte the
Sabboth that they were offended with Christe, because he healed sicke
men, and with his apostles, because they, beyng sore hungery, gathered the
eares of corne to eate upon that daye. And because his disciples wasshed
not their handes so often as the tradicions requyred, the Scribes and
Phariseis quereled with Christ, saiyng: why do thy disciples breake the
tradicions of the seniours? But Christ objected against them that they, for
to observe their awne tradicions, did teache men to breake the verye
commaundementes of God. For thei taught the people such a devocion
that they offered their goodes into the treasure house of the temple under
the pretense of Gods honor, leaving their fathers and mothers, to whom
they were chiefly bounde, unholpen: and so they brake the commaundementes of God to kepe theyr awne tradicions. They estemed more an othe
made by the golde or oblacion in the temple then an othe made in the
name of God hymselfe or of the temple. Thei wer more studious to pay
their tithes of smal thynges then to do the greater thynges commaunded of
God, as workes of mercye, or to do justice, or to deale syncerely, uprightly
and faythefully with God and man – these, saieth Christ, ought to be
doen, and the other not omitted. And to be shorte, they were of so blynd
judgement that they stombled at a strawe and leped over a blocke. They
would, as it were, nicely take a flye out of their cuppe, and drynke doune a
whole camell. And therfore Christe called them blynde guydes, warnynge
his disciples from tyme to tyme to eschewe their doctrine. For althoughe
they semed to the worlde to be moste perfect men, bothe in livyng and
teaching, yet was their life but hypocrisie, and their doctrine but sower
leven, mixte with supersticion, idolatry, and preposterous judgement,
setting up the tradicions and ordinaunces of man in the stede of Gods
commaundementes.

[The Third Part of the Sermon of Good Woorkes

That all men might rightly judge of good woorkes, it hath been declared
in the seconde parte of this sermon what kynde of good workes thei
bee that God would have his people to walke in, namely suche as he hath
commaunded in his Holy Scripture, and not suche woorkes as men have
immagined of their awne brayne of a blynde zeale and devocion, without

the Worde of God. And by mistakyng the nature of good woorkes,
manne hath moste highly displeased God, and hath goen from his will and
commaundement.

So] thus have you heard how muche the worlde from the beginnyng
until Christes tyme was ever ready to fall from the commaundementes of
God, and to seke other meanes to honor and serve hym, after a devocion
imagined of their awne heades, and how they extolled their awne tradicions as high or above Gods commaundementes, whiche hath happened
also in our tymes, the more it is to be lamented, no lesse then it did
emonge the Jewes, and that by the corrupcion, or at the least, by the
negligence of them that chiefly ought to have preferred Gods commaundementes, and to have preserved the syncere and heavenly doctrine left by
Christe.

What man havyng any judgement or learnyng, joyned with a true zeale
unto God, doeth not se and lament to have entred into Christes religion
suche false doctrine, supersticion, idolatrie, hipocrisy and other enormities
and abuses, so as by lytle and lytle, through the sower leven thereof, the
swete bread of Gods Holye Worde hath been muche hindered and layed
aparte? Never had the Jewes in their moste blyndenesse so many pilgrimages unto images, nor used so muche knelyng, kissyng and censyng of
them, as hath been used in oure tyme.

Sectes and feined religions were neither the forty parte so many emonge
the Jewes, nor more supersticiously and ungodly abused then of late
dayes they have been emonge us. Whiche sectes and religions had so many
hypocriticall woorkes in their state of religion, as they arrogantly named
it, that their lampes, as they sayd, ranne alwayes over, able to satisfye
not onely for their awne synnes, but also for all other their benefactors,
brothers and sisters of their religion, as moste ungodly and craftelye they
had perswaded the multitude of ignoraunt people, keping in diverse
places, as it were, martes or markettes of merites, beyng ful of their holy
reliques, images, shrines, and workes of supererogacion, redy to be solde.
And all thinges which they had were called holy: holy coules, holy girdels,
holy pardoned beades, holy shooes, holy rules, and all full of holynesse.
And what thyng can be more foolishe, more supersticious or ungodly then
that men, women and chyldren shoulde weare a friers coote to deliver
theim from agues or pestilence, or when they dye, or when they be buried,
cause it to be caste upon them in hope therby to be saved. Which supersticion, although, thankes be to God, it hath been lytle used in this realme,
yet in diverse other realmes it hath been, and yet is used, both emonge
many, bothe learned and unlearned. But to passe over the innumerable
supersticiousnesse that hath been in straunge apparell, in silence, in dormi-

torie, in cloyster, in chapter, in choyse of meates and in drinkes, and in
suche like thinges, let us consider what enormities and abuses have been in
the thre chiefe principal poyntes, whiche they called the thre essencialles
of religion, that is to saye, obedience, chastitie and wilfull povertye.

Fyrst, under pretense of obedience to their father in religion, whiche
obedience they made them selfes, they were exempted by their rules and
canons from the obedience of their natural father and mother, and from the
obedience of emperor and kyng and all temporall power, whom of verye
duetye by Godes lawes they were bound to obeye. And so the profession
of their obedience not due was a renunciacion of their due obedience.
And how their profession of chastitie was observed, it is more honesty to
passe over in silence, and let the world judge of that whiche is well
knowen then with unchaste woordes, by expressynge of their unchast lyfe,
to offende chast and godly eares. And as for theyr wylfull povertye, it
was such then, when in possessions, jewels, plate and riches thei were equal
or above merchauntes, gentlemen, barons, erles and dukes, yet by this
subtile sophistical terme, Proprium in communi, they deluded the worlde,
perswadyng that notwithstandyng all their possessions and riches, yet
they observed their vowe, and were in wilful povertie. But for al their
riches, thei might neither healpe father nor mother, nor other that were in
deede very nedye and poore without the licence of their father abbot,
prior, or warden. And yet they might take of every man, but thei might
not geve ought to any man, no, not to theim whom the lawes of God
bound them to helpe. And so through their tradicions and rules the lawes
of God could beare no rule with theim. And therefore of theim might
be moste truely sayed that which Christ spake unto the Pharises: you breake
the commaundementes of God by your tradicions; you honor God with
youre lippes, but your hartes be farre from him. And the longer praiers thei
used by day and by night, under pretense of suche holynes, to get the
favor of widowes and other simple folkes, that they might syng trentals
and servyce for theyr husbandes and frendes, and admitte them into their
suffrages, the more truely is verefyed of theim the saying of Christ: wo
be to you, Scribes and Phariseis, hypocrites, for you devoure widowes
houses under coloure of long praiers; therfore your dampnacion shalbe the
greater. Wo be to you, Scribes and Phariseis, hipocrites, for you go
about by sea and by land to make mo novices and newe brethren, and
when they be admitted of your secte, you make them the chyldren of
helle, worse then your selfes be.

Honor be to God, who did put light in the harte of his faithful and true
minister of moste famous memory, Kynge Henry the .viii., and gave
hym the knowledge of hys Worde, and an earnest affection to seke his

glory, and to put awaye all suche supersticious and pharisaicall sectes, by Antichrist invented and set up agaynst the true Worde of God and glory of hys moste blessed name, as he gave the lyke spirite unto the moste noble and famous prynces, Josaphat, Josias, and Ezechyas. God graunte all us, the Kynges hyghnesse faythfull and true subjectes, to fede of the swete and savorie breade of Gods awne Woorde and, as Christ commaunded, to eschewe all oure pharisaicall and papistical leven of mans feyned religion. Whiche, although it were before God moste abhominable, and contrary to Gods commaundementes and Christes pure religion, yet it was extolled to be a moste godly lyfe, and highest state of perfection. As though a man might be more godly and more perfecte by kepynge the rules, tradicions and professions of men then by kepynge the holy commaundementes of God.

And briefly to passe over the ungodly and counterfet religions, let us reherse some other kyndes of papisticall supersticions and abuses, as of beades, of Lady Psalters and rosaries, of .xv. Oos, of Sainct Bernardes Verses, of Sainct Agathes letters, of purgatory, of masses satisfactory, of stacions and jubilies, of feyned reliques, of halowed beades, belles, breade, water, palmes, candelles, fyre and suche other, of supersticious fastynges, of fraternities, of pardons, with suche lyke merchaundyse, whiche were so estemed and abused to the great prejudice of Gods glory and commaundementes that they were made moste high and moste holy thynges, whereby to atteyn to the eternall lyfe, or remission of sinne. Yea also, vayne invencions, unfruictfull ceremonies and ungodly lawes, decrees and counsayles of Rome, were in suche wyse advaunced that nothyng was thought comparable in aucthoritie, wisedom, learnynge and godlynes unto them. So that the lawes of Rome, as thei sayed, were to be receyved of all men as the foure Evangelistes, to the which all lawes of princes must geve place. And the lawes of God also partly were omitted and lesse estemed that the sayde lawes, decrees and counsayles, with theyr tradicions and ceremonies, myght be more duely observed and had in greater reverence. Thus was the people, through ignoraunce, so blynded with the goodly shewe and apparaunce of those thynges that they thought the observyng of them to be a more holynesse, a more perfecte service and honoryng of God, and more pleasyng to God then the kepyng of Gods commaundementes. Such hath been the corrupt inclinacion of man, ever supersticiously geven to make new honorynge of God of hys awn hedde, and then to have more affection and devocion to observe that then to searche out Gods holy commaundementes and to kepe them. And furthermore, to take Gods commaundementes for mennes commaundementes, and mennes commaundementes for Gods commaundementes, yea, and for the highest and moste perfect and holy of all Gods commaundementes. And so was all confused that scant well learned men, and but a small numbre of them, knewe, or at the least, would knowe and durst affirme the truth, to separate Gods commaundementes from the commaundementes of men: wherupon dyd growe muche error, supersticion, idolatry, vayne religion, preposterous judgement, greate contencion, with all ungodly livyng.

Wherfore, as you have any zeale to the right and pure honoryng of God, as you have any regard to your awn soules and to the life that is to come, which is both without payn and without end, applie your selfes chiefly above all thyng to reade and to heare Gods Worde: marke diligently therin what hys wyll is you shall do, and with all youre endevor, applye your selfes to folowe thesame. First you must have an assured faythe in God, and geve youre selfes wholy unto hym, love hym in prosperite and adversitie, and dread to offende hym evermore. Then, for hys sake, love all men, frendes and fooes, because they be his creacion and image, and redemed by Christ, as ye are. Caste in your mindes how you maye do good unto all men unto your powers, and hurt no man. Obey al your superiors and governors, serve youre masters faithfully and diligently, aswell in theyr absence as in theyr presence, not for dread of punishment onely, but for conscience sake, knowyng that you are bound so to do by Gods commaundementes. Disobey not your fathers and mothers, but honor them, helpe them, and please them to your power. Oppresse not, kil not, beat not, neyther slaunder, nor hate any man; but love all men, speake well of al men, helpe and succor every man, as you maye, yea, even your enemies that hate you, that speake evil of you and that do hurt you. Take no mans goodes, nor covete your neyghbors goodes wrongfully, but content your selfes with that which ye get truely, and also bestowe your awne goodes charitably, as nede and case requyreth. Flee all idolatryc, witchcraft and perjury; commit no maner of adultery, fornicacion, nor other unchastnesse in wil nor in dede with any other mannes wyfe, wydowe, mayde, or other wyse. And travailynge continually durynge your lyfe, thus in the observynge the commaundementes of God (wherein consisteth the pure, principal and direct honour of God, and which, wrought in faythe, God hath ordeyned to be the righte trade and pathe waye unto heaven) you shall not fayle, as Christe hath promised, to come to that blessed and eternall lyfe, where you shall live in glory and joye with God for ever. To whome be laude, honor, and imperie, for ever and ever.

Amen.

NOTES

103 *as a braunche ... do nothyng*: John 15:4–5.
     he pleased God ... please God: Heb 6:5–6.
     whatsoever ... it is sinne: Rom 14:23.
     gaie: attractive.
     '*wee muste set ... thintent of man*': Augustine *Enarratio in Ps 31* 2, 4 (PL 36:
     259).
104 *if thine iye ... darkenesse*: Matt 6:23.
     '*The iye doth signifie ... no light in it*': Augustine *De sermone Domini in monte*
     2, 13, 45 (PL 34: 1289).
     For good deedes ... thei bee doen: Cf Augustine *Contra Iulianum* 4, 21 (PL 44:
     749).
     If a heathen man ... workes to hym: Cf Augustine *Contra Iulianum* 4, 30 (PL
     44: 753–4).
     '*whether thou wilt ... is naught*': Augustine *Contra Iulianum* 4, 32 [on Rom
     14:23] (PL 44: 755).
     '*faithe, whiche worketh by charitie*': Augustine *Enarratio in Ps 89* 17 [on Gal
     5:6] (PL 37: 1149).
     vertues ... same faith: Cf Augustine *Contra Iulianum* 4, 19 (PL 44: 747).
     Augustine saieth: 'All ... best workes': The source is in fact Prosper of Aqui-
     taine *Liber sententiarum ex operibus S. Augustini delibatarum* 1, 106
     (PL 51: 441).
     psalme ... utterly lost: Augustine *Enarratio in Ps 83* 7 [ie 84:3] (PL 37:
     1060–1).
     '*he that by nature ... is vice*': Ambrosiaster *De vocatione gentium* 1, 3 (PL 17:
     1078).
     '*you shall finde ... never justified any man*': Pseudo-Chrysostom *De fide et lege
     naturae* 1 (PG 48: 1081–2). Pseudo-Chrysostom quotes John 6:29.
105 *What woorkes ... whiche commaundementes?*: Matt 19:16–18.
106 *Thou shalte not ... as thy self*: Matt 19:18–19.
     his awne birde: 'a bird of one's own brain' is proverbial for 'a conception of
     one's own.'
107 *new gods ... worshipped it*: Exod 32:1–6.
     folowed ... the Moabites god: Num 25:1–5.
     Baall ... and many other: Judg 2:13; Amos 5:26; 1 Kings 11:5, 7, 33; Hos 9:10;
     2 Kings 18:4 and 23:5, 13. For Bel and the Dragon, see Bel:1–42. For
     Priapus, see Vg 3 Reg 15:13, where AV 2 Chron 15:16 has "made an idol in
     a grove." The twelve signs probably refers to Gen 49, where the insig-
     nias of Israel's tribes, according to *The Book of Jewish Knowledge* ed
     Nathan Ausubel (New York: Crown Publishers 1964) sv 'animals, "clean"
     and "unclean," ' indicate totem-clans; signs are prohibited in Lev 19:28.
     censyng: offering incense before.

no sacrifice ... but in Jerusalem: References to the propriety of sacrificing in Jerusalem occur throughout 2 Chron.

Achab ... groves: 1 Kings 18:19, 22.

noble kynges ... God for ever: 2 Chron 17:3–6, 30:14, 31:1, 34:2–7.

108 *Wo be to you ... parte cleane*: Matt 23:25, 26.

ravyn: rapine.

Hypocrites ... your awne tradicions: Matt 15:7–9, quoting Isa 29:13–14.

positive: conventional, enacted.

your tradicions ... before God: Luke 16:15.

109 *Scribes and Phariseis ... that daye*: Matt 12:1–14.

his disciples ... verye commaundementes of God: Matt 15:1–6.

they brake ... tradicions: Mark 7:9.

an othe ... of the temple: Matt 23:16–22.

tithes ... God and man: Matt 23:23.

stombled ... blocke: OED *stumble* 2e cites the homily to illustrate this proverbial saying, also found in a citation dated 1530.

flye ... camell: Matt 23:24.

sower leven: Matt 13:33 and 16:6.

110 *syncere*: pure.

lampes ... satisfye: The Council of Trent (1563) confirmed that in accord with the doctrine of satisfaction (earthly suffering undergone in reparation for sin) the souls detained in purgatory are comforted by the suffrages, or intercessory prayers, of the faithful. The lamps lit betoken the prayers offered for those joined in the mystical body of Christ.

workes of supererogacion: Based on Luke 10:35 (Vg 'quodcumque supererogaveris') and the parable of the good Samaritan, these are deeds that surpass in virtue acts of duty or obligation. They are explicitly rejected by Article 14 of the Thirty-nine Articles. Becon says that *opera supererogationis* could justly be termed *opera superarrogantiae* (*Prayers and Other Pieces* ed John Ayre, Parker Society 4 [Cambridge: Cambridge University Press 1844] 200). Cf Tyndale *Doctrinal Treatises* ed Henry Walker, Parker Society 47 (Cambridge: Cambridge University Press 1848) 85–7.

all thinges ... holynesse: Cf Becon's preface to 'A Comfortable Epistle to the Afflicted People of God': 'The church of Christ knoweth none other armours against Satan, but faith, prayer, and the word of God. The synagogue of Satan teacheth that, if a man will fight and prevail against Satan, he must flee for succour unto holy bread, holy water, holy palms, holy candles, holy bells, holy beads, holy laces etc.' (*Prayers and Other Pieces* 198).

friers coote: In 'Acts of Christ and Antichrist,' Becon says that Antichrist 'sendeth us to a grey-friar's cowl, and willeth us to be buried in that, promising us by that means both remission of sins and everlasting life' (*Prayers and Other Pieces* 518–19). Cf Grindal *Remains* ed William

Nicholson, Parker Society 23 (Cambridge: Cambridge University Press 1843) 30.

111   *thre essencialles*: Vows of obedience, chastity, and poverty were first taken by the twelfth-century Hermits of St Augustine. Although, as evangelical counsels, they are works of supererogation, Innocent III made them essential to the monastic vocation (see NCE sv 'vow [practice and theology,/ of]').

Proprium in communi: Plato's community in which there is no 'meum' or 'tuum' is compatible with Christian teaching (Acts 2:44–5 and 4:32–5), according to Erasmus *Adagia* I i i: *Amicorum communia omnia* (*Opera omnia* ed J. Leclerc, 10 vols [Leiden 1703–6] II 14); Augustine had prescribed communism for cenobitic institutions (*Epistola 211 5*; PL 33: 960). Revived by anabaptists during the sixteenth century, the idea that property should be held in common is condemned by Article 38 of the Thirty-nine Articles.

you breake ... farre from him: Matt 15:3, 8.

trentals: A sequence of thirty requiem masses said on consecutive days, a liturgical usage that depends on a story told by Gregory the Great in *Dialogorum libri* 4, 55 (PL 77: 416–21).

suffrages: prayers.

Wo be to you ... your selfes be: Matt 23:14–15.

112   *beades, of Lady Psalters and rosaries*: A string of beads is used to count the 150 Hail Marys of the Dominican rosary, called the Lady Psalter, since 150 is the number of the Psalms.

.xv. Oos: A very popular devotion, each prayer of which begins with 'O ...' It is included, for example, in *Hore Beatissime Virginis Marie* (Paris 1534), a book of hours, the 1530 edition of which, once owned by Thomas More, is now in the Beinecke Library at Yale. The introduction to these prayers states that 'these be the .xv. oos the whyche the holy virgin saint brigitte [of Sweden] was wounte to say dayly before the holy rode in saint Paules chyrche at Rome: who so say this a hole yere he shall delever .xv. soules out of purgatory of hys nexte kyndreed, and converte other .xv. synners to goode lyf & other .xv. ryghtuouse men of hys kynde shall persever in goode lyf. And what ye desyre of god ye shall have it / yf it be to the salvacyon of your sowle' (f 59).

Sainct Bernardes Verses: *Versus sancti bernardi* also appear in the *Hore*, which explains: 'Whan saint Bernard was in hys prayers the dyvell sayd unto hym: I knowe that there be certeyne verses in the sawter who that say them dayly shall not perysshe and he shall have knowledge of the daye that he shall dye / but the fende wolde noth shewed hym [sic] to saint bernard. [T]han saint bernard: I shall say dayly the hole sawter. [T]he fende considerynge that saint bernard shall do so moche profyte to laboure so, he shewed hym this verses' (f 125).

Sainct Agathes letters: Agatha, who is commemorated on 5 February, was martyred in AD 251, her breasts having been cut off by Quintianus. 'Her intervention was credited with stilling an eruption of Mt Etna the year after her burial; and in the Middle Ages ... bread, candles, fruits and letters were blessed in her name to ward off destruction by fire' (NCE sv 'Agatha, St.'). The letters are also mentioned disparagingly in the homily 'Against Peril of Idolatry,' found in the second book of homilies, and in James Pilkington *The Works* ed James Scholefield, Parker Society 38 (Cambridge: Cambridge University Press 1842) 177.

purgatory ... jubilies: An attack on the Roman Catholic doctrine of satisfaction, particularly 'trafficking' in indulgences, forms of vicarious satisfaction held to assist the imperfect soul during its purification in purgatory. Stations, in this context, are days of partial fast often associated with the granting of indulgences. Jubilees (see Lev 25:25–54), celebrated every hundred years and sometimes more often, are occasions for the dispensing of plenary indulgences. See NCE sv 'Holy Year.'

feyned reliques: Virtually all the reformers attacked the cult of relics as an example of image-worship. For a spirited but cautious defence, which includes an account of relics discovered at Barking Abbey, see Thomas More *A Dialogue concerning Heresies* [1530] ed T.M.C. Lawler, Germain Marc'hadour, and R.C. Marius (New Haven: Yale University Press 1981) 217–25.

halowed beades ... fyre: Becon decries the consecration of liturgical things in 'The Monstrous Marchandise of the Romish Bishops,' *The Works* (London 1564) III 207–14, and 232–3. This treatise is not among those printed in the three Parker Society volumes devoted to Becon's writings.

fraternities: Probably a reference to letters of fraternity, which entitled the benefactor of a convent to share in the benefits won by its prayers and good works.

counsayles of Rome: For a typical protestant objection to councils, which, according to Roman Catholic theology, have supernatural power tantamount to the pope's, see Nicholas Ridley *The Works* ed Henry Christmas, Parker Society 40 (Cambridge: Cambridge University Press 1843) 129–36. Cf the twenty-first of the Thirty-nine Articles.

113   *scant*: scarcely, hardly.
Caste ... mindes: consider.
case: occasion.
imperie: dominion.

TEXTUAL APPARATUS

103   An Homelie, or Sermon] A Sermon *1559, 1623*. acceptable] accepted *1623*. Enoche] Eunoch *1559*; the Eunuch *1623*. eternall] everlasting *1559, 1623*. without it no worke] without, no worke *1559*; without fayth, no worke *1623*.

set not] set no *1559, 1623*. any good worke] any good works *1623*. a horse]
104 an horse *1623*. light in it] light in them *1559, 1623*. dissevered] discerned
1549, 1559, 1623. thei bee doen] they were doen *1623*. commende the woorke]
commende the word *1559*. other workes] other good workes *1623*. pitie]
105 pietie *1559*. yet is it] yet it is *1549, 1559, 1623*. did justify] justified *1559, 1623*.
objecte] say agayne *1559, 1623*. this is the effecte] this the effecte *1547*.
eternall] everlastyng *1559, 1623*. Of the three] Of three *1559*. procede] go
forth *1559*; go forward *1623*. parte, whiche in the former sermon was noted
of faithe, that is to say] part, that is, *1559, 1623*. eternall] everlasting *1559*,
106 *1623*. the eternall life] the everlasting life *1559*; everlasting life *1623*. lawes of
God] lawe of God *1559, 1623*. and mother] and thy mother *1623*. eternall]
everlastinge *1559, 1623*. taken] taked *1547*. his succession] that came of hym
1559, 1623. decline] fall *1559, 1623*. unto salvacion] of salvacion *1549*. Jupiter,
Juno] Jupiter, some, Juno *1549*. region] countrey *1559, 1623*. people after]
107 people ter *1623*. reprehende] reprove and rebuke *1559, 1623*. shal you find]
you shall find *1623*. inconstant] unstedfast *1559, 1623*. Mechom] Melchom
1623. Beel] Bell *1623*. preciously deckyng and censyng] precious decking and
sensing *1559, 1623*. better then theim] better then they *1559, 1623*. avarice]
covetousnes *1559, 1623*. seduced] deceived *1559, 1623*. elect] chosen *1559, 1623*.
108 reduced] brought again *1559, 1623*. iniquitie] wickednes *1559, 1623*. repetyng]
rehearsyng *1559, 1623*. worship] worshypped *1547, 1549*. so highly extolled]
set up so high *1559, 1623*. a ryght and syncere] a ryght syncere *1549*; a ryght
and pure *1559*; rught and pure *1623*. omitted] left of *1559*; left off *1623*.
mannes lawes, beyng not contrary to] mens lawes not being contrary unto
1623. good and necessarye] good as necessarye *1547*. induce] bring in
1559; bring *1623*. observe] kepe *1559, 1623*. consequently] or folowyngly *added*
1559, 1623. other temporall] our temporall *1549*. to be the moste high] for
109 the moste high *1623*. transgression] or breakyng *added, 1559, 1623*. the
observyng] the kepyng *1559*; keeping *1623*. objected against them] layde to
theyr charge *1559, 1623*. observe] kepe *1559, 1623*. omitted] left undone
1559, 1623. mixte] mingled *1559, 1623*. preposterous] overtwhart *1559*; overthwart *1623*. in the stede] in stead *1623*. immagined] studyed out of *1559*,
110 *1623*. commaundement] commendements *1623*. thus have you heard] *1549*;
Thus have you heard *1547*; that thus you have heard *1559, 1623*. imagined of]
found out *1559, 1623*. extolled] did set up *1559, 1623*. preferred ... syncere]
preferred ... pure *1559*; preserved the pure *1623*. forty] fourtieth *1623*.
hypocriticall] and fayned *added 1559, 1623*. of their religion] of religion *1559*,
1623. supererogacion] overflowinge abboundance *1559, 1623*. holy pardoned
beades] holy Pardons, beades *1559, 1623*. is used, both emonge] is used
111 emonge *1623*. in drinkes] drinks *1623*. thre essencialles] or thre chiefe
foundations *added 1559, 1623*. pretense] or color *added 1559, 1623*. exempted]
made free *1559, 1623*. renunciacion] forsaking *1559, 1623*. observed] kept
1559, 1623. Proprium in communi] that is to say, proper in common *added*
1559, 1623. deluded] mocked *1559, 1623*. notwithstandyng] notwitstandyng

1547. observed] kept *1559, 1623.* neither healpe] never healpe *1559, 1623.* tradi-
cions] aditions *1623.* your hartes] you hartes *1547.* pretense] or colour
added 1559, 1623. admitte] or receive *added 1559, 1623.* suffrages] prayers *1559,
1623.* wo be to you] wo be unto you *1623.* admitted] let in or receaved
112 *1559, 1623.* set up agaynst] set up againe *1623.* Kynges] Quenes *1559;* Kings
1623. extolled] praysed *1559, 1623.* counterfet religions] counterfet religion
1623. palmes] Psalmes *1623.* fraternities] or brotherheades *added 1559, 1623.*
eternall] everlasting *1559, 1623.* remission of sinne] remission of synnes
1549. omitted] left of *1559;* left off *1623.* observed] kept *1559, 1623.* observyng]
113 kepyng *1559, 1623.* observe] keepe *1559, 1623.* separate] or sever *added 1559,
1623.* preposterous] overtwhart *1559;* overthwart *1623.* above all thyng] above
all thynges *1623.* love all men] love of all men *1549.* witchcraft] withcraft
1547. fornicacion, nor] fornicacion or *1623.* wydowe, mayde] wydowe
or mayde *1623.* durynge your lyfe] during this life *1623.* the observynge] the
kepyng *1559;* keeping *1623.* consisteth] standeth *1559, 1623.* direct] right
1559, 1623. eternall] everlasting *1559, 1623.* laude] prayse *1559, 1623.*

6   An Homelie of Christian Love and Charitie

Of all thynges that be good to bee taught unto Christian people, there is nothynge more necessarye to bee spoken of and dayely called upon then charitie, aswell for that all maner of woorkes of righteousnes be conteyned in it, as also that the decay therof is the ruyne of the worlde, the banishment of vertue, and the cause of all vice. And for so muche as almoste every man maketh and frameth to hymself charitie after hys awne appetite, and howe detestable soever his lyfe be, both unto God and man, yet he perswadeth hymself stil that he hath charitie, therfore you shall heare now a true and playn descripcion of charitie, not of mennes imaginacion, but of the very woordes and example of our savior Jesus Christ, in which descripcion every man, as it were in a glasse, maye considre himself and se plainly without error, whether he be in the true charitie or not.

Charitie is to love God with al our harte, al our lyfe and all our powers and strength: with all our harte, that is to say, that our hartes, mynd and studye be set to beleve his Worde, to trust in him, and to love hym above al other thynges that we love best in heaven or in yearth; with al our lyfe, that is to saye, that our chief joye and delight be set upon him and his honor, and our whole lyfe geven unto the service of hym above all thynges, with hym to lyve and dye, and to forsake all other thynges rather then hym, for he that loveth hys father or mother, sonne or daughter, house or lande, more then me, sayeth Christ, is not worthy to have me; with all our powers, that is to saye, that with our handes and fete, with our eyes and eares, our mouthes and tongues, and with all other partes and powers, both of body and soule, we should be geven to the kepyng and fulfillyng of his commaundementes. This is the fyrste and principall parte of charitie, but it is not the whole, for charitie is also, to love every man, good and evil, frende and foo, and whatsoever cause be geven to the contrary, yet nevertheles to beare good wil and harte unto every man, to

use our selfes wel unto them aswell in woordes and countenaunce as in all
our outwarde actes and deedes. For so Christ himself taught and so also
he performed in dede. Of the love of God he taught in thys wyse unto a
doctor of the law that asked hym which was the great and chiefe commaundemente in the lawe: Love thy lord God, saied Christ, with all thy
hart, with all thy lyfe and with al thy mynde. And of the love that we
ought to have emong our selfes eche to other, he teacheth us thus: you
have heard it taught in tymes paste, thou shalt love thy frende and hate thy
foe, but I tell you, love youre enemyes, speake wel of them that diffame
you and speake evill of you, do well to theim that hate you, praye for
them that vexe and persecute you, that you maye be the chyldren of your
Father that is in heaven. For he maketh hys sunne to ryse both upon
the evyl and good, and sendeth rayne to juste and unjuste. For yf you love
them that love you, what rewarde shall you have? Do not the Publicans
likewyse? And if you speake well onely of them that be your brethren and
derebeloved frendes, what great matter is that? Do not the heathen thesame
also? These be the very woordes of our savior Christ himself touchyng
the love of our neighbor. And for asmuche as the Phariseis with their
moste pestilente tradicions and false interpretacions and gloses had corrupted and almost clerely stopped up this pure wel of Gods lively Worde,
teachyng that this love and charitie perteyned onely to a mannes frendes
and that it was sufficiente for a man to love them which do love hym and
to hate his fooes, therfore Christ opened thys welle agayn, pourged it,
and scoured it, by gevyng unto his godly lawe of charitie a true and clere
interpretacion, which is this: that we ought to love every man, both
frende and fooe, addyng thereto what commoditie we shal have thereby
and what incommoditie by doynge the contrary. What thyng can we wishe
so good for us as the eternall heavenly Father to repute and take us for
hys chyldren? And this shal we be sure of, sayeth Christe, if we love every
man withoute exception. And if we doo otherwyse, saieth he, we be no
better then the Phariseis, Publicans and heathen and shal have our rewarde
with them, that is, to be excluded from the number of Gods electe chyldren
and from hys everlastynge inheritaunce in heaven.

   Thus of true charitie Christ taught that every man is bounde to love
God above all thynges and to love every man, frend and fooe. And thus
likewyse he did use hymselfe, exhortynge hys adversaries, rebukynge
the faultes of hys adversaryes, and when he coulde not amende them, yet
he prayed for them. Firste he loved God hys Father above all thinges:
so muche that he soughte not hys awne glory and wil, but the glory and
wyl of hys Father. I seke not, said he, myne awne wyl, but the wyl of hym
that sent me. Nor he refused not to dye to satisfie his Fathers wil, saiyng,

if it maye be, let this cuppe of death go from me; if not, thy wyll be doen, and not myne. He loved not onely his frendes, but also hys enemyes, which in their hartes bare exceeding great hatred against hym, and in their tongues spake all evill of hym, and in their actes and dedes pursued hym with all their might and power even unto death. Yet al this notwithstand-ynge, he withdrewe not hys favor from them, but styll loved them, preached unto theim, of love rebuked theyr false doctryne, theyr wycked livyng, and did good unto them, paciently accepting whatsoever they spake or did agaynst hym. When they gave hym evill woordes, he gave none evyll agayn; when they did stryke hym, he did not smyte agayne; and when he suffered death, he dyd not sle them, nor threaten them, but prayed for them, and referred all thinges to hys Fathers wyl. And as a shepe that is led unto the shambles to be slayn and as a lambe that is shorne of hys fleese make no noyse nor resistence, even so wente he unto his death without any repugnaunce or openynge of his mouth to saye any evil.

Thus have I described unto you what charitie is aswel by the doctryne as by the example of Christ himself. Wherby also every man maye without error know hymself, what state and condicion he standeth in, whether he be in charitie, and so the chyld of the Father in heaven, or not. For althoughe almoste every man perswadeth hymself to be in charitie, yet let hym examine none other man, but his awne hart, his life and conversa-cion, and he shal not be deceived, but truly decerne and judge whether he be in perfecte charitie or not. For he that foloweth not hys awne appetite and wil, but geveth hymself earnestly to God to do al his wil and com-maundementes, he may be sure that he loveth God above all thinges and els surely he loveth him not, whatsoever he pretend. As Christ said, if ye love me, kepe my commaundementes. For he that knoweth my com-maundementes and kepeth them, he it is, said Christ, that loveth me. And again he saith, he that loveth me will kepe my Worde, and my Father will love him, and we will both come to him and dwel with hym. And he that loveth me not will not kepe my wordes. And likewise, he that beareth good hart and mynde, and useth wel his tongue and dedes unto every man, frend and foo, he may knowe therby that he hath charitie. And then he is sure also that almightie God taketh hym for hys dere beloved Sonne, as S. Jhon saith: hereby manifestly are knowen the children of God from the chyldren of the devill, for whosoever doth not love hys brother belongeth not unto God.

[The Second Parte of the Sermon of Charitie

You have heard a plaine and a fruitful descripcion of charitie and how profitable and necessarie a thing charite is, how charitie extendeth it selfe both to God and man, frend and fooe, and that by the doctrine and example of Christ. And also who maie certefie hym selfe whether he be in perfit charitie or not, now as concerning thesame matter it foloweth.]

The perverse nature of man, corrupt with sin and destitute of Gods Worde and grace, thinketh it against al reason that a man should love his enemy and hath many perswasions, whiche induce hym to the contrary. Agaynst all whiche reasons we ought aswel to set the teachyng as the livyng of our savior Christ, who loving us, when we wer his enemies, doth teache us to love our enemies. He did paciently take for us many reproches, suffered beatyng and most cruell death. Therfore, we be no membres of hym if we will not folowe hym. Christe, sayeth S. Peter, suffered for us, leavyng an example that we should folowe hym.

Furthermore, we muste consider that to love our frendes is no more but that whiche thiefes, adulterers, homicides and al wicked persons do, in so much that Jewes, Turkes, infidels and all brute beastes do love them that be their frendes, of whom thei have their livyng or any other benefites. But to love enemies is the proper condicion onely of them that be the chyldren of God, the disciples and folowers of Christe. Notwithstandyng, mannes froward and corrupt nature weigheth over depely many tymes the offence and displeasure doen unto hym by enemies and thinketh it a burden intollerable to be bounde to love them that hate hym. But the burden should be easy enough, if on the otherside every man would consider what displeasure he hath doen to hys enemye agayn and what pleasure he hath received of his enemy. And if we find no equal recompense neither in receiving pleasures of our enemy, nor in renderyng displeasures unto hym agayn, then let us pondre the displeasures whiche we have doen against almightye God, how often and how grevously we have offended hym. Wherof, if we will have of God forgevenesse, there is none other remedye but to forgeve the offences doen unto us, whiche be very small in comparison of our offences doen against God.

And if we considre that he whiche hath offended us deserveth not to be forgeven of us, let us consider again that we muche lesse deserve to be forgeven of God. And although our enemy deserve not to be forgeven for his awne sake, yet we ought to forgeve hym for Gods love, consideryng how great and many benefites we have received of hym without our desertes, and that Christ hath deserved of us, that for his sake we should

forgeve them their trespasses committed against us. But here may ryse
a necessary question to be dissolved: if charitie require to thynke, speake
and do well unto every man, bothe good and evill, how can magistrates
execute justice upon malefactors with charitie? How can they cast evill
men in prison, take away their gooddes and somtyme their lifes accordyng
to lawes, if charitie wil not suffre them so to do?

Hereunto is a plain and a breif aunswere: that plagues and punishmentes
be not evill of them selfes, if they be wel taken of innocentes. And to an
evil man thei are bothe good and necessary, and maye be executed accordyng to charitie, and with charitie should be executed. For declaracion
wherof you shal understand that charitie hath .ii. offices: thone contrary to
the other, and yet both necessary to be used upon men of contrary sort
and disposicion. The one office of charitie is to cherish good and innocent
men, not to oppresse them with false accusacions, but to encorage them
with rewardes to do wel and to persever in wel doyng, defendyng them
with the swourd from their adversaries. And the office of bishops and
pastors is to prayse good men for well doynge that they maye persever
therein, and to rebuke and correct by the Worde of God the offences and
crimes of all evill disposed persones. For the other office of charitie is
to rebuke, correct and punish vice without acceptacion of persones, and
thys to be used against them onely that be evil men and malefactors. And
that it is aswell the office of charitie to rebuke, punysh and correct them
that be evill as it is to cherishe and reward them that be good and innocent,
S. Paule declareth, writyng to the Ro., saiyng that the hygh powers are
ordeyned of God not to be dreadful to them that do wel, but unto malefactors, to draw the swourd to take vengeaunce of him that committeth
the sinne. And S. Paule biddeth Timothe constantly and vehemently to
rebuke synne by the Woorde of God. So that bothe offices should be
diligently executed to impugne the kyngdom of the devill: the preacher
with the Worde and the governor with the swourde, els they love neither
God, nor them whom thei governe, if for lacke of correccion thei wilfully
suffre God to be offended and them whom thei governe to perishe. For
as every lovyng father correcteth hys naturall sonne when he doth amisse,
or els he loveth hym not, so all governors of realmes, countreis, townes,
and houses should lovingly correcte theim whiche be offendors under their
governaunce and cherish them which live innocently, if they have any respect either unto God and their office, or love unto them of whom thei
have governaunce. And suche rebukes and punishementes of them that of-
fend must be doen in due tyme, least by delay the offendors fal hedlynges
into al maner of mischief, and not onely be evill themselfes, but also
do hurt unto many men, drawyng other by their evil example to sinne and
outrage after them. As one thief may both robbe many men and also

make many thefes, and one sedicious person may allure many and noye a whole towne or countrey. And suche evil persons that be so great offendors of God and the common weale, charitie requireth to be cut of from the body of the common weale, lest thei corrupt other good and honest persons, like as a good surgion cutteth away a putrified and festered membre for love he hath to the whoole body, least it infect other membres adjoyning to it.

Thus it is declared unto you what true charitie or Christian love is, so plainly that no man nede to be deceived. Which love whosoever kepeth not only towardes God, whom he is bound to love above al thinges, but also towardes his neighbor, aswel frend as foe, it shal surely kepe him from al offence of God and just offence of man. Therfore, beare well awai this one short lesson: that by true Christian charitie God ought to be loved above all thinges, and all men ought to be loved, good and evill, frend and foo, and to all suche we ought, as we maye, to do good; those that be good, of love to encourage and cherish because they be good, and those that be evill, of love to procure their correction and due punishment that thei may therby either be brought to goodnes, or at the leaste that God and the common wealth may be the lesse hurt and offended. And if we thus direct our life by Christian love and charitie, then Christ doth promise and assure us that he loveth us, that we be the children of our heavenly Father, reconciled to hys favor, very membres of Christ, and that after this short time of this present and mortall life, we shal have with hym eternal lyfe in his everlastynge kyngdom of heaven. Therfore, to hym, with the Father and the Holy Ghost, be al honor and glory, now and ever.

Amen.

NOTES

120 *appetite*: inclination.
   Charitie ... strength: Matt 22:37; Deut 6:5.
   he that loveth ... not worthy to have me: Matt 10:37.
121 *Love thy lord ... thy mynde*: Matt 22:37.
   you have heard ... thesame also: Matt 5:43–7.
   scoured: cleaned by removing dirt and weeds.
   repute ... for: regard as.
   I seke not ... sent me: John 5:30.
122 *if it maye be ... not myne*: Matt 26:39, 42.
   as a shepe ... any evil: Isa 53:7; Acts 8:32.
   if ye love ... loveth me: John 14:15, 21.
   he that loveth ... my wordes: John 14:23–4.

hereby ... not unto God: 1 John 3:10.
123 *Christe ... folowe hym*: 1 Pet 2:21.
froward: perverse.
124 *dissolved*: solved.
plagues ... maye be executed accordyng to charitie: Bonner suggests that those
unharmed by plagues and punishments may tolerate them as measures
both good and necessary for the correction of sinners. His subsequent
argument helps to explain the 'bloody' part he played in the Marian
persecutions; see G. Alexander 'Bonner and the Marian Persecutions'
History 60 (1975) 374–91.
acceptacion of persones: favouritism.
hygh powers ... committeth the sinne: Rom 13:1, 4.
constantly ... Woorde of God: 1 Tim 5:20.
125 *noye*: aphetic form of 'annoy.'

TEXTUAL APPARATUS

120 An Homelie] A Sermon *1559, 1623*. conteyned] conteiged *1549*. ruyne] or fall
added 1559, 1623. descripcion] or setting furth *added 1559, 1623*. descripcion]
or settyng forth *added 1559, 1623*. lyfe] soule *1623*. hartes] heart *1623*. our
lyfe] your life *1547*. our powers] your powers *1549*; our power *1623*. contrary]
121 conttary *1549*. countenaunce] countenaunces *1623*. saied Christ] saith Christ
1549. thy lyfe] thy soule *1623*. diffame you and] defame and *1623*. to
juste] t o juste *1547*; to the juste *1623*. tradicions and false] tradicions, false
1547. gevyng] gevyug *1547*. repute] reken *1559, 1623*. excluded] shut out
1559, 1623. electe] chosen *1559, 1623*. thus likewyse] this likewyse *1623*.
122 above] abovee *1547*. death go] death pass *1623*. in their tongues] with their
tongues *1623*. accepting] takyng *1559, 1623*. smyte agayne] smyte him
againe *1623*. fle] slay *1623*. referred] did put *1559, 1623*. make] maketh *1559,
1623*. wente he unto] hee went to *1623*. described] set forth *1559, 1623*.
example] examples *1623*. then he is sure also that] when he is sure that *1623*.
123 descripcion] settyng forth *1559, 1623*. The perverse] But the perverse *1547*.
induce] bringe *1559, 1623*. proper condicion onely of them] porper ... them
1559; proper condicion of them *1623*. equal] or even *added 1559, 1623*.
124 renderyng] requyttinge *1559, 1623*. against] unto *1623*. malefactors] or evil
doers *added 1559, 1623*. innocentes] the harmelesse *1559, 1623*. innocent]
harmelesse *1559, 1623*. persever] continue *1559, 1623*. And the office] as the
office *1623*. persever] continue *1559, 1623*. For the other] The other *1623*.
acceptacion] regarde *1559, 1623*. thys to be used] is to be used *1559, 1623*.
malefactors] or evil doers *added 1559, 1623*. innocent] harmelesse *1559, 1623*.
committeth the sinne] commiteth sinne *1549*. constantly and vehemently]
stoutely and earnestlye *1559, 1623*. impugne] fight agaynste *1559, 1623*.
125 the governor] Governours *1623*. love neither] neither love *1623*. noye]

annoye *1623*. countrey] couutrey *1549*. offendors of] offendors to *1623*. cut of from] cut from *1623*. body] dody *1549*. putrified] rotten *1559, 1623*. adjoyning to] adjoyning unto *1623*. God ought to be loved above ... loved, good] God ought to be loved, good *1623*. procure] and seke *added 1559, 1623*. the lesse hurt] lesse hurt *1623*. eternal] everlastynge *1559, 1623*. now and ever] now and forever *1623*.

7   Against Swearyng
and Perjury

Almightie God, to the intent his moste holy name should be had in honor
and evermore be magnified of the people, commaundeth that no man
shoulde take hys name vainly in his mouth, threatenyng punishmente unto
hym that unreverently abuseth it by swearyng, forswearyng and
blasphemy. To the intent, therfore, that thys commaundement maye be
the better knowen and kepte, it shalbe declared unto you bothe howe it is
lawfull for Christian people to sweare, and also what perill and daunger
it is vainly to sweare, or to be forsworne.

Firste, when judges require othes of the people for declaracion of the
truth, or for execucion of justice, thys maner of swearynge is lawfull. Also,
when men make faythfull promises with attestacion of the name of God
to observe covenauntes, honest promises, statutes, lawes and good customes, as Christian princes do in their conclusions of peace for conservacion
of common wealthes, and private persones promyse their fidelitie in
matrimonie or one to another in honeste and true frendshippe, and al men
when they do sweare to kepe common lawes or locall statutes and good
customes for due ordre to be had and contynued emong men, when
subjectes do sweare to be true and faythefull to their kynge and sovereygne
lorde, and when judges, magistrates and officers sweare truely to execute
their offices, and when a man woulde affirme the trueth to the settynge
furthe of Gods glory for the salvacion of the people in open preachynge of
the Gospell, or in gevyng of good counsayll, privately for their soules
health: all these maner of swearynges, for causes necessary and honest, be
lawfull. But when men do sweare of custome in reasonynge, biyng and
sellynge, or other daily communicacion, as many be common and greate
swearers, suche kynde of swearyng is ungodly, unlawefull and prohibited
by the commaundement of God. For suche swearyng is nothyng els but
takynge of Gods holy name in vayn. And here is to be noted that lawfull

swearynge is not forbidden, but commaunded of almightie God. For
we have examples of Christ and godly men in Holy Scripture that did
sweare themselfes and required othes of other likewise. And Gods commaundement is: Thou shalte dreade thy lorde God and shalt sweare by hys
name. And almighty God by his prophet David sayeth: all men shalbe
praysed that sweare by hym.

Thus did oure savior Christe sweare diverse tymes, saiyng: verely, verely.
And S. Paule sweareth thus: I call God to witnesse. And Abraham,
waxyng olde, required an othe of hys servaunt that he shoulde procure a
wyfe for his sonne Isaac whiche should come of his awne kyndred, and the
servaunt did sweare that he would perfourme hys masters will. Abraham,
also beynge required, dyd sweare unto Abimelech, the King of Geraris,
that he should not hurte hym, nor his posteritie, and so likewyse did Abimelech sweare unto Abraham. And David did sweare to be and continue
a faithfull frende to Jonathas, and Jonathas did sweare to become a faithfull
frende unto David.

Also, God once commaunded that if a thynge were laied to pledge to
any man or left with him to kepe, if thesame thing wer stolne or lost, that
the keper therof should be sworne before judges that he did not convey
it away, nor used any deceipt in causyng thesame to be conveyed away by
hys consent or knowledge. And S. Paule saieth that in al matters of
controversy betwene two persones, whereas one saieth yea, and the other
nay, so as no due profe can be had of the truthe, the ende of every suche
controversy muste be an othe ministered by a judge.

And moreover, God by the prophet Jeremy saieth: thou shalt sweare the
Lord liveth, in truth, in judgement, in righteousnesse. So that whosoever
sweareth when he is required of a judge, let hym be sure in his conscience
that hys othe have these thre condicions, and he shall never nede to be
afraied of perjurie. First, he that sweareth must sweare truly, that is, he
muste, secludynge all favor and affeccion to the parties, have the truthe
onely before hys eyes, and for love thereof saye and speake that which he
knoweth to be truth, and no further. The seconde is: he that taketh an
othe must do it with judgemente, not rasshely and unadvisedly, but soberly,
considerynge what an othe is. The thyrde is: he that sweareth muste
sweare in righteousnesse, that is, for the very zeale and love which he
beareth to the defence of innocency, to the maintenaunce of the truth, and
to the righteousnes of the matter or cause, all profite, disprofite, all love
and favor unto the persone for frendship or kyndred layed a parte. Thus an
othe, if it have with it these thre condicions, is a parte of Gods glory,
which we are bounde by his commaundement to geve unto hym. For he
willeth that we shall sweare onely by his name, not that he hath pleasure in

oure othes, but like as he commaunded the Jewes to offre sacrifices unto hym, not for any delight that he had in theim, but to kepe the Jewes from committyng of idolatrie. So he, commaundyng us to sweare by his holy name, doth not teache us that he delighteth in swearyng, but he thereby forbiddeth all men to geve his glory to any creature in heaven, yearth or water.

Hetherto you se that othes lawfull are commaunded of God, used of patriarches and prophetes, of Christe hymself and of his apostle Paule. Therefore, Christian people muste thinke lawful othes bothe godly and necessary. For by lawfull promises and covenauntes confirmed by othes princes and their countreys are confirmed in common tranquillitie and peace. By holy promises, with attestacion of Gods name, wee bee made lively membres of Christ, when we professe his religion, receivyng the sacrament of baptisme. By like holy promise, the sacrament of matrimony knitteth man and wife in perpetuall love that thei desire not to be sepe-rated for any displeasure or adversitie that shall after happen. By lawfull othes which kynges, princes, judges and magistrates doo sweare, common lawes are kept inviolate, justice is indifferently ministered, innocent per-sones, orphanes, widdowes and poore men are defended from murtherers, oppressors and thiefs, that they suffre no wrong, nor take any harme. By lawfull othes, mutuall societie, amitie and good ordre is kepte contin-ually in all commonalties, as boroughes, citees, tounes and villages. And by lawful othes, malefactors are searched out, wrong doers are punished, and thei whiche sustein wrong are restored to their righte. Therefore, lawfull swearyng cannot be evill whiche bryngeth unto us so many godly, good and necessarie commodities. Wherfore, when Christe so earnestly forbad swearyng, it maie not so bee understanded as though he did forbid all maner of othes, but he forbiddeth all vain swearyng and forswearyng, bothe by God and by his creatures, as the common use of swearyng in biyng, sellyng and in our daily communicacion, to the intent every Christian mannes worde should be aswell regarded in suche matters, as if he should confirme his communicacion with an othe. For 'every Christian mannes worde,' saieth Sainct Hierome, 'should be so true that it should bee regarded as an othe.' And Chrisostome, witnessyng thesame, saieth: 'It is not convenient to sweare, for what nedeth us to sweare when it is not lawfull for one of us to make a lye unto another?'

Peradventure some will saie, I am compelled to sweare, for els men that do common with me, or do bye and sell with me, wil not beleve me. To this aunswereth .S Chrisostome that he that thus saieth sheweth hymself to be an unjust and a deceiptfull persone, for if he wer a trustie man and his deedes taken to agree with his wordes, he should not nede to sweare at

al. For he that useth truthe and plainnesse in his bargainyng and communicacion, he shal have no nede by such vain swearyng to bryng hymself in
credence with his neighbours, nor his neighbours will not mistruste his
saiynges. And if his credence bee so muche loste in deede that he thynketh
no man will beleve hym without he sweare, then he maie well thynke his
credence is cleane gone. For truthe it is, as Theophilactus writeth, that 'no
manne is lesse trusted then he that useth muche to sweare.' And almightie
God by the Wiseman saieth: that man whiche sweareth muche shalbee
full of synne, and the scourge of God shall not depart from his house.

But here some menne will saie, for excusyng of their many othes in
their daily talke, why should I not sweare when I sweare truely? To suche
men it maie be saied that though thei sweare truely, yet in swearyng
often, unadvisedly, for trifles, without necessitie and when thei should not
sweare, thei be not without faulte, but do take Gods moste holy name
in vain. Muche more ungodly and unwise men are thei that abuse Gods
moste holy name, not onely in biyng and sellyng of small thynges daily in
al places, but also in eatyng, drinkyng, plaiyng, commonyng and reasonyng. As if none of these thynges mighte bee dooen, excepte in doyng
of theim the moste holy name of God be commonly used, and abused
vainly, and unreverentely talked of, sworne by and forsworne, to the
breakyng of Gods commaundement and procurement of his indignacion.

[The Seconde Parte of the Sermon of Swearyng

You have ben taught in the first part of this sermon against swearing and
perjurie what greate daunger it is to use the name of God in vain, and
that all kynde of swearyng is not unlawful, neither against Godes commaundement, and that there bee three thynges required in a lawfull othe:
firste, that it be made for the mayntenaunce of the truthe; second, that
it be made with judgement, not rashely and unadvisedly; thirdely, for the
zeale and love of justice. Ye heard also what commodities commeth of
lawfull othes and what daunger commeth of rasshe and unlawfull othes.
Now as concerning the rest of thesame matter, ye shall understande that]
aswell thei use the name of God in vain that by an othe make lawfull
promises of good and honeste thynges, and performe them not, as thei
which do promise evill and unlawfull thynges, and do performe thesame.

Of such men that regard not their godly promises confirmed by an othe,
but wittyngly and wilfully breaketh theim, wee do reade in Holy Scripture
twoo notable punishementes. Firste, Josue and the people of Israell made

a league and faithfull promise of perpetuall amitie and frendshippe with the
Gabaonites: notwithstandyng, afterward in the dayes of wicked Saule,
many of these Gabaonites wer murdered contrary to thesaid faithfull
promise made. Wherewith almightie God was so sore displeased that he
sent an universall famyne upon the whole countrey, whiche continued
by the space of three yeres. And God would not withdrawe his punishement, untill thesaied offence was revenged by the death of vii. sonnes,
or next kinsmen, of Kyng Saule. Also, whereas Sedechias, Kyng of Jerusalem, had promised fidelitie to the Kyng of Chaldea, afterwarde, when
Sedechias, contrary to his othe and allegeaunce, did rebell against Kyng
Nabugodonosor, this heathen Kyng, by Gods permission invadyng the land
of Jewry and besiegyng the citee of Jerusalem, compelled thesaied Kyng
Sedechias to flee, and in fleyng toke hym prisoner, slewe his sonnes before
his face, and putte out bothe his iyes, and bindyng hym with cheines led
hym prisoner miserably into Babilon.

Thus doth God shewe plainly how muche he abhorreth breakers of
honeste promises confirmed by an othe made in his name. And of them
that make wicked promises by an othe and wil perfourme the same, wee
have example in the Scripture chiefly of Herode, of the wicked Jewes,
and of Jephthah. Herode promised by an othe unto the damosel whiche
daunsed before hym to geve unto her whatsoever she should aske, when
she was instucted before of her wicked mother to aske the hedde of
Sainct Jhon Baptist. Herod, as he toke a wicked oth, so he more wickedly
performed thesame and cruelly slewe the mooste holy prophete. Likewise
did the malicious Jewes make an othe, cursyng themselfes if thei did
either eate or drinke, untill thei had slain .S. Paule. And Jephthah, when
God had geven to him victory of the children of Ammon, promised
of a foolishe devocion unto God to offre for a sacrifice unto hym that
persone whiche of his awne house should firste meete with hym after
his returne home. By force of whiche fonde and unadvised othe he did sle
his awne and onely doughter, whiche came out of his house with mirthe
and joy to welcome hym home. Thus the promise whiche he made moste
foolishly to God, against Gods eternall will and the lawe of nature, moste
cruelly he performed, so committyng against God double offence. Therefore, whosoever maketh any promise, bindyng hymself thereunto by an
othe, let him forese that the thyng whiche he promiseth bee good, honest,
and not against the commaundement of God, and that it be in his awne
power to performe it justely. And suche good promises muste all men
kepe evermore assuredly. But if a man at any tyme shall, either of ignoraunce or of malice, promise and sweare to do any thing whiche is either

against the lawe of almightie God, or not in his power to performe, let
hym take it for an unlawfull and ungodly othe.

Now some thyng to speake of perjurie, to the intent you should knowe
how great and grevous an offence against God this wilfull perjurie is, I
wyll shew you what it is to take an othe before a judge upon a booke.
Firste, when they, laiyng their handes upon the gospell boke, do sweare
truely to enquyre and to make a true presentment of thinges wherwith they
be charged, and not to let from saiyng the truthe and doyng truely, for
favor, love, dreade, or malice of any persone, as God may healpe them and
the holy contentes of that boke, they muste consider that in that boke is
conteyned Gods everlasting truth, his moste holy and eternall Woorde,
whereby we have forgevenes of our synnes and be made inheritors of
heaven to lyve for ever, with Godes angels and hys sainctes, in joy and
gladnes. In the gospell boke is conteyned also Godes terrible threates to
obstinate synners that will not amende their lyfes, nor beleve the truthe of
God, his Holy Worde, and the everlastyng payn prepared in helle for
idolaters, hypocrites, for false and vain swearers, for perjured men, for false
witnes berers, for false condempners of innocent and giltles men and for
theim whiche, for favoure, hide the crimes of malefactors that thei should
not bee punished. So that whosoever wilfully forsweareth hymself upon
Christes holy evangely, thei utterly forsake Gods mercy, goodnes and
truth, the merites of our savior Christes nativitie, lyfe, passion, death,
resurrection and ascencion. They refuse the forgevenesse of synnes promised to all penitent sinners, the joyes of heaven, the company with angels
and sainctes for ever, all whiche benefites and comfortes are promised
unto true Christian persones in the Gospel. And thei, so being forsworne
upon the Gospel, do betake theim selfes to the devilles service, the master
of all lyes, falshed, deceipt and perjurie, provokyng the great indignacion
and curse of God against them in this lyfe and the terrible wrath and
judgement of our savior Christ at the great daye of the Laste Judgement,
when he shall justly judge both the quicke and the dedde accordyng to
their workes. For whosoever forsaketh the truthe for love or displeasure of
any man, or for lucre and profite to hymself, doth forsake Christ and
with Judas betraieth him.

And although suche perjured mennes falsehode be nowe kept secrete,
yet it shalbe opened at the last daye, when the secretes of all mennes hartes
shalbe manifest to al the worlde. And then the truth shal appere and
accuse them, and their awne conscience, with all the blessed company of
heaven, shal beare witnesse truly against them. And Christ the righteous
judge shal then justly condempne theim to everlastyng shame and death.

This sinne of perjurie, almightye God by the prophet Malachie, doth threaten to punyshe sore, saiyng unto the Jewes: I wil come to you in judgement, and I wyl be a swift witnesse and a sharpe judge upon sorcerers, adulterers and perjured persons. Whiche thyng to the prophet Zacharye God declareth in a vision wherein the prophet sawe a boke fliyng, which was twentie cubites long and tenne cubites broode, God sayenge then unto hym: This is the curse that shal go furth upon the face of the earth for falshod, false swearyng and perjurye. And this curse shall entre into the house of the false man and into the house of the perjured man, and it shal remain in the middest of his house and consume hym, the timber and stones of his house. Thus you se how much God doth hate perjury and what punishement God hath prepared for false swearers and perjured persones.

Thus you have heard how and in what causes it is lawfull for a Christian man to sweare; ye have heard what properties and condicions a lawfull othe muste have, and also how suche lawfull othes are bothe godly and necessarie to bee observed; ye have heard that it is not lawfull to sweare vainly, that is, other waies then in suche causes and after suche sort as is declared; and finally, ye have heard how dampnable a thyng it is either to forsweare our selfes, or to kepe an unlawfull and an unadvised oth. Wherefore, lette us earnestly call for grace, that all vain swearyng and perjurie set apart, we maie onely use suche othes as bee lawfull and godly, and that we may truly, without al fraude, observe thesame accordyng to Gods will and pleasure. To whom, with the Sonne and Holy Ghoste, bee all honor and glory.

Amen.

NOTES

128 *Almightie God ... blasphemy*: Exod 20:7.
attestacion: calling to witness.
all these maner of swearynges ... be lawfull: Article 39 of the Thirty-nine Articles condones oath taking, but not 'vain and rash swearing.' The use of plural adjectives with 'maner' is preserved in the modern English phrase 'all manner of ...'
129 *Thou shalte dreade ... hys name*: Deut 6:13.
all men ... by hym: Ps 63:11.
verely, verely: John 3:3, 5, 11.
I call God to witnesse: 2 Cor 1:23.
Abraham ... masters will: Gen 24:1–9.
Abraham, also ... unto Abraham: Gen 21:22–34.

David ... unto David: 1 Sam 18:3 and 20:16, 17, 42.

God once commaunded ... knowledge: Exod 22:10, 11.

laied to pledge: put up as security.

S. Paule saieth ... by a judge: Heb 6:16.

Jeremy saieth ... righteousnesse: Jer 4:2.

thre condicions: also mentioned in Article 39. Elaboration on Jeremiah's conditions for lawful oath taking is a commonplace in discussions of swearing. See, for instance, Heinrich Bullinger 'The Third Sermon of the Second Decade,' in *Decades* tr H.I., 4 vols, ed Thomas Harding, Parker Society 9–12 (Cambridge: Cambridge University Press 1849–52) I 249–50.

secludynge: barring.

130   *forbiddeth ... water*: Isa 42:8; Ps 150:6.

commonalties: communities.

understanded: a common form of the past participle.

'*every Christian ... othe*': Jerome *In Evangelium Matthaei* 1, 6 [on Matt 5:34–7] (PL 26: 41).

'*It is not convenient ... another?*': Chromatius *Tractatus 10 in Evangelium Matthaei* 2 (PL 20: 352). Griffiths conjectures that the mistaken attribution to Chrysostom, found also in Becon's 'Invective Against Swearing,' resulted from the common abbreviation 'Chr.' (76 n 3).

common: converse.

Chrisostome ... sweare at al: Chrysostom *In Epistolam ad Ephesios, Hom* 2 4 (PG 62: 21).

131   *without*: unless.

'*no manne ... muche to sweare*': Theophylactus *Enarratio in Evangelium Matthaei* 5, 37 (PG 123: 199–200).

that man whiche sweareth ... his house: Sir 23:11.

commonyng: conversing.

Josue ... Gabaonites: Josh 9:15–16.

132   *almightie God ... Kyng Saule*: 2 Sam 21:1–14.

Sedechias ... Babilon: 2 Kings 24:17–25:7.

Herode promised ... holy prophete: Matt 14:7–12.

Jewes ... S. Paule: Acts 23:12.

Jephthah ... hym home: Judg 11:30–40.

133   *presentment*: a legal declaration.

let from: desist.

evangely: OED cites the homily as an instance of the Gospels' being used as something to swear on.

134   *I wil come ... perjured persons*: Mal 3:5.

prophet sawe ... stones of his house: Zech 5:1–4.

fraude: deception.

TEXTUAL APPARATUS

128 Against] A Sermon Against *1623*. declaracion] or openynge *added 1559, 1623*. attestacion] callynge to witnes *1559, 1623*. observe] kepe *1559, 1623*. lawes or locall] lawes and locall *1623*. communicacion, as] communicacion s(*1623*.

129 prohibited] forbidden *1559, 1623*. commaunded of] commaunded by *1623*. othes of other] othes of others *1623*. Isaac] Isahac *1623*. and so likewyse] and likewyse *1623*. these thre] three *1623*. must sweare] may sweare *1623*. secludynge] setting apart *1559, 1623*. to the righteousnes] of the righteousnes

130 *1623*. For by lawfull promises] *1559*; For lawfull promises *1547, 1549*; For lawfull promise *1623*. covenauntes] covevauntes *1549*. confirmed by] confirmed by by *1547*. attestacion of Gods name] calling the name of God to witnesse *1559, 1623*. innocent persones, orphanes] harmlesse persones, fatherlesse chyldren *1559, 1623*. bee understanded] bee understood *1623*.

131 common] commune *1623*. do take] to take *1549*. also in eatyng] *1623*; also eatyng *1547, 1549, 1559*. commonyng] communing *1623*. second] Secondly *1623*. aswell] And aswell *1547*. lawfull promises] unlawfull promises *1623*. confirmed] bounde *1559, 1623*. famyne] hunger *1559, 1623*. Also, whereas] And, whereas *1623*. permission] and suffraunce *added 1559, 1623*. Jewry] Jurie

132 *1623*. confirmed] bounde *1559, 1623*. she should aske] she would aske *1623*.

133 eternall will] everlasting will *1559, 1623*. God double] God a double *1623*. or malice] nor malice *1547*. hys sainctes] Sainctes *1623*. witnes berers] witnes beares *1549*. malefactors] evyl doers *1559, 1623*. forsweareth hymself] forsweare themselves *1623*. profite to] profite of *1623*. betraieth] betray *1623*.

134 fliyng] fleeing *1623*. house and ... the timber] house ... and the timber *1623*. not lawfull] not lafull *1549*. an unlawfull and an unadvised not lafull *1549*. an unlawfull and an unadvised oth] unlawfull and unadvised othes *1549*. observe] keepe *1559, 1623*.

8 A Sermon,
How Daungerous a Thynge It Is
To Declyne from God

Of our goyng from God, the Wyseman sayeth that pryde was the first
beginning, for by it mans harte was turned from God hys maker. For
pryde, saieth he, is the fountain of all synne; he that hath it shalbe ful
of cursynges, and at the ende it shall overthrow hym. And, as by pride and
sinne we go from God, so shall God and al goodnes with hym go from
us. And the prophet Ozee doeth plainlye affirme that they which go awaye
still from God by vicious livyng and yet would go about to pacifye him
otherwise by sacrifice, and enterteigne him thereby, they laboure in vayn.
For notwithstandyng al their sacrifice, yet he goeth styll away from them.
For so much, saieth the prophete, as they do not applye their myndes
to returne to God, although thei go about with whole flockes and herdes
to seke the Lord, yet they shall not fynde hym, for he is gone away
from them. But as touchyng our turnyng to God, or from God, you shall
understande that it maye be doen diverse wayes. Some tymes directly
by idolatrye, as Israel and Juda then dyd; some tymes men go from God
by lacke of fayth and mistrustyng of God, wherof Esaie speaketh in
this wyse: Wo to them that go doune into Egypt to seke for healp, trustyng
in horses and havyng confidence in the numbre of chariottes and puissaunce of horsemen. They have no confidence in the holy God of Israell,
nor seeke for the Lorde. But what foloweth? The Lorde shall let his hande
fall upon them, and doune shall come bothe the healper and he that is
holpen: they shalbe destroyed altogether.

Some tyme men go from God by the neglectyng of hys commaundementes concerning their neighbours, whiche commaundeth them to expresse hartye love towardes every man, as Zachary sayde unto the people
in Gods behalfe: Geve true judgement, shewe mercye and compassion
every one to hys brother; ymagen no deceipt towardes widowes or children
fatherles and motherles, towardes straunger or the poore; let no man

forge evill in hys harte against his brother. But these thinges they passed
not of: thei turned their backes and went their waie; they stopped their
eares that they might not heare; they hardened their hartes, as an adamant
stone, that they might not lysten to the lawe and the woordes that the
Lorde had sent through his Holy Spirite by hys auncient prophetes. Wherfore the Lorde shewed his great indignacion upon them: it came to passe,
sayeth the prophet, even as I tolde them: as they woulde not heare, so
when they cryed they were not heard, but wer dispersed into all kingdomes
which they never knewe, and their lande was made desolate. And to be
short, all they that may not abyde the Word of God, but folowyng the
perswasions and stubbernes of their awne hartes, go backewarde and
not forward, as it is sayd in Jeremy, they go and turne away from God. In
so muche that Origene saieth: 'He that with mynde, with study, with
dedes, with thought and care, applieth himself to Gods Worde and thinketh
upon his lawes, day and night, geveth himself wholy to God and in hys
preceptes and commaundementes is exercised: this is he that is turned
to God.' And on the other part he saieth: 'Whosoever is occupied with
fables and tales when the Word of God is rehersed, he is turned from
God. Whosoever in time of reading Gods Worde is careful in hys mynd of
worldly busines, of money or of lucre, he is turned from God. Whosoever
is entangled with the cares of possessions, filled with coveteousnes of
ryches, whosoever studieth for the glory and honor of this worlde, he is
turned from God.' So that after hys mynd, whosoever hath not a speciall
mynde to that thynge that is commaunded or taught of God, he that
doth not listen unto it, embrace and print it in hys hart, to the intent that
he may duely fashion hys lyfe thereafter, he is plainly turned from God,
although he do other thinges of hys awne devocion and mynde which to
him seme better, and more to Gods honor.

   Whiche thyng to be true, we be taught and admonyshed in the Holye
Scripture by the example of Kyng Saul, who beyng commaunded of God
by Samuel that he should kyll all the Amalechites and destroye them
clerely with their goodes and cattals, yet he, beynge moved partely with
pitie and partely, as be thought, with devocion unto God, saved Agag,
their kyng, and all the cheif of their cattail, therwith to make sacrifice unto
God. Wherwithal God, beynge displeased highly, sayd unto the prophete
Samuel: I repente that ever I made Saul a kyng, for he hath forsaken
me and not folowed my wordes; and so he commaunded Samuel to shewe
hym. And when Samuel asked wherfore, contrary to Gods Woorde, he
had saved the cattail, he excused the matter, partely by feare, saiynge he
durst do none other for that the people would have it so, partely for
that they were goodly beastes, he thought God would be content, seynge

it was done of a good intent and devocion to honor God with the sacrifice of them. But Samuel, reprovyng all suche intentes and devocions, seme they never so muche to Gods honor, if they stande not with his Woorde whereby we maye be assured of hys pleasure, sayde in this wyse: Would God have sacrifices and offeringes, or rather that hys Word should by obeyed? To obey him is better then offerynges, and to listen to hym is better then to offre the fatte of rammes: yea, to repine agaynst hys voice is as evil as the sinne of divinacion, and not to agre to it is like abhominable ydolatry. And now, forasmuche as thou hast cast awaye the Worde of the Lorde, he hath cast awaye the, that thou shouldest not be kynge.

By all these examples of Holy Scripture we maye knowe that as we forsake God so shall he ever forsake us. And what miserable state doth consequently and necessariely folow therupon, a man maye easely consider by the terrible threatenynges of God. And although he considre not al the sayde miserie to the uttermost, beyng so great that it passeth any mans capacitie in this lyfe sufficiently to consydre thesame, yet he shal soone perceyve somuch therof that if his hart be not more then stony or harder then the adamant, he shall feare, tremble and quake to call thesame to hys remembraunce.

Fyrste, the displeasure of God towardes us is commonly expressed in the Scripture by these twoo thinges: by shewyng his fearefull countenaunce upon us, and by turnyng his face or hiding it from us. By shewyng his dreadful countenaunce is signifyed his great wrath, but by turnynge hys face or hidinge therof is many tymes more signified, that is to saye, that he clerely forsaketh us and geveth us over. The whiche significacions be taken of the properties of mens maners, for men towardes them whome they favour commonly beare a good, a chearefull and a loving counten-aunce, so that by the face or countenaunce of a man it doth commonly appere what wyl or minde he beareth towardes other. So when God doeth shew hys dreadfull countenaunce towardes us, that is to say, doeth send dreadful plagues of sword, famyne or pestilence upon us, it appereth that he is greatly wroth with us. But when he withdraweth from us hys Woorde, the righte doctryne of Christe, hys gracious assistence and ayde, which is ever joyned to hys Worde, and leaveth us to our awne wit, our awne wyll and strength, he declareth then that he beginneth to forsake us. For where as God hath shewed to all them that truely beleve his Gospel his face of mercy in Jesus Christ, whiche doeth so lighten theyr hartes that they, if they beholde it as they ought to do, be transformed to hys image, bee made partakers of the heavenly light and of hys Holy Spirite, and bee fashioned to him in all goodnes requisite to the children of God: so, if they after do neglecte thesame, if they bee unthankefull unto hym, if they ordre not their lyfes accordynge to hys example and doctryne and to the settyng furth of hys glory, he wyll take awaye from them hys kyngdom, his Holy Word wherby he should reigne in them, because they bryng not furth the fruit therof that he loketh for. Nevertheles, he is so mercifull and of so long-sufferaunce that he doth not shewe upon us that great wrathe sodainly. But when we beginne to shrinke from his Worde, not beleving it, or not expressing it in oure livinges, firste he doeth send hys messengers, the true preachers of his Worde, to admonish us of our dutie, that as he for hys part for the great love he bare unto us delivered his awn Sonne to suffre death, that we, by hys death, myghte be delivered from death and be restored to the lyfe eternall, evermore to dwel with hym and to be partakers and inheritors with hym of hys everlast-yng glory and kingdome of heaven: so agayn, that we for our partes shoulde walke in a godly lyfe, as becommeth hys chyldren to do. And if thys wyl not serve, but stil we remayne disobedient to hys Worde and wyll, not knowyng him, not loving him, not fearing him, not puttyng our whole trust and confidence in him, and on the otherside, to our neighbors behaving us uncharitably, by disdayne, envye, malice, or by committyng murther, robbery, adultry, gluttony, deceipt, liyng, swearyng, or other like detestable workes and ungodly behavioure, then he threateneth us by terryble comminacions, swearynge in great angree that whosoever doeth these workes shall never entre into his reste, whiche is the kyngdome of heaven.

[The Second Parte of the Sermon of Declinyng from God

In the former parte of this sermon ye have learned how many maner of wayes men fal from God: some by idolatrye, some for lacke of faithe, some by the neglectyng of their neighbours, some by not hearing Godes Worde, some by the pleasure they take in the vanities of worldly thynges. Ye have also learned in what misery that man is which is gone from God, and how that God yet of his infinite goodnes to cal againe man from that his miserye useth first gentil admonycions by his preachers – after, he laieth on terrible thretinynges.]

Now, if this gentle monicion and comminacion together do not serve, then God will shewe his terrible countenaunce upon us, he will powre intollerable plagues upon our hedes, and after, he wyll take away from us all hys ayde and assistence, wherwith before he did defend us from all such maner of calamitie. As the evangelical prophet Esaye, agreyng with Christes parable, doth teache us, saiyng, That God had made a goodly vineyarde for hys beloved children: he hedged it, he walled it rounde about, he planted it with chosen vynes and made a turret in the myddes therof, and therein also a wine presse. And when he loked that it should bryng hym furth good grapes, it brought furth wylde grapes. And after it foloweth: Now shall I shew you, saieth God, what I will do with my vyneyarde: I wil pluck doune the hedges that it may perysh; I will breake doune the walles that it may be troden under fote; I wil let it lie wast; it shall not be cutte, it shall not be digged, but briers and thornes shall overgrowe it, and I shall commaunde the cloudes that they shall no more rayne upon it.

By these threatenynges we ar monyshed that if we whiche are the chosen vyneyarde of God bryng not furth good grapes, that is to say, good workes, that may be delectable and pleasaunt in hys sight, when he loketh for them, when he sendeth his messengers to cal upon us for them, but rather bring furth wyld grapes, that is to say, sower workes, unswete, unsavery and unfruictfull, then wil he plucke away all defence and suffre grevous plagues of famyne and battaile, dearth and death, to light upon us. Finally, if these do not yet serve, he wil let us lie wast, he wil geve us over, he wyl turne away from us, he will dygge and delve no more aboute us, he wil let us alone and suffre us to brynge furthe even such fruite as we wyl, to bryng furth brambles, bryers and thornes, all naughtynes, all vice, and that so abundantlye, that they shal cleane overgrow us, suffocate, strangle and utterly destroye us. But they that in thys worlde lyve not after God, but after theyr awne carnal libertie, perceyve not thys greate wrath of God towardes them, that he wyll not dygge, nor delve any more about them, that he doeth let them alone even to them selfes. But they take thys for a great benefite of God to have all theyr awne libertye, and so they live as carnall libertye were the true libertye of the Gospel. But God forbidde, good people, that ever we should desyre such libertie. For although God suffre sometymes the wicked to have their pleasure in thys world, yet the end of ungodly livyng is at length eternall destruction.

The murmuryng Israelites had that they longed for: they had quayles enough, yea, til they were wery of them. But what was the end therof? Their swete meate had soure sauce: even whiles the meat was in theyr mouthes, the plague of God lighted upon them, and sodainely they died. So if we live ungodly, and God suffreth us to folowe our awne wylles, to have our awne delightes and pleasures, and correcteth us not with some plague, it is no doubt but he is almost utterly displeased with us. And although it be long or he strike, yet many tymes when he striketh such persons, he striketh them at once, for ever. So that when he doth not stryke us, when he ceaseth to afflict us, to punysh or beate us, and suffreth us to runne hedlinges into al ungodlines and pleasures of thys world that

we delight in without punyshment and adversitie, it is a dreadfull token
that he loveth us no lenger, that he careth no lenger for us, but hath geven
us over to our awne selfes. As long as a man doeth proyne his vines,
doeth digge at the rootes, and doth laye freashe yearth to theim, he hath a
mynde to theim, he perceiveth some token of fruitfulnes that may be
recovered in them, but when he wil bestowe no more suche cost and labor
aboute them, then it is a signe that he thinketh they will never bee good.
And the father, as long as he loveth his chyld, he loketh angrely, he
correcteth hym when he doeth amisse, but when that serveth not, and
upon that he ceaseth from correction of hym and suffereth hym to do
what he liste himself, it is a signe that he intendeth to disinherite hym and
to cast him away for ever. So surely, nothyng should perce our hart so
sore and put us in suche horrible feare as when we knowe in our conscience
that wee have grevously offended God and do so continue, and that yet
he striketh not, but quietely suffereth us in the naughtines that we have
delight in. Then specially it is tyme to crye, and to crye agayne, as David
did: Caste me not awaie from thy face and take not away thy Holy Spirit
from me. Lorde turne not away thy face from me; cast not thy servaunt
away in displeasure. Hide not thy face from me, least I be lyke unto them
that go doune to hel. The whiche lamentable praiers of him, as they do
certify us what horrible daunger thei be in from whom God turneth
his face, for that time and as long as he so doth, so should thei move us to
crye upon God with all our harte, that we maie not be brought into that
state whiche, doubtles, is so sorowful, so miserable and so dreadfull as
no toungue can sufficiently expresse or any hart can thynke.

  For what deadly greif may a man suppose it is to be under the wrath of
God, to be forsaken of hym, to have his Holy Spirit, the aucthor of all
goodnesse, to be taken from hym, to be brought to so vile a condicion
that he shalbe left mete for no better purpose then to be for ever condempned to hel? For not onely such places of David do shewe that upon
the turnyng of Gods face from any persons thei shalbe left bare from al
goodnesse and far from hope of remedy, but also the place, recited last
before of Esaie, doeth meane thesame, which sheweth that God at length
doth so forsake his unfruitful vineyard that he wil not only suffre it to
bryng furth wedes, breirs and thornes, but also, further to punish the un-
fruitfulnesse of it; he saith: he wil not cut it, he wil not delve it, and he
will commaunde the cloudes that they shal not rain upon it, wherby
is signified the teachyng of his Holy Worde, whiche Sainct Paule, after a
like maner, expresseth by plantyng and wateryng, meanyng that he will
take that awaye from theim. So that thei shalbe no lenger of his kyngdom;
they shalbe no lenger governed by his Holy Spirite; thei shalbe frustrated

of the grace and benefites that thei had and ever might have enjoyed through Christ. Thei shalbe deprived of the heavenly light and life whiche they had in Christe whiles they abode in hym. They shalbe, as thei wer once, as men without God in this worlde, or rather in worse takyng. And to be short, they shalbe geven into the power of the devil, which beareth the rule in al them that be cast awaie from God, as he did in Saule and Judas, and generally in all suche as worke after their awne willes, the children of diffidence and infidelitie.

Let us beware, therfore, good Christian people, least that we, rejecting Gods Worde, by the whiche we obteyn and reteine true faith in God, be not at length cast of so farre that we become as the children of infidelitie, whiche be of two sortes farre diverse, yea, almoste cleane contrary, and yet bothe bee very far from returnyng to God. The one sort, onely waiyng their sinful and detestable livyng with the right judgement and strayghtnes of Gods ryghteousnes, be so destitute of counsail and be so comfortles, as all they must nedes be from whom the spirit of counsaill and comfort is gone, that they will not be perswaded in theyr hartes, but that either God cannot, or els that he will not take them again to his favor and mercy. The other, hearyng the lovynge and large promises of Gods mercye, and so not conceivyng a ryght faith therof, make those promises larger then ever God did, trusting that although thei continue in their synful and detestable livyng never so long, yet that God at the ende of their life will shewe his mercie upon theim and that then they wil returne. And bothe these two sortes of men be in a dampnable state, and yet neverthelesse God, who willeth not the death of the wicked, hath shewed meanes wherby both thesame, if thei take hede in ceason, may escape.

The first, as they do dread Gods rightfull justice in punishing sinners, wherby they should be dismaid and should dispaire in dede as touchyng any hope that may be in themselfes, so if thei would constantly beleve that Gods mercie is the remedy appoynted against such dispaire and distrust, not onely for them, but generally for all that bee sory and truely repentaunt, and will therewithall sticke to Gods mercie, they maie be sure thei shal obtein mercie and entre into the porte or haven of savegarde, into the whiche whosoever doth come, be thei before tyme never so wicked, thei shalbe out of daunger of everlastyng dampnacion. As God by Ezechiel saieth: what tyme soever the wicked doeth returne and take earnest and true repentaunce, I will forget all his wickednesse.

The other, as they be redy to beleve Gods promises, so they should be as redy to beleve the threatenynges of God: aswel thei should beleve the lawe as the Gospel; aswel that there is an hell and everlastyng fyre as that there is an heaven, and everlasting joye; aswel they should beleve

dampnacion to be threatened to the wicked and evyll doers as salvacion to be promised to the faithfull in worde and workes; aswel they should beleve God to bee true in the one, as in the other. And the synners that continue in their wycked livyng ought to thynke that the promises of Gods mercie and the Gospell perteyn not unto theim, beynge in that state, but onely the lawe and those Scriptures whiche conteyne the wrathe and indignacion of God and his threatenynges, which should certifye them that as thei do over boldely presume of Gods mercy and live dissolutely, so doeth God still more and more withdrawe his mercie from theim, and he is so provoked thereby to wrathe at lenght that he destroyeth suche presumers many tymes sodainly. For of suche, Saincte Paule sayed thus: when they shall saye, it is peace, there is no daunger, then shall sodayn destruction come upon theim. Let us beware, therfore, of suche naughtie boldenesse to synne, for God, whiche hath promised his mercie to them that bee truely repentaunte, although it bee at the latter ende, hath not promised to the presumpteous synner either that he shall have long life, or that he shal have true repentaunce at the laste ende. But for that purpose hath he made every mannes deathe uncertayne, that he should not put his hope in thend, and in the meane season, to Gods highe displeasure, lyve ungodly. Wherfore, let us folowe the counsaill of the Wiseman: let us make no tariyng to turne unto the Lord; let us not put of from daie to day, for sodainly shal his wrath come, and in tyme of vengeaunce he shal destroye the wycked. Let us, therefore, turne betymes, and when we turne, let us praye to God, as Ozee teacheth, saiyng: Forgeve us all oure synnes; receyve us graciously. And if we turne to him with an humble and a very penitent harte, he wil receive us to his favor and grace for his holy names sake, for his promise sake, for his truthe and mercies sake, promysed to all faithefull belevers in Jesus Christ, his onely naturall Sonne. To whom the onely saviour of the world, with the Father and the Holy Ghost, bee all honor, glory and power, world without end.
Amen.

NOTES

137 *Wyseman sayeth ... overthrow hym*: Sir 10:12–13 (Vg 'Initium superbiae hominis apostare a Deo: quoniam ab eo qui fecit illum recessit cor eius. Quoniam initium omnis peccati est superbia: qui tenuerit illam adimplebitur maledictis, et subvertet eum ad finem').
they do not applye ... away from them: Hos 5:4, 6.
Israel and Juda: Hos 4:12 and 5:5.

Wo ... destroyed altogether: Isa 31:1, 3.
puissaunce: power.
Geve true judgement ... made desolate: Zech 7:8–14.
138 *passed not of*: cared not for.
go backewarde and not forward: Jer 7:24.
'*He that with mynde ... worlde, he is turned from God*': Origen *In Exodum*,
     Hom 12 2 (PG 12: 383).
example of Kyng Saul: 1 Sam 15:1–3.
Wherwithal: Whereupon.
I repente ... folowed my wordes: 1 Sam 15:11.
for that: because.
139 *Would God ... not be kynge*: 1 Sam 15:22–3 (Vg 1 Reg 15:23 'Quoniam quasi
     peccatum ariolandi est, repugnare: et quasi scelus idolatriae, nolle
     acquiescere').
repine: murmur.
transformed ... children of God: 2 Cor 3:18 and 4:6.
140 *take awaye ... hys kyngdom*: Matt 21:43.
comminacions: denunciations.
whosoever doeth these workes ... into his reste: Heb 4:1–13; Ps 95:10–11.
That God had made ... rayne upon it: Isa 5:1–7; Matt 21:33–41.
141 *monyshed*: admonished.
suffre: allow.
Israelites ... wery of them: Num 11:4, 31–3.
whiles the meat ... they died: Ps 78:30–1.
or he strike: before he strike.
142 *proyne*: prune.
Caste me not ... to hel: Pss 51:11, 17:9, and 143:7.
Sainct Paule ... wateryng: 1 Cor 3:6–9.
143 *men without ... worlde*: Eph 2:12.
Saule and Judas: 1 Sam 15:24–35; Luke 22:3.
the children of diffidence and infidelitie: Eph 2:2; Col 3:6 (in both cases AV
     renders 'children of disobedience').
the spirit of counsaill: Isa 11:2.
willeth not the death of the wicked: Ezek 18:23, 32 and 33:11.
what tyme ... his wickednesse: Ezek 33:12–16.
144 *lenght*: a form of 'length.'
when they shall saye ... come upon theim: 1 Thess 5:3.
make no tariyng ... destroye the wycked: Sir 5:7 (Vg 5:9 'Subito enim veniet ira
     illius, Et in tempore vindictae disperdet te').
Forgeve us ... graciously: Hos 14:2.

TEXTUAL APPARATUS

137 To Declyne] To Fall *1559, 1623.* goeth] geeth *1623.* not applye] no applye
1547. puissaunce] or power *added 1559, 1623.* ymagen no] ymagen to *1547.*
138 towardes straunger] toward strangers *1623.* dispersed] scattered *1559, 1623.*
backewarde] barkewarde *1549.* applieth] and geveth *added 1559, 1623.* as
be thought] as he thought *1623.* their kyng] the kyng *1559, 1623.* Saul a
139 kyng] Saul Kyng *1623.* repine] repugne *1559, 1623.* divinacion] southsaying
140 *1559, 1623.* withdraweth] writhdraweth *1549.* admonish] and warne *added*
1559, 1623. eternall] everlastinge *1559, 1623.* not loving] nor loving *1623.*
behaving us] behaving ourselves *1559, 1623.* The Seconde Parte of the Sermon
of Declinyng from God] The Second ... Falling from God *1559, 1623.*
hearing Godes Worde] hearing of Gods Worde *1559, 1623.* comminacion]
communicacion *1549;* threatning *1559, 1623.* goodly vineyarde] godly vine-
141 yarde *1559.* wine presse] vine-press *1623.* wylde grapes] wylde graps *1623.*
digged] didged *1547.* monyshed] and warned *added 1559, 1623.* unswete] *not
in 1623.* not yet serve] serve not *1623.* suffocate] choke *1559, 1623.* as carnall]
as if carnall *1623.* eternall] endlesse *1559, 1623.* doubt] boubt *1559.* it be
142 long or] he be long ere *1623.* token that he loveth] token loveth, *with* that
he *as catchword 1547.* doth laye] doeh laye *1547.* for that time] for the
time *1623.* move] and stirre *added 1559, 1623.* or any hart] nor any hart *1623.*
recited] rehersed *1559, 1623.* teachyng] reachyng *1547.* expresseth] expressed
143 *1559, 1623.* frustrated of] put from *1559, 1623.* diffidence and infidelitie]
mistrust and unbelyefe *1559, 1623.* rejecting] or casting away *added 1559, 1623.*
reteine] retin *1547.* infidelitie] unbeleif *1559, 1623.* destitute of] without
1559, 1623. all they must] they all must *1623.* constantly] or stedfastly *added*
1559, 1623. dispaire] dspaire *1559.* the wicked] the which *1559;* a sinner
144 *1623.* take earnest] dake earnest *1559.* he shal destroye] he will destroye *1549,*
1559, 1623. for his truthe and mercies sake] *not in 1549.*

9 An Exhortation
agaynst the Feare of Death

It is not to be marveyled that worldly men do feare to dye, for death
depriveth them of all worldly honors, riches and possessions, in the fruition
whereof the worldely man compteth hymself happie, so long as he maye
enjoye theim at hys awne pleasure, and other wyse, if he be dispossessed of
thesame, without hope of recovery, then he can none other thinke of
himself but that he is unhappie, because he hath loste hys worldely joye
and pleasure. Alas, thinketh this carnall man, shall I now depart for ever
from all my honors, all my treasures, from my countrey, frendes, riches,
possessions and worldly pleasures, whiche are my joy and hartes delight?
Alas, that ever that daie shal come when all these I muste bid farewell
at once, and never to enjoye any of them after. Wherfore, it is not without
greate cause spoken of the Wiseman: O death, how bitter and sower is
the remembraunce of thee to a man that liveth in peace and prosperitie in
his substaunce, to a man livyng at ease, leading his life after his awne
mind without trouble, and is therwithal well pampered and fed! There be
other men whom this world doth not so greatly laugh upon, but rather
vexe and oppresse with povertye, sickenesse, or some other adversitie,
yet thei do fear death, partly because the fleashe abhorreth naturally his
awne sorowful dissolucion whiche death doth threaten unto theim, and
partely by reason of sickenesses and paynfull diseases, whiche be moste
strong pangues and agonies in the fleshe, and use commonly to come to
sicke men before death, or at the leaste, accompany death, whensoever
it commeth.
   Although these twoo causes seme great and weightie to a worldly man,
wherupon he is moved to feare death, yet there is another cause much
greater then any of these afore rehersed for whiche, in dede, he hath juste
cause to feare death, and that is the state and condicion wherunto, at
the last ende, death bryngeth all them that have their hartes fixed upon

this world without repentaunce and amendement. This state and condicion is called the second death, whiche unto all suche shall insue after this bodily deathe. And this is that death whiche in deede ought to be dread and feared, for it is an everlasting losse, without remedy, of the grace and favor of God, and of everlastyng joy, pleasure and felicite. And it is not onely the losse for ever of all these eternall pleasures, but also it is the condempnacion, both of body and soule – without either appellacion, or hope of redempcion – unto everlastynge paynes in hell. Unto this state death sent the unmercyfull and ungodly richeman, that Luke speaketh of in his Gospell, who livyng in all wealthe and pleasure in this worlde and cherishyng himself daily with daintie fare and gorgeous apparel, despiced poore Lazarus, that lay pitifully at his gate, miserably plagued, and full of sores, and also grevously pined with hunger. Bothe these twoo were arrested of deathe, whiche sent Lazarus, the poore miserable man, by aungels anone unto Abrahams bosome, a place of rest, pleasure and consolacion. But the unmerciful richman descended doune into hel, and beyng in tormentes, he cried for comforte, complainyng of the intollerable payn that he suffered in that flamme of fire, but it was to late. So unto this place bodily death sendeth all them that in this world have their joye and felicite: all them that in this world be unfaithfull unto God and uncharitable unto their neighbors, so diyng without repentaunce and hope of Gods mercie. Wherfore it is no marvaile that the worldly man feareth death, for he hath muche more cause so to do then he himself doeth considre.

Thus we se thre causes why worldly men feare death. One, because thei shal lose therby their worldely honors, riches, possessions and all their hartes desires; another, because of the painfull diseases and bitter pangues, which commonly men suffre either before, or at the tyme of death; but the chiefe cause, above al other, is the dread of the miserable state of eternall dampnacion, bothe of body and soule, whiche they feare shal folow after their departyng out of the worldly pleasures of this present life.

For these causes be all mortall men whiche be geven to the love of this world both in feare and state of death through syn, as the holy apostle saieth, so long as thei live here in this world. But everlastyng thankes be to almighty God for ever, there is never one of al these causes, no, nor yet thei altogether, that can make a true Christian man afraied to dye, whiche is the very membre of Christe, the temple of the Holy Ghoste, the Sonne of God and the very inheritor of the everlastyng kyngdom of heaven, but plainly contrary, he conceiveth great and many causes, undoubtedly grounded upon the infallyble and everlastynge truth of the Woorde of God, whiche move hym not onely to put away the feare of bodiely death,

but also for the manifolde benefites and singuler commodities whiche
ensue unto every faithfull person by reason of thesame to wish, desire and
longe hartely for it. For death shall be to hym no death at all, but a very
deliveraunce from death, from all paynes, cares, and sorowes, miseries
and wretchednes of this world, and the very entry into rest, and a beginnyng of everlastyng joye, a tastyng of heavenly pleasures so great that
neither toungue is able to expresse, neither eye to se, nor eare to heare
them, no, nor anye earthly mans hart to conceyve them. So excedinge
greate benefites thei be whiche God our heavenly Father, by his mere
mercye and for the love of his Sonne Jesus Christe, hathe layed up in store
and prepared for theim that humbly submitte themselfes to Gods wil and
evermore unfainedly love him from the botome of their hartes. And we
oughte to beleve that death, beyng slayne by Christe, cannot kepe any man
that stedfastly trusteth in Christ under his perpetuall tiranny and subjection, but that he shall ryse from death agayne unto glory at the last daye,
appoynted by almighty God, lyke as Christ oure head did ryse agayne,
accordinge to Gods appoyntement, the thyrde daye. For Sainct Augustine
saieth: The head goynge before, the membres trust to folowe and come
after. And Sainct Paule saieth: if Christe be rysen from the dead, we shall
ryse also from thesame. And to comforte all Christen persons herein,
Holye Scripture calleth this bodiely death a slepe, wherin mans senses be,
as it were, taken from hym for a ceason, and yet when he awaketh, he
is more freash then he was when he went to bed. So, althoughe we have
our soules seperated from our bodyes for a ceason, yet at the general
resurreccion we shalbe more freash, beautifull and perfite then we be now.
For now we be mortall, then we shal be immortall; now infect with
divers infirmities, then clerely voyde of all mortall infirmities; now we be
subject to all carnall desyres, then we shalbe al spirituall, desiryng nothynge
but Gods glory and thinges eternal. Thus is this bodiely death a doore,
or entrynge unto lyfe, and therfore not so muche dreadfull, if it be rightly
considered, as it is comfortable; not a mischief, but a remedy of all
mischief; no enemy, but a frende; not a cruel tyraunt, but a gentle guide
leadyng us not to mortalitie, but to immortalitie, not to sorow and payne,
but to joye and pleasure, and that to endure for ever, if it be thankefully
taken and accepted as Gods messenger, and paciently borne of us for
Christes love that suffered most paynfull death for oure love, to redeme us
from death eternall. Accordynge hereunto, Saincte Paule saieth: our lyfe
is hidde with Christ in God, but when our lyfe shall appere, then shall we
also appere with hym in glorye.

Why then shall we feare to dye, consideryng the manifolde and comfortable promises of the Gospell and of Holy Scriptures? God the Father

hath geven us everlastynge lyfe, saieth S. Jhon, and thys lyfe is in hys Sonne: he that hath the Sonne hath lyfe, and he that hath not the Sonne hath not lyfe. And this I wrote, saieth S. Jhon, to you that beleve in the name of the Sonne of God, that you maye knowe that you have everlastynge lyfe and that you do beleve upon the name of the Sonne of God. And our savior Christ sayeth: he that beleveth in me hath lyfe everlastynge, and I wyll rayse him from death to lyfe at the last day. Sainct Paule also sayeth that Christe is ordeyned and made of God oure righteousnes, our holynes and redemption, to the entent that he which wyll glory should glory in the Lorde. Sainct Paule did contemne and set litle by all other thynges, estemynge them as dunge whiche before he had in very greate pryce that he might be found in Christ to have everlasting lyfe, true holynes, righteousnes and redempcion. Finally, S. Paule maketh a playne argument in this wise: If our heavenly Father woulde not spare his awne naturall Sonne, but dyd geve hym to death for us, how can it be that with him he shoulde not geve us all thynges? Therfore, if we have Christ, then have we with him and by him all good thinges, whatsoever we can in our hartes wish or desire: as victorie over death, sinne and hel; we have the favor of God, peace wyth hym, holynes, wysedome, justice, power, lyfe and redempcion; we have by hym perpetuall health, wealth, joye and blysse everlastynge.

[The Second Parte of the Sermon of the Feare of Deathe

It hath been heretofore shewed yow that ther be thre causes wherfore men do commonly feare death: first, the sorowful departyng from worldlie goodes and pleasures; the second, the feare of the panges and paynes that come wyth deathe; last and principall cause is the horrible feare of extreme miserie and perpetuall damnacion in tyme to come. And yet none of these three causes troubleth good men, because they staie them selfes by true faith, perfit charitie and sure hope of the perpetual joye and blisse everlastyng.]

   All those, therefore, have great cause to be full of joye that be joyned to Christ with true faythe, stedfast hope and perfyt charitie, and not to feare death nor everlastynge dampnacion. For deathe cannot deprive them of Jesu Christ, nor any sinne can condempne them that are graffed surely in him, which is their onely joy, treasure and lyfe. Let us repent our synnes, amend our lyfes, trust in hys mercy and satisfaction, and death can neyther take hym from us, nor us from hym. For then, as S. Paul saieth, whether we lyve or dye, we be the Lordes awne. And agayne he sayeth: Christ did dye and rose agayne, because he should be Lord both of the dead and quicke. Then, if we be the Lordes awne when we be dead, it must nedes folowe that suche temporall deathe not onely cannot harme us, but also that it shall muche be to our profit and joyne us unto God more perfectly. And therof the Christian hart may surely be certified by the infallible truth of Holye Scripture. It is God, sayeth Sainct Paule, which hath prepared us unto immortalitie, and thesame is he which hath geven us an earnest of the spirite. Therfore, let us be alwaies of good comforte, for we knowe that so longe as we be in the body, we be, as it were, farre from God in a straunge countrey, subject to many perils, walkyng without perfite sighte and knowledge of almighty God, onely seynge hym by faythe in Holy Scriptures. But we have a courage and desire rather to be at home with God, and oure savior Christe, farre from the body, where we maye behold hys Godhead as he is, face to face, to oure everlastyng comfort. These be Saincte Paules wordes, in effecte, wherby we may perceyve that the lyfe in this world is resembled to a pilgrimage in a straunge countrie far frome God and that death, deliverynge us from our bodyes, doth sende us straight home into our awne countrey and maketh us to dwell presently with God for ever in perpetuall rest and quietnesse. So that to dye is no losse, but profite and winnynge to all true Christen people.

What lost the thefe that hanged on the crosse with Christ by hys bodiely death? Yea, how much dyd he gayne by it? Did not our saviour say unto hym, thys daye thou shalt be with me in Paradyse? And Lazarus, that pitifull person that lay before the richemans gate, payned with sores and pined with hungre, did not death highlye profite and promote hym, which by the ministery of aungels sent hym unto Abrahams bosome, a place of rest, joye and heavenly consolacion? Let us thinke none other, good Christen people, but Christ hath prepared thesame joye and felicitie for us that he prepared for Lazarus and the thefe. Wherfore, let us sticke unto his salvacion and gracious redempcion, and beleve hys Worde, serve hym from our hartes, love and obeye hym, and whatsoever we have done heretofore contrarye to hys moste holy wyll, now let us repent in tyme, and hereafter study to correct our lyfe, and doubt not but we shall finde hym as mercifull unto us as he was either to Lazarus or to the thefe: whose examples are written in Holy Scripture for the comfort of them that be sinners, and subjecte to sorowes, miseries and calamities in this worlde, that thei should not despayre in Gods mercy, but ever truste therby to have forgivenesse of their synnes and lyfe everlastinge, as Lazarus and the thefe had. Thus I trust every Christen man perceyveth by the infallible Woorde of God that bodiely death cannot harme nor hinder theim that truly beleve in Christ, but contrary, shal profit and promote the Christen soules whiche beynge truly penitent for their offences departe hence in perfect charitie and in sure truste that God is mercifull to them, forgivinge theyr synnes for the merites of Jesus Christe, hys onely naturall Sonne.

The second cause why some do feare death is sore sickenesse and grevous paynes, whiche partly come before death, and partely accompayneth deathe whensoever it cometh. This feare is the feare of the frayle fleashe and a naturall passion belonginge unto the nature of a mortall man. But true fayth in Gods promyses and regarde of the paynes and pangues whiche Christe upon the crosse suffered for us miserable synners, with consideracion of the joye and everlastyng lyfe to come in heaven, wil mitigate those paynes and moderate thys feare, that it shall never be able to overthrowe the hartie desire and gladnesse that the Christian soule hath to be seperated from thys corrupt body, that it maye come to the gracious presence of our saviour Jesus Christ. If we beleve stedfastly the Woorde of God, we shal perceyve that suche bodiely sickenesse, pangues of death, or whatsoever dolorous paynes we suffre either before or with death, be nothynge els in Christen men but the rodde of our heavenly and lovynge Father, wherwith he mercifully correcteth us, either to trie and declare the faythe of hys pacient chyldren that they maye be founde laudable, glorious and honorable in hys sight, when Jesus Christ shalbe openly shewed to be the judge of al the worlde, or els to chastise and amende in them whatsoever offendeth hys fatherly and gracious goodnesse, lest they shoulde peryshe everlastingly. And this hys correctynge rodde is common to all them that be truly hys. Therfore, let us caste away the burden of synne that lyeth so hevye in our neckes, and returne unto God by true penaunce and amendemente of our lyfes. Let us with pacience runne thys course that is appoynted, sufferyng for hys sake that dyed for our salvacion al sorowes and pangues of death and death it selfe joyfully, when God sendeth it to us, havynge our eyes fixed ever upon the heade and capitayn of our fayth, Jesus Christe, who, considerynge the joye that he shoulde come unto, cared neyther for the shame, nor payne of deathe, but willingly, conformyng hys wyll to hys Fathers wyll, moste paciently suffered the moste shamefull and paynefull deathe of the crosse, beyng innocent. And now, therfore, he is exalted in heaven and everlastingly sitteth on the right hande of the throne of God the Father. Let us call to our remembraunce, therfore, the lyfe and joyes of heaven that are kepte for al them that paciently doo suffre here with Christe, and consider that Christe suffered all hys paynfull passion by synners and for synners, and then we shall with pacience, and the more easyly, suffre suche sorowes and paynes when they come. Let us not set at light the chastisinge of the Lorde, nor grudge at hym, nor fall from hym when of hym we be corrected, for the Lorde loveth them whom he doth correcte and beateth every one

whom he taketh to be hys chylde. What chylde is that, saieth Saincte
Paule, whome the father loveth and doth not chastice? If ye be without
Gods correction, which al hys welbeloved and true children have, then be
you but bastardes, smally regarded of God and not hys true chyldren.
Therfore, seynge that when we have in earth our carnall fathers to be our
correctors, we do feare them and reverently take their correction, shall
we not much more be in subjeccion to God, our spirituall Father, by
whome we shall have eternal lyfe? And our carnall fathers some tyme
correct us even as pleaseth them, without cause, but this Father justely
correcteth us, either for our synne to the intent we should amende, or
for our commoditie and wealthe to make us therby partakers of his holynesse. Furthermore, all correction whiche God sendeth us in thys present
tyme semeth to have no joye and comforte, but sorowe and payne, yet it
bringeth with it a taste of Gods mercye and goodnes towardes them
that be so corrected, and a sure hope of Godes everlastyng consolacion in
heaven. If then these sorowes, diseases and sickenesses, and also death
it selfe, be nothyng els but our heavenly Fathers rod, wherby he certifieth
us of hys love and gracious favor, wherby he trieth and purifieth us,
wherby he geveth unto us holynesse and certifieth us that we by hys children and he our mercifull Father, shall not we then with all humilitie,
as obedyent and lovyng chyldren, joyfully kysse our heavenly Fathers rod,
and ever saye in oure harte with oure savior Jesus Christe: Father, if
this anguishe and sorowe, which I fele, and death, which I se approche,
maye not passe, but that thy wyll is that I muste suffre them, thy wyll be
done.

[The Thyrde Parte of the Sermon of the Feare of Deathe

In this homelye agaynst the feare of death two causes were declared which
comonly move worldly men to be in muche feare to dye. And yet thesame
do nothyng trouble the faithfull and good lyvers when death cometh,
but rather geveth them occasion greatly to rejoyce, consyderinge that they
shall be delyvered from the sorow and miserie of this world and be
brought to the great joye and felicitie of the life to come.]
   Now the thirde and speciall cause why death in deede is too be feared is
the miserable state of the worldly and ungodly people after their death.
But this is no cause at all why the godly and faytheful people should feare
death, but rather contrariwise, their godly conversacion in thys lyfe and
beliefe in Christ, cleaving continually to hys merites, should make them to
longe sore after that lyfe that remayneth for them undoubtedly after this
bodely death. Of this immortall state after thys transitory lyfe, where

we shal live evermore in the presence of God in joye and reste, after victory
over all sickenes, sorowes, sinne and death, there be many playn places
of Holy Scripture which confirme the weake conscience agaynst the feare
of al suche dolours, sickenesses, synne and death corporal, to asswage
such trembling and ungodly feare, and to encourage us with comforte and
hope of a blessed state after thys life. Sainct Paule wissheth unto the
Ephesians that God the Father of glory woulde geve unto theim the spirite
of wisedome and revelacion, that the eyes of their hartes might have light
to knowe him and to perceyve how great thinges he had called them
unto, and how riche inheritaunce he hath prepared after this life for them
that pertyene unto hym. And Sainct Paul himself declareth the desire of
his hart, which was to be dissolved and losed from hys body and to
be with Christ, which, as he sayde, was much better for him, althoughe to
them it was more necessary that he should live, which he refused not for
their sakes. Even like as Sainct Martyn sayde: 'Good Lorde, if I be necessary
for thy people to do good unto them, I will refuse no labor, but els for
myne awne selfe, I beseche the to take my soule.'

   Now the holy fathers of the olde lawe and all faythful and righteous
men which departed before our savior Christes ascencion into heaven dyd
by death departe from troubles unto rest, from the handes of theyr enemies into the handes of God, from sorowes and sickenesses unto joyful
refreashing, into Abrahams bosome, a place of al comfort and consolacion,
as Scriptures do plainly by manifest wordes testifie. The boke of Wisedom
saith that the righteous mens soules be in the hand of God, and no torment
shal touche them. They semed to the eyes of folishe men to dye, and
their death was compted miserable, and theyr departing out of this worlde,
wretched, but thei be in rest. And another place saieth that the righteous
shall live for ever, and their rewarde is with the Lorde, and their myndes be
with God who is above al. Therfore they shall receyve a glorious kyngdome and a beautifull croune at the Lordes hand. And in another place,
thesame boke saieth: the righteous, though he be prevented with sodain
death, neverthelesse he shalbe there where he shalbe refreshed. Of Abrahams bosome Christes wordes be so playne that a Christen man nedeth no
more profe of it. Now then, if thys were the state of the holy fathers and
righteous men before the comminge of our savior, and before he was
glorified, how much more then oughte all wee to have a stedfast faith and
a sure hope of this blessed state and condicion after our death, seynge
that oure savior now hath perfourmed the whole worke of oure redempcion, and is gloriously ascended into heaven to prepare oure dwellinge
places with hym, and saied unto hys Father: Father, I will that, where I
am, my servauntes shalbe with me. And we knowe that whatsoever Christe

wyll, hys Father will the same; wherfore it cannot be but if we be his faythfull servauntes, our soules shalbe with hym after oure departynge out of this present life. Sainct Stephin, when he was stoned to death, even in the middest of hys tormentes what was hys mynde moste upon? When he was full of the Holy Ghoste, sayeth Holye Scripture, havynge hys eyes lifted up into heaven, he sawe the glory of God and Jesus standinge on the righte hande of God. The which truth after he had confessed boldely before the enemies of Christ, they drewe hym oute of the citie, and there they stoned hym, who cried unto God saiynge: Lorde Jesu Christe, take my spirite. And doeth not oure savior saye playnely in Saincte Jhons Gospel: Verely, verely, I saye unto you, he that heareth my Woorde and beleveth on hym that sente me hath everlastynge lyfe, and commeth not into judgement, but shall passe from death to lyfe? Shall we not then thinke that death to be precious by the whiche we passe unto lyfe? Ther-fore, it is a true saiynge of the prophete: the death of the holy and righteous men is precious in the Lordes sighte. Holy Simeon, after that he had hys hartes desire in seynge oure savior that he ever longed for all hys lyfe, he embraced hym in his armes and sayde: Now Lord, let me departe in peace, for myne eyes have beholden that savior which thou haste prepared for all nacions.

It is truthe, therefore, that the death of the righteous is called peace and the benefite of the Lord, as the church saieth in the name of the righteous departed out of this world: My soule turne the to thy rest, for the Lorde hath bene good to the and rewarded the. And we se by Holy Scripture and other auncient histories of martyrs that the holy, faithfull and righteous, ever syns Christes ascencion, in their death did not doubte but that they went to be with Christe in spirite, whiche is oure lyfe, healthe, wealth and salvacion. Jhon in his holy Revelacion saw a .C.xl. and .iiii.M. virgins and innocentes of whome he saide: These folow the lambe Jesu Christ wheresoever he goeth. And shortly after, in thesame place he saieth, I heard a voyce from heaven, saiyng unto me: Write, happye and blessed are the dead whiche dye in the Lorde; from hencefurthe surelye, saieth the spirite, they shall reste from theyr paynes and labours, for their woorkes do folow them. So that then they shall reape with joye and comforte that whiche they sowed with labors and paynes. They that sowe in the spirit, of the spirit shall reape everlastynge lyfe. Let us, therefore, never be wery of well doynge, for when the tyme of reapynge or reward commeth, we shal reape without any werines everlastynge joye. Therfore, whyle we have time, as Saincte Paule exhorteth us, let us doo good to all men and not lay up our treasures in earth, where ruste and mothes corrupt it, whiche ruste, as Sainct James saieth, shall beare witnes against us at the great daye, condempne us, and shal like most brennynge fyre tormente oure fleashe. Let us beware, therefore, as we tendre oure awne wealthe, that we be not in the numbre of those miserable coveteous men, whiche Sainct James biddeth mourne and lament for their gredy gatherynge and ungodly kepynge of goodes. Let us be wise in time and learne to folowe the wise example of the wicked stuarde. Let us so prudently dispose oure goodes and possessions, committed unto us here by God for a ceason, that we maye truely heare and obeye this commaundement of oure savior Christes: I saye unto you, sayeth he, make you frendes of the wicked Mammon, that they maye receive you into everlastynge tabernacles. Ryches he calleth wicked, because the worlde abuseth them unto all wickednes, which are otherwise the good gifte of God and the instrumentes whereby Gods servauntes do truely serve hym in usynge of thesame. He commaunded them not to make them ryche frendes, to get hyghe dignities and worldly possessions, to geve great giftes to ryche men that have no neede therof, but to make theim frendes of poore and miserable men, unto whome, whatsoever they geve, Christe accepteth it as geven to hymselfe. And to these frendes Christe in the Gospell geveth so greate honor and preeminence that he sayeth: they shall receyve theyr benefactors into everlastynge houses, not that men shalbe oure rewarders for our well doyng, but that Christ will rewarde us and take it to be done unto hymselfe, whatsoever is doone to suche frendes. Thus makynge poore wretches oure frendes, we make oure savioure Christe oure frende, whose membres they are, whose miserie as he taketh for hys awne misery, so theyr reliefe, succour and helpe he taketh for hys succoure, reliefe and helpe, and will asmuche thanke us and rewarde us for oure goodnes shewed to them, as if he him selfe had receyved lyke benefite at oure handes, as he witnesseth in the Gospell, saiynge, Whatsoever ye have done to any of these symple persones, whiche do beleve in me, that have ye doen to my selfe.

Therfore, let us diligently forese that our fayth and hope whiche we have conceyved in almightie God and in oure savioure Christe waxe not faynte, nor that the love whiche we pretende to beare to hym waxe not coulde, but let us studye dayly and diligently to shewe oure selfes to be the true honorers and lovers of God, by kepynge of his commaundementes, by doyng of good dedes unto our nedy neighbors, relevynge, by all meanes that we can, their povertye with our abundaunce, their ignoraunce with oure wisedome and learnynge, and comforte their weakenesse with oure strength and aucthoritie, calling all men backe from evill doynge by godly counsayll and good example, perseverynge styll in well doynge so longe as we lyve. So shall we not nede to feare death for any of those three causes afore mencioned, nor yet for any other cause that can be imagined. But contrary, consideryng the manifold sickenesses, troubles and sorowes of this present lyfe, the daungers of this perilous pilgrimage, and the greate encombraunce whiche oure spirite hath by thys synful fleshe and frayle body subject to death; considerynge also the manifolde sorowes and daungerous deceiptes of this world on every side, the intollerable pride, coveteousnes and lechery in tyme of prosperitie, the impacient mur-murynge of them that be worldly in tyme of adversitie, whiche cease not to withdrawe and plucke us from God oure savioure Christe, from oure life, wealth or eternal joy and salvacion; considerynge also the innumerable assaultes of oure ghostly enemy, the devill, with al his fiery dartes of ambicion, pryde, lechery, vainglory, envie, malice, detraction, with other hys innumerable deceiptes, engines and snares whereby he goeth busely aboute to catche al men under his dominion, ever lyke a roreynge lyon, by all meanes searchynge whome he maye devoure: the faythfull Christian man which considereth al these miseries, perilles and incommodities, where-unto he is subjecte so longe as he here liveth upon earthe, and on the other part, considereth that blessed and comfortable state of the heavenly lyfe to come and the swete condicion of them that departe in the Lorde, howe they are delivered from the continuall encombraunces of their mortall and synfull bodye, from all the malice, craftes and deceiptes of this world, from al the assaultes of their ghostly enemy, the devil, to live in peace, reste and perpetuall quietnes, to live in the felowship of innumerable aungelles and with the congregacion of perfecte juste men, as patriarches, prophetes, martyrs and confessors, and finally, unto the presence of al-mighty God and oure savior Jesus Christe: he that doeth consider all these thinges, and beleveth theim assuredly, as they are to be beleved, even from the botome of his harte, beynge established in God in thys true faythe, havynge a quiete conscience in Christe, a firme hope and assured trust in Gods mercy, through the merites of Jesu Christe, to obteyne thys quietnes, reste and eternall joye, shal not onely be without feare of bodiely deathe when it commeth, but certainlye, as Saincte Paule did, so shall he gladly, accordynge to Gods will, and when it pleaseth God to call hym oute of thys lyfe, greatly desyre in hys harte that he maye be rid from al these occasions of evil and live ever to Gods pleasure, in perfecte obedience of hys will, with our savior Jesus Christe. To whose gracious presence, the Lorde of hys infinite mercye and grace brynge us to reigne with hym in lyfe everlastyng. To whome, with oure heavenly Father and the Holy Ghoste, be glorye in worldes without ende.

   Amen.

NOTES

147 *O death ... and fed*: Sir 41:1.
148 *the second death*: Rev 21:8.
    dread: an archaic form of the past participle.
    appellacion: action of appealing to a higher court.
    richeman ... but it was to late: Luke 16:19–31.
    daintie: choice.
    pined: enfeebled.
    arrested of: seized by.
    the holy apostle saieth: Heb 2:14–15.
    temple of the Holy Ghoste: 1 Cor 3:16 and 6:19.
149 *neither eye ... conceyve them*: 1 Cor 2:9.
    The head goynge before ... after: Augustine *Enarratio in Ps 65* 1 [on Col 1:18]
        (PL 36: 786).
    if Christe ... from thesame: 1 Cor 15:20–3.
    a slepe: John 11:11–14; Acts 7:60; 1 Thess 4:13–18.
    our lyfe ... with hym in glorye: Col 3:3–4.
    God the Father ... upon the name of the Sonne of God: 1 John 5:11–13.
150 *he that beleveth ... last day*: John 6:40.
    Christe is ordeyned ... glory in the Lorde: 1 Cor 1:30–1.
    all other thynges ... found in Christ: Phil 3:7–11.
    If our heavenly ... us all thynges: Rom 8:32.
    nor any sinne can condempne them: Rom 8:1.
    graffed: grafted.
    whether we lyve ... quicke: Rom 14:8–9.
151 *It is God ... face to face*: 2 Cor 5:5–8; 1 John 3:2; 1 Cor 13:12.
    thys daye ... in Paradyse: Luke 23:43.
    Lazarus ... consolacion?: Luke 16:20–2.
152 *let us caste away ... beyng innocent*: Heb 12:1–2.
    exalted in heaven ... throne of God: Phil 2:9; Heb 12:2.
    Christe suffered ... but sorowe and payne: Heb 12:3–13.
153 *Father ... thy wyll be done*: Matt 26:42.
154 *that God the Father ... have light*: Eph 1:17–18.
    desire of his hart ... he should live: Phil 1:23–6 (Vg 'Desiderium habens
        dissolvi, et esse cum Christo').
    'Good Lorde ... take my soule': Sulpicius Severus *Epistola* 3 (*ad Bassulam*) (PL
        20: 182).
    righteous mens soules ... thei be in rest: Wisd 3:1–3.
    the righteous shall live ... Lordes hand: Wisd 5:15–16.
    the righteous ... refreshed: Wisd 4:7 (Vg 'Justus autem si morte praeoccupatus
        fuerit, In refrigerio erit').
    prevented with: forestalled by.
    Christes wordes: Luke 16:22–31.

to prepare ... shalbe with me: John 14:2–3, 17:24, and 12:26.
155 *When he was full ... take my spirite*: Acts 7:55–9.
Verely ... death to lyfe: John 5:24 (Vg 'Sed transiit a morte in vitam').
the death of the holy ... Lordes sighte: Ps 116:15.
he embraced ... nacions: Luke 2:28–31.
My soule ... rewarded the: Ps 116:7 (Vg 114:7 'Convertere, anima mea, in requiem tuam, Quia Dominus benefecit tibi'). ·
These folow ... do folow them: Rev 14:1–5, 13.
reape ... paynes: Ps 126:5–6.
They that sowe ... corrupt it: Gal 6:8–10; Matt 6:19.
whiche ruste ... oure fleashe: James 5:3.
156 *brennynge*: burning.
Sainct James biddeth: James 5:1–6.
wicked stuarde: Luke 16:1–9.
stuarde: steward.
I saye unto you ... tabernacles: Luke 16:9.
Whatsoever ye have done ... to my selfe: Matt 25:40, 10:42, and 18:6.
157 *lyke a roreynge ... maye devoure*: 1 Pet 5:8.
felowship ... juste men: Heb 12:22–3.
Saincte Paule ... in hys harte: Phil 1:23.

TEXTUAL APPARATUS

147 other thinke] otherwise thinke *1623*. carnall] fleshely *1559*. agonies in] agonies or battaylles and in *1559*. accompany] or affelowshyp *added 1559*.
148 fixed] or nayled *added 1559*. insue] and folowe *added 1559*. eternall] everlastynge *1559*. and ungodly] and the ungodly *1623*. pitifully] pitifull *1623*. miserably] miserable *1559*. descended] went *1559*. unfaithfull] untfaythfull *1559*. departyng out of] departyng from *1623*. never one] never a one *1623*. nor yet thei] nor yet them *1623*. whiche is the very] who is the very *1623*.
149 infallyble] or undeceaveable *added 1559*. move] mooveth *1623*. nor anye earthly] *1623*; nor for anye earthly *1547, 1549, 1559*. perpetuall] everlastyng *1559*. mans senses] man senses *1623*. resurreccion] and rising againe *added 1559*. we shal be immortall] shall we be immortall *1623*. infect] infected *1623*. infirmities] infirmittes *1549*. remedy of] remedy for *1623*. accepted]
150 receyved *1559*. eternall] everlastynge *1559*. lyfe is in] lyfe in is *1547*. this I wrote] this I write *1623*. our holynes] or holynes *1623*. perpetuall health]
151 everlastinge health *1559*. perpetual joye] endelesse joye *1559, 1623*. shall muche be] shall be much *1623*. infallible] or undeceavable *added 1559, 1623*. resembled] and likened *added 1559, 1623*. perpetuall] everlastinge *1559, 1623*. prepared] and made readye before *added 1559, 1623*. whatsoever] whatever *1559*. lyfe everlastinge] life and everlastinge *1559*. infallible] or undecevable
152 *added 1559, 1623*. contrary] contrarily *1623*. accompayneth] or commeth with

1559; or come with *1623.* a mortall man] mortall man *1559.* mitigate] and
asswage less *added 1559, 1623.* moderate] or bryng into a meane *added 1559,
1623.* lyeth so hevye] lyeth to hevye *1549, 1559, 1623.* fixed] and set fast
added 1559, 1623. conformyng] and framyng *added 1559, 1623.* innocent] and
153 harmelesse *added 1559, 1623.* right] rigtht *1547.* eternal] everlastynge *1559,
1623.* as pleaseth them] as it pleaseth them *1623.* sorowe, which] sorrow,
wich *1547.* homelye] sermon *1559, 1623.* felicitie] felicie *1549.* merites] mercies
154 *1623.* many playn] *1623;* many both playn *1547, 1549, 1559.* death corporal]
bodely death *1559, 1623.* have light] geve light *1559;* give life *1623.* into
Abrahams bosome] in Abrahams bosome *1623.* as Scriptures] as the Scrip-
155 tures *1623.* departynge] departure *1623.* all hys lyfe] in hys lyfe *1623.* em-
braced] or toke *added 1559;* and tooke *added 1623.* righteous departed] righteousnes departed *1547.* ascencion] or going up *added 1559, 1623.* to be
156 with Christe] to Christe *1623.* spirite] syirite *1547.* prudently dispose] wysely
order *1559, 1623.* tabernacles] or dwellinges *added 1559, 1623.* Ryches he
calleth] Ryches bee called *1623.* gifte] giftes *1623.* possessions] promotyons
1559, 1623. accepteth] taketh *1559, 1623.* theyr benefactors] them that doe
good unto them *1559, 1623.* pretende to beare] beare in hande to beare *1559,
157 *1623.* abundaunce] and plenty *added 1559, 1623.* contrary] contrarily *1623.*
eternal] everlastynge *1559, 1623.* detraction] or backebityng *added 1559, 1623.*
ever] even *1549.* perpetuall] endelesse *1559, 1623.* eternall] everlastyng *1559,
1623.* infinite] infinitie *1547.*

10 An Exhortacion concernyng Good Ordre and Obedience to Rulers and Magistrates

Almightie God hath created and appointed all thinges in heaven, yearth and waters in a moste excellent and perfect ordre. In heaven, he hath appoynted distinct orders and states of archangelles and angels. In yearth, he hath assigned kynges, princes, with other governors under them, all in good and necessary ordre. The water above is kept and raineth doune in due time and ceason. The sunne, mone, sterres, rainbow, thunder, lightning, cloudes and al birdes of the aire do kepe their ordre. The yearth, trees, seedes, plantes, herbes, corne, grasse and all maner of beastes kepe them in their ordre. All the partes of the whole yeare, as winter, somer, monethes, nightes and dayes, continue in their ordre. All kyndes of fishes in the sea, rivers and waters, with all fountaynes, sprynges, yea, the seas themselfes, kepe their comely course and ordre. And man hymself also hath al his partes, both within and without, as soule, harte, mynd, memory, understandyng, reason, speache, withall and singuler corporall membres of his body, in a profitable, necessary and pleasaunt ordre. Every degre of people, in their vocacion, callyng and office, hath appoynted to them their duetie and ordre. Some are in high degre, some in lowe, some kynges and princes, some inferiors and subjectes, priestes and laimen, masters and servauntes, fathers and chyldren, husbandes and wifes, riche and poore, and every one have nede of other: so that in all thinges is to be lauded and praysed the goodly ordre of God, without the whiche, no house, no citie, no common wealth can continue and endure. For where there is no right ordre, there reigneth all abuse, carnall libertie, enormitie, syn and babilonicall confusion. Take awaye kynges, princes, rulers, magistrates, judges and such states of Gods ordre, no man shal ride or go by the high waie unrobbed, no man shall slepe in his awne house or bed unkilled, no man shall kepe his wife, children and possessions in quietnes:

all thynges shal be common, and there must nedes folow all mischief and utter destruction, both of soules, bodies, goodes and common wealthes.

But blessed be God, that we in this realme of England fele not the horrible calamities, miseries and wretchednes which al thei undoubtedly fele and suffre that lacke this godly ordre. And praised be God, that we knowe the great excellent benefite of God shewed towards us in this behalfe. God hath sente us his high gifte, our most dere sovereigne lord, King Edward the Sixt, with godly, wise and honorable counsail, with other superiors and inferiors in a beautifull ordre. Wherefore, let us subjectes do our bounden duties, geving hartie thankes to God and praiyng for the preservacion of this godly ordre. Let us al obey even from the botome of our hartes al their godly procedynges, lawes, statutes, proclamacions and injunctions, with al other godly orders. Let us considre the Scriptures of the Holy Ghost, whiche perswade and commaunde us all obediently to be subject: first and chiefly, to the Kynges majestie, supreme hed over all, and next, to his honorable counsail, and to all other noble men, magistrates and officers, which by Gods goodnes be placed and ordered. For almightie God is the onely aucthor and provider of thys forenamed state and ordre, as it is written of God in the boke of the Proverbes: through me kynges do reigne; through me counsailors make just lawes; through me doo princes beare rule and all judges of the yearth execute judgment: I am lovyng to them that love me.

Here let us marke wel and remembre that the high power and aucthoritie of kynges, with theyr makyng of lawes, judgementes and officers, are the ordinaunces not of man, but of God, and therfore is this word 'through me' so many tymes repeted. Here is also well to be considered and remembred that this good ordre is appoynted of Gods wisedom, favor and love, specially for them that love God, and therfore he saith, I love them that love me. Also, in the boke of Wisedom we may evidently learne that a kynges power, aucthoritie and strength is a greate benefite of God, geven of his great mercy to the comfort of our greate misery. For thus wee rede there spoken to kynges: Heare, o ye kynges, and understand; learne, ye that be judges of thendes of the yearth; geve eare, ye that rule the multitudes: for the power is geven you of the Lord, and the strength from the highest. Let us learne also here by the infallible Word of God that kinges and other supreme and higher officers are ordeined of God, who is most highest, and therfore they are here diligentely taught to apply themselfes to knowledge and wisedom necessary for the orderynge of Gods people to their governaunce committed. And they be here also taught by almighty God that thei should reknowledge themselfes to have al their power and strength not from Rome, but immediatly of God most highest.

We rede in the boke of Deuteronomy that al punishement perteineth to God by this sentence: vengeaunce is mine, and I will reward. But this sentence we must understand to pertein also unto the magistrates, which do exercise Gods roume in judgement and punishing by good and godly lawes here in yearth. And the places of Scripture whiche seme to remove from emong al Christian men judgement, punishment or kyllyng ought to be understand that no man, of his awne private aucthoritie, may be judge over other, may punish, or may kil. But we must refer al judgement to God, to kynges and rulers, and judges under them, which be Gods officers, to execute justice and by plain wordes of Scripture have their aucthoritie and use of the swourd graunted from God, as we are taught by S. Paule, the dere and elect apostle of our savior Christ, whom we ought diligently to obeye even as we would obey our savior Christ, yf he wer present. Thus .S. Paule writeth to the Roma.: Let every soule submit hymself unto the aucthoritie of the higher powers, for there is no power but of God; the powers that be, be ordeined of God; whosoever, therfore, resisteth the power, resisteth the ordinaunce of God, but they that resist shal receive to themselfes dampnacion, for rulers are not fearful to them that do good, but to them that do evill. Wilt thou be without feare of the power? Do well then, and so shalt thou be praysed of the same, for he is the minister of God, for thy wealthe. But and if thou do that whiche is evill, then feare, for he beareth not the swourde for naught, for he is the minister of God, to take vengeaunce on hym that doth evill. Wherfore ye must nedes obey, not onely for feare of vengeaunce, but also because of conscience, and even for this cause paie ye tribute, for they are Gods ministers, servyng for the same purpose.

Here let us al learne of S. Paule, the elect vessel of God, that all persones having soules – he excepteth none, nor exempteth none, neither priest, apostle, nor prophet, saieth .S. Chriso. – do owe of bounden duetie, and even in conscience, obedience, submission and subjection to the hygh powers, which be constituted in aucthoritie by God, forasmuch as thei be Gods livetenauntes, Gods presidentes, Gods officers, Gods commissioners, Gods judges, ordeyned of God hymself, of whom onely thei have al their power and all their aucthoritie. And thesame .S. Paule threateneth no lesse pain then everlasting dampnacion to al disobedient persons, to al resisters against this generall and common aucthoritie, forasmuch as they resist not man, but God, not mannes devise and invencion, but Gods wisedom, Gods ordre, power and aucthoritie.

[The Second Part of the Sermon of Obedience

Forasmuche as God hath created and disposed all thynges in a comely ordre, wee have been taught in the first parte of this homelie, concernyng good ordre and obedience, that we also ought in all common wealthes to observe and kepe a due ordre, and to be obedient to the powers, their ordinaunces and lawes, and that al rulers are appoyncted of God for a godly ordre to be kepte in the worlde, and also how the magistrates ought to lerne how to rule and governe, accordyng to Gods lawes. And that al subjectes are bounden to obeye theim as Goddes ministers: yea, although thei bee evill, not onely for feare, but also for conscience sake.]

And here, good people, let us all marke diligently that it is not lawfull for inferiors and subjectes in any case to resist the superior powers, for .S. Paules wordes be playn, that whosoever resisteth shall get to themselfes dampnacion: for whosoever resisteth, resisteth the ordinaunce of God. Our savior Christe him self and his apostles received many and diverse injuries of the unfaithfull and wicked men in aucthoritie, yet we never rede that thei, or any of them, caused any sedicion or rebellion agaynst aucthoritie. We rede oft that they paciently suffered al troubles, vexacions, slaunders, pangues and paines, and death it self obediently, without tumulte or resistence. They committed their cause to him that judgeth righteously and prayed for their enemyes hartely and earnestly. They knew that the aucthoritie of the powers was Gods ordinaunce, and therfore, bothe in their wordes and dedes, they taught ever obedience to it and never taught, nor did the contrary. The wicked judge, Pilat, sayd to Christe, knowest thou not that I have power to crucifye the and have power also to lose the? Jesus aunswered, Thou couldest have no power at all against me, except it were geven the from above. Wherby Christe taught us plainly that even the wicked rulers have their power and aucthoritie from God. And therfore it is not lawfull for their subjectes by force to resyst them, although they abuse their power, muche lesse then it is lawfull for subjectes to resiste their godly and Christian princes whiche do not abuse their aucthoritie, but use thesame to Gods glory and to the profyte and commoditie of Gods people.

The holy apostle S. Peter commaundeth servauntes to be obedient to their masters, not onely if they be good and gentle, but also if they be evil and froward, affirmyng that the vocation and callyng of Gods people is to bee pacient and of the sufferyng syde. And there he bringeth in the pacience of our savior Christ to perswade obedience to governors, yea, although they be wycked and wrong dooers. But let us now heare S. Peter himself speake, for his awn wordes certifye best our conscience. Thus he

uttereth them in his firste Epistle: Servauntes, obeye your masters with
feare, not onely if they be good and gentle, but also if they bee frowarde.
For it is thanke worthy, if a man for conscience towarde God suffereth
grief and suffreth wronge undeserved, for what praise is it, when ye be
beaten for your faultes, if ye take it paciently? But when ye do wel, if
you then suffre wrong and take it paciently, then is there cause to have
thanke of God, for hereunto verely were ye called. For so did Christ suffre
for us, leavyng us an example that we should folow his steppes. Al these
be the very wordes of .S. Peter.

S. David also teacheth us a good lesson in this behalfe, who was many
tymes most cruelly and wrongfullye persecuted of Kyng Saule and many
tymes also put in jeoperdy and daunger of his life by Kyng Saule and
his people, yet he never resysted, neither used any force or violence against
Kyng Saule, his mortall enemy, but did ever to his liege lorde and master,
Kyng Saule, moste true, most diligent, and most faithfull service. In so
muche that when the lord God had geven Kyng Saule into Davides handes
in his awn cave, he would not hurt him, when he myght without all
bodily perill easly have slain hym; no, he would not suffre any of his
servauntes once to lay their handes upon Kyng Saule, but praied to God in
this wise: Lord, kepe me from doyng that thyng unto my master, the
Lordes anoynted; kepe me that I laye not my hande upon him, seyng he is
the anoynted of the Lorde. For as truly as the Lorde liveth, except the
Lorde smyte him, or except his day come, or that he go doune to warre
and in battaill perishe, the Lorde be mercifull unto me, that I lay not
my hand upon the Lordes anoynted. And that David mighte have killed
his enemye, Kyng Saule, it is evidently proved in the first boke of the
Kynges, both by the cuttyng of the lap of Saules garment and also by the
playn confession of Kyng Saule. Also another time, as it is mencioned
in the same boke, when the most unmercifull and most unkynd Kyng Saule
did persecute poore David, God did agayn geve Kyng Saule into Davides
handes by castyng of Kyng Saul and his whole army into a dead slepe,
so that David and one Abisai with him came in the night into Saules hoste
wher Saule lay slepyng and his speare stacke in the ground at his hed.
Then said Abisai unto David, God hath delivered thyne enemy into thy
handes at this tyme; now, therfore, let me smyte him once with my spear
to the yearth, and I will not smyte him agayn the seconde tyme meanyng
thereby to have kylled hym with one stroke and to have made him sure
for ever. And David answered, and sayd to Abisai, destroy him not,
for who can lay his handes on the Lordes anoynted and be giltles? And
David said furthermore: as sure as the Lord liveth, the Lord shal smite
him, or his day shall come to dye, or he shall descend into battaill, and

there perish. The Lord kepe me from laiyng my handes upon the Lordes anoynted. But take thou now the speare that is at his head and the cruse of water, and let us go: and so he did.

Here is evidently proved that we may not resyst, nor in any wayes hurt an anoynted kyng, which is Gods liuetenaunt, vicegerent and highest minister in that countrey where he is kyng. But peradventure, some here would saye that David in his awne defence might have killed Kyng Saule lawfully and with a safe conscience. But holy David did knowe that he might in no wise resist, hurt, or kyl his sovereigne lorde and kyng; he dyd knowe that he was but King Saules subject, though he wer in great favor with God, and his enemy, King Saule, out of Gods favor. Therefore, though he wer never so much provoked, yet he refused utterly to hurt the Lordes anoynted. He durst not, for offending God and his awne consci- ence, although he had occasion and opportunitie, once lay his handes upon Gods high officer, the King, whom he did know to be a person reserved, for his office sake, onely to Gods punishment and judgement. Therfore, he prayeth so ofte and so earnestly that he laye not his handes upon the Lordes anoynted. And by these .ii. examples S. David, beyng named in Scripture a man after Gods awne hart, geveth a general rule and lesson to all subjectes in the world not to resist their liege lord and king, not to take a sweard by their private aucthoritie against their king, Gods anointed, who onely beareth the sweard by Gods aucthoritie for the maintenaunce of the good and for the punishment of the evil, who onely by Gods law hath the use of the swearde at his commaundement, and also hath all power, jurisdiction, regiment and coercion as supreme gover- nor of all his realmes and dominions, and that, even by the aucthoritie of God and by Gods ordinaunces.

Yet another notable story and doctrine is in the second boke of the Kynges that maketh also for this purpose. When an Amalechite, by King Saules awn consent and commaundement, had kylled Kyng Saul, he went to David supposing to have had great thanke for his message that he had killed Davids mortall enemy, and therfore he made great hast to tel to David the chaunce, bringyng with him Kyng Saules croune that was upon his hed and his bracelet that was upon his arme to perswade his tidynges to be true. But godly David was so farr from rejoysyng at these newes that immediatly he rent his clothes of his backe; he mourned and wepte, and sayde to the messenger, how is it that thou wast not afraied to laie thy handes on the Lordes anoynted to destroy him? And by and by, David made one of his servauntes to kil the messenger, saiyng, thy bloud be on thine awne hed, for thy awn mouth hath testified against the, grauntyng that thou hast slain the Lordes anoynted. These examples being so mani-

fest and evident, it is an intollerable ignoraunce, madnesse and wickednesse
for subjectes to make any murmuryng, rebellion, resistence, commocion
or insurrection agaynst their moste dere and most dread sovereigne lorde
and kyng, ordeined and appoynted of Gods goodnesse for their commoditie, peace and quietnes.

Yet let us beleve undoubtedly, good Christian people, that we may not
obey kynges, magistrates, or any other, though thei be our awne fathers,
if thei would commaunde us to do any thyng contrary to Gods commaundementes. In such a case, we ought to say with the apostles, we must
rather obeye God then man. But nevertheles in that case, we maye not in
any wyse resist violently or rebell against rulers, or make any insurrection,
sedicion or tumultes, either by force of armes or other waies, against
the anoynted of the Lord or any of his appointed officers. But we must in
suche case paciently suffre all wronges and injuries, referryng the judgement of oure cause onely to God. Let us feare the terrible punishment of
almightie God against traitors or rebellious persones by the example of
Chore, Dathan and Abiron, whiche repined and grudged against Gods
magistrates and officers, and therfor the earth opened, and swallowed
them up a live. Other, for their wicked murmuryng and rebellion, wer by
a sodain fire sent of God utterly consumed. Other, for their froward
behaviour to their rulers and governors, Gods ministers, were sodainly
stricken with a foule leprosy. Other wer stinged to death with wonderful
straunge firy serpentes. Other wer sore plagued, so that ther was killed
in one day the numbre of fourtene thousand and seven hundred for rebellion agaynst them whom God had appoynted to be in aucthoritie. Absalon
also, rebelling against his father King David, was punished with a straunge
and notable death.

[The Third Part of the Sermon of Obedience

Ye have heard before in this homelie of good ordre and obedience manifestly proved, bothe by Scriptures and examples, that all subjectes are
bounden to obeye their magistrates and for no cause to resist, rebell, or
make any sedicion against them, yea, although thei be wicked men.] And
lette no man thynke that he can escape unpunished that committeth
treason, conspiracy, or rebellion agaynste his sovereigne lorde, the kynge,
though he commit thesame never so secretly, either in thought, woorde,
or dede, never so prively, in hys privie chambre by hymselfe, or openly
communicatyng and consultyng with other. For treason will not be hid;
treason will out at the length. God will have that moste detestable vice
bothe opened and punished, for that it is so directly against hys

ordinaunce and agaynste hys hygh principall judge and anoynted in yearth. The violence and injury that is committed against aucthoritie is committed agaynste God, the common weale and the whole realme, whiche God wyll have knowen and condignely punished, one way or other. For it is notably wrytten of the Wiseman in Scripture, in the boke called Ecclesiastes, wishe the kyng no evyll in thy thought, or speake no hurt of hym in thy privy chambre, for a byrde of the aire shall betraye thy voyce, and with her fethers shall she bewraye thy wordes. These lessons and examples are writen for our learnyng.

Let us al, therfore, feare the moste detestable vice of rebellion, ever knowyng and remembring that he that resisteth common aucthoritie resisteth God and his ordinaunce, as it may be proved by many other mo places of Holy Scripture. And here let us take hede that we understand not these or suche other like places whiche so streightly commaunde obedience to superiors, and so streightly punisheth rebellion and disobedience to thesame to be meant in any condicion of the pretensed power of the Bishop of Rome. For truely the Scripture of God alloweth no suche usurped power, full of enormities, abusions and blasphemies. But the true meanyng of these and suche places be to extol and set furthe Gods true ordinaunce and the aucthoritie of Gods anointed kynges, and of their officers appoynted under them.

And concernyng the usurped power of the Bishop of Rome, which he most wrongfully chalengeth, as the successor of Christe and Peter, we maye easely perceive how false, feined and forged it is, not onely in that it hath no sufficient grounde in Holy Scripture, but also by the fruites and doctrine therof. For our savior Christ and S. Peter teacheth most earnestly and agreably obedience to kynges, as to the chief and supreme rulers in this world, next under God. But the Bishop of Rome teacheth immunities, priviledges, exempcions, and disobedience, moste clearly agaynst Christes doctrine and S. Peters. He ought, therefore, rather to be called Antichriste and the successor of the Scribes and Phariseis then Christes vicar, or S. Peters successor, seyng that not only in this poynt, but also in other weightie matters of Christian religion, in matters of remission of synnes and of salvacion, he teacheth so directly agaynst both S. Peter and against our savior Christe, who not onely taught obedience to kynges, but also practised obedience in their conversacion and livyng. For we rede that they both paied tribute to the kyng. And also we rede that the holye virgyn Mary, mother to our savior Christ, and Joseph, who was taken for his father, at the emperors commaundemente went to the citie of David, named Bethleem, to be taxed emong other and to declare their obedience to the magistrates for Gods ordinaunces sake. And here let us not forget the blessed virgin Maries obedience, for although she was highly in Gods favor and Christes naturall mother, and was also great with chylde that same time, and so nigh her travaile that she was delivered in her journey, yet she gladly, without any excuse or grudgyng, for conscience sake did take that cold and foule winter journey, beyng in the meane ceason so poore that she lay in the stable, and there she was delivered of Christ.

And according to thesame, lo how S. Peter agreeth, writing by expresse wordes in his first Epistle: submit your selfes, saieth he, unto kinges, as unto the chief heddes or unto rulers, as unto them that are sent of hym for the punishment of evill doers and for laude of them that do well, for so is the wil of God. I nede not to expound these wordes: they be so plain of themselfes. S. Peter doth not say, submit your selfes unto me, as supreme hed of the Churche; neither he saith, submit your selfes from time to time to my successors in Rome. But he saith, submit your selfes unto your kyng, your supreme head, and unto those that he appoynteth in aucthoritie under hym. For that ye shal so shew your obedience, it is the wil of God. God will that you be in subjection to your hed and king. That is Gods ordinaunce, Gods commaundement and Gods holy will, that the whole body of every realme and al the membres and partes of thesame shalbe subject to their hed, their kynge, and that, as S. Peter writeth, for the Lordes sake and, as S. Paule writeth, for conscience sake, and not for feare onely. Thus we learne by the Worde of God to yeld to our kyng that is dewe to oure kyng, that is, honor, obedience, paimentes of dewe taxes, customes, tributes, subsidies, love and feare.

Thus we knowe partly our bounden dueties to common aucthoritie. Nowe let us learne to accomplishe thesame. And let us moste instauntly and hartely praye to God, the onely aucthor of all aucthoritie, for all them that be in aucthoritie, according as S. Paule willeth, writyng thus to Timothe in his first Epistle: I exhort, therfore, that above all thynges, prayers, supplicacions, intercessions and geving of thankes be doen for all men: for kynges and for all that bee in aucthoritie, that we maye live a quiete and a peaceable life with al godlines and honestie, for that is good and accepted in the sight of God our savior. Here S. Paule maketh an earnest and an especiall exhortacion, concernyng gevyng of thankes and praier for kynges and rulers, saiyng above al thynges, as he might say in any wise principally and chiefly, let prayer be made for kynges. Let us hartely thanke God for his greate and excellent benefite and providence concernyng the state of kynges. Let us pray for them, that they may have Gods favor and Gods proteccion. Let us pray that they may ever in al thinges have God before their eyes. Let us pray, that they may have wisedom, strength, justice, clemencie, and zeale to Gods glory, to Gods

veritie, to Christian soules, and to the common wealth. Let us praye that they maye rightly use their swourde and aucthoritie for the maintenaunce and defence of the catholique faith, conteined in Holy Scripture, and of their good and honest subjectes, and for the feare and punishement of the evill and vicious people. Let us praye that they may faithfully folowe the moste faithfull kynges and capitaines in the Bible: David, Ezechias, Josias and Moses, with such other. And let us praye for our selfes, that we maye live godly, in holy and Christian conversacion: so we shal have God of our side. And then let us not feare what man can do against us: so we shall live in true obedience, bothe to oure moste mercifull Kynge in heaven and to oure moste Christian kynge in earthe. So shall we please God, and have the excedynge benefite, peace of conscience, reste and quietnesse here in this worlde, and after thys lyfe we shall enjoye a better lyfe, rest, peace and the eternal blisse of heaven, whiche he graunt us all, that was obedient for us al, even to the death of the crosse, Jesus Christ: to whom with the Father and the Holy Ghost be al honor and glory, bothe now and ever.
    Amen.

NOTES

161 *assigned*: designated.
   Take awaye ... there must nedes folow: This passage, which Shakespeare seems to have recalled in composing Ulysses' famous speech on degree (*Troilus and Cressida* 1.iii.75–137), has numerous analogues. One of them, a passage in Richard Rainolde's *The Foundacion of Rhetorike* (London 1563) f 36, leads to the homilist's likely source, pseudo-Demosthenes' *Oration Against Aristogeiton* 1, 15–17, 20–27 (*Demosthenes* III ed J.H. Vince [London: William Heinemann 1956] 523–531). See Clifford J. Ronan 'Daniel, Rainolde, Demosthenes, and the Degree Speech of Shakespeare's Ulysses' *Renaissance and Reformation* n s 9, 2 (1985) 111–18.
162 *bounden*: morally obligatory.
   through me ... that love me: Prov 8:15–17 (Vg 'Per me reges regnant, Et legum conditores justa decernunt; Per me principes imperant, Et potentes decernunt justitiam').
   Heare ... from the highest: Wisd 6:1–3.
163 *vengeaunce ... reward*: Deut 32:35.
   roume: authority.
   Let every soule ... the same purpose: Rom 13:1–7.
   wealth: spiritual well-being.
   the elect vessel of God: Acts 9:15.

he excepteth none ... S. Chriso.: Chrysostom *In Epistolam ad Romanos, Hom 23* I (PG 60: 615).

164 *whosoever resisteth ... ordinaunce of God*: Rom 13:2.
committed ... righteously: I Pet 2:23.
Pilat ... geven the from above: John 19:10–11.
S. Peter ... folow his steppes: I Pet 2:18–21.

165 *S. David ... most faithfull service*: I Sam 18–20.
Lord, kepe me ... Lordes anoynted: I Sam 24:6–7 (Vg 24:6 and 26:10 'Propitius sit mihi Dominus, ne faciam hanc rem domino meo, christo Domini, ut mittam manum meam in eum, quia christus Domini est ... Vivit Dominus, quia nisi Dominus percusserit eum, aut dies eius venerit ut moriatur, aut in praelium descendens perierit: propitius sit mihi Dominus ne extendam manum meam in christum Domini').
proved in the first ... and so he did: I Sam 26:7–12.
stacke: a form of the past participle of 'stick.'

166 *cruse*: pot.
vicegerent: deputy.
named in Scripture ... Gods awne hart: Ps 139:3, 20, 26; Acts 13:22.
regiment: rule.
second boke of the Kynges ... slain the Lordes anoynted: 2 Sam 1:1–16.

167 *we must rather obeye ... man*: Acts 5:29.
Chore, Dathan and Abiron: Num 16:1–33.
murmuryng ... utterly consumed: Num 11:1.
their froward behaviour ... to be in aucthoritie: Num 12:1–15, 21:5–6, and 16:41–9.
Absalon ... notable death: 2 Sam 18:9–17.
opened: disclosed.

168 *condignely*: appropriately.
wishe ... thy wordes: Eccles 10:20.
bewraye: archaic form of 'betray.'
streightly: directly.
they both paied tribute: Matt 17:24–7.
also we rede ... ordinaunces sake: Luke 2:1–7.

169 *there she was delivered of Christ*: Following this in Bodleian 4°1 6 (2) Th. Seld. is a passage found in no other edition of 1547: 'Our savior Christ refused the office of a worldly Judge, and so he dyd the office of a worldly Kyng: Commaunding his disciples, and al that beleve in him, that they should not contende for superioritie, nether for worldly dominion in this worlde. For ambicion and pryde is detestable in al Christian persones of every degre. And the Apostles in that place, do not represent the persones of Bisshoppes, and Priestes only, but also (as auncient authores do write) they represent the persones of Kynges and Princes: Whose worldly rule and governaunce, they then ambiciously desired. So that in that place Christ teacheth also Christen Emperours,

Kinges and Princes, that they shoulde not rule their subjectes by will, and to their awne commoditie, and pleasure onely: But that they shoulde governe their subjectes, by good and Godly lawes. They shoulde not make themselfes so to be lordes over the people, to do with them and their goodes what they list, and to make what lawes they list, without drede of God and of his lawes, without consideracion of their honor, and office, wherunto God hath called them, (as Heathen kynges and Princes do) but to thynke them selfes to be Gods officers, ordeined by God to be his ministres unto the people, for their salvacion, common quyetnes and wealth: to punyshe malefactors, to defend innocentes, and to cherish well doers.' The scriptural passages referred to in the margin are Luke 12, John 6, and Matt 18.

submit your selfes ... wil of God: 1 Pet 2:13–15.

S. Peter ... not for feare onely: 1 Pet 2:13; Rom 13:5.

we learne ... love and feare: Matt 22:21; Rom 13:7.

I exhort ... God our savior: 1 Tim 2:1–3.

170 *God of our side*: Jdt 5:17, 21.

obedient ... death of the crosse: Phil 2:8.

TEXTUAL APPARATUS

161 An Exhortacion] A Exhortacion *1549*. distinct] or severall *added 1559*; and severall *added 1623*. assigned] and appoynted *added 1559, 1623*. all in good] in all good *1623*. kepe them in their] kepe themselves in their *1559*; kepe themselves in *1623*. thinges] thinged *1547*. lauded] laudes *1547*. endure] or last *added 1559, 1623*. states] estates *1559, 1623*. quietnes: all] quietne: sall *1547*.

162 lord, King Edward the Sixt] lady Quene Elizabeth *1559*; lord King James *1623*. beautifull ordre] and goodly *added 1559*; and godly *added 1623*. Kynges majestie] quenes majestie, *with* kynges *as catchword 1559*. supreme hed] supreme governour *1623*. and next] and the next *1623*. his honorable] her honorable *1559*. provider of] provider for *1623*. officers] offices *1623*. appoynted of] appoynted by *1623*. power is geven] power geven *1623*. infallible] and undeceuable *added 1559, 1623*. diligently taught] taught diligently *1623*. apply] and geve *added 1559, 1623*. to their governaunce committed] or whom to governe they ar charged of God *added 1559, 1623*. reknowledge] acknowledge *1623*. seme to] seemeto *1623*. the dere and elect] the dere and chosen *1559*; that dere and chosen *1623*. resisteth the power, resisteth] with standeth the power, withstandeth *1559, 1623*. resist] or are against *added 1559*; or are against it *added 1623*. the power] that power *1623*. to take vengeaunce] to make vengeaunce *1547*. elect] chosen *1559, 1623*. consti-

164 tuted]sette *1559, 1623*. wee have been taught] we have have been taught *1623*. this homelie] this sermon *1559*; the sermon *1623*. godly ordre] goodly *1623*. resist] or stand against *added 1559*; and stand against *added 1623*. resisteth ...

resisteth, resisteth] withstandeth ... withstandeth, withstandeth *1559, 1623*.
lose the] loce the *1559*. by force to resyst] by force to withstand *1559*; to
withstand *1623*. resiste their godly] withstande their godly *1559, 1623*. suffer-
165 yng syde] sufferyng sides *1623*. suffereth] endureth *1623*. S. David] Holy
David *1623*. never resysted] never withstode *1559*; neither withstood *1623*.
mortall] or deadlye *added 1559*; and deadly *1623*. their handes] their hand
1623. my hande] my handes *1549*. in battaill perishe] perish in battaile *1623*.
by the playn] by plain *1623*. as it is mencioned] as is mencioned *1623*.
166 descend] or go doune *added 1559, 1623*. resyst] withstand *1559, 1623*. viceger-
ent] vecegerent *1547*. resist] withstand *1559, 1623*. although he had occasion]
althought he had occasion *1547*. reserved] and kept *added 1559, 1623*. resist]
withstand *1559, 1623*. a sweard] the sweard *1549*. commaundement] command
1623. and coercion] coercion and punishment *1559*; correction and punishment *1623*. thanke] thankes *1549, 1623*. mortall] deadly *1559, 1623*. chaunce]
chanunce *1623*. these newes] this newes *1623*. immediatly] and forthwith
added 1559, 1623. thy awn mouth] thine own mouth *1623*. testified] and wit-
167 nessed *added 1559, 1623*. resistence] or withstanding *added 1559, 1623*. resist]
withstande *1559, 1623*. insurrection] insurrectio *1623*. his appointed officers]
his officers *1623*. traitors or rebellious] traitors and rebellious *1623*. whiche
repined] whiche repugned *1559*; whiche hee repugned *1623*. behaviour]
behavour *1549*. homelie] sermon *1559, 1623*. by Scriptures] by the Scriptures
1623. resist] or withstande *added 1559*; or withstand or *added 1623*. either
in thought] either *followed by* his *as catchword 1549*. at the length] *1547, 1559*;
168 at length *1549, 1623*. condignely] or woorthelye *added 1559, 1623*. or speake]
nor speake *1559, 1623*. a byrde] the byrde *1623*. her fethers] their feathers
1549. shall she bewraye] shall he betraye *1549*; shall betraye *1559, 1623*. Let us
al, therfore] therefore let us al *1559, 1623*. resisteth ... resisteth] or withstandeth ... or withstandeth *added 1559, 1623*. punisheth] punished *1623*. disobedience to] disobedience of *1549*. pretensed] or couloured *added 1559, 1623*.
forged it is] forged it it *1547*. teacheth ... disobedience] teacheth that
thei that ar under him ar fre from al burdens and charges of the common
welth and obedience towardes their prince *1559, 1623*. Christian religion]
169 Christes religion *1549*. remission] and forgevenes *added 1559, 1623*. chylde
that] chylde at that *1623*. the stable] a stable *1623*. submit your selfes] or be
subject *added 1559*; and be subject *added 1623*. for laude] for the laude
1549; for the praise *1559, 1623* neither he saith] neither sayth hee *1623*. selfes]
sels *1547*. That is Gods] This is Gods *1623*. their kynge] the kynge *1549*.
accepted] or alowable *added 1559, 1623*. clemencie, and zeale] *1623*; clemencie,
170 zeal *1547, 1549, 1559*. and for the feare] for the feare *1623*. may faithfully ...
moste faithfull kynges] may most faithfully ... kynges *1623*. we shal have
God of] shall we have God on *1623*. Christian kynge] Christian Quene *1559*.
worlde] worde *1547*. eternal blisse] everlastyng blesse *1559*; everlasting
blisse *1623*.

11 An Homelie of Whoredome and Unclennesse

Although there want not, good Christian people, great swarmes of vices worthi to be rebuked – unto such decai is true godlynes and verteous livinge now come – yet above other vices the outragious seas of adultery, whoredome, fornicacion and unclennesse have not onelye braste in, but also overflowed almoste the whoole worlde, unto the greate dishonor of God, the excedyng infamie of the name of Christ, the notable decay of true religion and the utter destruction of the publique wealthe. And that so abundantly, that through the customable use thereof thys vice is growen into suche an height that in a maner among many it is compted no sin at al, but rather a pastyme, a dalliaunce, and but a touche of youthe, not rebuked but winked at, not punyshed but laughed at. Wherfore, it is necessarye at this presente to entreat of the syn of whoredom and fornicacion, declaringe unto you the greatnes of this syn, and how odious, hatefull and abhominable it is, and hath alwaye been reputed before God and al good men; and how grevously it hath been punished bothe by the lawe of God and the lawes of diverse princes; again, to shewe you certayne remedies whereby ye maye, through the grace of God, eschew this moste detestable synne of whoredom and fornicacion, and lead youre lyfes in all honestie and cleannesse.

   And that ye maye perceive that fornicacion and whoredome are in the sight of God moste abhominable synnes, ye shall call to remembraunce this commaundement of God: thou shalte not commit adultery. By the whiche woorde, adultery, although it bee properly understande of the unlawful commixcion of a maryed manne with any woman beside his wife, or of a wife with any man beside her husbande, yet therby is signified also all unlawfull use of those partes whiche bee ordeined for generacion. And this one commaundement forbiddyng adultery dooth sufficiently painte and sette out before our iyes the greatnesse of this synne of whoredome, and manifestly declareth how greatly it ought to bee abhorred of all honest and faithfull persones. And that none of us all shall thynke hymselfe excepted from this commaundement, whether we be old or young, maried or unmaried, man or woman, heare what God the Father saieth by his mooste excellent prophete, Moses: there shalbee no whore emong the daughters of Israell, nor no whoremongers emong the sonnes of Israell.

Here is whoredome, fornicacion and all unclennesse forbidden to all kyndes of people, all degrees and all ages, without excepcion. And that wee shall not doubt but that this precept perteineth to us in deede, heare what Christe, the perfecte teacher of all truthe, saieth in the Newe Testament: ye have heard, saieth Christe, that it was saied to theim of the old tyme, thou shalte not commit adultery, but I saie unto you, whosoever seeth a woman to have his lust of her hath committed adultery with her all ready in his harte. Here our savior Christe doth not onely confirme and stablishe the lawe agaynste adultery, geven in the Olde Testament of God the Father by his servaunt Moses, and make it of full strength, continually to remain emong the professors of his name in the newe lawe, but he also, condempnyng the grosse interpretacion of the Scribes and Phariseis, whiche taught that the aforesaied commaundement onely required to abstein from the outward adultery, and not from the filthie desires and unpure lustes, teacheth us an exacte and full perfeccion of puritie and clennesse of life, bothe to kepe our bodies undefiled and our hartes pure and fre from all evill thoughtes, carnall desires and fleshly consentes. Howe can wee then bee free from this commaundement, where so greate charge is laied upon us? Maie a servaunt do what he will in any thyng, havyng a commaundement of his master to the contrary? Is not Christe our master? Are not wee his servauntes? Howe then maie wee neglecte our masters will and pleasure, and folowe oure awne will and phantasie? Ye are my frendes, saieth Christe, if you kepe those thynges that I commaunde you. Nowe hath Christe, our master, commaunded us that we should forsake all unclennesse and lecherie, bothe in body and spirite: this therfore must we do, if we loke to please God. In the Gospell of Sainct Matthewe we reade that the Scribes and Phariseis were grevously offended with Christe, because his disciples did not kepe the tradicions of the fore fathers, for thei washed not their handes when thei went to diner or supper, and emong other thynges, Christ aunswered and saied: heare and understand: not that thyng whiche entereth into the mouthe defileth the man, but that whiche commeth out of the mouthe defileth the man. For those thinges whiche procede out of the mouthe come furth from the hart, and thei defile the man. For out of the hart procede evill thoughtes, murders, breakyng of wedlocke, whoredome, theftes, false witnes, blasphemies:

these are the thynges whiche defile a man. Here maie we se that not onely murder, thefte, false witnes and blasphemie defile men, but also evill thoughtes, breakyng of wedlocke, fornicacion and whoredome.

Who is nowe of so litle witte that he will esteme whoredome and fornicacion to bee thynges of smal importaunce and of no waight before God? Christe, whiche is the truthe and cannot lye, saieth that evill thoughtes, breakyng of wedlocke, whoredome and fornicacion defile a manne, that is to saie, corrupte bothe the body and soule of manne, and make theim, of the temples of the Holy Ghoste, the filthy dunghill or dungeon of all uncleane spirites, of the mansion of God, the dwellyng place of Sathan. Agayne, in the Gospell of Saincte Jhon, when the woman taken in adultery was broughte unto Christe, saied not he unto her: Go thy waie and synne no more? Dooth not he here call whoredome synne? And what is the rewarde of synne, but everlastyng deathe? If whoredome bee synne, then is it not lawful for us to commit it. For .S. Jhon saith: he that committeth synne is of the devill. And our savior saith: Every one that committeth syn is the servaunt of syn. If whoredom had not been syn, surely S. Jhon Baptist would never have rebuked Kyng Herode for takyng his brothers wife, but he tolde him plainly that it was not lawfull for him to take his brothers wife. He wynked not at the whoredom of Herode, although he wer a kyng of greate power, but boldely reproved hym for his wicked and abhominable livyng, although for thesame he lost his hedde. But he would rather suffre deathe then see God so dishonored by the breakyng of his holy precept, then to suffre whoredome to be unrebuked, even in a kyng. If whoredome had been but a pastyme, a daliaunce and a thyng not to bee passed of (as many coumpt it now a daies), truely Jhon had been more then twyse madde, if he would have had the displeasure of a king, if he would have been cast into prison and lost his hedde for a trifle. But Jhon knewe right well how filthy, stynkyng and abhominable the synne of whoredome is in the sight of God; therefore would not he leave it unrebuked, no, not in a kyng. If whoredome bee not lawfull in a kyng, neither is it lawfull in a subject. If whoredome bee not lawfull in a publique officer, neither is it lawfull in a private persone. If it bee not lawfull neither in kyng, nor subjecte, neither in common officer, nor private persone, truely then is it lawfull in no man, nor woman, of whatsoever degree or age thei bee. Furthermore, in the Actes of the Apostles, we reade that when the apostles and elders with the whole congregacion were gathered together to pacifie the hartes of the faithfull dwellyng at Antioche, whiche were disquieted through the false doctryne of certain Jewishe preachers, thei sente worde to the brethren that it semed good to the Holy Ghost and to them to charge them with no more then with necessary thynges: emong other, thei willed them to abstein from idolatry and fornicacion, from which, said thei, if ye kepe your selfes, ye shal do wel.

Note here how these holy and blessed fathers of Christes churche would charge the congregacion with no mo thynges then wer necessary. Marke also how emong those thynges from the whiche thei commaunded the brethren of Antioche to abstein, fornicacion and whoredom is numbred. It is, therfore, necessary, by the determinacion and consent of the Holy Ghost and the apostles and elders, with the whole congregacion, that as from idolatry and supersticion, so likewise we must abstein from fornicacion and whoredom. Is it necessary unto salvacion to abstein from idolatry? So is it to abstein from whoredom. Is there any nigher waie to leade unto dampnacion then to bee an idolater? No; even so, neither is there a nerer waie to dampnacion then to be a fornicator and an whoremonger.

Now, where are those people whiche so lightly esteme breakyng of wedlocke, whoredom, fornicacion and adultery? It is necessary, saieth the Holy Ghost, the blessed apostles, the elders, with the whole congregacion of Christ – it is necessary to salvacion, saie thei, to abstein from whoredom. If it bee necessary unto salvacion, then wo be to them whiche, neglectyng their salvacion, geve their myndes to so filthye and stinkyng sinne, to so wicked vice, to suche detestable abhominacion.

[The Second Part of the Sermon against Adultrie

You have ben taught in the first parte of thys sermon againste adultrie howe that vice at thys daie reygneth mooste above all other vices; and what is mente by thys woorde 'adulterie,' and how Holy Scripture disswadeth from doyng that fylthy sinne; and fynally what corrupcion commeth to mans soule through the synne of adultrie. Nowe to procede further,] lette us heare what the blessed apostle Sainct Paule saith to this matter. Writyng to the Romaynes, he hath these wordes: Let us cast awaie the woorkes of darkenes, and put on the armours of light. Let us walke honestly, as it wer, in the daie tyme, not in eatyng and drynkyng, neither in chambrynges and wantonnesse, neither in striefe and enviyng, but put ye on the lorde Jesus Christ, and make not provision for the fleshe, to fulfill the lustes of it. Here the holy apostle exhorteth us to caste awaie the workes of darkenesse, whiche, emong other, he calleth gluttonous eatyng, drinkyng, chamberyng and wantonnesse, whiche all are ministeries unto that vice and preparacions to induce and bring in the filthy synne of the fleshe. He calleth theim the deedes and woorkes of darkenes, not onely because thei are customably dooen in darkenesse, or in the night

tyme – for every one that doth evill hateth the light, neither commeth he
to the light, least his workes should be reproved – but that thei lead
the right waie unto that utter darkenesse, where wepyng and gnashyng of
teethe shalbee. And he saieth in another place of thesame Epistle: Thei
that are in the fleshe cannot please God. We are debtors to the fleshe, not
that wee should live after the fleshe, for if ye live after the fleshe, ye
shall dye. Agayn he saieth: Flye from whoredome, for every synne that a
manne committeth is without his bodye, but whosoever committeth
whoredome synneth against his awne body. Dooe ye not knowe that youre
membres are the temple of the Holy Ghoste whiche is in you, whom
also ye have of God, and ye are not youre awne? For ye are derely bought;
glorifie God in your bodies &c. And a litle before, he saieth: Dooe ye
not knowe that your bodies are the membres of Christe? Shall I then take
the membres of Christ and make them the membres of an whore? God
forbid. Do ye not knowe that he whiche cleveth to an whore is made one
body with her? There shalbee two in one fleshe, saith he, but he that
cleveth to the Lorde is one spirite. What godly reasons doth the blessed
apostle S. Paule bryng furth here to disswade us from whoredom and
al unclennesse! Your membres, saieth he, are the temple of the Holy
Ghoste, whiche whosoever doth defile, God wil destroy him, as saieth S.
Paule. If we be the temple of the Holy Ghoste, how unfittyng then is it to
drive that Holy Spirite from us through whoredome and in his place to
set the wicked spirites of unclennesse and fornicacion, and to be joyned,
and do service to theim! Ye are derely bought, saieth he; therefore,
glorifie God in your bodies. Christ, that innocent lambe of God, hath
bought us from the servitude of the devil not with corruptible gold and
silver, but with his most precious and dere harte bloudde. To what intente?
That wee should fall again unto our olde unclennesse and abhominable
livyng? Naie verely: but that wee should serve hym all the daies of our life
in holinesse and righteousnesse; that we should glorifie hym in our bodies
by puritie and clennesse of life. He declareth also that our bodies are the
membres of Christe. How unsemely a thyng is it, then, to cease to bee
incorporate and one with Christe, and through whoredome to be joyned
and made all one with an whore! What greater dishonor or injurie can
we do to Christ then to take awaie from hym the membres of his body,
and to joyne them to whores, devils and wicked spirites? And what more
dishonoure can we do to our selfes then through unclennesse to lose so
excellent a dignitie and fredome, and to become bonde slaves and miserable
captives to the spirites of darkenesse? Lette us, therefore, considre first
the glory of Christe, and then our state, our dignitie and fredome wherein
God hath set us by gevyng us his Holy Spirite, and lette us valeauntly

defende thesame against Sathan and all his craftie assautes, that Christ maie
bee honored and that we loose not our libertie, but still remain in one
spirite with hym.

Moreover, in his Epistle to the Ephesians, the blessed apostle willeth us
to bee so pure and free from adultery, fornicacion and all unclennesse
that we not once name them emong us, as it becommeth sainctes, nor
filthinesse, nor foolishe talkyng, nor jestyng, whiche are not commely, but
rather gevyng of thankes. For this ye knowe, saieth he, that no whoremonger, either uncleane person or coveteous persone, whiche is an idolater,
hath any inheritaunce in the kyngdome of Christe and God. And that
we should remembre to bee holy, pure and free from all unclennesse, the
holy apostle calleth us sainctes, because we are sanctified and made holy
in the bloud of Christe through the Holy Ghoste. Now, if we bee sainctes,
what have we to do with the maners of the heathen? Saincte Peter saieth:
as he whiche called you is holy, even so bee ye holy also in all your
conversacion, because it is written: Be ye holy, for I am holy.

Hetherto have we heard how grevous a synne fornicacion and whoredome is, and howe greatly God doth abhorre it throughout the whole
Scripture. Howe can it any otherwyse be then a synne of moste abhominacion, seyng it once may not be named emonge the Christians, muche
lesse it may in any poynt be committed. And surely if we would weyghe
the greatnes of this synne and consydre it in the right kynde, we shoulde
fynde the synne of whoredom to be that most fylthy lake, foule puddle
and stynkyng synke, wherinto all kyndes of synnes and evils flow, wher also
they have their restynge place and abydinge. For hath not the adulterer a
pryde in hys whoredome? As the Wiseman sayeth: They are glad when
they have done evyl, and rejoyse in thinges that are starke naught. Is not
the adulterer also ydle, and delighteth in no godly exercise, but onely
in that his most filthy and beastly pleasure? Is not his minde abstracte and
utterlye drawen awaye from all vertuous studyes and fruicteful labours,
and onely gyven to carnall imaginacions? Doth not the whoremonger geve
his mynde to glottonye, that he maye be the more apte to serve hys
lustes and carnall pleasures? Doeth not the adulterer geve hys mynde to
covetuousnes and to pollyng and pillyng of other, that he maye be the
moreable to mainteyne his harlottes and whores, and to contynue in hys
filthye and unlawfull love? Swelleth he not also with envye agaynst other,
fearynge that his preye shoulde be allured and taken awaye from hym?
Agayne, is he not yrefull and replenished with wrath and displeasure even
agaynste his beste beloved, if at any tyme his beastly and devyllishe
requeste be letted? What synne or kynde of synne is it that is not joyned
with fornicacion and whoredom? It is a monstre of manye heades: it

receyveth all kyndes of vices and refuseth all kyndes of vertues. If one severall synne bryngeth dampnacion, what is to be thought of that synne which is accompanyed with all evyls, and hath waytynge on it whatsoever is hatefull to God, dampnable to man and pleasunt to Sathan?

Great is the dampnacion that hangeth over the heades of fornicatours and adulterers. What shal I speake of other incommodities which issue and flowe out of this stinkynge puddell of whoredome! Is not that treasure which before all other is most regarded of honest persons, the good fame and name of man and woman, loste through whoredome? What patrimony, what substaunce, what goodes, what riches doth whoredome shortly consume and brynge to naughte! What valiauntnes and strengthe is many times made weake and destroyed with whoredome? What wyt is so fyne that is not doted and defaced throughe whoredome? What beautye, althoughe it were never so excellent, is not obscured through whoredome?

Is not whoredome an enemy to the pleasaunte flour of youth? And bringeth it not gray heares and olde age before the tyme? What gyft of nature, although it were never so precious, is not corrupted with whoredom? Come not the Frenche pockes, with other diverse diseases, of whoredome? From whence come so many bastardes and misbegotten children, to the hyghe displeasure of God and dishonoure of holy wedlocke, but of whoredome? How many consume all their substaunce and goodes, and at the laste falle into suche extreme poverty that afterward they steale and so are hanged, through whoredome! What contencion and manslaughter commeth of whoredom! How many maydens be deflowred, how many wyfes corrupted, howe many wydowes defyled, through whoredom! How much is the publique weale impoveryshed and troubled through whoredom! How muche is Gods Worde contempned and depraved by whoredome and whoremongers!

Of this vice commeth a great parte of the divorces whiche now a dayes be so commonly accustomed and used by mens private aucthoritie, to the great displeasure of God and the breache of the most holy knotte and bonde of matrimonye. For when this most detestable sinne is once crept into the breaste of the adulterer so that he is entangled with unlawfull and unchaste love, streyghtwayes hys true and lawfull wyfe is despyced, her presence is abhorred, her companye stynketh and is lothsome, whatsoever she doth is despraysed, there is no quietnes in the house so longe as she is in sighte: therefore, to make shorte tale, muste she awaye, for her husbande can brooke her no lenger. Thus, through whoredome, is the honest and innocent wyfe put awaye, and an harlot received in her stede; and in lyke sorte, it happeneth many tymes in the wyfe towardes her husbande. O abhominacion! Christ, oure saviour, very God and man, commynge to restore the lawe of hys heavenly Father unto the righte sense, understandinge and meanynge, emong other thinges refourmed the abuse of this law of God. For where as the Jewes used, of a long sufferaunce, by custome, to put away their wyfes at their pleasure for every cause, Christ, correctyng that evyl custome, did teache that if any man put awaye his wyfe and marieth an other, for any cause, except onely for adultery, which then was death by the law, he was an adulterer, and forced also hys wyfe, so divorced, to committe adulterye, if she were joyned to any other man, and the man also, so joyned with her, to committe adultery.

In what case, then are those adulterers which for the love of an whore put awaye their true and lawfull wyfe, againste all lawe, ryght, reason and conscience? O, dampnable is the state wherin thei stande! Swifte destruction shall fall on them, if they repent not and amende not, for God wyll not ever suffer holy wedlocke thus to be dishonoured, hated and despyced. He will once punishe this carnal and licencious maner of living, and cause that his holy ordinaunce shalbe had in reverence and honoure. For surely wedlocke, as the apostle saieth, is honorable emonge all men, and the bed undefyled, but whoremongers and fornicatours God wyll judge, that is to saye, punishe and condempne. But to what purpose is this labour taken to describe and set furth the greatnes of the synne of whoredome and the incommodities that issue and flowe out of it, seynge that breath and toungue shall soner fayle any man then he shall or maye be able to set it out, according to the abhominacion and haynousnes therof? Notwithstandynge, thys is spoken to the entent that all men shoulde flee whoredome and lyve in the feare of God. God graunt that it maye not be spoken in vayne.

[The Thirde Part of the Sermon against Adulterie

In the second part of this sermon againste adulterie that was laste red, you have learned howe earnestlie the Scripture warneth us to avoyde the synne of adulterie and to enbrace clennes of lyfe; and that throughe adulterie wee fall into all kyndes of synnes and are made bonde slaves to the Devell; thorow clennes of lyfe wee are made membres of Christe; and finally howe farre adultery bringeth a man from al goodnes and driveth him headlong into al vices, mischief and miserie.] Now wyll I declare unto you, in ordre, with what grevous punishmentes God in tymes paste plagued adulterye, and howe certayne worldly princes also dyd punishe it, that ye maye perceave that whoredom and fornicacion be synnes no lesse detestable in the sight of God and of all good men then I have hytherto uttered.

In the fyrst boke of Moyses we reade that when mankynd began to be
multiplyed upon the yearth, the men and women gave their myndes so
greatlye to carnall delectacion and fylthy pleasure thay they lyved without
all feare of God. God, seynge this their beastlye and abhominable livynge,
and perceyvynge that they amended not, but rather encreased dayly more
and more in their synfull and uncleane maners, repented that he ever
had made man, and to shewe how greatly he abhorred adultery, whoredome, fornicacion and all unclennes he made all the fountaynes of the
depe yearth to burste out and the sluces of heaven to be opened so that the
rayne came downe upon the yearth by the space of forty dayes and forty
nyghtes, and by thys meanes destroyed the whole world and all mankynde,
eighte persons onely excepted, that is to saye, Noe, the preacher of righteousnes, as Sainct Peter calleth hym, and his wyfe, his three sonnes and
their wyfes. O what a grevous plague dyd God cast here upon all
lyvyng creatures for the synne of whordome! For the which, God toke
vengeaunce not onely of man, but also of beastes, foules and all lyvynge
creatures. Manslaughter was committed before, yet was not the worlde
destroyed for that, but for whoredome all the worlde, fewe onely excepte,
was overflowed with waters and so peryshed: an example worthye to be
remembred, that ye maye learne to feare God.

We reade agayne that for the fylthye synne of uncleannes Sodome and
Gomorre and the other cytyes nyghe unto them were destroyed with
fyre and brymstone from heaven, so that there was neither man, woman,
chylde, nor beaste, nor yet anye thynge that grewe upon the yearth there
lefte undestroyed. Whose harte trembleth not at the hearynge of this
hystorie? Who is so drowned in whoredome and uncleannes that wil not
nowe for ever after leave this abhominable livynge, seynge that God so
grevously punysheth uncleannes, to rayne fyre and brymstone from heaven,
to destroye whole cyties, to kyll man, woman and chylde, and all other
livynge creatures there abydyng, to consume wyth fyre all that ever grewe?
What can be more manyfest tokens of Gods wrathe and vengeaunce
against uncleannes and impuritie of lyfe? Marke this hystorye, good people,
and feare the vengeaunce of God. Do we not reade also that God dyd
smyte Pharao and his house with great plagues, because that he ungodly
desyred Sara, the wyfe of Abraham? Lykewyse reade we of Abimelech,
Kynge of Gerar, although he touched her not by carnal knowledge. These
plagues and punyshmentes did God caste upon fylthye and uncleane
persones before the law was geven, the lawe of nature onely reignynge in
the hartes of men, to declare howe greate love he had to matrimonye,
and agayne, howe muche he abhorred adulterye, fornicacion and all uncleannes. And when the lawe that forbad whoredome was geven by Moyses

to the Jewes, dyd not God commaunde that the transgressours thereof
shoulde be put to death? The wordes of the lawe be these: Who so committeth adulterye with anye mans wyfe shal dye the death, bothe the
man and the woman, because he hath broken wedlocke wyth hys neighbours wyfe. In the lawe also it was commaunded that a damosell and
a man taken together in whoredome should be both stooned to death. In
an other place we also reade that God commaunded Moyses to take all
the heade rulers and princes of the people, and to hang them upon gybbets
openly that every man might see them, because they eyther committed
or dyd not punishe whoredom. Agayne, dyd not God sende suche a plague
emonge the people for fornication and uncleannes that they dyed in one
daye three and twenty thousande?

I passe over for lacke of tyme many other historyes of the Holy Byble
which declare the grevous vengeaunce and heavy displeasure of God
agaynste whoremongers and adulterers. Certes, this extreme punyshment
appoynted of God sheweth evidently how greatly God hateth whoredom.
And let us not doubte but that God at thys present abhorreth all maner
of uncleannes no lesse then he did in the olde lawe, and wyll undoubtedly
punishe it, both in this worlde and in the worlde to come. For he is a
God that can abyde no wyckednes: therefore, oughte it to be eschewed of
all that tendre the glorye of God and the salvacion of theyr awne soules.

Sainct Paule saieth: all these thynges are written for oure example and to
teache us the feare of God and the obedience to his holy lawe. For if
God spared not the naturall braunches, neither wyll he spare us that be
but graftes, if we commit lyke offence. If God destroyed many thousandes
of people, many cyties, yea the whole worlde, for whoredome, let us not
flatter oure selfes and thinke we shal eschape free and without punishment.
For he hath promised in hys holy lawe to sende moste grevous plagues
upon them that transgresse his holy commaundementes.

Thus have we hearde howe God punisheth the synne of adulterye; let us
nowe heare certayn lawes which the cyvile magistrates devised, in dyvers
countrays, for the punishment therof, that we maye learne how unclennes
hath ever bene detested in all well ordered cyties and common wealthes
and emonge all honeste persons. The lawe emong the Lepreians was thys:
that when any were taken in adultery, they were bound and caried three
daies through the cytie, and afterward, as longe as they lyved, were they
despiced, and with shame and confusyon reputed as persones desolate
of all honestye. Emonge the Locrensians the adulterers had bothe theyr
eyes thrust oute. The Romayns, in tymes paste, punyshed whoredome
sometyme by fyre, sometyme by swourde. If a man emonge the Egyptians
had bene taken in adulterye, the lawe was that he shoulde openly in the

presence of all the people be scourged naked with whippes unto the
number of a thousande strypes. The woman that was taken with hym had
her nose cut of whereby she was knowen ever after to be an whore, and
therfore to be abhorred of all men. Emong the Arabians they that were
taken in adulterye had theyr heades striken from their bodyes. The Athenians punyshed whoredome by death in lyke maner. So lykewyse dyd the
barbarous Tartarians. Emong the Turkes, even at thys day, they that bee
taken in adultery, bothe man and woman, are stoned streightewayes to
death without mercy. Thus se we what godly actes were devised in tymes
paste of the high powers for the puttyng awaye of whoredome, and for
the mainteynyng of holy matrimony and pure conversacion. And the
aucthors of these actes were no Christians, but heathen, yet were they so
enflammed withe the love of honestye and purenes of lyfe that for the
maintenaunce and conservacion of that, they made godly statutes, suffering
neyther fornicacion, nor adultery to reigne in their realmes unpunished.
Christ sayde to the people: The Ninivites shall ryse at the judgement with
thys nacion (meanyng the unfaythful Jewes) and shal condempne them.
For they repented at the preachyng of Jonas, but beholde, sayeth he,
a greater then Jonas is here (meanynge hymselfe), and yet they repent not.
Shall not, thynke you, likewise the Locrensians, Arabians, Athenians,
with suche other, ryse up at the judgement and condempne us, for asmuche
as they ceased from whoredome at the commaundement of man, and we
have the law and manifest preceptes of God, and yet forsake we not
our filthy conversacion? Truly, truly, it shalbe easier at the daye of judgement to these heathen then to us, except we repent and amende. For
althoughe death of body semeth to us a grevous punyshment in this worlde
for whoredome, yet is that payn nothynge, in comparison of the grevous
tormentes whiche adulterers, fornicatours and all uncleane persons shall
suffer after thys lyfe. For all suche shalbe excluded and shut out of the
kingdome of heaven, as S. Paule saieth: Be not deceived, for neyther
whoremongers, nor worshippers of images, nor adultrers, nor softelinges,
nor sodomites, nor thefes, nor covetous persons, nor dronkards, nor
cursed speakers, nor pyllers shall inherite the kyngdom of God. And S.
Jhon in hys Revelacion saieth that whoremongers shall have their parte
with murderers, sorcerers, enchaunters, liars, ydolaters and such other
in the lake whiche burneth with fyre and brimstone, which is the seconde
death. The punyshmente of the bodye, although it be death, hath an
ende, but the punishment of the soule, which S. Jhon calleth the second
death, is everlasting. There shalbe fyre and brimstone; there shall be
wepinge and gnashing of tethe; the worme that shall there gnawe the
conscience of the dampned shall never dye. O whose hart distilleth not

even droppes of bloud to heare and consydre these thinges? If we tremble
and shake at the hearyng and naming of these paynes, oh, what shal they
do that shall feele them, that shall suffer theim, yea, and ever shal suffer,
worldes without ende? God have mercy upon us. Who is now so drowned
in synne and past all godlynes that he wyll set more by a fylthy and
stynkyng pleasure, whiche sone passeth away, then by the losse of everlasting glory? Againe, who will so geve himselfe to the lustes of the fleshe
that he feareth nothynge at all the paynes of hell fyre?

But let us heare howe we maye eschewe the synne of whoredome and
adultery, that we maye walke in the feare of God and bee free from those
moste grevous and intollerable tormentes whiche abyde all uncleane
persons. To avoyde fornicacion, adultery and all unclennes, let us provide
that above all thynges we maye kepe oure hartes pure and cleane from
all evill thoughtes and carnal lustes. For if that be once infected and corrupte, we fall hedlonge into all kynde of ungodlynes. Thys shal we easly do,
if, when we fele inwardly that Sathan, oure olde enemy, tempteth us
unto whoredom, we by no meanes consente to hys craftye suggestions,
but valiauntly resiste and withstande hym by stronge fayth in the Woorde
of God, objectinge agaynst hym alwayes in oure harte this commaundemente of God: Scriptum est, non moechaberis. It is written, thou shalt not
commit whoredome. It shall be good also for us ever to lyve in the feare
of God, and to set before oure eyes the grevous threateninges of God
agaynste all ungodly synners, and to consider in oure mynde howe fylthye,
beastly and shorte that pleasure is, wherunto Sathan moveth us, and
agayn, how the payne appoynted for that sinne is intollerable and everlasting. Moreover, to use a temperaunce and sobrietie in eatyng and drynkyng, to eschewe uncleane communicacion, to avoyde al fylthy company, to
flee ydlenes, to delight in readynge Holy Scripture, to watche in godly
prayers and vertuouse meditacions, and at all tymes to exercise some godly
travayles shall helpe greatly unto the eschewynge of whoredome.

And here are all degrees to be monyshed, whether they be maryed or
unmaryed, to love chastitie and clennes of lyfe. For the maryed are bounde
by the lawe of God so purely to love one an other that neyther of them
seke any straunge love. The man muste onley cleve to hys wyfe, and
the wyfe agayne onely to her husband: they muste so delighte one in an
others companye that none of them covit any other. And as they are
bounde thus to lyve together in al godlines and honesty, solikewyse is their
duetye vertuously to brynge up their chyldren and to provide that they
fall not into Sathans snare, nor into any unclennes, but that they come pure
and honeste unto holy wedlocke, when tyme requyreth. So likewyse
ought all masters and rulers to provide that no whoredome, nor any poynte

of unclennes be used emonge their servauntes. And agayne, they that are
single and feele in theim selfes that they cannot live without the company
of a woman, let them get wifes of theyr awne and so lyve godly together.
For it is better to mary then to burne. And to avoyde fornicacion, saieth
the apostle, lette every man have hys awne wyfe, and everye woman her
awne husbande. Finally, all suche as feele in themselfes a sufficiency
and habilitie, throughe the operacion of Gods spirite, to leede a sole and
contynent lyfe, let them prayse God for his gifte and seke all meanes
possible to maynteyne thesame: as by readyng of Holy Scriptures, by godly
meditations, by continuall prayers and suche other vertuous exercises. If
we all on this wyse wyll endevour our selfes to eschewe fornicacion,
adultery and all unclennes, and leade oure lyfes in all godlynes and honestye, servynge God with a pure and cleane harte and glorifiynge hym in
oure bodies by leadynge an innocente lyfe, we maye be sure to bee in the
numbre of those of whome oure savioure Christe speaketh in the Gospell
on this maner: Blessed are the pure in harte, for they shall see God: to
whome alone be all glory, honour, rule and power, worldes withoute ende.
  Amen.

NOTES

174 *braste*: a form of 'burst.'
     thys vice ... laughed at: Cf Thomas Becon's preface to Heinrich Bullinger
     The Christen State of Matrimony tr Miles Coverdale (London 1543):
     'Certes it is a thynge much to be wondered at, that whoredome shoulde
     growe up into suche heyght, among them, that professe the fruytes
     of the spirite. But what marvel ys it, seynge that whoredome nowe a
     dayes is become, but a lusty courageous pastyme of youth, & reputed
     almoste for no synne at all' (sig Bvi').
     entreat of: discuss.
     thou shalte not commit adultery: Exod 20:14.
     commixcion: copulation.
175 *there shalbee no whore ... sonnes of Israell*: Deut 23:17.
     whoremongers: AV 'sodomite'; Vg 'scortator.'
     ye have heard ... in his harte: Matt 5:27–8.
     Ye are my frendes ... commaunde you: John 15:14.
     heare and understand ... whiche defile a man: Matt 15:10–11, 18–19.
176 *whiche is the truthe and cannot lye*: John 14:6; Titus 1:2.
     Go thy waie ... no more: John 8:11.
     rewarde of synne ... deathe: Rom 6:23.
     he that committeth ... devill: 1 John 3:8.

Every one that committeth ... servaunt of syn: John 8:34; Rom 6:16.
S. Jhon Baptist ... rebuked Kyng Herode: Matt 14:3–12.
Actes of the Apostles: Acts 15:22–9.

177 *from which ... ye shal do wel*: Acts 15:29.
Let us cast ... lustes of it: Rom 13:12–14.
armours: military equipment in the broadest sense.
chambrynges: sexual lewdness.
ministeries: a form of 'ministries.'

178 *every one that doth evill ... shalbee*: John 3:20; Matt 13:42, 50.
Thei that are in ... ye shall dye: Rom 8:12–13.
Flye ... bodies &c: 1 Cor 6:18–20.
Dooe ye not knowe ... one spirite: 1 Cor 6:15–17.
members ... destroy him: 1 Cor 2:16–17.
If we be the temple ... service to theim: Cf Bullinger *The Christen State of Matrimony*: 'Is it not an horryble defylyng of gods temple / to set that vycious harlot Venus / euen in the place where god shuld reigne with his spirite / & to be ioyned & do seruice vnto her with body & soule?' (f xxvᵛ).
not with corruptible ... harte bloudde: 1 Pet 1:18–19.
serve hym ... our life: Luke 1:74–5; Isa 38:20.

179 *free from adultery ... Christe and God*: Eph 5:3–5.
any inheritance: Gal 5:19–21, the marginal gloss, alludes to an analogue that is not quoted.
apostle calleth us sainctes: 1 Cor 6:9–11.
as he whiche called ... for I am holy: 1 Pet 1:15, quoting Lev 11:44 and 19:2.
They are glad ... starke naught: Prov 2:14 (Vg 'Qui laetantur cum malefecerint, Et exsultant in rebus pessimis').
abstracte: detached.
pollyng and pillyng: literally, making bare of hair and skin, ie plundering and extorting.

180 *doted*: decayed.
How many consume ... through whoredome: Cf *The Christen State of Matrimony*: 'How many a man hath consumed all his substaunce & goodes with harlottes / and at the last hath bene hanged / drawned or headed?' (f xxviᵛ).

181 *Christ, correctyng ... to committe adultery*: Matt 19:8–9.
case: plight.
surely wedlocke ... God wyll judge: Heb 13:4.

182 *fyrst boke of Moyses*: Gen 6 and 7.
the preacher of righteousnes: 2 Pet 2:5.
Manslaughter ... before: Gen 4:8.
Sodome and Gomorre: Gen 19:1–29.
God dyd smyte ... wyfe of Abraham?: Gen 12:17.
Abimelech: Gen 20.

183 *Who so committeth ... neighbours wyfe*: Lev 20:10.
　　In the lawe ... stooned to death: Deut 22:23–4.
　　In an other place ... punishe whoredom: Num 25:1–4.
　　gybbets: gallows.
　　dyd not God ... three and twenty thousande: Num 25:9; 1 Cor 10:8.
　　a God that can abyde no wyckednes: Ps 5:4.
　　tendre: cherish.
　　all these thynges ... example: 1 Cor 10:6, 11.
　　if God spared ... braunches: Rom 11:21–2.
　　eschape: escape.
　　lawes which the cyvile magistrates devised: The homily takes, almost verbatim,
　　　the following information on the Lepreians, the Locrensians, and the
　　　Romans from Coverdale's translation of *The Christen State of Matrimony*
　　　chapter 11, which is concerned with the methods by which various
　　　secular authorities punished adultery. It takes, again almost verbatim, its
　　　information on the Egyptians, Arabians, Athenians, Tartarians, and
　　　Turks from Becon's preface to Bullinger's work. The customs of the first
　　　four nations are canvassed in Andreas Tiraquellus *De legibus connubialibus
　　　et iure maritali* (Paris 1524) ff cxxxviiiʳ–cxrᵛ; the customs of the last four
　　　appear in Joannes Boemus *Repertorium librorum trium ... de omnium
　　　gentium ritibus* (Paris 1520) II, 1.10.11.
184 *The Ninivites ... yet they repent not*: Matt 12:41.
　　Be not deceived ... kyngdom of God: 1 Cor 6:9–10; Gal 5:19–21; Eph 5:5.
　　softelinges: effeminate men.
　　whoremongers ... seconde death: Rev 21:8.
　　wepinge ... never dye: Matt 13:42; Luke 3:17; Isa 66:24.
186 *For it is better ... her awne husbande*: 1 Cor 7:9, 2.
　　Blessed ... shall see God: Matt 5:8.

TEXTUAL APPARATUS

174 An Homelie of] A Sermon agaynste *1559, 1623*. adultery] or breakyng of
　　wedlocke *added 1559, 1623*. publique] common *1549*. height] heigth *1549, 1559*.
175 commixcion] or joynyng together *added 1559, 1623*. whoremongers] whore-
　　monger *1623*. all unclennesse] all other unclennesse *1623*. precept] or
　　commaundement *added 1559, 1623*. was saied] is saied *1549*. of the old] of
　　old *1623*. havyng a commaundement] havyng commaundement *1623*. lech-
176 erie] filthinesse *1623*. Christe, whiche] Christe, who *1623*. mansion] house
　　1559, 1623. of greate power] or power *1623*. precept] or commaundement
　　added 1559; and commandement *added 1623*. and a thyng not] and not *1623*.
　　filthy, stynkyng] filthy and stynkng *1623*. publique] or common *added*

177 *1559, 1623.* is it lawfull] is it lauful *1559.* Is it necessary] It is necessary *1549, 1623.* an whoremonger] a whoremonger *1623.* saie thei] saie the *1547.* vice, to suche] vice, and to suche *1549.* disswadeth] or discounsayled *added 1559, 1623.* lette us heare] But lette us heare *1547.* all are ministeries] *1547;* all are ministers *1549;* are all mynysters *1559, 1623.* customably dooen in] customa-
178 bly in *1623.* debtors to ... not that] debtors not to ... that *1559, 1623.* Flye] flee *1623.* reasons] words *1623.* disswade] or discounseyle *added 1559;* and discounsell *added 1623.* unto our olde] into our olde *1623.* incorporate and one] or imbodyed *added after* incorporate *1559;* or imbodyed and made one *added 1623.* joyned] enjoyned *1559, 1623.* injurie] injury *1549.* and then
179 our state] and then our estate *1559;* then our estate *1623.* libertie] or freedom *added 1559, 1623.* either uncleane] neither uncleane *1623.* holy in] holy by *1623.* in all your] in your *1623.* once may not be] once may not once be *1623.* weyghe] weight *1559.* wherinto] whereunto *1559, 1623.* abstracte] pluckte *1559, 1623.* vertuous] vertous *1547;* verteous *1549.* carnall imaginacions] carnall and fleshly imaginacion *1559, 1623.* It is a monstre] Is it a monstre *1547.*
180 patrimony] or livelehode *added 1559;* or livelode *added 1623.* valiauntnes] valiauntes *1547, 1549.* doted] besotted *1623.* obscured] disfigured *1559, 1623.* the Frenche pockes, with other diverse] many foule and most loathsome *1623.* publique] and commune *added 1559, 1623.* depraved by] depraved through *1623.* despraysed] desprapied *1547.* tale, muste she awaye] worke,
181 shee must away *1623.* innocent] harmelesse *1559, 1623.* used, of a long] used, a long *1623.* those adulterers] these adulterers *1623.* O, dampnable ... state] O, how dampnable ... estate *1623.* not ever suffer] not suffer *1623.* carnal] fleshelye *1559, 1623.* his holy] this holy *1549, 1623.* incommodities] discommodities *1623.* grevous] grevos *1549.* plagued] plauged *1559.* and
182 of] to *1623.* carnall delectacion] fleshely delight *1559, 1623.* repented that he ever] repented that ever he *1623.* plague] plauge *1559.* also of beastes] of all beastes *1623.* with fyre] by fyre *1623.* Do we not reade] Do you not reade *1623.* plagues] plages *1559.* matrimonye] or wedlock *added 1559;* and wed-
183 locke *added 1623.* transgressours] breakers *1559, 1623.* no wyckednes] none wyckednes *1559.* salvacion] salvacions *1549.* transgresse] or breake *added 1559, 1623.* in dyvers] in their *1623.* reputed] coumpted *1559, 1623.* desolate] voyde *1559, 1623.* Locrensians] Locreusyans *1547, 1549.* had bothe] have
184 bothe *1559, 1623.* ever after] even after *1547, 1549.* streightewayes] streigth-wayes *1549.* Thus se we] Thus we see *1623.* matrimony] or wedlock *added 1559, 1623.* but heathen] but the heathen *1623.* conservacion] or kepynge up *added 1559, 1623.* nor adultery] or adultery *1623.* meanynge hymselfe] meamyng himself *1549.* Locrensians] Locreusians *1547, 1549.* ryse up at] ryse up in *1623.* from whoredome] from the whoredome *1623.* preceptes] and commaundementes *added 1559, 1623.* whoredome] woredome *1623.*
185 softelinges] effeminate persons *1623.* by a fylthy] by fylthy *1623.* To avoyde] Now to avoyde *1623.* objectinge] aleadgynge *1559, 1623.* Sathan moveth]

Sathan continuallie stirreth and moveth *1623*. Holy Scripture] Holy Scriptures *1623*. vertuouse] verteouse *1549*. solikewyse is] solikewyse it is *1623*.
186   and to provide] and provide *1623*. operacion] workynge *1559, 1623*. by
leadynge] by the leadynge *1623*. innocente] and harmelesse *added 1559, 1623*.

12 An Homelie agaynst Contencion and Braulynge

Thys daye, good Christen people, shalbe declared unto you the unprofit-ablenes and shamfull unhonesty of contencion, stryfe and debate: to the entente that when you shall se, as it were in a table paynted before your eyes, the evilfavorednes and deformitie of this most detestable vice, your stomackes maye be moved to ryse agaynst it, and to detest and abhorre that synne which is so much to be hated and so pernicious and hurtful to al men. But emong all kyndes of contencion, none is more hurtfull then is contencion in matters of religion.

Eschewe, saieth Sainct Paul, foolish and unlearned questions, knowyng that they breed strife. It becommeth not the servaunt of God to fighte or stryve, but to be meke towarde all men. This contencion and strife was in Saincte Paules tyme emonge the Corinthians, and is at this time emonge us Englishe men. For to many there be which upon the alebenches or other places delight to propounde certayne questions, not so muche per-teyning to edificacion as to vainglory and ostentacion: and so unsoberly to reason and dispute that when neyther partye wil geve place to other, they fall to chydynge and contencion, and somtyme from hote wordes to further inconvenience. Sainct Paul could not abyde to heare emong the Corinthians these wordes of discorde or dissencion: I holde of Paule, I of Cephas, and I of Apollo. What would he then say, if he hearde these woordes of contencion, whiche be now almoste in every mans mouth: he is a Pharisei, he is a gospeler, he is of the new sorte, he is of the olde faythe, he is a new broched brother, he is a good catholique father, he is a papist, he is an heretique? Oh how the churche is divided! Oh how the cyties be cutte and mangled! Oh how the coote of Christ, that was without seame, is all to-rent and torne! Oh body misticall of Christe: where is that holy and happy unitie, out of the which whosoever is, he is not in Christ? If one membre be pulled from another, where is the body? If the body be drawen from the head, where is the lyfe of the body? We cannot be joynted to Christ our head, except we be glued with concord and charitie, one to another. For he that is not in this unitie is not of the churche of Christ, whiche is a congregacion or unitie together, and not a division.

Sainct Paul saieth that as long as emulacion, contencion and factions be emonge us, we be carnal, and walke according to the fleshly man. And Sainct James saieth: If you have bitter emulacion and contencion in your hartes, glory not of it, for where as contencion is, there is inconstancy and al evill deades. And why do we not heare S. Paule, which prayeth us, where as he might commaund us, saiyng, I beseche you, in the name of our lord Jesus Christ, that you wil speake al one thinge and that there be no dissencion emong you, but that you wil be one whole body, of one mynd and of one opinion in the truth. If his desire be reasonable and honest, why do we not graunt it? If his request be for our profit, why do we refuse it? And if we list not to heare hys peticion of praier, yet let us heare his exhortacion, wher he saith: I exhorte you that you walke, as it becommeth the vocacion in the whiche you be called, with all submission and mekenes, with lenitie and softenes of mynde, bearynge one another by charitye, studiyng to kepe the unitie of the spirit by the bond of peace: for there is one body, one spirit, one fayth, one baptisme. There is, he saieth, but one body, of the whiche he can be no lively membre that is at variaunce with the other membres. There is one spirit, whiche joyneth and knitteth all thynges in one. And how can this one spirit reigne in us, when we emonge oure selfes be divided? There is but one fayth, and howe can we then saye, he is of the olde fayth, and he is of the new faythe? There is but one baptisme, and then shall not all they whiche be baptised be one? Contencion causeth division, wherfore it oughte not to be emong Christians, whome one faith and baptisme joyneth in an unitie. But if we contempne Saincte Paules requeste and exhortacion, yet at the least let us regarde hys obtestacion, in the whiche he doeth very earnestly charge us and, as I may so speake, conjure us in thys fourme and maner: If there be any consolacion in Christe, if there be any comforte of love, if you have any communion of the spirite, if you have any bowelles of pitie and compassion, fulfyll my joye, beyng all like affected, havynge one charitie, beinge of one mynd, of one opinion, that nothyng be done by contencion or vainglory. Who is he that hath any bowelles of pitie that wyll not be moved with these wordes so pithy? Whose hart is so stony but that the sworde of these wordes, whiche bee more sharpe then any two edged swoorde, maye not cutte and breake a sondre? Wherfore, let us endevour

our selfes to fulfil S. Paules joye, here in thys place, whiche shalbe at length to our greate joye in another place.

Let us so reade the Scripture that by readynge therof we maye be made the better livers, rather then the more contencious disputers. If any thyng is necessary to be taught, reasoned, or disputed, let us do it with all mekenes, softnes and lenitie. If any thyng shall chaunce to be spoken uncomly, let one beare anothers frailtie. He that is faulty, let hym rather amende then defend that which he hath spoken amisse, lest he falle by contencion from a foolish erroure into an obstinate heresie, for it is better to geve place mekely then to winne the victory with the breach of charitie – which chaunceth where every man will defende hys opinion obstinately. If we be Christen men, why do we not folowe Christe, whiche saieth: learne of me, for I am meeke and lowely in hart? A disciple muste learne the lesson of his scholemaster, and a servaunt must obey the commaundement of hys master. He that is wise and learned, saieth S. James, let hym shewe hys goodnes by hys good conversacion and sobernes of hys wysedome. For where there is envy and contencion, that wysedome commeth not from God, but is worldly wysedome, mans wysedome and devilishe wysedome. For the wysedome that commeth from above, from the spirit of God, is chast and pure, corrupted with no evil affeccions; it is quiet, meke and peaceable, abhorringe all desyre of contencion; it is tractable, obedient, not grudgyng to learne and to geve place to them that teache better for their reformacion. For there shall never be an ende of strivinge and contencion, if we contende who in contencion shalbe master and have the overhande, if we shall heape erroure upon errour, if we continue to defend that obstinately which was spoken unadvisedly. For truth it is that stifnes in mainteyning an opinion bredeth contencion, braulyng and chiding, whiche is a vice, emong all other, most pernicious and pestilent to common peace and quietnes.

And as it standeth betwixt two persons and parties, for no man commonly doth chide with him self, so it comprehendeth two most detestable vices: the one is picking of querelles with sharpe and contencious wordes; the other standeth in froward answering and multipliyng evil wordes againe. The first is so abhominable that Saincte Paule saieth: if any that is called a brother be a worshipper of ydols, a brauler, or piker of querels, a thefe or an extorcioner, with hym that is suche a man se that ye eate not. Now here considre that Saincte Paule numbreth a scolder, a brauler, or a picker of querels emong thiefes and ydolaters, and many tymes commeth lesse hurt of a thief then of a raylyng tongue: for the one taketh away a mannes good name; the other taketh but hys richesse, which is of muche lesse value and estimacion then is hys good name. And a thief hurteth but him from whom he stealeth, but he that hath an evill tongue troubleth al the towne where he dwelleth, and sometyme the whole countrey. And a raylynge tongue is a pestilence so full of contagion that Sainct Paule willeth Christian men to forbeare the company of suche and neyther to eate nor drynke with theim. And where as he will not that a Christian woman shoulde forsake her husband, although he be an infidele, nor that a Christian servaunt should departe from hys master whiche is an infidele and heathen, and so suffre a Christian man to kepe company with an infidel, yet he forbiddeth us to eat or drink with a scolder or a querel picker. And also, in the .vi. chapi. to the Cor., he saieth thus: Be not deceyved, for neither fornicators, neither worshippers of ydols, neyther thiefes, nor dronkards, neither cursed speakers shall dwell in the kyngdom of heaven. It must nedes be a great fault that doth move and cause the father to disherite hys natural sonne. And how can it otherwise be, but that this cursed speakynge must nedes be a most dampnable synne, the whiche doeth cause God, our moste merciful and loving Father, to deprive us of hys moste blessed kyngdom of heaven?

Agaynst the other synne, that standeth in requiting taunt for taunte, speaketh Christe himselfe: I saye unto you, saieth oure savior Christe, resiste not evill, but love your enemies and saye well by them that saye evill by you, do well unto theim that do evill to you, and praye for them that do hurte and pursue you, that you maye be the chyldren of youre Father whiche is in heaven, whoo suffereth hys sunne to ryse bothe upon good and evill, and sendeth hys rayn both to the juste and unjuste. To thys doctryne of Christe agreeth very well the teaching of Sainct Paul, that electe vessell of God, who ceaseth not to exhorte and call upon us, saiynge, blesse them that curse you, blesse, I saye, and curse not; recompense to no man evill for evill; if it be possible, asmuche as lieth in you, lyve peaceablye with all men.

[The Second Part of the Sermon of Contencion

It hath ben declared unto you, in this sermon against strief and braulyng, what greate inconvenience commeth therby and specially of suche contencion as groweth in matters of religion; and how, when as no man will geve place to another, there is none ende of contencion and discord; and that unitie whiche God requireth of Christians is utterly thereby neglected and broken; and that this contencion standeth chiefly in twoo poynctes, as in pickyng of querels and makyng froward answeres. Now you shall here Sainct Paules wordes, saiyng,] Dearely beloved, avenge not youre

selfes, but rather geve place unto wrath, for it is written: vengeaunce
is myne; I will revenge, saieth the Lorde. Therfore, if thyne enemye honger,
fede hym; if he thirst, geve hym drinke; be not overcome with evill, but
overcome evil with goodnes. All these be the woordes of S. Paule.

But they that be so full of stomacke, and sette so muche by them selfes
that they may not abyde so muche as one evill woorde to bee spoken
of them peradventure wyll saye: if I be evil reviled, shal I stand stil like a
goose, or a foole, with my finger in my mouth? Shall I be such an
ydiot and diserde to suffre every man to speake upon me what thei list, to
rayle what they liste, to spewe out al their venyme agaynst me at their
pleasures? Is it not convenient that he that speaketh evill shoulde be aunswered accordingly? If I shall use this lenitie and softnes, I shal both
encrease mine enemies frowardnesse and provoke other to do lyke. Suche
reasons make they that can suffre nothynge for the defence of their
impacience. And yet, if by froward aunsweryng to a froward persone there
were hope to remedy his frowardnesse, he should lesse offende that
should so aunswer, doyng thesame not of yre or malice, but onely of that
intent that he that is soo frowarde or malicious may be refourmed. But
he that can not amende another mans faulte, or cannot amende it without
hys awn faulte, better it were that one should perishe then two. Then,
if he cannot quiete hym with gentle woordes, at the least let hym not
folowe him in wicked and uncharitable wordes. If he can pacifie him with
suffering, let him suffre; and if not, it is better to suffre evil, then to do
evil, to saye wel, then to say evill. For to speake well agaynst evill commeth
of the spirite of God, but to rendre evill for evill commeth of the contrary
spirite. And he that cannot temper ne rule hys awn yre is but weake
and feble, and rather more lyke a woman or a child then a stronge man.
For the true strength and manlines is to overcome wrath, and to despice
injury and other mennes folishnes. And besides this, he that shall despice·
the wronge dooen unto hym by his enemye, every man shall perceyve that
it was spoken or doen withoute cause, where as contrary, he that doeth
fume and chafe at it shall help the cause of hys adversary, gevynge suspicion
that the thing is true. And so in goynge about to revenge evil we shew
our selfes to be evil, and while we will punysh and revenge another mannes
foly, we double and augment our awne foly.

But many pretenses fynd they that be wilful to colour theyr impacience.
Myne enemy, saye they, is not worthy to have gentle wordes or deedes,
beynge so ful of malice or frowardnes. The lesse he is worthy, the more
arte thou allowed of God, the more arte thou commended of Christe,
for whose sake thou shoulde render good for evyll, because he hath commaunded the and also deserved that thou shouldest so do. Thyne neighbor

hath peradventure with a worde offended the: call thou to thy remembraunce with howe many wordes and dedes, how grevously, thou hast
offended thy lord God. What was man when Christe dyed for hym? Was
he not hys enemye, and unworthy to have hys favor and mercye? Even
so, with what gentlenes and pacience doeth he forbeare and tollerate the,
although he is dayly offended by the! Forgeve, therfore, a lighte tresspace
to thy neighbor, that Christ maye forgeve the many thousandes of trespasses, which arte every daye an offendor. For if thou forgeve thy brother,
beynge to the a trespasser, then hast thou a sure signe and token that
God wyll forgeve the, to whom all men be debtors or trespassers. How
wouldest thou have God merciful to the, if thou wilt be cruell unto thy
brother? Canste thou not find in thyne hart to do that towardes an
other that is thy felowe which God hath done to the that arte but hys
servaunt? Ought not one sinner to forgeve another, seyng that Christ
which was no synner did praye to hys Father for theim that withoute mercy
and dispitfully put hym to death? Who, when he was reviled, did not
use revilyng wordes again, and when he suffred wrongfully, he did not
threaten, but gave all vengeaunce to the judgemente of hys Father, whiche
judgeth rightefully. And what crakest thou of thy hed, if thou labor not
to be in the body? Thou canste be no membre of Christ, if thou folow not
the steppes of Christ, who, as the prophete saieth, was led to death like
a lambe, not openynge hys mouth to revilyng, but openyng hys mouth to
praiynge for them that crucified hym, saiynge: Father, forgeve them, for
they cannot tel what they do. The whiche example, anone after Christ,
Sainct Stephin did folow, and after, Sainct Paule: We be evill spoken of,
saieth he, and we speake well; we suffre persecucion and take it paciently;
men curse us, and we gently entreate. Thus S. Paul taught that he did,
and he dyd that he taughte: Blesse you, sayeth he, them that persecute you;
blesse you, and curse not. Is it a great thyng to speake wel to thyne
adversary, to whom Christ doth commaund the to do wel? David, when
Semei dyd call him al to naught, did not chide agayn, but saide paciently:
suffre hym to speake evil, if perchaunce the Lorde will have mercy on me.

   Hystories be full of examples of heathen men that toke very mekely
bothe opprobrious wordes and injurious dedes. And shall those heathen
men excel in pacience us that professe Christ, the teacher and example
of all pacience? Lisander, when one did rage agaynst him in revilinge of
him, he was nothing moved, but said: 'go to, go to; speke agaynst me
asmuch and as oft as thou wilt, and leave out nothynge, if perchaunce by
thys meanes thou maiest discharge the of those naughtie thynges with
the which it semeth that thou arte full laden.' Many men speake evill of all
men, because thei can speake wel of no man. After this sorte, thys wyse

man avoyded from him the injurious wordes spoken unto hym, imputyng and laiyng them to the naturall sickenes of hys adversary. Perycles, when a certain scolder, or a raylyng felowe, dyd revile him, he aunswered not a word again, but went into a galery, and after toward night, when he wente home, thys scolder folowed hym, ragyng still more and more because he sawe the other to set nothyng by hym. And after that he came to hys gate, beyng darke night, Perycles commaunded one of hys servauntes to light a torche and to bryng the scolder home to his awn house. He did not only with quietnes suffre thys brawler paciently, but also recompensed an evil turne with a good turne, and that to hys enemye. Is it not a shame for us that professe Christe to be worse then heathen people in a thynge chiefly perteyning to Christes religion? Shall philosophie perswade them more then Gods Woorde shall perswade us? Shal natural reason prevaile more with them then religion shall do with us? Shall mans wisedome leade them to that thyng whereunto the heavenly doctryne cannot leade us? What blyndenesse, wilfulnesse, or rather madnesse is this? Perycles, beyng provoked to angre with many contumelious wordes, aunswered not a worde. But we stirred but with one litle woorde, what tragedies do we move? How do we fume, rage, stampe and stare like madde men? Many men of every trifle will make a great matter, and of the sparke of a litle worde wyll kindle a great fyre, takyng all thinges in the worste parte. But how muche better is it, and more lyke to the example and doctryne of Christe, to make rather of a great faulte in our neighbour a smal fault, reasoning with our selfes after this sort: he spake these wordes, but it was in a sodaine heate, or the drinke spake them and not he, or he spake them at the mocion of some other, or he spake them beyng ignoraunt of the truth; he spake them not agaynste me, but agaynste hym whome he thoughte me to be.

But as touching evill speakyng, he that is ready to speake evyl against other men fyrste lette hym examyne himself, whether he be faultlesse and cleare of the faulte whiche he fyndeth in an other. For it is a shame when he that blameth an other for any faulte is giltye hymselfe either in thesame faulte, eyther in a greater. It is a shame for hym that is blynde to call an other man blynde, and it is more shame for hym that is whole blynde to call hym blinkerd that is but pore-blynd. For this is to se a strawe in another mannes iye, when a man hath a blocke in his awne iye. Then let hym considre that he that useth to speake evill shal commonly be evil spoken of again. And he that speaketh what he will for his pleasure shalbe compelled to hear that he would not, to his displeasure. Moreover, lette hym remembre that saiyng that we shall geve an accompte for every idle woorde. How muche more then shall we make a reconyng for our

sharpe, bitter, braulyng and chidyng woordes, whiche provoke our brother
to be angery and so to the breach of his charitie!

And as touchyng evill aunsweryng, although we be never so muche
provoked by other mennes evill speakyng, yet we shall not folow their
frowardnes by evill aunsweryng, if we considre that anger is a kynde
of madnesse and that he whiche is angery is, as it wer, for that tyme in a
phrenesie. Wherfore, let hym beware, least in his fury he speake any
thyng wherof afterward he maie have juste cause to be sory. And he that
will defende that anger is no fury, but that he hath reason, even when
he is moste angery, then let hym reason thus with himself, when he is
angery: now I am so moved and chafed that within a litle while after
I shalbe otherwaies minded. Wherfore, then, should I now speake any
thyng in mine anger, whiche hereafter, when I would fainest, cannot
be chaunged? Wherfore shall I do any thyng now, beyng, as it wer, out of
my witte, for the whiche, when I shall come to my self again, I shalbe
very sadde? Why doth not reason? Why dooth not godlinesse? Yea, why
doth not Christ obtein the thyng now of me, which hereafter, tyme shall
obtein of me? If a man be called an adulterer, usurer, drunkarde, or by
any other contumelious name, let hym consider earnestly whether he be so
called truly or falsly: if truly, let hym amende his fault, that his adversarie
maie not after worthely charge hym with suche offences; if these thynges
be laid against him falsly, yet let hym consider whether he hath geven
any occasion to be suspected of suche thynges, and so he maie bothe cut
of that suspicion wherof this slaunder did arise, and in other thynges
shall live more warely. And thus usyng our selfes, wee maie take no hurte,
but rather muche good by the rebukes and slaunders of our enemie. For
the reproche of an enemy may be to many men a quicker spurr to the
amendement of their life then the gentle monicion of a frend. Phillippus,
the Kyng of Macedony, when he was evill spoken of by the chiefe rulers of
the citee of Athens, he did thanke them hartely, because by theim he was
made better, bothe in his woordes and deedes: 'for I study,' saied he,
'bothe by my saiynges and doynges to prove theim liars.'

[The Third Part of the Sermon of Contencion

Ye heard in the last lesson of the sermon against strief and braulyng how
we maie answere theim whiche maintein their froward saiynges in contencion and that will revenge with woordes suche evill as other men do to
them; and finally, how we maie, accordyng to Gods will, ordre our selfes,
and what to consider towardes theim, when wee are provoked to contencion with railyng wordes. Now to procede in thesame matter, you shall

knowe the right waie howe to disprove and overcome your adversarie and enemie.]

This is the best waie to refell a mannes adversary: so to live that all whiche shall knowe his honestie maie beare witnesse that he is slaundered unworthely. If the faulte whereof he is slaundered be suche that for the defence of his honestie he must nedes make aunswere, yet let hym aunswere quietly and softely, on this fashion, that those faultes be laid against hym falsly. For it is truth that the Wiseman saith: a soft aunswer asswageth anger, and a hard and sharpe aunswer doth stirre up rage and fury. The sharpe aunswer of Nabal did provoke David to cruel vengeaunce, but the gentle wordes of Abigaill quenched the fire again that was all in a flamme. And a speciall remedy against malicious toungues is to arme our selfes with pacience, mekenes and silence, least with multipliyng wordes with the enemy we bee made as evill as he.

But thei that cannot beare one evil worde peradventure for their awne excusacion wil alledge that which is written: He that despiceth his good name is cruell. Also wee read: aunswere a foole accordyng to his folish-nesse. And our lorde Jesus did hold his peace at certain evil saiynges, but to some he aunswered diligently. He heard men call him a Samaritain, a carpenters sonne, a wine drinkar, and he helde his peace; but when he heard theim saie, thou haste a devill within thee, he aunswered to that ear-nestly. Truthe it is in deede that there is a tyme when it is convenient to aunswere a foole accordyng to his folishenesse, least he should seme in his awne conceipt to be wise. And sometyme it is not profitable to aunswer a foole accordyng to his foolishnesse, least the wise manne bee made like to the foole. When our infamie is joyned with the perill of many, then is it necessarie, in aunsweryng, to be quicke and ready. For we reade that many holy men of good zeales have sharpely and fiercely both spoken and aunswered tyrauntes and evil men: whiche sharp wordes proceded not of anger, rancor, or malice, or appetite of vengeaunce, but of a fervent desire to bryng them to the true knowledge of God and from ungodly livyng, by an earnest and sharpe objurgacion and chidyng. In this zeale Sainct Jhon Baptiste called the Phariseis, adders broode, and S. Paule called the Galathians, fooles, and the men of Crete he called liars, evill beastes, and sloggishe bellies, and the false apostles he called dogges and craftie workemen. And this zeale is godly, and to be allowed, as it is plainly proved by the example of Christ, who although he wer the fountain and spryng of all mekenesse, gentilnes and softnesse, yet he calleth the obstinate Scribes and Phariseis blynd guydes, fooles, painted graves, hypocrites, serpentes, adders brode, a corrupte and wicked generacion. Also he rebu-keth Peter egerly, saiyng: go behind me Sathan. Likewise S. Paule reprov-

eth Elimas, saiyng: O thou full of all craft and guile, enemie to al justice,
thou ceasest not to destroy the right waies of God, and now, lo, the hande
of the Lorde is upon thee, and thou shalt be blynde and not se for a
tyme. And S. Peter reprehendeth Ananias very sharpely, saiyng: Ananias,
how is it that Sathan hath filled thy harte that thou shouldest lye unto
the Holy Ghost? This zeale hath been so fervent in many good men that it
hath stirred them not onely to speake bitter and eger wordes, but also to
do thynges whiche might seme to some to be cruell, but in deede thei
be very juste, charitable and godly, because thei were not doen of ire,
malice or contencious mynde, but of a fervent mynd to the glory of God
and the correccion of synne, executed by men called to that office. For
in this zeale our lorde Jesus Christ did drive with a whippe the biars and
sellers out of the temple. In this zeale Moses brake the two tables whiche
he had received at Gods hand, when he sawe the Israelites daunsyng
aboute a calfe, and caused to be killed .xxiii. M. of his awne people. In
this zeale Phinees, the sonne of Eleasar, did thruste throughe with his
sword Zambry and Cozby, whom he found together joyned in the act of
lechery.

Wherfore, now to returne again to contencious wordes, and specially in
matters of religion and Gods Worde, which would be used with all
modestie, sobernesse and charitie, the wordes of S. James ought to be well
marked and borne in memory, where he saith that of contencion riseth
al evill. And the wise Kyng Salomon saieth: honor is due to a manne that
kepeth hymself from contencion, and all that mingle themselfes therwith
bee fooles. And because this vice is so muche hurtefull to the societie
of a common wealthe, in all well ordred cities these common braulers and
skolders bee punished with a notable kynde of pain: as to bee sette on
the cokyngstole, pillery, or suche like. And thei be unworthy to live in a
common wealthe the whiche do asmuche as lieth in theim, with braulyng
and skoldyng, to disturbe the quietnes and peace of thesame. And whereof
commeth this contencion, strief and variaunce, but of pride and vain
glory? Let us therefore humble oure selfes under the mightie hande of
God, whiche hath promised to reste upon them that bee humble and lowe
in spirite. If we bee good and quiete Christian men, let it appere in our
speache and tongues. If we have forsaken the devil, let us use no more
devillish toungues. He that hath been a railyng skolder, now let him be a
sober counsailoure. He that hath been a malicious slaunderor, nowe let
hym bee a lovyng comforter. He that hath been a vain railer, now let him
be a ghostly teacher. He that hath abused his tongue in cursyng, now
let him use it in blessyng. He that hath abused his tong in evill speakyng,

now lette hym use it in speakyng well. All bitternesse, anger, railyng
and blasphemy, let it be avoyded from you. If you may, and it be possible,
in nowise be angery. But if you maie not bee cleane voyde of this passion,
then yet so temper and bridle it that it stirre you not to contencion and
braulyng. If you be provoked with evil speaking, arme your self with pacience, lenitie and silence, either speakyng nothyng, or els beyng very soft,
meke and gentle in aunsweryng. Overcome thine adversaries with benefites
and gentlenes. And above all thynges kepe peace and unite: bee no peace
breakers, but peace makers. And then there is no doubt but that God,
the aucthor of comforte and peace, will graunte us peace of conscience and
suche concord and agrement that with one mouthe and mynde wee maie
glorifie God, the Father of our lorde Jesus Christe: to whom bee all glory
now and ever.
   Amen.

[Advertisement]

Hereafter shal folow homelies of fastyng, praiyng, almose dedes; of the
Nativite, Passion, Resurreccion and Ascencion of our savior Christ; of the
due receivyng of his blessed body and bloud under the forme of bread
and wine; against idlenesse, against gluttony and drunkennesse, against
coveteousnesse, against envy, ire and malice, with many other matters
aswell fruitefull as necessarie to the edifiyng of Christian people and the
increase of godly livyng. Amen.
   God save the kyng.

NOTES

191 *table*: tablet, or picture.
   stomackes: dispositions.
   Eschewe ... meke towarde all men: 1 Tim 1:4; 2 Tim 2:23–4.
   I holde ... of Apollo: 1 Cor 1:12 and 3:4.
   new broched brother: The term 'brother' had been used by Barnes, Frith,
      Tyndale, and other early reformers to describe colleagues of evangelical
      belief. Thomas More mocked the novelty of the term in several works in
      which he contended against 'the false fraternitie' of reformers. See J.B.
      Trapp ed *The Apologye* (New Haven: Yale University Press 1979) 14
      and 313 n 14/23.
   coote: coat.
   to-rent: from OE *torendan*, 'to rend in pieces.'

192 *joynted ... charitie:* Eph 4:15–16.
    as long as emulacion ... fleshly man: 1 Cor 3:3.
    If you have ... evill deades: James 3:14, 16.
    I beseche you ... of one opinion: 1 Cor 1:10.
    I exhorte you ... baptisme: Eph 4:1–5.
    lenitie: gentleness.
    obtestacion: adjuration.
    If there be any consolacion ... vainglory: Phil 2:1–3.
    more sharpe ... swoorde: Heb 4:12.
193 *learne ... hart:* Matt 11:29.
    He that is wise ... their reformacion: James 3:13–17.
    if any ... ye eate not: 1 Cor 5:11.
    thief ... hys good name: proverbial: cf Shakespeare *Othello* III.iii.157–61.
194 *he will not ... with an infidel:* 1 Cor 7:12–14; 1 Tim 6:1.
    Be not deceyved ... kyngdom of heaven: 1 Cor 6:9–10.
    disherite: disinherit.
    I saye unto you ... juste and unjuste: Matt 5:39, 44–5.
    electe vessell ... with all men: Acts 9:15; Rom 12:14, 17–18.
    Dearely beloved ... with goodnes: Rom 12:19–21, quoting Deut 32:35. That the dividing of the homilies into parts (1549) broke in half the quotation from Rom 12 suggests that the revisions were sometimes casually and carelessly made.
195 *goose:* simpleton, since the goose was proverbial for its stupidity.
    finger: the phrase 'with one's finger in one's mouth' was proverbial for a person who looked foolish.
    diserde: blockhead; a term first found c 1520, according to the OED, which cites the homily's use of it.
    fume and chafe: express irritation.
196 *Christ ... death:* Luke 23:34.
    Who, when he was reviled ... rightefully: 1 Pet 2:23.
    crakest: boasts.
    led to death like a lambe: Isa 53:7.
    Father, forgeve ... what they do: Luke 23:34.
    Sainct Stephin did folow: Acts 7:59–60.
    We be evill spoken ... entreate: 1 Cor 4:12–13.
    Blesse you ... curse not: Rom 12:14.
    suffre hym ... mercy on me: 2 Sam 16:11–12.
    'go to ... full laden': For Lysander's saying, see Plutarch *Moralia* ed and tr F.C. Babbit et al, 15 vols (London: William Heinemann 1927–69) III 376–7.
197 *Perycles ... to his awn house:* See Plutarch *Lives* ed and tr B. Perrin, 11 vols (London: William Heinemann 1914–26) III 12–13.
    blinkerd: derogatory term for a blind or dim-sighted person.
    strawe ... his awne iye: Matt 7:3.

pore-blynd: partially blind.

geve an accompte: Matt 12:36.

198 *Phillippus ... liars'*: See Plutarch *Moralia* III 43.

199 *refell*: refute.

a soft aunswer ... rage and fury: Prov 15:1.

aunswer of Nabal ... flamme: 1 Sam 25:10–35.

excusacion: defence.

he that despiceth ... is cruell: Augustine *Sermo 355: De vita et moribus clericorum suorum* I (PL 39: 1569), cited in Gratian's *Decretum, Pars secunda*, C 12 q I C 10 (PL 187: 886).

aunswere a foole ... his folishnesse: Prov 26:5.

hold his peace: John 19:9.

a Samaritain ... to that earnestly: John 8:48; Matt 13:55 and 11:19.

aunswer a foole ... like to the foole: Prov 26:5, 4.

objurgacion: rebuke.

Phariseis ... craftie workemen: Matt 3:7; Gal 3:1; Titus 1:12; Phil 3:2.

he calleth ... wicked generacion: Matt 23:16–33.

go behind me Sathan: Matt 16:23.

200 *O thou full ... not se for a tyme*: Acts 13:10–11.

Ananias ... the Holy Ghost: Acts 5:3.

Christ did drive ... the temple: John 2:15.

Moses brake ... his awne people: Exod 32:15–19, 27–8 (Vg 32:28 'quasi viginti tria millia hominum'; AV 'about three thousand men').

Phinees ... act of lechery: Num 25:8, 14–15; a marginal note says: 'But these examples are not to be folowed of everbody but as men be called to office and set in aucthoritie.'

of contencion riseth al evill: James 3:16.

honor is due ... bee fooles: Prov 20:3.

cokyngstole: the *cathedra stercoris*, a chair in which scolds were fastened and humiliated.

pillery: another instrument for punishing scolds and like offenders.

humble oure selfes ... hande of God: 1 Pet 5:6.

promised to reste ... lowe in spirite: Luke 1:52.

201 *All bitternesse ... avoyded from you*: Eph 4:31.

and it be possible: if it be possible.

with one mouthe ... lorde Jesus Christe: Rom 15:6.

TEXTUAL APPARATUS

191 An Homelie] A Sermon *1559, 1623*. Braulynge] Barwlinge *1559*. and so pernicious] and pernicious *1623*. This contencion] Tis contencion *1549*. propounde] set forth *1559, 1623*. ostentacion] shewynge forth of theyr

192 conning *1559, 1623*. partye] parte *1559, 1623*. joynted] joyned *1623*. in this

unitie] of this unitie *1623*. emulacion] or envyinge *added 1559, 1623*. factions]
or sectes *added 1559, 1623*. emulacion] or envying *added 1559, 1623*. incon-
stancy] undedfastnes *1559*; unstedfastnesse *1623*. vocacion in the whiche] vocacion in which *1623*. he saieth] saith he *1623*. obtestacion] earnest entreatyng
1559, 1623. communion] felowshyp *1559, 1623*. nothynge] nohynge *1559*.

193 stony but that the] stony the *1559*; stony that the *1623*. is necessary] be
necessary *1623*. He that] He tha *1549*. chaunceth where] chaunceth when
1623. be Christen] be the Christen *1623*. whiche saieth] whiche saieth
he *1549*. worldly] wordely *1549*. desyre of contencion] desyre and contencion
1623. their reformacion] the reformacion *1623*. And as it] and it *1623*. tymes

194 commeth] tymes there commeth *1623*. muche] muh *1547*. contagion]
contagiousnes *1559, 1623*. infidele, nor] infidele, or *1623*. or a querel] or
querel *1623*. neither cursed] nor cursed *1623*. doth move] doeeh move *1547*.
standeth] staudeth *1547*. Christe himselfe:] Christe himselfe saying *1623*.
saieth oure savior Christe] *not in 1623*. evill to] evill unto *1623*. pursue] persecute *1559, 1623*. sunne] sonne *1549*; Sunne *1623*. rayn both to] rayn both
upon *1623*. electe] chosen *1559, 1623*. Sermon of Contencion] Sermon
agaynste Contencion *1559, 1623*. and specially] specially *1623*. makyng fro-

195 ward] makyng of froward *1623*. I will revenge] and I will revenge *1623*. so
full] full *1623*. be evil reviled] be reviled *1623*. should so aunswer] so
should aunswer *1623*. ne rule] nor rule *1623*. yre] anger *1559, 1623*. injury]
injuries *1623*. contrary] contrarily *1623*. And so in] And in so *1623*. impaci-
ence] impacient *1549*. thou allowed] thou therefore allowed *1623*. God,

196 the more] God, and the more *1623*. offended] offendde *1549*. tollerate] and
suffer *added 1559, 1623*. debtors or] debtors and *1623*. reviled, did] reviled,
he did *1623*. and we speake] and speake *1547, 1549, 1559*. wel to thyne] wel to
of and thyne *1547*. opprobrious] and reprocheful *added 1559, 1623*. injurious]
or wrongful *added 1559, 1623*. heathen men excel] heathen excel *1559, 1623*.

197 injurious] reprocheful *1559, 1623*. a raylyng felowe] raylyng felowe *1549, 1623*.
Is it not a shame] It is a shame *1549*. shall do with us] shall with us *1623*.
that thyng] those things *1623*. contumelious] vilainous *1559, 1623*. stirred but
with] stirred with *1549*. tragedies ... move] foule worke ... make *1559, 1623*.
rather of a great] rather a great *1549*. eyther in a greater] or in a greater

198 *1623*. blinkerd] winkarde *1549*. hear that] hear what *1623*. that tyme] the
tyme *1549, 1623*. phrenesie] phenesy *1547*. no fury] not fury *1623*. the thyng]
that thyng *1623*. contumelious] shamefull *1559, 1623*. study,' saied] studse,
saied *1547*; studie, sayeth *1623*. Sermon of Contencion] Sermon against
Contencion *1559, 1623*. do to them] do them *1623*. contencion] and stryfe

199 *added 1559, 1623*. refell] improve *1559, 1623*. yet let hym] let hym *1623*. hard
and] *not in 1549*. did provoke] provoked *1623*. excusacion] excuse *1559,
1623*. haste a] hast the *1623*. infamie] or the reproche that is done unto us
added 1559, 1623. is it necessarie] it is necessarie *1623*. zeales] zeale *1623*.
proceded] came *1559, 1623*. appetite] desyer *1559, 1623*. objurgacion] rebuke
1559, 1623. this zeale] his zeale *1623*. yet he calleth] ye he called *1547*; yea

200   he called *1549*. unto the Holy Ghost] upon the Holy Ghost *1559*. been] bee
1547. because thei were not] bbeecause they were not *1559*. a calfe] the calfe
1623. thruste] thurst *1549*. Zambry] Zimri *1623*. lechery] uncleannesse

201   *1623*. charitie] chastity *1623*. All bitternesse] And bitternesse *1549*. stirre you
not to] stirre you to *1547*. adversaries] adversary *1623*. now and ever]
now and for ever *1623*.

[*Advertisement*]
homelies] sermons *1559, 1623*.

AN HOMELIE AGAINST
DISOBEDIENCE AND
WYLFULL REBELLION

An Homelie against Disobedience and Wylfull Rebellion

The first part.

As God, the creator and Lorde of all thinges, appointed his angels and heavenly creatures in all obedience to serve and to honour his majestie: so was it his wil that man, his chiefe creature upon the earth, should live under the obedience of him, his creator and Lorde; and for that cause, God, assoone as he had created man, gave unto him a certaine precept and lawe, which he, being yet in the state of innocencie, and remayning in paradise, shoulde observe as a pledge and token of his due and bounden obedience, with denunciation of death if he did transgresse and breake the said lawe and commaundement. And as God woulde have man to be his obedient subject, so dyd he make all earthly creatures subject unto man, who kept their due obedience unto man, so long as man remayned in his obedience unto God: in the whiche obedience yf man had continued still, there had ben no povertie, no diseases, no sicknesse, no death, nor other miseries where with mankynde is nowe infinitely and most miserablie afflicted and oppressed. So here appeareth the originall kyngdome of God over angels and man, and universallie over all thinges, and of man over earthly creatures whiche God had made subject unto him, and withall the felicitie and blessed state which angels, man, and all creatures had remayned in, had they continued in due obedience unto God their king. For as long as in this first kingdome the subjectes continued in due obedience to God their kyng, so long dyd God embrace all his subjectes with his love, favour, and grace, whiche to enjoy, is perfect felicitie. Whereby it is evident, that obedience is the principal vertue of al vertues, and in deede the very roote of all vertues, and the cause of all felicitie. But as all felicitie and blessednesse shoulde have continued with the continuance of obedience: so with the breache of obedience, and breakyng in

of rebellion, al vices and miseries dyd withall breake in, and overwhelme
the worlde. The first aucthour of which rebellion, the roote of all vices and
mother of all mischiefes, was Lucifer, first Gods most excellent creature
and most bounden subject, who by rebelling against the majestie of God,
of the brightest and most glorious angell is become the blackest and
most foulest feende and devill, and from the height of heaven is fallen into
the pit and bottome of hell.

Here you may see the first aucthour and founder of rebellion and the
rewarde thereof: here you may see the graunde captayne and father of all
rebels, who perswadyng the folowyng of his rebellion agaynst God,
their creator and Lorde, unto our first parentes Adam and Eve, brought
them in high displeasure with God, wrought their exile and banishment
out of paradise, a place of all pleasure and goodnesse, into this wretched
earth and vale of all miserie, procured unto them sorowes of their mindes,
mischiefes, sicknesse, diseases, death of their bodyes, and which is farre
more horrible then all worldly and bodyly mischiefes, he had wrought
thereby their eternall and everlasting death and dampnation, had not God
by the obedience of his sonne Jesus Christe repaired that which man by
disobedience and rebellion had destroyed, and so of his mercie had pardoned and forgeven him: of whiche all and singuler the premises, the
Holy Scriptures do beare recorde in sundry places. Thus you do see that
neither heaven nor paradise coulde suffer any rebellion in them, neither be
places for any rebels to remayne in. Thus became rebellion, as you see,
both the first and greatest, and the very roote of all other sinnes, and the
first and principall cause both of all worldly and bodyly miseries, sorowes,
diseases, sicknesses, and deathes, and which is infinitely worse then all
these, as is saide, the very cause of death and dampnation eternal also.

After this breache of obedience to God and rebellion agaynst his majestie,
al mischiefes and miseries breaking in therwith and overflowyng the
world, lest all thinges should come unto confusion and utter ruine, God
foorthwith, by lawes geven unto mankynd, repayred agayne the rule
and order of obedience thus by rebellion overthrowen, and besides the
obedience due unto his majestie, he not onlye ordayned that in families and
housholdes the wyfe shoulde be obedient unto her husbande, the children
unto their parentes, the servantes unto their maisters: but also when
mankinde increased and spread it selfe more largelie over the worlde, he
by his Holy Worde dyd constitute and ordayne in cities and countreyes
severall and speciall governours and rulers, unto whom the residue of
his people shoulde be obedient. As in readyng of the Holye Scriptures, we
shall finde in very many and almost infinite places, aswell of the Olde
Tastament, as of the Newe, that kinges and princes, aswell the evill as the

good, do raigne by Gods ordinaunce, and that subjectes are bounden
to obey them; that God doth geve princes wysdome, great power, and
aucthoritie; that God defendeth them agaynst their enemies and destroyeth
their enemies horribly; that the anger and displeasure of the prince is as
the roaring of a lion, and the verye messenger of death; and that the
subject that provoketh him to displeasure sinneth agaynst his owne soule –
with many other thinges concerning both the aucthoritie of princes and
the dutie of subjectes.

But here let us rehearse two special places out of the New Tastament,
which may stand in steade of all other. The first out of Saint Paules Epistle
to the Romanes and the 13 chapter, where he wryteth thus unto all
subjectes, 'Let every soule be subject unto the higher powers, for there is
no power but of God, and the powers that be are ordayned of God.
Whosoever, therfore, resisteth the power, resisteth the ordinaunce of God;
and they that resist shall receave to them selves damnation. For princes
are not to be feared for good works, but for evil. Wilt thou then be without
feare of the power? Do well, so shalt thou have prayse of the same: for
he is the minister of God for thy wealth. But if thou do evyl, feare: for he
beareth not the sworde for naught, for he is the minister of God to take
vengeaunce upon hym that doth evyll. Wherefore ye must be subject,
not because of wrath only, but also for conscience sake: for, for this cause
ye pay also tribute, for they are Gods ministers, serving for the same
purpose. Geve to every man therefore his duetie: tribute, to whom tribute
belongeth; custome, to whom custome is due; feare, to whom feare
belongeth; honour, to whom ye owe honour.' Thus farre are Saint Paules
wordes. The seconde place is in Saint Peters first Epistle, and the second
chapter, whose wordes are these, 'Submit yourselves unto al maner ordinaunce of man for the Lordes sake, whether it be unto the kyng, as unto
the cheefe head, eyther unto rulers, as unto them that are sent of hym
for the punishment of evyll doers, but for the cherishing of them that do
well. For so is the wyl of God, that with well doyng ye may stoppe the
mouthes of ignoraunt and foolishe men: as free, and not as having the
libertie for a cloke of malitiousnesse, but even as the servauntes of God.
Honour all men, love brotherly felowship, feare God, honour the kyng.
Servauntes obey your masters with feare, not only if they be good and
curteous, but also though they be frowarde.' Thus farre out of Saint Peter.
By these two places of the Holy Scriptures it is most evident that kinges,
queenes, and other princes (for he speaketh of aucthoritie and power, be it
in men or women) are ordayned of God, are to be obeyed and honoured
of their subjectes; that such subjectes as are disobedient or rebellious
against their princes disobey God and procure their owne damnation; that

the government of princes is a great blessing of God geven for the common wealth, specially of the good and godly, for the comfort and cherishing of whom God geveth and setteth up princes, and on the contrary part, to the feare and for the punishment of the evyll and wicked. Finally that if servauntes ought to obey their maisters, not only beyng gentle, but such as be froward, aswell and much more ought subjectes to be obedient, not only to their good and curteous, but also to their sharpe and rigorous princes. It commeth therfore neither of chaunce and fortune (as they tearme it) nor of thambition of mortall men and women clymyng up of theyr owne accorde to dominion, that there be kynges, queenes, princes, and other governours over men beyng theyr subjectes: but all kinges, queenes and other governours are speciallye appoynted by the ordinaunce of God. And as God him selfe, being of an infinite majestie, power and wysdome, ruleth and governeth all thynges in heaven and in earth as the universall Monarche and only King and Emperour over all, as being only able to take and beare the charge of all: so hath he constitute, ordayned and set earthly princes over particular kingdomes and dominions in earth, both for the avoydyng of all confusion, whiche els woulde be in the world if it should be without such governours, and for the great quiet and benefite of earthly men, their subjects, and also that the princes them selves, in aucthoritie, power, wisdome, providence and righteousnes in government of people and countreys committed to their charge, should resemble his heavenly governance, as the majestie of heavenly things may by the bacenesse of earthly thinges be shadowed and resembled. And for that similitude that is betweene the heavenly Monarchie and earthly kingdomes wel governed, our saviour Christe in sundrye parables sayth that the kyngdome of heaven is resembled unto a man, a kyng, and as the name of the king is very often attributed and geven unto God in the Holy Scriptures, so doth God him selfe in the same Scriptures somtime vouchsafe to communicate his name with earthly princes, tearming them gods: doubtlesse for that similitude of government, which they have or should have, not unlike unto God, their King. Unto the which similitude of heavenly government, the nearer and nearer that an earthly prince doth come in his regiment, the greater blessing of Gods mercy is he unto that countrey and people over whom he raigneth; and the further and further that an earthly prince doth swarve from the example of the heavenly government, the greater plague he is of Gods wrath, and punishment, by Gods justice, unto that countrey and people over whom God for their sinnes hath placed such a prince and governour. For it is in deede evident, both by the Scriptures and by dayly experience, that the maintenaunce of al vertue and godlynesse, and, consequently, of the wealth

and prosperitie of a kingdome and people, doth stande and rest more in
a wise and good prince on the one part, then in great multitudes of other
men being subjectes; and on the contrary part, the overthrowe of all
vertue and godlynesse, and consequently the decay and utter ruine of a
realme and people, doth growe and come more by an undiscrete and evyll
governour then by many thousandes of other men being subjectes. Thus
say the Holy Scriptures, 'Well is thee, O thou lande (saith the Preacher)
whose kyng is come of nobles, and whose princes eate in due season,
for necessitie, and not for lust.' Agayne, 'a wyse and righteous kyng maketh
his realme and people wealthy: and a good, mercyfull, and gratious
prince is as a shadowe in heate, as a defence in stormes, as deawe, as sweete
shoures, as freshe water springes in great droughtes.' Agayne, the Scriptures of undiscrete and evyll princes speake thus, 'Wo be to thee (O thou
lande) whose kyng is but a chylde, and whose princes are early at their
bankettes.' Agayne, 'When the wicked do raigne, then men go to ruine.'
And agayne, 'A foolishe prince destroyeth the people, and a covetous kyng
undoeth his subjectes.' Thus speake the Scriptures, thus experience testifieth of good and evyll princes.

What shall subjectes do then? Shall they obey valiaunt, stoute, wyse and
good princes, and contemne, disobey and rebell against chyldren beyng
their princes, or against undiscrete and evyll governours? God forbid. For
first what a perilous thing were it to commit unto the subjectes the
judgement which prince is wyse and godly and his government good, and
whiche is otherwise, as though the foote must judge of the head – an
enterprise very heynous, and must needes breede rebellion. For who else
be they that are most inclined to rebellion, but suche hautie spirites? From
whom springeth suche foule ruine of realmes? Is not rebellion the greatest
of all mischeefes? And who are most redie to the greatest mischeefes,
but the worst men? Rebelles, therefore, the worst of all subjectes, are most
redie to rebellion, as beyng the worst of all vices and furthest from the
dutie of a good subject; as on the contrary part, the best subjectes are most
firme and constant in obedience, as in the speciall and peculier vertue of
good subjectes. What an unworthy matter were it then to make the
naughtiest subjectes, and most inclined to rebellion and all evyll, judges
over their princes, over their government and over their counsellers,
to determine whiche of them be good or tollerable, and whiche be evyll
and so intollerable that they must needes be removed by rebels, being ever
redie, as the naughtiest subjectes, soonest to rebell against the best princes,
specially if they be young in age, women in sexe, or gentle and curteous
in governement, as trusting by their wicked boldnesse easyly to overthrow
their weakenesse and gentlenesse, or at the least so to feare the mindes

of such princes that they may have impunitie of their mischeevous doynges. But where as in deede a rebel is worse then the worst prince, and rebellion worse then the worst governement of the worst prince that hytherto hath ben, both are rebels unmeete ministers and rebellion an unfit and unwholsome medicine to refourme any small lackes in a prince, or to cure any litle greefes in governement, suche leude remedies beyng farre worse then any other maladies and disorders that can be in the body of a common wealth. But whatsoever the prince be, or his governement, it is evident that for the most part those princes whom some subjectes do thinke to be very godly and under whose governement they rejoyce to live, some other subjectes do take the same to be evyll and ungodly, and do wishe for a chaunge. If, therfore, all subjectes that mislyke of their prince shoulde rebell, no realme shoulde ever be without rebellion. It were more meete that rebels shoulde heare the advise of wise men and geve place unto their judgement, and folowe the example of obedient subjectes – as reason is that they whose understanding is blinded with so evyll an affection shoulde geve place to them that be of sounde judgement, and that the worse should geve place to the better – and so might realmes continue in long obedience, peace, and quietnesse.

But what if the prince be undiscrete and evyll in deede, and it also evident to all mens eyes that he so is? I aske agayne, what if it be long of the wickednesse of the subjectes, that the prince is undiscrete or evyll? Shall the subjectes both by their wickednesse provoke God for their de-served punishment to geve them an undiscrete or evyll prince, and also rebell against hym, and withall against God, who for the punishment of their sinnes dyd geve them suche a prince? Wyll you heare the Scriptures concerning this point? God (say the Holy Scriptures) maketh a wicked man to raigne for the sinnes of the people. Agayne, God geveth a prince in his anger (meaning an evyll one) and taketh away a prince in his displeasure (meaning specially when he taketh away a good prince for the sinnes of the people): as in our memorie he toke away our good Josias, Kyng Edwarde, in his young and good yeres for our wickednesse. And contraryly, the Scriptures do teache that God geveth wysdome unto princes, and maketh a wyse and good kyng to raigne over that people whom he loveth, and who loveth hym. Agayne, 'If the people obey God, both they and their kyng shall prosper and be safe, els both shall perishe,' saieth God by the mouth of Samuel. Here you see that God placeth aswell evyll princes as good, and for what cause he doth both. If we, therfore, wyll have a good prince eyther to be geven us or to continue nowe we have such a one, let us by our obedience to God and to our prince move God therunto. If we will have an evyl prince (when God shall

sende such a one) taken away and a good in his place, let us take away
our wickednesse, which provoketh God to place such an one over us, and
God wyll eyther displace hym or of an evyll prince make hym a good
prince: so that we first wyll chaunge our evyll into good. For wyll you
heare the Scriptures? 'The heart of the prince is in Gods hande; whiche way
soever it shall please hym, he turneth it.' Thus say the Scriptures. Wherefore let us turne from our sinnes unto the Lorde with all our heartes,
and he wyll turne the heart of the prince unto our quiet and wealth: Els
for subjectes to deserve through their sinnes to have an evyll prince,
and then to rebell against hym, were double and treble evyll, by provoking
God more to plague them. Nay, let us either deserve to have a good
prince, or let us paciently suffer and obey such as we deserve.

And whether the prince be good or evill, let us accordyng to the counsell
of the Holy Scriptures pray for the prince, for his continuaunce and
increase in goodnesse, yf he be good, and for his amendement, yf he be
evyll. Wyll you here the Scriptures concerning this most necessarie point?
'I exhort therefore' saith Saint Paul, 'that, above al thinges, prayers,
supplications, intercessions, and geving of thankes be had for all men, for
kinges, and all that are in aucthoritie, that we may live a quiet and peaceable lyfe with all godlynesse: for that is good and acceptable in the sight
of God our saviour.' etc. This is Saint Paules counsell. And who, I pray
you, was prince over the most part of Christians, when Gods holy spirite
by Saint Paules pen gave them this lesson? Forsooth, Caligula, Clodius,
or Nero, who were not onlye no Christians, but pagans, and also either
foolishe rulers, or most cruell tyrauntes. Wyll you yet heare the Worde
of God to the Jewes, when they were prisoners under Nabuchodonozor,
King of Babylon, after he had slaine their king, nobles, parentes, children
and kinsfolkes, burned their countrey, cities, yea, Hierusalem it selfe,
and the holy temple, and had caryed the residue remayning alive captives
with him unto Babylon? Wyll you heare yet what the prophete Baruch
sayth unto Gods people being in this captivitie? 'Pray you,' sayth the
prophete, 'for the lyfe of Nabuchodonozor, Kyng of Babylon, and for the
lyfe of Balthaser, his sonne, that their dayes may be as the dayes of
heaven upon the earth, that God also may geve us strength and lighten
our eyes, that we may live under the defence of Nabuchodonozor, King of
Babylon, and under the protection of Balthaser, his sonne, that we may
long do them service, and finde favour in their sight. Pray for us also unto
the Lord our God, for we have sinned agaynst the Lord our God.' Thus
farre the prophete Baruch his wordes: whiche are spoken by him unto
the people of God of that kyng who was an heathen, a tyraunt and cruel
oppressour of them, and had ben a murtherer of many thousandes of their

nation and a destroyer of their countrey, with a confession that their sinnes had deserved such a prince to raigne over them.

And shall the olde Christians, by Saint Paules exhortation, pray for Caligula, Clodius or Nero, shall the Jewes pray for Nabuchodonozor, these emperours and kinges being straungers unto them, being pagans and infidels, being murtherers, tyrauntes and cruell oppressours of them, and the destroyers of their countrey, countreymen and kinsmen, the burners of their villages, townes, cities and temples? And shall not we pray for the long, prosperous and godly raigne of our naturall prince, no straunger (which is observed as a great blessing in the Scriptures), of our Christian, our most gratious Soveraigne, no heathen, nor pagan prince? Shall we not pray for the health of our most mercifull, most loving Soveraigne, the preserver of us and our countrey in so long peace, quietnes and securitie, no cruell person, no tyraunt, no spoyler of our goodes, no shedder of our bloods, no burner and destroyer of our townes, cities and countrey, as were those for whom yet, as ye have heard, Christians, being their subjectes, ought to pray? Let us not commit so great ingratitude agaynst God and our Soveraigne as not continually to thanke God for this government, and for his great and continuall benefites and blessinges powred upon us by such government. Let us not commit so great a sinne agaynst God, agaynst our selves and our countrey as not to pray continually unto God for the long continuaunce of so gratious a ruler unto us and our countrey. Els shal we be unworthy any longer to enjoy those benefites and blessinges of God which hitherto we have had by her, and shalbe most worthy to fall into all those mischiefes and miseries whiche we and our countrey have by Gods grace through her government hitherto escaped. What shall we say of those subjectes – may we call them by the name of subjectes? – who neither be thankfull nor make any prayer to God for so gratious a Soveraigne; but also them selves take armor wickedly, assemble companies and bandes of rebels to breake the publike peace so long continued, and to make, not warre, but rebellion, to endaunger the person of such a gratious Soveraigne, to hazard the estate of their countrey (for whose defence they shoulde be redie to spende their lives) and being Englishemen, to robbe, spoyle, destroy and burne, in Englande, Englishemen, to kill and murther their owne neighbours and kinsfolke, their owne countreymen, to do all evill and mischiefe, yea, and more to then forraigne enemies woulde or coulde do? What shall we say of these men who use them selves thus rebelliously agaynst their gratious Soveraigne – who, yf God for their wickednes had geven them an heathen tyraunt to raigne over them, were by Gods Word bound to obey him and to pray

for him? What may be spoken of them, so farre doth their unkindnes, un-
naturalnesse, wickednesse, mischevousnesse in their doinges passe and
excel any thing and all thinges that can be expressed or uttered by wordes?
Only let us wishe unto all such most speedie repentaunce, and with so
greevous sorow of heart, as such so horrible sinnes against the majestie of
God do require, who in most extreme unthankfulnesse do rise not only
against their gratious prince, agaynst their naturall countrey, but agaynst
all their countremen, women and children, against them selves, their wives,
children and kinsfolkes, and by so wicked an example agaynst all Christendome and agaynst whole mankinde of all maner of people throughout
the wyde worlde: suche repentaunce, I say, suche sorowe of heart, God
graunt unto all such whosoever ryse of private and malitious purpose, as is
meete for suche mischeeves attempted and wrought by them.

And unto us and all other subjectes, God of his mercy graunt that we
may be most unlyke to all such, and most lyke to good, naturall, loving and
obedient subjectes: nay, that we may be such in deede, not only shewing
all obedience our selves, but as many of us as be able to the uttermost
of our power, habilitie and understanding, to stay and represse all rebels
and rebellions against God, our gratious prince, and natural countrey,
at every occasion that is offered unto us. And that whiche we all are hable
to do, unlesse we do it, we shall be most wicked and most worthy to
feele in the ende suche extreme plagues as God hath ever powred upon
rebels. Let us all make continuall prayers unto almightie God, even from
the bottome of our heartes, that he wyll geve his grace, power and strength
unto our gratious Queene Elizabeth to vanquishe and subdue all, aswell
rebels at home as forraine enemies, that all domesticall rebellions beyng
suppressed and pacified, and all outwarde invasions repulsed and abandoned, we may not only be sure and long continue in all obedience unto
our gratious Soveraigne and in that peaceable and quiet life whiche
hytherto we have lead under her Majestie with all securitie, but also that
both our gratious Queene Elizabeth and we her subjectes may altogether,
in al obedience unto God, the King of all kinges, and unto his holy
lawes, leade our lives so in this worlde in all vertue and godlinesse, that in
the worlde to come we may enjoy his everlasting kyngdome. Whiche I
beseche God to graunt, aswell to our gratious Soveraigne, as unto us all,
for his Sonne our saviour Jesus Christes sake, to whom with the Father
and the Holy Ghost, one God and King immortall, be all glory, prayse,
and thankes geving, worlde without ende. Amen.

Thus have you heard the first part of this Homilie; nowe good people
let us pray.

THE PRAYER

O most mightie God, the lorde of hoastes, the governour of all creatures, the only gever of all victories, who alone art hable to strengthen the weake against the mightie, and to vanquishe infinite multitudes of thyne enemies with the countenaunce of a fewe of thy servauntes calling upon thy name and trusting in thee: Defende, O Lorde, thy servaunt and our governour under thee, our Queene Elizabeth, and all thy people committed to her charge, and especially at this tyme, O Lorde, withstande the crueltie of all those which be common enemies aswel to the trueth of thy eternall Worde, as to their owne natural prince and countrey, and manifestly to this crowne and realme of Englande, whiche thou hast of thy divine providence assigned in these our dayes to the governement of thy servaunt, our Soveraigne and gratious Queene. O most mercifull Father, if it be thy holy wyll, make soft and tender the stonie heartes of all those that exalt them selves against thy trueth, and seeke eyther to trouble the quiet of this realme of Englande, or to oppresse the crowne of the same; and convert them to the knowledge of thy Sonne, the only saviour of the worlde, Jesus Christe, that we and they may joyntly glorifie thy mercies. Lighten, we besech thee, their ignoraunt heartes to embrace the trueth of thy Worde, or els so abate their crueltie, O most mightie Lorde, that this our Christian region, with others that confesse thy holy Gospel, may obtaine by thine ayde and strength suretie from al enemies without shedding of Christian blood, wherby all they whiche be oppressed with their tyrannie may be relieved, and they which be in feare of their crueltie may be comforted; and finally that all Christian realmes, and specially this realme of Englande, may by that defence and protection continue in the trueth of the Gospell, and enjoy perfect peace, quietnesse and securitie; and that we for these thy mercies, joyntly altogether with one consonant heart and voyce, may thankfully render to thee all laude and prayse, that we, knit in one godly concorde and unitie amongst our selves, may continually magnifie thy glorious name, who with thy Sonne, our saviour Jesus Christe, and the Holy Ghost, art one eternall, almightie and most mercifull God. To whom be all laude and prayse, worlde without ende. Amen.

The Seconde Part of the Homilie against Disobedience and Wylfull Rebellion

The seconde part.

As in the first part of this treatie of obedience of subjectes to their princes, and against disobedience and rebellion, I have alleaged divers sentences

out of the Holy Scriptures for profe: so shall it be good for the better both
declaration and confirmation of the sayde holsome doctrine to alleage
one example or two out of the same Holy Scriptures of the obedience of
subjectes, not only unto their good and gratious governours, but also unto
their evyll and unkinde princes.

As Kyng Saule was not of the best, but rather of the worst sort of
princes, as beyng out of Gods favour for his disobedience against God in
sparing in a wrong pitie the Kyng Agag, whom almightie God
commaunded to be slayne, according to the justice of God against his
sworne enemie: and although Saule of a devotion ment to sacrifice such
thinges as he spared of the Amalechites to the honour and service of God,
yet Saul was reproved for his wrong mercie and devotion, and was told
that obedience woulde have more pleased him then such lenitie; whiche
sinfull humanitie (sayth holy Chrisostome) is more cruell before God
then any murder or sheding of blood, when it is commaunded of God.
But yet how evill soever Saul the Kyng was and out of Gods favour,
yet was he obeyed of his subject David, the very best of al subjectes and
most valiaunt in the service of his prince and countrey in the warres,
the most obedient and loving in peace, and alwayes most true and faythfull
to his soveraigne and lorde, and furdest of from all maner rebellion. For
the which his most painfull, true and faythfull service, Kyng Saul yet
rewarded him not only with great unkindnes, but also sought his destruction and death by al meanes possible: so that David was faine to save
his lyfe, not by rebellion, nor any resistance, but by flight and hiding him
selfe from the Kynges sight. Whiche notwithstandyng, when King Saul
upon a time came alone into the cave where David was, so that David
might easely have slaine him, yet would he neither hurt him him selfe,
neither suffer any of his men to lay handes uppon him. An other time also
David entring by night with one Abisai, a valiaunt and a fearce man,
into the tent where Kyng Saul dyd lye a sleepe, where also he might yet
more easely have slayne him, yet woulde he neither hurt hym him selfe, nor
suffer Abisai, who was wylling and readie to slea kyng Saul, once to
touche him. Thus dyd David deale with Saul his prince, notwithstandyng
that Kyng Saul continually sought his death and destruction. It shall
not be amisse unto these deedes of David to adde his wordes, and to shewe
you what he spake unto such as encouraged him to take his oportunitie
and advauntage to slea Kyng Saul, as his mortall enemie, when he might.
'The Lord keepe me,' sayth David, 'from doing that thing, and from
laying handes upon my lorde, Gods annoynted. For who can lay his hande
uppon the Lordes annoynted and be giltlesse? As truely as the Lorde
liveth, except that the Lord do smyte him, or his dayes shall come to dye,
or that he go downe to warre and be slaine in battell, the Lorde be

mercifull unto me, that I lay not my hande upon the Lordes annointed.'
These be Davids wordes spoken at sundry times to divers his servauntes
provoking him to slay Kyng Saul, when oportunitie served him thereunto.
Neither is it to be omitted and left out howe, when an Amalechite had
slaine Kyng Saul even at Saules owne bidding and commaundement (for
he would live no longer nowe, for that he had lost the feelde agaynst
his enemies, the Philistines), the saide Amalechite makyng great hast to
bryng first worde and newes thereof unto David, as joyous unto him
for the death of his mortall enemie, bringing withall the crowne that was
upon Kyng Saules head and the bracelet that was upon his arme, both
as a proofe of the trueth of his newes and also as fit and pleasaunt presentes
unto David, beyng by God appoynted to be Kyng Saul his successour in
the kyngdome, yet was that faythfull and godly David so farre from
rejoycing at these newes that he rent his clothes, wept, and mourned, and
fasted; and so farre of from thankesgeving to the messenger, either for
his deede in kyllyng the Kyng, though his deadly enemie, or for his message
and newes, or for his presentes that he brought, that he sayde unto him,
'Howe happened it that thou wast not afrayde to lay thy handes uppon the
Lordes annoynted to slea him?' Whereupon, immediatly he commaunded
one of his servauntes to kill the messenger, and said, 'Thy blood be upon
thine owne head, for thyne owne mouth hath witnessed agaynst thy selfe
in confessing that thou hast slaine the Lordes annoynted.'

This example, dearely beloved, is notable, and the circumstances thereof
are well to be consydered, for the better instruction of all subjectes in their
bounden duetie of obedience, and perpetual fearing of them from attempt-
ing of any rebellion or hurt agaynst their prince. On the one part, David
was not only a good and true subject, but also such a subject as both
in peace and warre had served and saved his princes honour and lyfe, and
delivered his countrey and countreymen from great daungers of infidels,
forrayne and most cruell enemies, horribly invading the king and his
countrey: for the whiche David was in singuler favour with all the people,
so that he might have had great numbers of them at his commaundement,
yf he woulde have attempted any thing. Besides this, David was no
common or absolute subject, but heyre apparant to the crowne and kyngdome, by God appoynted to raigne after Saul: which, as yt increased
the favour of the people that knewe it towardes David, so dyd it make
Davids cause and case much differring from the case of common and
absolute subjectes. And, which is most of all, David was highlie and singu-
larlie in the favour of God. On the contrary part, Kyng Saul was out of
Gods favour, for that cause whiche is before rehearsed, and he, as it were,
Gods enemie, and therefore lyke in warre and peace to be hurtfull and

pernitious unto the common wealth, and that was knowen to many of his
subjectes, for that he was openlye rebuked of Samuel for his disobedience
unto God, which myght make the people the lesse to esteeme him. King
Saul was also unto David a mortall and deadly enemie, though without
Davids deserving, who by his faythfull, painfull, profitable, yea most
necessarie service had well deserved as of his countrey, so of his prince;
but Kyng Saule farre otherwyse: the more was his unkindnesse, hatred and
crueltie towardes such a good subject both odious and detestable. Yet
woulde David neither hym selfe slea nor hurt such an enemie, for that he
was his prince and lord, nor would suffer any other to kyll, hurt or lay
hande upon hym, when he might have ben slayne without any sturre, tumult or daunger of any mans lyfe.

Nowe let David aunswere to suche demaundes as men desirous of
rebellion do use to make. Shall not we, specially being so good men as we
are, ryse and rebell against a prince hated of God, and Gods enemie, and
therefore lyke not to prosper eyther in warre or peace, but to be hurtfull
and pernitious to the common wealth? No, saith good and godly David,
Gods and such a kynges faythfull subject, and so convicting such subjectes
as attempt any rebellion against such a king to be neither good subjectes
nor good men. But say they, shall we not ryse and rebell against so unkinde
a prince, nothing consydering or regarding our true faythfull and payneful
service, or the safegarde of our posteritie? No, saith good David, whom no
suche unkindnesse coulde cause to forsake his due obedience to his soveraigne. Shall we not, say they, ryse and rebell against our knowen, mortall
and deadly enemie, that seeketh our lives? No, saith godly David, who
had learned the lesson that our Saviour afterwarde playnely taught, that we
shoulde do no hurt to our felowe subjectes, though they hate us and be
our enemies: muche lesse unto our prince, though he were our enemie.
Shall we not assemble an armie of such good felowes as we are, and by
hazarding of our lives and the lives of such as shall withstande us, and
withall hazarding the whole estate of our countery, remove so naughtie a
prince? No, saith godly David, for I, when I myght without assembling
force or number of men, without tumult or hazarde of any mans lyfe,
or shedding of any drop of blood have delivered my selfe and my countery
of an evyll prince, yet woulde I not do it. Are not they, say some, lustie
and couragious captaynes, valiaunt men of stomacke, and good mens
bodyes, that do venture by force to kyll or depose their kyng, beyng a
naughtie prince, and their mortall enemie? They may be as lustie, as
couragious as they list, yet, saith godly David, they can be no good nor
godly men that so do: for I not only have rebuked, but also commaunded
hym to be slayne as a wicked man which slue Kyng Saule, myne enemie,

though he, beyng wearie of his life for the losse of the victorie against
his enemies, desired that man to slay hym. What shall we then do to an
evyll, to an unkynde prince, an enemie to us, hated of God, hurtfull to the
common wealth etc.? Lay no violent hande upon hym, saith good David,
but let hym live untyll God appoint and worke his ende, eyther in warre by
lawfull enemies, not by trayterous subjectes, or by naturall death. Thus
would godly David make aunswere: and Saint Paule, as ye heard before,
wylleth us to pray also for such a prince. If Kyng David woulde make
these aunsweres, as by his deedes and wordes recorded in the Holy Scriptures in deede he doth make unto all such demaundes concerning rebelling
against evyll princes, unkinde princes, cruell princes, princes that be to
their good subjectes mortall enemies, princes that are out of Gods favour,
and so hurtfull, or like to be hurtfull to the common wealth, what aunswere, thinke you, would he make to those that demaunde whether they
(being naughtie and unkinde subjectes) may not, to the great hazarde
of the lyfe of many thousandes and the utter daunger of the state of the
common wealth and whole realme, assemble a sort of rebels to put in
feare, or to depose or destroy their naturall and loving Princes, enemie to
none, good to all, even to them the worst of all other, the mayntayner
of perpetuall peace, quietnesse and securitie, most beneficiall to the common wealth, most necessarie for the safegarde of the whole realme? What
aunswere would David make to their demaunde, whether they may not
attempt, cruelly and unnaturally, to destroy so peaceable and mercyfull a
Princes? What, I say, woulde David, so reverently speaking of Saule and so
paciently suffering so evyll a King, what woulde he aunswere and say to
such demaundes? What woulde he say, nay what would he do to such
hie attempters, who so said and dyd, as you before have hearde, unto hym
that slue the Kyng, his maister, though a most wicked prince? If he
punished with death, as a wicked doer, such a man, with what reproches
of wordes woulde he revyle such, yea, with what tormentes of most
shamefull deathes woulde he destroy suche hell houndes rather then evyll
men, suche rebels, I meane, as I last spake of? For if they who do disobey
an evyll and unkynde prince be most unlyke unto David, that good
subject, what be they who do rebell against a moste naturall and lovyng
prince? And if David, beyng so good a subject that he obayed so evyll a
kyng, was worthy of a subject to be made a kyng hym selfe, what be
they who are so evyll subjectes that they wyll rebell against their gratious
prince worthy of? Surely no mortall man can expresse with wordes, nor
conceave in mynde the horrible and most dreadfull dampnation that such
be worthy of, who, disdayning to be the quiet and happy subjectes of
their good prince, are most worthy to be the miserable captives and vyle

slaves of that infernall tyraunt Satan, with hym to suffer eternall slaverie and tormentes. This one example of the good subject David out of the Olde Testament may suffice, and for the notablenesse of it serve for all.

In the Newe Testament the excellent example of the blessed Virgin Marie, the mother of our saviour Christe, doth at the first offer it selfe. When proclamation or commaundement was sent into Jurie from Augustus, the Emperour of Rome, that the people there shoulde repaire unto their owne cities and dwellyng places, there to be taxed, neither dyd the blessed virgin, though both highly in Gods favour and also being of the royall blood of the auncient naturall kinges of Jurie, disdaine to obey the commaundement of an heathen and forraine prince, when God had placed such a one over them; neither dyd she alledge for an excuse that she was great with chylde, and most neare her time of deliveraunce; neither grudged she at the length and tediousnesse of the journey from Nazareth to Bethlehem, from whence and whyther she most go to be taxed; neither repined she at the sharpnesse of the dead time of winter, being the latter ende of December, an unhandsome time to travell in, specially a long journey for a woman being in her case: but, al excuses set a part, she obeyed, and came to the appoynted place, where at her comming she founde such great resort and throng of people, that finding no place in any inne, she was faine after her long, painefull and tedious journey, to take up her lodging in a stable, where also she was delivered of her blessed childe (and this also declareth howe neare her time she toke that journey). This obedience of this most noble and most vertuous ladie to a forraigne and pagan prince doth well teache us, who in comparison to her are most base and vile, what redie obedience we do owe to our naturall and gratious Soveraigne. Howebeit in this case the obedience of the whole Jewish nation (beyng otherwyse a stubberne people) unto the commaundement of the same forraigne heathen prince doth prove that such Christians as do not most readily obey their naturall gratious Soveraigne are farre worse then the stubberne Jewes, whom yet we accompt as the worst of all people.

But no example ought to be of more force with us Christians then the example of Christe, our maister and Saviour, who, though he were the Sonne of God, yet dyd alwayes behave him selfe moste reverently to such men as were in aucthoritie in the worlde in his time, and he not rebelliously behaved him selfe, but openly dyd teache the Jewes to pay tribute unto the Romane Emperour, though a forraigne and a pagan prince; yea, him selfe with his apostles payde tribute unto him; and finally, being brought before Pontius Pilate, a straunger borne, and an heathen man, beyng lord president of Jurie, he acknowledged his aucthoritie and power to be geven him from God, and obeyed paciently the sentence of most painefull and shameful death, which the sayde judge pronounced and gave moste unjustly agaynst hym, without any grudge, murmuring or evil word once geving. There be many other examples of the obedience to princes, even suche as be evil, in the Newe Testament, to the utter confusion of disobedient and rebellious people, but this one may be an eternal example, which the Sonne of God, and so the Lorde of all, Jesus Christ, hath geven to us, his Christians and servauntes, and such as may serve for al, to teache us to obey princes, though straungers, wicked and wrongfull, when God for our sinnes shall place such over us. Whereby it foloweth unavoydably that such as do disobey or rebell agaynst their owne naturall gratious soveraignes, howsoever they call them selves or be named of others, yet are they in deede no true Christians, but worse then Jewes, worse then heathens, and such as shall never enjoy the kingdome of heaven, which Christe by his obedience purchased for true Christians, being obedient to him the Kyng of al kynges, and to their prince whom he hath placed over them. The which kyngdome, the peculiar place of all such obedient subjectes, I beseche God our heavenly Father, for the same our saviour Jesus Christes sake, to graunt unto us, to whom with the Holy Ghost be all laude, honour and glory, now and for ever, Amen.

Thus have you heard the seconde part of this Homelie; nowe good people let us pray.

THE PRAYER: as before.

The Thirde Part of the Homilie against Disobedience and Wylfull Rebellion

The thirde part.

As I have in the first part of this treatise shewed unto you the doctrine of the Holye Scriptures as concerning the obedience of true subjects to their princes, even aswell to such as be evill as unto the good, and in the second part of the same treatie confirmed the sayde doctrine by notable examples likewyse taken out of the Holy Scriptures: so remaineth it nowe that I partly do declare unto you in this third part what an abhominable sinne agaynst God and man rebellion is, and howe dreadfully the wrath of God is kindled and inflamed agaynst all rebels, and what horrible plagues, punishmentes, and deathes, and finally eternal dampnation doth hang over their heades; as howe on the contrary part good and obedient subjects are in Gods favour, and be partakers of peace, quietnesse and securitie,

with other Gods manifolde blessinges in this worlde, and by his mercies
through our saviour Christe, of lyfe everlasting also in the worlde to come.
Howe horrible a sinne against God and man rebellion is can not possiblie
be expressed according unto the greatnesse therof. For he that nameth
rebellion, nameth not a singuler, or one only sinne, as is theft, robberie,
murther and such like, but he nameth the whole poodle and sinke of
all sinnes against God and man, against his prince, his countrey, his countreymen, his parentes, his children, his kinsefolkes, his freendes, and
against al men universally: al sinnes, I say, against God and all men heaped
together nameth he that nameth rebellion. For concerning the offence of
Gods majestie, who seeth not that rebellion ryseth first by contempt of
God and of his holy ordinaunces and lawes, wherin he so straightly commaundeth obedience, forbiddeth disobedience and rebellion? And besides
the dishonour done by rebels unto Gods holy name by their breaking
of the othe made to their prince with the attestation of Gods name and
calling of his majestie to witnesse, who heareth not the horrible othes and
blasphemies of Gods holy name that are used dayly amongst rebelles,
that is eyther amongst them or heareth the trueth of their behaviour? Who
knoweth not that rebels do not only them selves leave all workes necessarie
to be done upon workedayes undone, whyles they accomplishe their
abominable worke of rebellion, and do compell others that woulde gladly
be well occupied to do the same, but also howe rebels do not only leave
the sabbath day of the Lorde unsanctified, the temple and churche of
the Lorde unresorted unto, but also do by their workes of wickednesse
most horribly prophane and pollute the sabbath day, serving Satan, and by
doyng of his worke making it the devils day in steede of the Lordes day?
Besides that, they compell good men that woulde gladly serve the Lorde
assembling in his temple and church upon his day, as becommeth the
Lordes servauntes, to assemble and meete armed in the feelde to resist the
furie of such rebels. Yea, and many rebels, lest they should leave any
part of Gods commaundementes in the first table of his lawe unbroken or
any sinne against God undone, do make rebellion for the mainteynaunce
of their images and idols, and of their idolatrie committed or to be
committed by them, and, in despite of God, cut and teare in sunder his
Holy Worde, and treade it under their feete, as of late ye knowe was done.

As concerning the second table of Gods lawe, and all sinnes that may
be committed against man, who seeth not that they be all contayned
in rebellion? For first, the rebels do not only dishonour their prince, the
parent of their countrey, but also do dishonour and shame their naturall
parentes, if they have any, do shame their kinred and freendes, do disherite and undo for ever their chyldren and heyres. Theftes, robberies and

murthers, which of all sinnes are most lothed of most men, are in no men
so much, nor so pernitiously and mischeevously, as in rebels. For the
most errant theeves and cruellest murtherers that ever were, so long as they
refrayne from rebellion, as they are not many in number, so spreadeth
their wickednesse and damnation unto a fewe: they spoyle but a fewe, they
shead the blood but of few in comparison. But rebels are the cause of
infinite robberies and murthers of great multitudes, and of those also whom
they shoulde defende from the spoyle and violence of other; and, as
rebels are many in number, so doth their wickednesse and damnation
spread it selfe unto many. And if whordome and adulterie amongst suche
persons as are agreeable to suche wickednesse are (as they in deede be)
most damnable, what are the forceable oppressions of matrones and mens
wyves, and the violating and deflowring of virgins and maydes, which
are most ryfe with rebels, howe horrible and damnable, thinke you, are
they? Nowe, besides that rebels, by breache of their fayth geven and othe
made to their prince, be guyltie of most damnable perjurie, it is wonder-
ous to see what false colours and fayned causes, by sclaunderous lyes made
upon their prince and the counsellers, rebels wyll devise to cloke their
rebellion withall, which is the worst and most damnable of al false-witnesse-
bearing that may be possible. For what shoulde I speake of coveting or
desiring of other mens wives, houses, landes, goodes, and servauntes in
rebels, who by their willes would leave unto no man any thing of his
owne?

Thus you see that al Gods lawes are by rebels violated and broken, and
that all sinnes possible to be committed against God or man be contayned
in rebellion: which sinnes, if a man list to name by the accustomed
names of the seven capital or deadly sinnes, as pryde, envie, wrath, covetousnesse, slouth, gluttonie and lecherie, he shall finde them all in rebellion,
and amongst rebels. For first, as ambition and desire to be a loft, whiche
is the propertie of pryde, styrreth up many mens myndes to rebellion,
so commeth it of a luciferian pryde and presumption that a fewe rebellious
subjectes shoulde set them selves up against the majestie of their prince,
against the wysdome of the counsellers, against the power and force of all
nobilitie, and the faythfull subjectes and people of the whole realme. As
for envie, wrath, murther and desire of blood, and covetousnesse of other
mens goods, landes and livinges, they are the inseparable accidentes of
all rebels, and peculier properties that do usually stirre up wicked men unto
rebellion. Nowe such as by riotousnes, gluttonie, drunkennesse, excesse
of apparell, and unthriftie games have wasted their owne goodes unthriftily,
the same are most apt unto and most desirous of rebellion, whereby they
trust to come by other mens goodes unlawfully and violently. And where

other gluttons and drunkardes take to much of such meates and drinkes
as are served to tables, rebels wast and consume in short space all corne in
barnes, feeldes or elswhere, whole graners, whole storehouses, whole
cellers, devoure whole flockes of sheepe, whole droves of oxen and kine.
And as rebels that are maried, leaving their owne wives at home, do most
ungraciously, so much more do unmaried men worse then any stallands
or horses, being now by rebellion set at libertie from correction of lawes
which bridled them before, whiche abuse by force other mens wives
and daughters, and ravishe virgins and maydens most shamfullie, abomina-
blie and damnablie. Thus all sinnes, by all names that sinnes may be
named, and by all meanes that all sinnes may be committed and wrought,
do all wholly upon heapes folowe rebellion, and are to be founde altogether amongst rebelles.

Nowe wheras pestilence, famine and warre are by the Holy Scriptures
declared to be the greatest worldly plagues and miseries that lightly can be,
it is evident that all the miseries whiche all these plagues have in them
do wholly altogether folowe rebellion, wherein as all their miseries be, so
is there much more mischiefe then in them all. For it is knowen that in
the resorting of great companies of men together, whiche in rebellion happeneth both upon the part of true subjectes and of the rebels, by their
close lying together, and corruption of the ayre and place where they do
lye with ordure and much filth in the hoatte weather, by unholsome
lodging and lying often upon the grounde, specially in colde and wette
wethers in winter, by their unholsome dyet and feeding at all times, and
often by famine and lacke of meate and drinke in due time, and agayne
by taking to much at other tymes: it is wel knowen, I say, that aswell
plagues and pestilences, as al other kindes of sicknesse and maladies by
these meanes grow upon and amongst men, wherby moe men are consumed at the length then are by dint of sworde sodenly slaine in the feelde.
So that not only pestilences, but also al other sicknesse, diseases and
maladies do folowe rebellion, whiche are much more horrible then plagues,
pestilences and diseases sent directlye from God, as hereafter shall appeare
more playnely. And as for hunger and famine, they are the peculiar
companions of rebellion, for whiles rebels do in short time spoyle and
consume all corne and necessarie provision which men with their labours
had gotten and appoynted upon for their finding the whole yere after,
and also do let al other men, husbandmen and others, from their husband-
rie and other necessarie workes, whereby provision shoulde be made for
times to come, who seeth not that extreme famine and hunger must
needes shortlye ensue and folowe rebellion? Now whereas the wyse kyng
and godly prophete, David, judged warre to be worse then eyther famine

or pestilence, for that these two are often suffered by God for mans amendement, and be not sinnes of them selves, but warres have alwayes the sinnes and mischiefes of men upon the one side or other joyned with them, and therefore is warre the greatest of these worldly mischiefes – but of all warres, civill warre is the worst, and farre more abominable yet is rebellion then any civill warre, being unworthie the name of any warre, so farre it exceedeth all warres in all naughtinesse, in all mischiefe and in all abomination. And therefore our saviour Christe denounceth desolation and destruction to that realme that by sedition and rebellion is divided in it selfe. Nowe as I have shewed before that pestilence and famine, so is it yet more evident that al the calamities, miseries and mischiefes of warre be more greevous and do more folowe rebellion then any other warre, as beyng farre worse then all other warres. For not only those ordinarie and usuall mischiefes and miseries of other warres do folowe rebellion, as corne and other thinges necessarie to mans use to be spoyled, houses, villages, townes, cities to be taken, sacked, burned and destroyed, not only many wealthie men, but whole countreys to be impoverished and utterly beggered, many thousandes of men to be slaine and murthered, women and maides to be violated and deflowred: thinges, when they are done by forraigne enemies, we do much mourne, as we have great causes, yet are all these miseries without any wickednesse wrought by any our countreymen. But when these mischiefes are wrought in rebellion by them that shoulde be frendes, by countreymen, by kinsmen, by those that shoulde defende their countrey and countreymen from such miseries, the miserie is nothing so great as is the mischiefe and wickednes when the subjectes unnaturally do rebell against their prince, whose honour and life they shoulde defende, though it were with losse of their owne lives: countreymen to disturbe the publique peace and quietnesse of their coun-trey, for defence of whose quietnesse they should spende their lives; the brother to seeke and often to worke the death of his brother, the sonne of the father; the fathers to seeke or procure the death of his sonnes, being at mans age, and by their faultes to disherite their innocent children and kinsmen their heyres for ever, for whom they might purchase livinges and landes, as naturall parentes do take care and paynes and be at great costes and charges; and universally, in steade of al quietnesse, joy and feli-citie, which do folow blessed peace and due obedience, to bryng in all trouble, sorowe, disquietnesse of mindes and bodies, and all mischiefe and calamities, to turne all good order upside downe, to bryng all good lawes in contempt and to treade them under feete, to oppresse all vertue and honestie and all vertuous and honest persons, and to set all vice and wickednesse and all vicious and wicked men at libertie, to worke their wicked willes, whiche were before bridled by holsome lawes, to weaken, to overthrowe and to consume the strength of the realme, their naturall countrey, aswell by the spending and wasting of the money and treasure of the prince and realme, as by murthering of the people of the same, their owne countreymen, who shoulde defende the honour of their prince and libertie of their countrey against the invasion of forraigne enemies: and so finally to make their countrey, thus by their mischeefe weakened, redie to be a pray and spoyle to all outward enemies that wyl invade it, to the utter and perpetuall captivitie, slaverie and destruction of all their countreymen, their chyldren, their freendes, their kinsfolkes left alive, whom by their wicked rebellion they procure to be delivered into the handes of forraigne enemies, as much as in them doth lye. In forraigne warres our countreymen, in obtayning the victorie, wynneth the prayse of valiauntnesse; yea, and though they were overcommed and slayne, yet winne they an honest commendation in this worlde, and dyeth in a good conscience for serving God, their prince and their countrey, and be chyldren of eternall salvation. But in rebellion, howe desperate and strong soever they be, yet win they shame here in fighting against God, their prince and countrey, and therefore justly do fall headlong into hell if they dye, and live in shame and fearefull conscience, though they escape. But commonly they be rewarded with shamefull deathes, their heades and carkases set upon poles, or hanged in chaynes, eaten with kytes and crowes, judged unworthy the honour of buryall, and so their soules, if they repent not (as commonly they do not), the devyll harrieth them into hell, in the middest of their mischeefe. For which dreadfull execution Saint Paule sheweth the cause of obedience, not only for feare of death, but also in conscience to Godward, for feare of eternall damnation in the world to come.

Wherfore, good people, let us as the chyldren of obedience feare the dreadfull execution of God and lyve in quiet obedience to be the chyldren of everlasting salvation. For as heaven is the place of good obedient subjectes, and hell the pryson and dungeon of rebels against God and their prince, so is that realme happy where most obedience of subjectes doth appeare, being the very figure of heaven; and contrarywyse, where most rebellions and rebels be, ther is the expresse similitude of hell, and the rebels them selves are the very figures of feendes and devyls, and their captayne the ungratious paterne of Lucifer and Satan, the prince of darknesse, of whose rebellion, as they be folowers, so shall they of his damnation in hell undoubtedly be partakers; and as undoubtedly chyldren of peace the inheritours of heaven with God the Father, God the Sonne, and God the Holy Ghost, to whom be all honour and glory for ever and ever. Amen.

Thus have you heard the thirde part of this Homilie; nowe good people let us pray.

THE PRAYER: as before.

The Fourth Part of the Homilie against Disobedience and Wylfull Rebellion.

The fourth part.

For your further instruction, good people, to shewe unto you howe much almightie God doth abhorre disobedience and wylfull rebellion, specially when rebels advaunce them selves so hie that they arme them selves with weapon, and stand in feelde to fight against God, their prince and their countrey, it shall not be out of the way to shewe some examples set out in Scriptures, written for our eternall erudition.

We may soone know, good people, howe heynous offence the trecherie of rebellion is, if we call to remembraunce the heavie wrath and dreadfull indignation of almightie God against such subjectes as do only but inwardly grudge, mutter and murmure against their governours, though their inward treason so privyly hatched in their brestes come not to open declaration of their doinges; as harde it is, whom the devil hath so farre intised against Gods Word to kepe themselves there: no, he meaneth styl to blow the cole, to kindle their rebellious heartes to flame into open deedes, if he be not with grace speedyly withstanded. Some of the chyldren of Israel, beyng murmurers against their magistrates appoynted over them by God, were stricken with foule leprosie; many were burnt up with fire sodaynly sent from the Lorde; sometyme a great sort of thousandes were consumed with the pestilence; sometyme they were stinged to death with a straunge kind of firie serpentes; and (whiche is most horrible) some of the captaynes with their bande of murmurers, not dying by any usuall or naturall death of men, but the earth opening, they with their wives, chyldren and families were swalowed quicke downe unto hell. Whiche horrible destructions of such Israelites as were murmurers against Moyses, appoynted by God to be their head and cheefe magistrate, are recorded in the booke of Numbers and other places of the Scriptures for perpetuall memorie and warning to all subjectes howe highly God is displeased with the murmuring and evyll speaking of subjectes against their princes, for that, as the Scripture recordeth, their murmure was not against their prince onlye beyng a mortall creature, but against God hym selfe also. Nowe, if such straunge and horrible plagues dyd fall upon such subjectes as did only murmure and speake evyll against their heades, what shall become of those most wicked impes of the devil that do conspire, arme them selves, assemble great numbers of armed rebels, and lead them with them agaynst their prince and countrey, spoyling and robbing, killing and murthering all good subjectes that do withstand them, as many as they may prevaile against? But those examples are written to stay us, not onlye from such mischiefes, but also from murmuring or speaking once an evil word agaynst our prince, which though any shoulde do never so secretly, yet do the Holy Scriptures shewe that the verye birdes of the ayre wyll bewray them. And these so many examples before noted out of the same Holy Scriptures do declare that they shall not escape horrible punishment therefore.

Nowe concerning actuall rebellion, amongst many examples thereof set foorth in the Holy Scriptures, the example of Absolon is notable: who entering into conspiracie agaynst King David, his father, both used the advise of very wittie men, and assembled a very great and huge companie of rebels. The whiche Absolon, though he were most goodly of person, of great nobilitie, being the Kinges sonne, in great favour of the people, and so dearely beloved of the King hym selfe, so much that he gave commaundement that (notwithstandyng his rebellion) his lyfe shoulde be saved: when for these consyderations, most men were afrayd to lay their handes upon him, a great tree stretching out his arme, as it were for that purpose, caught him by the great and long bushe of his goodly heere, lapping about it as he fled hastyly bareheaded under the sayde tree, and so hanged him up by the heere of his head in the ayre, to geve an eternal document that neither comlinesse of personage, neither nobilitie, nor favour of the people, no, nor the favour of the king him selfe can save a rebell from due punishement: God, the King of all kinges, being so offended with hym, that rather then he shoulde lacke due execution for his treason, every tree by the way wyll be a gallous or gibbet unto him, and the heere of his owne head wylbe unto him in steade of an haulter to hang him up with, rather then he shoulde lacke one. A fearefull example of Gods punishment, good people, to consyder! Nowe Achitophel, though otherwyse an exceeding wyse man, yet the mischevous counseller of Absolon in this wicked rebellion, for lacke of an hangman, a convenient servitour for suche a traytour, went and hanged up him selfe: a worthie ende of all false rebelles, who, rather then they shoulde lacke due execution, wyll by Gods just judgement become hangmen unto them selves. Thus happened it to the captaynes of that rebellion, beside fourtie thousande of rascall rebels slaine in the feelde and in the chase. Likewyse is it to be seene in the Holy Scriptures howe that great rebellion which the traitor Seba moved in Israel was sodenly appeased, the head of the captaine traitour, by the meanes of a silie woman, beyng cut of.

And as the Holy Scriptures do shewe, so doth dayly experience prove, that the counsels, conspiracies and attemptes of rebels never toke effect, neither came to good, but to most horrible ende. For though God do often tymes prosper just and lawful enemies, whiche be no subjectes, agaynst their forraigne enemies, yet dyd he never long prosper rebellious subjectes agaynst their prince, were they never so great in aucthoritie or so many in number. Five princes, or kynges (for so the Scripture tearmeth them) with al their multitudes coulde not prevaile agaynst Chodorlaomor, unto whom they had promised loialtie and obedience, and had continued in the same certaine yeres, but they were all overthrowen and taken prisoners by him; but Abraham with his familie and kinsfolkes, an handfull of men in respect, owyng no subjection unto Chodorlaomor, overthrew him and all his hoast in battaile, and recovered the prisoners, and delivered them. So that though warre be so dreadful and cruel a thing, as it is, yet doth God often prosper a fewe in lawful warres with forraigne enemies agaynst many thousandes, but never yet prospered he subjectes being rebels against their natural soveraigne, were they never so great or noble, so many, so stout, so wittie and pollitike, but alwayes they came by the overthrow and to a shameful ende: so much doth God abhorre rebellion, more then other warres, though otherwyse being so dreadful and so great a destruction to mankinde. Though not only great multitudes of the rude and rascal commons, but sometime also men of great wit, nobilitie and aucthoritie have moved rebellions against their lawfull princes, (whereas true nobilitie shoulde most abhorre such vilanous and true wysdome shoulde most detest such frantike rebellion). Though they woulde pretende sundrie causes, as the redresse of the common wealth (whiche rebellion of all other mischiefes doth most destroy), or reformation of religion (wheras rebellion is most agaynst all true religion), though they have made a great shewe of holye meaning by beginning their rebellions with a counterfet service of God (as dyd wicked Absolon begin his rebellion with sacrificing unto God), though they display and beare about ensignes and banners, whiche are acceptable unto the rude ignorant common people, great multitudes of whom by suche false pretences and shewes they do deceave and drawe unto them: yet were the multitudes of the rebelles never so huge and great, the captaynes never so noble, politike and wittie, the pretences fained to be never so good and holie, yet the speedie overthrowe of all rebels of what number, state or condition soever they were, or what colour or cause soever pretended, is and ever hath ben such that God thereby doth shewe that he alloweth neither the dignitie of any person, nor the multitude of any people, nor the weight of any cause as sufficient for the which the subjectes may move rebellion against their princes. Turne over and reade the histories of all nations, looke over the chronicles of our owne countrey, call to mynde so many rebellions of olde tyme, and some yet freshe in memorie, ye shall not finde that God ever prospered any rebellion against their naturall and lawfull prince, but contrarywyse that the rebelles were overthrowen and slaine, and such as were taken prysoners dreadfully executed. Consyder the great and noble families of dukes, marquesses, earles and other lords, whose names ye shall reade in our chronicles, nowe cleane extinguished and gone, and seeke out the causes of the decay: you shall finde that not lacke of issue and heyres male hath so muche wrought that decay and waste of noble blooddes and houses as hath rebellion.

And for so much as the redresse of the common wealth hath of olde ben the usuall fayned pretence of rebels, and religion nowe of late beginneth to be a colour of rebellion, let all godly and discrete subjectes consyder well of both, and first concerning religion. If peaceable King Salomon was judged of God to be more meete to buylde his temple (wherby the ordering of religion is meant) then his father, King David, though otherwyse a most godly kyng, for that David was a great warrier and had shed much blood, though it were in his warres against the enemies of God, of this may al godly and reasonable subjectes consyder that a peaceable prince, specially our most peaceable and mercyfull Queene, who hath hytherto shed no blood at all, no, not of her most deadly enemies, is more lyke and farre meeter eyther to set up or to mayntayne true religion then are blooddy rebelles, who have not shead the blood of Gods enemies, as Kyng David had done, but do seeke to shead the blood of Gods freendes, of their owne countreymen, and of their owne most deare freendes and kynsefolke, yea, the destruction of their most gratious prince and naturall countrey, for defence of whom they ought to be redie to shead their blood if neede shoulde so require. What a religion it is that such men and by such meanes woulde restore may easyly be judged: even as good a religion, surely, as rebelles be good men and obedient subjectes, and as rebellion is a good meane of redresse and reformation, beyng it selfe the greatest deformation of all that may possiblie be. But, as the trueth of the Gospell of our saviour Christe beyng quietly and soberly taught, though it do cost them their lives that do teache it, is hable to mayntayne the true religion, so hath a frantike religion neede of such furious mainteynaunces as is rebellion, and of such patrons as are rebelles, beyng redie not to dye for the true religion, but to kill all that shall or dare speake against their false superstition and wicked idolatrie.

Nowe concerning pretenses of any redresse of the common wealth made by rebelles, every man that hath but halfe an eye may see howe vayne they be, rebellion beyng, as I have before declared, the greatest ruine and destruction of all common wealthes that may be possible. And who so looketh on the one part upon the persons and governement of the Queenes most honourable counsellers, by the experiment of so many yeres proved honorable to her Majestie, and most profitable and beneficiall unto our countrey and countreymen, and on the other part, consydereth the persons, state and conditions of the rebelles them selves, the reformers, as they take upon them, of the present governement, he shall finde that the most rash and harebrayned men, the most greatest unthriftes that have most leudely wasted their owne goodes and landes, those that are over the eares in debt, and such as for theftes, robberies and murthers dare not in any well governed common wealth, where good lawes are in force, shewe their faces, such as are of most leude and wicked behaviour and lyfe, and all such as wyll not, or can not live in peace, are alwayes most redie to move rebellion or to take part with rebelles. And are not these meete men, trowe you, to restore the common wealth decayed, who have so spoyled and consumed all their owne wealth and thrift? And very lyke to mende other mens maners, who have so vile vices and abominable conditions them selves? Surely that whiche they falsely call reformation is in deede not only a defacing or a deformation, but also an utter destruction of all common wealth, as would well appeare might the rebelles have their willes, and doth right well and to wel appeare by their doyng in such places of the countrey where rebelles do route: where, though they tary but a very litle whyle, they make such reformation that they destroy all places, and undo all men where they come, that the chylde yet unborne may rue it and shall many yeres hereafter curse them.

Let no good and discrete subjectes, therfore, folowe the flagge or banner displayed to rebellion, and borne by rebels, though it have the image of the plough paynted therin, with, God speede the plough, written under in great letters, knowing that none hinder the plough more then rebels, who will neither go to the plough them selves, nor suffer other that woulde go unto it. And though some rebelles beare the picture of the five woundes paynted agaynst those who put theyr only hope of salvation in the woundes of Christe, not those woundes which are painted in a clout by some leude paynter, but in those woundes whiche Christe hym selfe bare in his pretious bodye; though they, little knowing what the crosse of Christe meaneth, whiche neyther carver nor paynter can make, do beare the image of the crosse paynted in a ragge against those that have the crosse of Christ painted in their harts; yet though they paint withal in their flagges,

Hoc signo vinces (by this signe thou shalt get the victory) by a most fond
imitation of the posie of Constantinus magnus, that noble Christian
Emperour and great conquerer of Gods enemies, a most unmeete ensigne
for rebels, the enemies of God, their prince and countrey; or what other
banner soever they shall beare: yet let no good and godly subject, upon any
hope of victorie or good successe, folowe such standerd bearers of rebellion. For, as examples of such practises are to be founde as well in the
histories of olde as also of later rebellions in our fathers and our freshe
memorie, so, notwithstanding these pretences made and banners borne, are
recorded withal unto perpetual memorie the great and horrible murthers
of infinite multitudes and thousandes of the common people, slayne in
rebellion, the dreadfull executions of the aucthours and captaynes, the pitiful undoing of their wyves and children, and disheriting of the heyres of
the rebels for ever, the spoiling, wasting and destruction of the people and
countrey where rebellion was first begun, that the childe then yet unborne
might rue and lament it, with the finall overthrow and shameful deathes
of al rebels, set foorth as well in the histories of forraigne nations as in the
chronicles of our owne countrey, some thereof being yet in fresh memory,
which, yf they were collected together, woulde make many volumes and
bookes; but, on the contrary part, all good lucke, successe and prosperitie
that ever happened unto any rebels of any age, time or countrey may be
contayned in a very fewe lines, or wordes.

Wherefore, to conclude, let all good subjectes, consydering how horrible
a sinne against God, their prince, their countrey and countreymen, agaynst
al Gods and mans lawes rebellion is, being in deede not one severall
sinne, but all sinnes agaynst God and man heaped together, consydering
the mischevous life and deedes and the shameful endes and deathes of
al rebels hitherto, and the pitiful undoing of their wives, children and
families, and disheriting of their heyres for ever, and above all thinges,
consydering the eternall dampnation that is prepared for all impenitent
rebels, in hell, with Satan, the first founder of rebellion and graund
captayne of all rebels, let all good subjectes, I say, consydering these
thinges, avoyde and flee all rebellion as the greatest of all mischiefes and
embrace due obedience to God and our prince as the greatest of all vertues,
that we may both escape all evils and miseries that do folowe rebellion
in this worlde and eternall dampnation in the worlde to come, and enjoye
peace, quietnesse and securitie with all other Gods benefites and blessinges
whiche folowe obedience in this life, and finally may enjoy the kingdome
of heaven, the peculiar place of all obedient subjectes to God and their
prince in the worlde to come. Whiche I beseche God, the King of all
kinges, graunt unto us for the obedience of his Sonne, our saviour Jesus

Christe, unto whom with the Father and the Holy Ghost, one God
and Kyng immortall, all honour, service and obedience of all his creatures
is due for ever and ever, Amen.

Thus have you heard the fourth part of this Homilie; nowe good people
let us pray.

THE PRAYER: as before.

The Fifth Part of the Homilie against Disobedience and Wylfull Rebellion

The fifth part.

Whereas, after both doctrine and examples of due obedience of subjectes
to their princes, I declared lastly unto you what an abominable sin agaynst
God and man rebellion is, and what horrible plagues, punishementes
and deathes, with death everlasting finally, doth hang over the heades of
all rebels, it shall not be either impertinent or unprofitable nowe to declare
who they be whom the devyll, the first aucthour and founder of rebellion,
doth chiefely use to the stirring up of subjectes to rebell agaynst their lawful
princes: that, knowing them, you may flee them and their dampnable
suggestions, avoyde all rebellion and so escape the horrible plagues and
dreadful deathes, and dampnation eternall finally due to all rebels.

Though many causes of rebellion may be reckened, and almost as many
as there be vices in men and women, as hath ben before noted, yet in
this place I wyll only touche the principall and most usuall causes, as
specially ambition and ignoraunce. By ambition, I meane the unlawful and
restles desire in men to be of higher estate then God hath geven or
appoynted unto them. By ignoraunce, I meane no unskilfulnesse in artes
or sciences, but the lacke of knowledge of Gods blessed wil declared in his
Holy Word, whiche teacheth both extremely to abhorre all rebellion as
the roote of al mischiefe, and specially to delight in obedience as the beginning and foundation of al goodnes, as hath ben also before specified.
And as these are the two cheefe causes of rebellion, so are there specially
two sortes of men in whom these vices do raigne, by whom the devyll, the
aucthour of all evil, doth chiefely stirre up all disobedience and rebellion.
The restles ambitious having once determined by one meanes or other
to atchive to their intended purpose, when they can not by lawfull and
peaceable meanes clime so high as they do desire, they attempt the same by
force and violence: wherein, when they can not prevayle agaynst the
ordinarie aucthoritie and power of lawful princes and governours them

selves alone, they do seeke the ayde and helpe of the ignoraunt multitude, abusing them to their wicked purpose. Wherefore, seeing a fewe ambitious and malitious are the aucthours and heades, and multitudes of ignoraunt men are the ministers and furtherers of rebellion, the cheefe poynt of this part shalbe aswell to notifie to the simple and ignoraunt men who they be that have ben and be the usuall aucthours of rebellion, that they may know them, and also to admonishe them to beware of the subtill suggestions of such restlesse ambitious persons, and so to flee them: that rebellions (though attempted by a few ambitious) through the lacke of mainteynaunce by any multitudes may speedyly and easely without any great labour, daunger or damage be repressed and clearely extinguished.

It is well knowen, aswell by all histories as by dayly experience, that none have eyther more ambitiously aspired above emperours, kinges, and princes, nor have more perniitiously moved the ignoraunt people to rebellion against their princes, then certayne persons which falsely chalenge to them selves to be only counted and called spirituall. I must therefore here yet once agayne breefely put you, good people, in remembraunce out of Gods Holy Worde how our saviour Jesus Christe, and his holy apostles, the heades and cheefe of all true spirituall and ecclesiastical men, behaved them selves towardes the princes and rulers of their time, though not the best governours that ever were, that you be not ignoraunt whether they be the true disciples and folowers of Christe and his apostles, and so true spirituall men, that eyther by ambition do so highly aspire, or do most malitiously teache, or most perniciously do execute rebellion against their lawfull princes, being the worst of all carnall workes and mischeevous deedes. The Holy Scriptures do teach most expresly that our saviour Christ hym selfe and his holy apostle Saint Paule, Saint Peter, with others, were unto the magistrates and higher powers, which ruled at their being upon the earth, both obedient them selves, and did also diligently and earnestly exhort all other Christians to the lyke obedience unto their princes and governours. Whereby it is evident that men of the cleargie and ecclesiasticall ministers, as their successours, ought both them selves specially and before others to be obedient unto their princes, and also to exhort all others unto the same. Our saviour Christe likewise, teaching by his doctrine that his kyngdome was not of this world, dyd by his example in fleeing from those that woulde have made hym kyng confirme the same; expresly also forbidding his apostles, and by them the whole cleargie, all princely dominion over people and nations; and he and his holy apostles like wise, namely Peter and Paule, dyd forbid unto all ecclesiasticall ministers, dominion over the churche of Christe. And in deede whyles that ecclesiasticall ministers continued in Christes churche in that order

that is in Christes Worde prescribed unto them, and in Christian kyngdomes kept them selves obedient to their owne princes, as the Holy Scriptures do teache them, both was Christes churche more cleare from
ambitious emulations and contentions, and the state of Christian kyngdomes lesse subject unto tumultes and rebellions. But after that ambition
and desire of dominion entred once into ecclesiasticall ministers, whose
greatnesse, after the doctrine and example of our Saviour, should cheefly
stande in humbling of them selves, and that the Byshop of Rome, beyng by
the order of Gods Word none other then the byshop of that one see and
diocesse, and never yet well able to governe the same, dyd by intollerable
ambition chalenge not onlye to be the head of all the churche dispersed
throughout the worlde, but also to be lorde of all the kyngdomes of
the worlde, as is expresly set foorth in the booke of his owne Canon
Lawes, most contrary to the doctrine and example of our saviour Christe,
whose vicar and of his holy apostles, namely Peter, whose successour he
pretendeth to be. After this ambition entred, and this chalenge once made
by the Byshop of Rome, he became at once the spoyler and destroyer
both of the churche, whiche is the kyngdome of our saviour Christe, and
of the Christian Empire, and all Christian kyngdomes, as an universall
tyraunt over all. And whereas before that chalenge made, there was great
amitie and love amongst the Christians of all countreys, hereupon began
emulation and muche hatred betweene the Byshop of Rome and his
cleargie and freendes on the one part, and the Grecian cleargie and Christians of the East on the other part, for that they refused to acknowledge
any suche supreme aucthoritie of the Byshop of Rome over them: the
Byshop of Rome for this cause amongst others, not only naming them and
takyng them for schismatikes, but also never ceasyng to persecute them
and the Emperours who had their see and continuance in Greece, by styr-
ring of the subjectes to rebellion against their soveraigne lordes, and by
raysing deadly hatred and most cruell warres betweene them and other
Christian princes. And when the Bishoppes of Rome had translated the title
of the Emperour, and as muche as in them did lye, the Empire it selfe
from their lord, the Emperour of Greece, and of Rome also by right, unto
the Christian princes of the West, they became in short space no better
unto the West Emperours then they were before unto the Emperours of
Greece. For the usuall discharging of subjectes from their othes of fidelitie
made unto the Emperours of the West, their soveraigne lordes, by the
Byshoppes of Rome, the unnaturall stirring up of the subjectes unto rebellion agaynst their princes, yea, of the sonne agaynst the father, by the
Byshop of Rome, the most cruell and bloody warres raised amongst Christian princes of all kyngdomes, the horrible murder of infinite thousandes

of Christian men, beyng slayne by Christians, and whiche ensued there-
upon, the pitifull losses of so many goodly cities, countreys, dominions,
and kingdomes sometyme possessed by Christians in Asia, Africa, and
Europa, the miserable fall of the Empyre and church of Greece, sometime
the most florishing part of Christendome, into the handes of Turkes,
the lamentable diminishing, decay and ruine of Christian religion: the
dreadfull encrease of paganitie, and power of the infidels and miscreantes –
and al by the practise and procurement of the Byshop of Rome, chiefely,
is in the histories and chronicles written by the Byshop of Romes owne
favourers and freendes to be seene, and is well knowen unto all such as are
acquainted with the sayde histories.

The ambitious intent and most subtil drifts of the Byshops of Rome in
these their practises appeared evidently by their bolde attempt in spoyling
and robbing the Emperours of their townes, cities, dominions and kyngdomes in Italie, Lumbardie and Cicilie, of auncient ryght belonging unto
the Empire, and by the joyning of them unto their bishoprike of Rome,
or els geving them unto straungers to holde them of the churche and
Bishop of Rome as in capite, and as of the chiefe lordes thereof. By these
ambitious and in deede traiterous meanes, and spoyling of their soveraigne
lordes, the Bishops of Rome, of priestes, and none other by ryght then
the Bishops of one citie and diocesse, are by false usurpation become great
lordes of many dominions, mightie princes, yea, or emperours rather, as
clayming to have divers princes and kynges to their vassalles, leige men and
subjectes; as in the same histories written by their owne familiers and
courtyers is to be seene. And in deede, since the tyme that the Byshops of
Rome by ambition, treason and usurpation atcheeved and atteined to
this height and greatnesse, they behaved them selves more lyke princes,
kynges and emperours in al thinges, then remained lyke priestes, byshops
and ecclesiasticall, or (as they would be called) spirituall persons in any
one thing at all. For after this rate they have handled other kinges and
princes of other realmes throughout Christendome, aswell as their soveraigne lordes, the Emperours, usually dischargyng their subjectes of theyr
oth of fidelitie, and so stirring them up to rebellion agaynst theyr naturall
princes, whereof some examples shall in the last part hereof be notified
unto you.

Wherefore let all good subjectes, knowyng these speciall instrumentes
and ministers of the devyl to the stirryng up of al rebellions, avoyde and
flee them and the pestilent suggestions of suche forraigne usurpers and
theyr adherentes, and embrace all obedience to God and theyr naturall
princes and soveraignes, that they may enjoy Gods blessinges and theyr
princes favour in al peace, quietnesse and securitie in this world, and finally

attayne through Christ, our saviour, lyfe everlastyng in the worlde to
come. Which God the Father, for the same our saviour Jesus Christ his
sake, graunt unto us al, to whom with the Holy Ghost be al honour and
glory, world without ende. Amen.

Thus have you hearde the fifth part of this Homilie; nowe good people
let us pray.

THE PRAYER: as before.

The Sixt and Last Part of the Homilie agaynst Disobedience and Wylfull Rebellion

The sixt part.

Now whereas the injuries, oppressions, ravenie and tyrannie of the B. of
Rome, usurping aswell against their natural lordes, the Emperours, as
agaynst all other Christian kynges and kingdomes, and their continuall
stirring of subjectes unto rebellions agaynst theyr soveraigne lordes, whereof I have partlye admonyshed you before, were intollerable, and it may
seeme more then marvel that any subjectes would after such sort holde with
unnatural forraigne usurpers against their owne soveraigne lordes and
naturall countrey, it remayneth that I do declare the meane whereby they
compassed these matters, and so to conclude this whole treatie of due
obedience, and agaynst disobedience and wylfull rebellion.

You shall understande that by ignoraunce of Gods Worde, wherein they
kept all men, specially the common people, they wrought and brought
to passe all these thinges, making them beleve that all they sayde was true,
all that they dyd was good and godly, and that to holde with them in
all thinges, agaynst father, mother, prince, countrey and all men, was most
meritorious. And in deede what mischiefe wyll not blinde ignoraunce
leade simple men unto?

By ignoraunce, the Juish cleargie induced the common people to aske
the deliverie of Barabbas, the seditious murtherer, and to sue for the cruell
crucifiyng of our saviour Christe, for that he rebuked the ambition,
superstition and other vices of the high priestes and cleargie. For as our
saviour Christe testifieth, that those who crucified hym, wyst not what they
dyd: so doeth the holy apostle Saint Paul say, If they had knowen, yf
they had not ben ignoraunt, they woulde never have crucified the Lorde of
glory, but they knewe not what they dyd. Our saviour Christe hym selfe
also foreshewed that it should come to passe by ignorance that those who
shoulde persecute and murther his true apostles and disciples shoulde

thinke they dyd God acceptable sacrifice and good service: as it also is verified even at this day.

And in this ignoraunce have the Byshops of Rome kept the people of God, specially the common sort, by no meanes so much as by the withdrawyng of the Worde of God from them, and by keeping it under the vale of an unknowen straunge tongue. For as it served the ambitious humour of the Byshops of Rome to compell all nations to use the naturall language of the citie of Rome, where they wer byshops, whiche shewed a certaine acknowledging of subjection unto them, so yet served it much more their craftie purpose, therby to keepe all people so blinde, that they not knowing what they prayed, what they beleved, what they were commaunded by God, myght take all their commaundementes for Gods. For as they woulde not suffer the Holy Scriptures or churche service to be used or had in any other language then the Latine, so were very few even of the most simple people taught the Lordes Prayer, the Articles of the fayth and the Ten Commaundementes, other wyse then in Latine, whiche they understoode not: by whiche universall ignoraunce, all men were readie to beleve what soever they saide, and to do whatsoever they commaunded. For to imitate the apostles phrase: If the Emperours subjectes had knowen out of Gods Worde their dutie to their prince, they would not have suffered the Byshop of Rome to perswade them to forsake their soveraigne lord, the Emperour, against their oth of fidelitie, and to rebell against him, onlye for that he cast images (unto the whiche idolatrie was committed) out of the churches, whiche the Byshop of Rome bare them in hande to be heresie. If they had knowen of Gods Worde but as much as the Ten Commaundementes, they shoulde have founde that the Byshop of Rome was not onlye a traytour to the Emperour, his leige lord, but to God also, and an horrible blasphemer of his majestie in calling his Holy Worde and commaundement heresie: and that whiche the Byshop of Rome toke for a just cause to rebell agaynst his lawfull prince, they myght have knowen to be a dubbling and tripling of his most haynous wickednesse, heaped with horrible impietie and blasphemie. But lest the poore people shoulde knowe to muche, he woulde not let them have as muche of Gods Worde as the Ten Commaundementes wholly and perfectly, withdrawyng from them the seconde commaundement, that bewrayeth his impietie, by a subtill sacrilege. Had the Emperours subjectes likewyse knowen and ben of any understanding in Gods Worde, would they at other tymes have rebelled against their soveraigne lorde, and by their rebellion have holpen to depose him, only for that the Byshop of Rome dyd beare them in hande that it was symonie, and heresie to, for the Emperour to geve any ecclesiastical dignities or promotions to his learned chaplaines

or other of his learned cleargie, which all Christian Emperours before him
had done without controlement? Would they, I say, for that the Byshop
of Rome bare them so in hande, have rebelled by the space of more then
fourtie yeres together agaynst hym, with so much sheding of Christian
blood and murther of so many thousandes of Christians, and finally have
deposed their soveraigne lord, had they knowen, and had in Gods Worde
any understanding at all? Specially had they knowen that they dyd all
this to plucke from their soveraigne lorde and his successours for ever their
auncient right of the Empire, to geve it unto the Romishe cleargie and
to the Byshop of Rome, that he myght for the confirmation of one arch-
byshop, and for a Romishe ragge whiche he calleth a paule, scarce worth
twelve pence, receave many thousand crownes of golde, and of other
byshops lyke wyse great summes of money for their bulles, which is symonie in deede, woulde, I say, Christian men and subjectes by rebellion
have spent so muche Christian blood and have deposed their naturall,
most noble and most valiaunt prince to bryng the matter finally to this
passe, had they knowen what they dyd, or had any understanding in Gods
Worde at all? And as these ambitious usurpers, the Byshops of Rome,
have overflowed all Italie and Germanie with streames of Christian blood,
shed by the rebellions of ignoraunt subjectes against their naturall lordes,
the Emperours, whom they have styrred therunto by suche false pretenses,
so is there no countrey in Christendome whiche by their lyke meanes
and false pretenses hath not ben oversprinkled with the blood of subjectes
by rebellion against their naturall soveraignes, styrred up by the same
Byshops of Rome.

    And to use one example of our owne countrey: the Byshop of Rome
dyd pyke a quarell to Kyng John of Englande about the election of Steven
Langton to the bishoprike of Canterburie, wherein the Kyng had auncient
ryght, beyng used by his progenitours, all Christian kynges of Englande
before hym, the Byshop of Rome having no right, but had begun then to
usurpe upon the kynges of Englande, and all other Christian kinges, as
they had before done against their soveraigne lords, the Emperours: pro-
ceedyng even by the same wayes and meanes, and likewise cursing Kyng
John, and discharging his subjectes of their othe of fidelitie unto their
soveraigne lorde. Nowe, had Englishmen at that tyme knowen their dutie
to their prince set foorth in Gods Worde, woulde a great manye of the
nobles and other Englishmen, naturall subjectes, for this forraigne and unnatural usurper his vayne curse of the Kyng, and for his faygned discharging of them of their othe of fidelitie to their naturall lorde, uppon so
sclender or no grounde at all, have rebelled against their soveraigne lorde,
the Kyng? Woulde Englishe subjectes have taken part against the Kyng

of Englande and against Englishmen, with the Frenche king and Frenchmen, being incensed against this realme by the Byshop of Rome? Woulde
they have sent for and receaved the dolphin of Fraunce, with a great
armie of Frenchmen, into the realme of England; would they have sworne
fidelitie to the dolphin of Fraunce, breaking their othe of fidelitie to
their natural lorde, the Kyng of England, and have stande under the dol-
phins banner displayed against the Kyng of Englande? Woulde they
have expelled their soveraigne lorde, the Kyng of Englande, out of London,
the chiefe citie of England, and out of the greatest part of Englande
upon the southside of Trent, even unto Lincolne, and out of Lincolne it
selfe also, and have delivered the possession thereof unto the dolphin
of Fraunce, whereof he kept the possession a great whyle? Woulde they,
being Englishemen, have procured so great shedding of English blood and
other infinite mischiefes and miseries unto Englande, their naturall countrey, as dyd folowe those cruell warres and traiterous rebellion, the fruites
of the Bishop of Romes blessinges? Would they have driven their naturall
soveraigne lorde, the King of Englande, to such extremitie, that he was
inforced to submit him selfe unto that forraigne false usurper, the Byshop
of Rome, who compelled him to surrender up the crowne of England
into the handes of his legate, who in token of possession kept it in his
handes divers dayes, and then delivered it agayne to Kyng John upon that
condition that the Kyng and his successours, kynges of Englande, should
holde the crowne and kyngdome of Englande of the Byshop of Rome
and his successours, as the vassalles of the sayde byshops of Rome for ever:
in token whereof the kynges of Englande shoulde also pay an yerely
tribute to the sayd byshop of Rome as his vassals and liege men? Woulde
Englishemen have brought their soveraigne lorde and naturall countrey
into this thraldome and subjection to a false forraigne usurper, had they
knowen and had any understandyng in Gods Worde at all? Out of the
which most lamentable case, and most miserable tyrannie, raveny and
spoyle of the most greedie Romish wolves ensuing hereupon, the kynges
and realme of Englande could not rid them selves by the space of many
yeres after, the Byshop of Rome by his ministers continually not onlye
spoyling the realme and kynges of Englande of infinite treasure, but
also with the same money hyring and mainteining forraigne enemies against
the realme and kynges of Englande to kepe them in such his subjection,
that they shoulde not refuse to pay whatsoever those unsaciable wolves dyd
greedely gape for, and suffer what so ever those most cruell tyrauntes
woulde lay upon them. Would Englishe men have suffered this? Would
they by rebellion have caused this, trowe you, and al for the Bishop
of Romes causelesse curse, had they in those dayes knowen and under-

standed that God doeth curse the blessinges, and blesse the cursinges of
such wicked usurping bishops and tyrauntes, as it appeared afterwarde
in Kyng Henry the Eyght his dayes, and Kyng Edwarde the Sixt, and in
our gracious Soveraignes dayes that nowe is, where neither the Popes
curses, nor Gods manifolde blessinges are wanting. But in Kyng Johns
tyme the Byshop of Rome understanding the bruite blindnes, ignoraunce
of Gods Word and superstition of Englishe men, and howe much they
were enclined to worship the baylonicall beast of Rome, and to feare all his
threatninges and causeles curses, he abused them thus, and by their
rebellion brought this noble realme and kynges of Englande under his
most cruell tyranny, and to be a spoyle of his most vile and unsaciable
covetousnes and ravenie for a long and a great deale to long a time.

And to joyne unto the reportes of histories matters of later memorie,
coulde the Byshop of Rome have raysed the late rebellions in the North
and West countreys in the tymes of Kyng Henry and Kyng Edwarde,
our gratious Soveraignes father and brother, but by abusing of the ignoraunt people? Or is it not most evident that the Byshop of Rome hath
of late attempted by his Irish patriarkes and byshops sent from Rome with
his bulles (whereof some were deprehended) to breake downe the barres
and hedges of the publique peace in Irelande, only upon confidence easyly
to abuse the ignoraunce of the wylde Irishe men? Or who seeth not that
uppon lyke confidence yet more lately he hath likewyse procured the
breache of the publique peace in Englande (with the long and blessed
continuaunce whereof he is sore greeved) by the ministery of his disguised
chaplaines, creeping in lay mens apparel into the houses and whispering
in the eares of certayne Northen borderers, being men most ignoraunt of
their dutie to God and their prince of all people of the realme, whom,
therefore, as most meete and redie to execute his intended purpose, he
hath by the saide ignoraunt masse priestes, as blynde guydes leadyng
the blind, brought those seely blynde subjectes into the deepe dytche of
horrible rebellion, damnable to them selves and very daungerous to the
state of the realme, had not God of his mercy miraculously calmed that
raging tempest, not only without any shipwrake of the common wealth,
but almost without any shedding of Christian and Englishe blood at al.
And it is yet much more to be lamented, that not only common people,
but some other youthful or unskilfull princes also, suffer them selves to be
abused by the Byshop of Rome his cardinalles and byshops to the oppressing of Christian men, their faithfull subjectes, eyther them selves, or els
by procuring the force and strength of Christian men to be conveyed out
of one countrey to oppresse true Christians in an other countrey, and by
these meanes open an entrie unto Moores and infidels into the possession

of Christian realmes and countreys: other Christian princes, in the meane tyme, by the Bishop of Romes procuryng also, beyng so occupied in civil warres or so troubled with rebellions that they have neither leysure nor habilitie to conferre their common forces to the defence of their felowe Christians against such invasions of the common enemies of Christendome, the infidels and miscreantes. Woulde to God we myght only reade and heare out of histories of the olde, and not also see and feele these newe and present oppressions of Christians, rebellions of subjectes, effusion of Christian blood, destruction of Christian men, decay and ruyne of Christendome, increase of paganitie, most lamentable and pitifull to beholde, beyng procured in these our dayes, aswell as in tymes past, by the Bishop of Rome and his ministers, abusing the ignoraunce of Gods Worde, yet remaynyng in some Christian princes and people. By which sowre and bitter fruites of ignoraunce, al men ought to be moved to geve eare and credite to Goddes Worde, shewyng, as moste truely, so moste playnely, howe great a mischiefe ignoraunce is, and agayne howe great and howe good a gyft of God knowledge in Gods Worde is.

And to begyn with the cleargie, who though they do bragge nowe, as dyd sometime the Jewyshe cleargie, that they can not lacke knowledge, yet doth God by his holy prophetes both charge them with ignoraunce and threaten them also for that they have repelled the knowledge of Gods Worde and lawe from them selves and from his people, that he wyl repell them, that they shalbe no more his priestes. God lykewyse chargeth princes, aswell as priestes, that they shoulde endevour them selves to get understandyng and knowledge in his Worde, threatnyng his heavy wrath and destruction unto them yf they fayle thereof. And the Wyse man sayth to all men universally, princes, priestes and people: Where is no knowledge, there is no good, nor health to the soule: and that all men be vayne in whom is not the knowledge of God and his Holy Worde; that they who walke in darknes, wot not whither they go, and that the people that wyl not learne, shall fall into great mischiefes, as dyd the people of Israel, who, for their ignoraunce in Gods Word, were first ledde into captivitie. And when by ignoraunce, afterward, they woulde not knowe the tyme of their visitation, but crucified Christ our saviour, persecuted his holy apostles, and were so ignoraunt and blynde that when they dyd most wickedly and cruelly they thought they did God good and acceptable service (as do many by ignoraunce thynke even at this day), finally, through their ignoraunce and blindnes, their countrey, townes, cities, Hierusalem it selfe, and the holy temple of God were all moste horribly destroyed, the most chiefest part of their people slayne, and the rest ledde into most miserable captivitie. For he that made them had no pitie upon them, neither woulde spare them; and all for their ignoraunce. And the Holye Scriptures do teache that the people that will not see with their eyes, nor heare with their eares, to learne and to understand with their heartes, can not be converted and saved. And the wicked them selves, being damned in hell, shall confesse ignorance in Gods Worde to have brought them thereunto, saying: We have erred from the way of the trueth, and the lyght of ryghteousnesse hath not shined unto us, and the sunne of understandyng hath not rysen unto us; we have weeried our selves in the way of wickednesse and perdition, and have walked cumberous and crooked wayes: but the way of the Lorde, have we not knowen.   And aswel our Saviour him selfe as his apostle Saint Paul do teache that the ignoraunce of Gods Word commeth of the devil, is the cause of all errour and misjudging (as faleth out with ignoraunt subjectes, who can rather espie a litle mote in the eye of the prince, or a counseller, then a great beame in their owne) and universally it is the cause of al evil, and finally, of eternall damnation: Gods judgement being severe towardes those who, when the light of Christes Gospell is come into the worlde, do delight more in darknesse of ignoraunce, then in the light of knowledge in Gods Worde. For al are commaunded to reade or heare, to searche and studie the Holy Scriptures, and are promysed understandyng to be geven them from God, yf they so do; all are charged not to beleve eyther any dead man, nor yf an angell shoulde speake from heaven, much lesse yf the Pope do speake from Rome agaynst or contrary to the Worde of God, from the whiche we may not decline neither to the ryght hande nor to the left. In Gods Worde princes must learne how to obey God, and to governe men; in Gods Worde subjectes must learne obedience both to God and their princes. Old men and young, riche and poore, al men and women, al estates, sexes and ages are taught their severall duties in the Worde of God. For the Worde of God is bright, geving lyght unto all mens eyes, the shining lampe directing all mens pathes and steppes. Let us, therefore, awake from the sleepe and darknesse of ignoraunce, and open our eyes that we may see the lyght; let us ryse from the workes of darknes, that we may escape eternal darknesse, the due rewarde thereof: and let us walke in the lyght of Gods Worde whyles we have light, as becommeth the children of light, so directing the steps of our lives in that way whiche leadeth to light and lyfe everlasting that we may finally obtayne and enjoy the same. Which God, the father of lyghtes, who dwelleth in light incomprehensible and inaccessable, graunt unto us through the light of the world, our saviour Jesus Christ, unto whom with the Holy Ghost, one most glorious God, be all honour, prayse and thankes geving for ever and ever. Amen.

Thus have you hearde the sixt parte of this Homilie; nowe good people let us pray.

THE PRAYER: as before.

A Thankes Geving for the Suppression of the Last Rebellion.

O heavenly and most merciful Father, the defendour of those that put their trust in thee, the sure fortresse of all them that flee to thee for succour, who of thy most just judgementes for our disobedience and rebellion against thy Holy Word, and for our sinfull and wicked living nothing aunswering to our holy profession, wherby we have geven an occasion that thy holye name hath ben blasphemed amongst the ignoraunt, hast of late both sore abashed the whole realme and people of Englande with the terrour and daunger of rebellion, thereby to awake us out of our dead sleepe of carelesse securitie, and hast yet by the miseries folowyng the same rebellion more sharply punished part of our countrey men and Christian brethren, who have more neerely felt the same, and most dreadfully hast scourged some of the seditious persons with terrible executions, justly inflicted for their disobedience to thee and to thy servaunt, their Soveraigne, to the example of us all and to the warnyng, correction and amendement of thy servauntes, of thyne accustomed goodnesse, turnyng alwayes the wickednesse of evill men to the profite of them that feare thee, who, in thy judgementes remembring thy mercie, hast by thy assistaunce geven the victorye to thy servaunt our Queene, her true nobilitie and faithful subjectes, with so litle, or rather no effusion of Christian blood, as also myght justlye have ensued, to the exceedyng comfort of all sorowfull Christian heartes, and that of thy fatherly pitie and mercifull goodnesse only, and even for thyne owne names sake, without any our desert at all. Wherefore we render unto thee most humble and hartie thankes for these thy great mercies shewed unto us, who had deserved sharper punishment, most humbly beseching thee to graunt unto all us that confesse thy holy name and professe the true and perfect religion of thy Holye Gospell, thy heavenly grace to shewe our selves in our living accordyng to our profession: that we, truely knowyng thee in thy blessed Word, may obediently walke in thy holy commaundementes, and that we, being warned by this thy fatherly correction, do provoke thy just wrath agaynst us no more, but may enjoy the continuance of thy great mercies towarde us, thy ryght hande, as in this, so in all other invasions, rebellions and daungers, continually saving and defendyng our churche, our realme, our

Queene and people of Englande that all our posterities ensuing, confessing thy holy name, professing thy Holy Gospell, and leadyng an holye lyfe, may perpetually prayse and magnifie thee, with thy onlye Sonne, Jesus Christe our saviour, and the Holy Ghost, to whom be all laude, prayse, glory and empyre for ever and ever. Amen.

NOTES

209　*appointed ... his creator and Lorde*: Pss 97:7, 103:20, and 148:2; Song of the Three Young Men:37; Dan 7:10; Matt 26:53; Col 1:16; Heb 1:4, 14; Rev 19:10.

certaine precept and lawe: Gen 2:17.

denunciation: threatening announcement.

God woulde have man ... subject unto man: Gen 1:28.

kyngdome: sovereignty.

first aucthour: Matt 4:9 and 25:41; John 8:44; 2 Pet 2:4; Jude:6; Rev 12:7.

210　*aucthour*: instigator.

perswadyng ... Adam and Eve: Gen 3:1 etc and Wisd 2:24. The use of 'etc' here and in subsequent notes to this homily reflects its use in the marginal references of the original edition. The homilist supplies specific references for the passages quoted, but suggests with 'etc' that other unspecified biblical passages corroborate his citation.

brought them ... death of their bodyes: Gen 3:8–9 etc, 17, 23, 24.

everlastyng death and dampnation: Rom 5:12 etc, 19 etc.

all and singuler: each and every of.

premises: the foregoing.

by lawes geven unto mankynd: Gen 3:17.

in families and housholdes ... unto their maisters: Gen 3:16; Eph 6:1–5.

largelie: widely.

the residue: the rest.

very many ... places: Job 34:30 (Vg 'Qui regnare facit hominem hypocritam Propter peccata populi') and 36:7; Eccles 8:2 and 10:16–17, 20; Pss 18:50, 20:6, 21:1, and 145:1; Prov 8:15.

211　*the anger and displeasure ... his owne soule*: Prov 19:12, 16:14, and 20:2.

'*Let every soule ... ye owe honour.*': Rom 13:1–7.

'*Submit yourselves ... though they be frowarde.*': 1 Pet 2:13–18.

al maner: the construction, without 'of,' usually takes the plural.

212　*universall Monarche*: Pss 10:16, 45:6 etc, and 47:2.

hath he constitute ... dominions in earth: Sir 17:17.

constitute: a form of the past participle.

sundrye parables ... a kyng: Matt 18:23 and 22:2.

name of the king: Pss 10:16, 45, and 47:2 etc; Matt 22:13 and 25:34.

communicate: bestow in order to share with.

tearming them gods: Ps 82:6.

regiment: reign.

213 '*Well is thee … droughtes.*': Eccles 10:17; Prov 16:15 and 29:4; Isa 32:1–2.

undiscrete: imprudent.

'*Wo be to thee … bankettes.*': Eccles 10:16.

'*When the wicked do raigne … undoeth his subjectes.*': Prov 28:12, 16 and 29:4.

foote … head: proverbial: cf Shakespeare *The Tempest* I.ii.470.

214 *leude*: worthless.

long of: on account of.

maketh a wicked … sinnes of the people: Job 34:30 (Vg 'Qui regnare facit hominem hypocritam Propter peccata populi').

God geveth … in his displeasure: Hos 13:11.

Josias, Kyng Edwarde: See above 21 n 29

contraryly, the Scriptures do teache … loveth hym: 2 Chron 2:11–12 and 9:8, 23; Prov 16:10.

'*If the people … both shall perishe*': 1 Sam 12:14–15, 25.

placeth: appoints.

215 '*The heart of the prince … he turneth it.*': Prov 21:1; Ezra 7:27.

'*I exhort … saviour.*': 1 Tim 2:1–3.

Caligula, Clodius, or Nero: tyrannical Roman emperors, AD 37–41, 41–54, and 54–68 respectively.

'*Pray you … Lord our God.*': Bar 1:11–13 (Vg 'et ut det Dominus virtutem nobis, et illuminet oculos nostros, ut vivamus … et serviamus … et inveniamus gratiam in conspectu').

216 *observed as a great blessing*: Deut 17:15.

estate: property.

218 *consonant*: harmonious.

treatie: treatise.

219 *Kyng Saule … such lenitie*: 1 Sam 15:11, 23, 35.

whiche sinfull humanitie … commaunded of God: Chrysostom *Adversus Judaeos Oratio* 4 1 (PG 48: 873).

how evill soever … out of Gods favour: 1 Sam 16:14–15, 18:10, 12, and 19:9–20.

most valiaunt … in the warres: 1 Sam 17:26 etc, 18:27, 19:5, 8; also 1 Sam 23 and 27.

most obedient … in peace: 1 Sam 16:23; 19:4; 24:9.

sought his destruction and death: 1 Sam 18:9, 25, and 29.

save his lyfe … by flight and hiding: 1 Sam 19:19; also 1 Sam 21 and 22.

into the cave where David was: 1 Sam 24:3–8.

entring … into the tent: 1 Sam 26:6, 9.

'*The Lord keepe me … upon the Lordes anointed.*': 1 Sam 24:4, 6 etc; 1 Sam 26:9–10 etc.

220 *Amalechite … Saules owne bidding*: 2 Sam 1:7, 9.

bringing withall the crowne … and the bracelet: 2 Sam 1:10.

David ... wept: 2 Sam 1:11–12.

'*Howe happened ... the Lordes annoynted.*': 2 Sam 1:13–16.

invading: attacking.

in singuler favour: 1 Sam 18:16, 30.

absolute: disengaged.

by God appoynted to raigne after Saul: 1 Sam 16:12 etc.

David ... in the favour of God: 1 Sam 18:12.

Saul was out of Gods favour: 1 Sam 15:11 and 18:10, 12.

221   *openlye rebuked of Samuel*: 1 Sam 15:19, 22, 26.

unkinde: unnatural.

our Saviour ... playnely taught: Matt 5:44.

estate: welfare.

list: like.

222   *a sort of*: a multitude of.

Princes: Princess.

223   *When proclamation or commaundement ... she obeyed*: Luke 2:1 etc.

unhandsome: unpleasant.

no place in any inne: Luke 2:7.

obedience of the whole Jewish nation: Luke 2:3.

openly dyd teache the Jewes: Matt 17:25 etc; Mark 12:17; Luke 20:25.

Pontius Pilate ... acknowledged his aucthoritie: Matt 27:2; Luke 23:1; John
     19:11.

224   *obeyed paciently the sentence*: Matt 27:26; Luke 23:24.

peculiar: special; appointed.

225   *rebellion ryseth first*: 'The first table of God's law broken by rebellion and
     the sins of rebels against God' (marginal note).

he so straightly commaundeth ... rebellion: Rom 13:1–7.

cut ... as of late ye knowe was done: See J. Raine *Depositions and Other
     Ecclesiastical Proceedings from the Courts of Durham* Surtees Society 21
     (1846) 132–3, 166–70, and 187–8 for the indignities suffered by the service
     books in 1569.

in sunder: apart.

second table: marginal notes refer the reader to the fifth, sixth, eighth,
     seventh, ninth, and tenth commandments, to all of which this paragraph
     alludes.

226   *forceable oppressions*: rapes.

a loft: a form of 'aloft.'

accidentes: accompanying non-essentials, logically distinct from 'substance.'

unthriftie: wanton.

227   *graners*: granaries.

kine: cattle.

stallands: stallions.

pestilence ... lightly can be: 2 Sam 24:13.

appoynted upon for their finding: set aside as their supply for.

let ... from: keep from.

David, judged warre ... pestilence: 2 Sam 24:14.

228 *And therefore our saviour ... divided in it selfe*: Matt 12:25.

229 *shoulde defende the honour of their prince*: Prov 14:28.

overcommed: a form of the past participle.

harrieth: carries off.

Saint Paule sheweth ... the world to come: Rom 13:1–7.

230 *weapon*: the uninflected plural was common before the seventeenth century.

erudition: instruction.

chyldren of Israel: Num 11:1, 12:10, 16:35 and 46–9, 21:5–6, Ps 78:31.

stinged to death: a common phrase, now obsolete.

the earth opening: Num 16:27–34.

quicke: alive.

memory: memento.

their murmure ... God hym selfe also: Exod 16:7.

231 *impes*: evil offspring.

birdes ... bewray them: Eccles 10:20.

the example of Absolon: 2 Sam 15:12, 17:1 etc and 11, 18:7–8.

gave commaundement ... and so hanged him: 2 Sam 18:5, 9.

lapping: wrapping.

document: warning.

haulter: a rope with a noose.

Achitophel ... the mischevous counseller: 2 Sam 15:12, 16:21 and 23, 17:23.

servitour: servant.

captaynes of that rebellion ... in the chase: 2 Sam 18:7–8.

rascall: common.

232 *Seba ... cut of*: 2 Sam 20:1–22.

appeased: pacified.

silie: simple.

counsels ... never toke effect: Ps 21:11 (Vg 20:12 'Cogitaverunt consilia quae non potuerunt stabilire').

Five princes ... delivered them: Gen 14.

frantike: insanely foolish.

Absolon ... sacrificing unto God: 2 Sam 15:12.

233 *meete*: fit.

David ... shed much blood: 2 Chron 22:7–10.

234 *unthriftes*: spendthrifts.

leudely: stupidly.

leude: ignorant.

trowe: think.

mende: aphetic for 'amend.'

route: assemble.

banner displayed to rebellion ... God speede the plough: By displaying the banner depicting the Five Wounds, the rebels recalled its use during both

the Pilgrimage of Grace (1536), the Lincolnshire rising for which 'old
Norton' had marched, and the Western rising, the so-called 'Prayer Book'
rebellion (1549), in the course of which the Devonshire rebels hoisted
such a flag at Fenny Bridge. See J.K. Lowers *Mirrors for Rebels: A Study
of Polemical Literature Relating to the Northern Rebellion in* 1569 University
of California Publications, English Studies 6 (Berkeley: University of
California Press 1953) 30. R.R. Reid, in 'The Rebellion of the Earls, 1569'
TRHS n s 20 (1906), claims that a second group carried an ensign on
which was written 'God speed the plough.' For allusions to the plough
motto, see Thomas Norton's 'To the Quenes Majesties Poor Deceived
Subjects in the North Countrey' (1569) and William Elderton's ballad,
'Prepare Ye the Plough,' both pamphlets inspired by the rising.

235 *Hoc signo vinces*: 'In reporting Constantine's preparation for the battle of
the Milvian bridge, Lactantius claimed (*De morte [persecutorum]*, 44) that
the Emperor saw Christ in a dream and was told to paint on his army's
shields an inverted "X" with one stem curved over ... This formed
the Christian monogram ✝. In the *Vita Constantini* (PL 8: 22), Eusebius
maintains that at noon, before the battle, Constantine and his army,
while he was praying to the god of his father, saw a cross over the sun
with the inscription "In this sign, conquer." That night Christ appeared
to him and told him to paint the cross on the shields of his soldiers.
Eusebius described this sign as the Labarum (used after 325) with the
Chi-Rho monogram ✗' (NCE, sv 'Constantine I, The Great, Roman
Emperor'). The 'fond imitation' of this inscription by the insurgents in
1569 must have been particularly galling inasmuch as Constantine, the
first Christian emperor, was often evoked by protestants as a prefiguration
of Elizabeth.

237 *spirituall*: as opposed to 'temporal.' Here begins the explicit attack on the
papacy.
   Scriptures do teach most expresly: Matt 17:25; Mark 12:17; Luke 20:25; Matt 27;
   Luke 23; Rom 13:1 etc; 1 Tim 2:1–2; 1 Pet 2:13.
   Christe ... confirme the same: John 6:15 and 18:36.
   expresly also forbidding ... nations: Matt 20:25; Mark 10:42; Luke 22:25.
   Peter and Paule ... churche of Christe: Matt 23:8; Luke 9:46; 2 Cor 1:24; 1
   Pet 5:3.

238 *doctrine and example of our Saviour*: Matt 18:4 and 20:28; Luke 9:48 and
   22:27.
   Canon Lawes: 'Totius enim orbis Papa tenet principatum' (*Liber Sextus
   Decretalium* [Venice 1600] 3.16.1, gloss 'Partibus,' page 379); 'Excipitur
   autem civitas Romana ab hac poena: si enim ipsa in hoc puniretur,
   privarentur etiam inferiores ecclesiae: cum totius orbis episcopus sit Ro-
   manus Pontifex' (ibidem 5.9.5, gloss 'Privata,' page 473).
   this ambition entered: the verb is a past participle.
   Christians of the East: Estrangement between Rome and Constantinople

began with the eastern heresies of the fifth and sixth centuries, intensified
during the ninth century, and caused open schism from 1054 onward,
despite attempts at *rapprochement* in 1274 and 1439. See Stephen Runciman
*The Eastern Schism: A Study of the Papacy and the Eastern Churches
during the Eleventh and Twelfth Centuries* (Oxford: Clarendon Press 1955).
translated: transferred.

239 *losses ... in Asia, Africa and Europa*: Cf John Foxe *Christus triumphans* (Basel
1556): 'Now, I, Ecclesia, am left alone with three offspring: Asia, Africa,
and Europe; and in my misery am despoiled of these, whom Nomocrates,
the implacable tyrant, has cast into the most sordid prison' (Quoted in
V.N. Olsen *John Foxe and the Elizabethan Church* [Berkeley: University of
California Press 1973] 61).

Turkes: The Turks took Constantinople in 1453.

histories and chronicles: The homily probably alludes to the same writers
Foxe named: 'besides our Monkes of England (for every Monastery almost had hys Chronicler) I might also recite both Italian, and other
countrey authors as Platina, Sabellicus, Nauclerus, Martinus, Antoninus,
Vincentius, Onuphrius, Laziardus, Georgius Lilius, Pollid. Virgilius,
with many more'; see *The Volume of the Ecclesiastical History* (London
1576) f ii.

drifts: designs.

Italie, Lumbardie, Cicilie: Wedged between Lombardy in the north and
Sicily in the south, the papal state sought to consolidate its power, especially during the twelfth and thirteenth centuries. Innocent III (1198–
1216) was successful in annexing the duchy of Spoleto and the march of
Ancora; he became patron of the league of Tuscan cities and ally of
the Lombard cities, thereby weakening the control of the Hohenstaufen
emperors; he won from Constance, queen of Sicily, recognition of
papal suzerainty. Frederick II (1227–1250) was baffled in his attempts to
reassert imperial claims by popes Gregory IX and Innocent IV.

in capite: from the Latin legal expression *tenere in capite*, which refers to the
tenure of land by the king. The word 'tenant' derives from this phrase.

after this rate: according to this manner of conduct.

oth of fidelity: Although the allusion is purposely vague, it may refer to
Innocent III, who required senators and prefects, for instance, who had
held imperial commissions, to swear oaths of fidelity to him. See A.C.
Flick *The Rise of the Mediaeval Church* (1909; facs repr New York: Burt
Franklin n d) 549. The spectre of *Regnans in excelsis* is behind the
reference, however vague.

240 *after such sort*: in such a way.

ignoraunce of Gods Worde: 'Of ignorance of the simple people. The latter
part' [marginal note].

By ignoraunce ... the deliverie of Barabbas: Matt 27:20; Luke 23:18.

those who crucified hym ... knewe not what they dyd: Luke 23:34; 1 Cor 2:8.

The clause 'if they had known' is the hinge on which much of the following turns: a marginal note says simply *si cognovissent*.

wyst: knew.

Christe hym selfe ... good service: John 15:21 and 16:2–3.

241 *cast images ... out*: 'Gregorius II, and III. Anno Dom. 726 etc.' (marginal
note). During the papacy of Gregory II (715–31), the emperor, Leo
III, led an iconoclastic campaign that included, in 727, the razing of a
depiction of Christ found on the imperial palace. When the pope declared
the emperor's actions heretical, rebellions emerged in northern Italy.
Pope Gregory III (731–41) spoke against iconoclasm at a synod of Italian
bishops held in 731.

bare them in hande: maintained.

holpen: past participle of 'help,' common until the seventeenth century.

heresie ... to this passe: 'Henricus IV. Gregorius VII. Anno Dom. 1076. Pas-
chalis II. Anno 1099' (marginal note). Emperor Henry IV (1056–1106)
clashed with Hildebrand, Pope Gregory VII (1073–85), who as archdeacon
had recommended papal support for William the Conqueror's invasion
of Britain. For defying the pope over the issue of lay investiture, Henry
was excommunicated and ordered deposed; he was absolved only after
his public submission to papal authority at Canossa in 1076. Paschal
II (1099–1118) renewed the papal claims to investiture and helped to per-
petuate the struggle with secular power that was temporarily resolved
by the Concordat of Worms in 1122.

symonie: trading in ecclesiastical preferments, from Simon Magus in Acts
8:18–19.

242 *controlement*: restraint.

paule: pall; the *pallium*, or papal vestment, conferred on all metropolitans.

bulles: papal edicts.

example of our owne countrey: 'King John. Innocentius III. Philip, French
King. Lewes, Dolphin of France. Pandolphus' (marginal note). The
contest between John (1199–1216) and Innocent III (1198–1216) over who
should appoint the archbishop of Canterbury began in 1205. John
chose John de Grey, the bishop of Norwich, to succeed Hubert; the
pope chose Stephen Langton. In 1210, Innocent excommunicated John,
and in 1212 deposed him from the kingship. A year later John bowed
to conditions delivered by Pandulph, the papal legate, which made England a fief of the Roman church. The capitulation proved astute, since
John received papal support two years later when Innocent rejected
the Magna Carta, which the barons had drawn up against their king; the
barons supported Louis, the Dauphin of France, as king of England.
See Sidney Painter *The Reign of King John* (Baltimore: Johns Hopkins
University Press 1949) 151–202; on the evidence for the pope's relieving
subjects of their oaths of fidelity, 187; on the pope's support for a
French invasion of England, 191 n 169. Note that in the homily events

are shaped to highlight papal interference: Innocent is seen as the instigator of the baronial revolt, and the revolt precedes John's submission to Pandulph. A marginal note in Foxe typifies the homily's treatment of this 'most prodigious tumult' (253): 'The pope, author of rebellion & disobedience of subjectes towardes their prince' (255).

243 *stande*: a form of the past participle.

case: plight.

rid them selves ... after: 'See the Acts of Parliament in King Edwarde the Third his days' (marginal note). During the reign of Edward III (1327–77), the 'usurped' power of the papacy was challenged by the Statute of Provisors (1351) and the first and second Statutes of Praemunire (1353, 1365). This legislation, essentially fiscal, resulted from a general belief 'that the revenues which the pope and other foreigners derived from English churches went to sustain the King's enemies abroad.' See May McKisack *The Fourteenth Century* 1307–1399 The Oxford History of England v (Oxford: Clarendon Press 1959) 273 and 280–3.

244 *God doeth curse the blessinges*: Mal 2:2.

late rebellions in the North and West: For introductory accounts of the 'Pilgrimage of Grace' (1536) and the Western Rebellion (1549), see Anthony Fletcher *Tudor Rebellions* (London: Longmans 1968).

Irish patriarkes: The rebellion of Shane O'Neill, 'defensor fidei in partibus Hiberniae,' occurred in 1566–7. According to the English, the *agent provocateur* was Richard Creagh who, when appointed archbishop of Armagh and primate of Ireland by the pope, carried letters to O'Neill that extolled his continuing fidelity to Rome. When Sir Henry Sidney wrote to Elizabeth on 5 March 1570, he advised her to punish Creagh 'and specially his trayterous ayding & assisting the pernicious Rebell Shane O'Nele.' Also suspected of fomenting rebellion was David Wolf, the Jesuit nuncio, who from 1560 was papal legate in Ireland. As early as 1561 Elizabeth complained that he 'had been sent from Rome to Ireland to excite disaffection against her crown.' Wolf was eventually arrested and imprisoned in 1566 (DNB). In 1569, Counter-Reformation activity again emerged when James Fitzmaurice Fitzgerald proclaimed that he was resisting Elizabeth's attempt to foist protestantism on those of the Catholic faith. See R.D. Edwards *Church and State in Tudor Ireland* (1935; repr New York: Russell and Russell 1972) 226–31 and 'Ireland, Elizabeth I and the Counter-Reformation,' in *Elizabethan Government and Society* ed S.T. Bindoff, J. Hurstfield, and C.H. Williams (London: Athlone Press 1961), 315–39; and N.P. Canny *The Elizabethan Conquest of Ireland* (New York: Barnes and Noble 1976) 147–57. Note that the earl of Sussex, who had to contend with the Northern Rebellion, was appointed to the presidency of the North after his resignation from the position of lord-lieutenant of Ireland.

deprehended: detected.

upon confidence: with the expectation.

almost without ... blood: 'Almost,' of course, is a relative term. Grindal reported to Bullinger that the insurrection was curbed 'without bloodshed, except that five hundred of the rebels were afterwards executed' (*Zurich Letters* 332). After examining the papers of Sir George Bowes, H.B. McCall observed that of approximately seven hundred 'appointed' to die, a smaller number 'did directly suffer.' In Richmondshire, where the lists seem complete, 57 died of 215 appointed to die. See 'The Rising in the North: A New Light upon One Aspect of It' *Yorkshire Archaeological Journal* 18 (1905) 74–87. McCall remarks, however, that the queen was 'inexorable, and sent down repeated messages urging severity' (85).

245   *bragge ... no more his priestes*: Jer 18:18; Ezek 7:26; Hos 4:6.

God lykewyse chargeth ... fayle thereof: Ps 2:10–12.

Where is no knowledge ... Holy Worde: Prov 19:2 (Vg 'Ubi non est scientia animae, non est bonum'); Wisd 13:1 (Vg 'Vani autem sunt omnes homines In quibus non subest scientia Dei').

they who walke ... mischiefes: Prov 17:24; Eph 4:17–18; John 12:35.

people of Israel ... captivitie: Isa 5:13.

not knowe the tyme of their visitation: Luke 19:44 and 23:34.

persecuted his holy apostles: 'Actes multis locis' [marginal note].

thought ... acceptable service: John 16:2.

For he that made them ... for their ignoraunce: Isa 27:11; Hos 4:6; Bar 3:10–14, 28.

246   *Holye Scriptures ... saved*: Isa 6:9; Matt 13:14–15; John 12:40.

We have erred ... not knowen: Wisd 5:6–7.

ignoraunce of Gods Word ... eternall damnation: Matt 13:19; 2 Cor 4:3–4; Matt 7:3.

light ... then in the light: John 3:19.

al are commaunded ... yf they so do: Matt 11:15 and 13:9, 43; Luke 8:8; John 5:39; Ps 1:1–3; Matt 7:7; Luke 11:9.

all are charged ... nor to the left: Luke 16:30–1; Gal 1:8; Deut 5:32 (Vg 'Non declinabitis neque ad dexteram, neque ad sinistrum').

In Gods Worde ... their princes: Deut 17:14–15 etc; Rom 13:1–7; 1 Pet 2:13–17.

Old men ... Worde of God: Ps 119:9.

Worde of God ... and steppes: Pss 19:8 (18:9 Vg 'Praeceptum Domini lucidum, illuminans oculos') and 119:105.

awake ... lyght: Eph 5:14; 1 Thess 5:4–6.

let us walke ... enjoy the same: John 12:35–6.

father of lyghtes: James 1:17; 1 Tim 6:16; John 3:19.

TEXTUAL APPARATUS

209 obedience of him, his] obedience of his *B, 1623.* nowe] new *1623.* father of
210 all rebels] father of rebels *1623.* vale of all miserie] vale of miserie *1623.* Thus
you do see] Thus doe you see *1623.* and greatest] and the greatest
211 *1623.* 13] thirteenth *1623.* Peters first Epistle] Peters epistle *1623.* al maner
212 ordinaunce] al maner of ordinaunces *1623.* without such governours]
without governours *1623.* plague he is] plague is he *1623.* by dayly experi-
213 ence] dayly by experience *1623.* furthest] farthest *1623.* gentle and curteous]
214 *B, 1623;* gentle, and curteous *A.* both are rebels] both rebels are *1623.*
215 worse] worst *1623.* it also evident] is also evident *1623.* such an one] such a
one *B, 1623.* part of Christians] part of the Christians *1623.* temple, and] *B,*
216 *1623;* temple, ano *A.* olde Christians] *B, 1623;* olde Christ-stians *A.* and the
destroyers] and destroyers *1623.* shedder of our bloods] shedder of bloods
1623. this government] his government *1623.* her, and shalbe] her
217 shalbe *1623.* expressed or uttered] expressed and uttered *1623.* us all make
continuall] *B;* us all make continnall *A;* us make continuall *1623.* King
218 of all kinges] King of kinges *1623.* Amen] *omitted B.* The prayer] The Prayer,
as in that time it was published *1623.* charge, and especially at this tyme,
O] *A;* charge. O *B;* charge, O *1623.* region] realm *1623.* The seconde part]
219 *omitted 1623.* same Holy Scriptures] *B, 1623;* same holy sriptures *A.* in
220 the warres] *B, 1623;* iu the warres *A.* and a fearce] and fearce *1623.* Philis-
tines] Philistims *1623.* commaunded] *B, 1623;* commaundyng *A.* daungers]
221 daunger *B, 1623.* in singuler] in a singuler *1623.* hazarding] harzarding *B.*
222 kyll or depose] kyll and depose *1623.* lustie, as] lustie and *1623.* eyther in
warre by lawfull enemies, not by trayterous subjectes, or by naturall death]
eyther by naturall death or in warre ... subjectes *B, 1623.* to pray also]
also to pray *1623.* to put in feare, or to depose or destroy] either to depose,
to put in feare or to destroy *1623.* Princes] Prince *1623.* who so] whoso
1623. they who] they, which *1623.* expresse with wordes] expresse
223 worth wordes *B.* tediousnesse of the journey] tedious journey *1623.* un-
224 handsome] unfit *1623.* yet we accompt] we yet account *1623.* many other]
many and divers other *1623.* unavoydably] *B, 1623;* unadvoydably *A.*   The
prayer: as before] The Prayer as in that time it was published *the complete*
prayer, as printed after Part One, follows 1623. The thirde part] *omitted*
225 *1623.* abominable worke] abominable worste *1623.* be all contayned] be
226 contayned *1623.* disherite] disinherite *1623.* blood but of few] blood but of a
few *1623.* Gods lawes] good lawes *1623.* presumption] *A, 1623;* presumtion
227 *B.* graners] garners *1623.* stallands or horses] *A, 1623;* allandes o r horses *B.*
before, whiche abuse] before) abuse *1623.* that all sinnes] that sinnes *1623.*
lightly] likely *1623.* miseries whiche] miseries that *1623.* wethers] weather
1623. kindes of sicknesse] kindes of sicknesses *1623.* grow upon and amongst]
grow upon and spring amongst *1623.* al other sicknesse] al other sickenesses

228 *1623.* name of] *A, 1623;* nam eof *B.* abomination ... selfe. Nowe as] *B, 1623;*
abomination. And as *A.* many wealthie] many very wealthie *1623.*
deflowred: thinges] deflowred: which thinges *B, 1623.* any our countreymen]
any of our countreymen *1623.* with losse] with the losse *1623.* disherite]
229 disinherite *1623.* calamities] calamitie *1623.* of the money] of money *1623.*
murthering of the people] murthering the people *1623.* handes of forraigne]
handes of the forraigne *1623.* wynneth] win *1623.* dyeth] die *1623.* and
their countrey] and countrey *1623.* heades] handes *1623.* harrieth] hurrieth
230 *1623.* The prayer: as before] The Prayer as in that time it was published *the
complete prayer, as printed after Part One, follows 1623.* The fourth part]
omitted 1623. against such subjectes] against subjectes *1623.* withstanded]
231 withstood *1623.* or speaking] and speaking *1623.* Scriptures howe that]
233 Scriptures, show that *1623.* shoulde so require] so shoulde require *B.* such
234 men and by] such men by *1623.* possiblie] possible *1623.* mende] amende
1623. rebelles beare ... folowe] *B, 1623;* rebelles litle knowing what the
crosse of Christe meaneth, which neither carver nor paynter can make, do
beare the image of the crosse paynted in a ragge, against those that have
the crosse of Christe printed in their heartes: though they beare the picture
of the five wounds paynted, against those who put their only hope of
salvation in the woundes of Christe, not those wounds which are painted
in a cloute by some leude paynter, but in those woundes whiche Christe
hym selfe bare in his pretious body: yet let no good and godly subject
235 folowe ... *A.* later] latter *1623.* the dreadfull] dreadfull *1623.* The prayer: as
236 before] The Prayer as in that time it was published *the complete prayer, as
printed after Part One, follows 1623.* The fifth part] *omitted 1623.* nowe to
declare] *B, 1623;* nowe lastly to declare *A, the homily then consisting of just
five parts.* so escape] to escape *1623.* deathes] death *1623.* due to all rebels.
¶Though] *B, 1623;* rebels, and embrasing all obedience to God and your
natural princes, may enjoy Gods blessinges and your princes favour in
all peace, quietnes and securitie in this world, and finally attaine through
Christe our saviour lyfe everlasting in the worlde to come: and so to
conclude this whole treatie of due obedience, and agaynst dampnable rebellion. ¶Though *A, the homily then consisting of just five parts.* sciences]
237 siences *A.* as the roote] as beeing the roote *1623.* be the usuall] be usuall
1623. damage] domage *B, 1623.* apostle] apostles *1623.* before others] before
238 other *1623.* humbling of them] humbling them *1623.* all the kyngdomes] all
kyngdomes *1623.* this ambition] his ambition *B, 1623.* amongst others]
amongst other *B, 1623.* when the Bishoppes] *B, 1623;* when the byshop *A.*
othes] othe *B.* lordes, by the Byshoppes] *B, 1623;* lordes, by the Byshop
239 *A.* Christian] *B, 1623;* Christ ian *A.* paganitie] paganisme *1623.* is well
knowen] aswell knowen *1623.* by the joyning] by joyning *1623.* lordes
thereof.] lordes thereof, in which tenure they hold the most part thereof,
even at this day *1623.* By these ambitious] But these ambitious *1623.*
Emperours, usually ... Amen] *B, 1623, the added matter preparing for the sixth*

240   part of the homily; Emperours. *A*. Thus have you ... pray.] *1623; omitted
      A*; ... the sixt part ... *B*. The prayer, as before] *B; omitted A*; The Prayer as
      in that time it was published *the complete prayer, as printed after Part
      One, follows 1623*. The Sixt ... Rebellion] *B, 1623; omitted A*. The sixt part]
      B; omitted A, 1623. Now whereas ... intollerable] *B, 1623*; Nowe where these
      things were intollerable *A*. countrey, it remayneth ... ¶You shall under-
      stande] *B*; countrey. It remayneth ... understande *1623*; countrey: you shall
      understande *A*. all they sayde] all that they sayde *1623*. aske the
241   deliverie] as ke the deliverie *1623*. by the withdrawyng] by withdrawyng *1623*.
242   depose] *A, 1623*; dispose *B*. a Romishe ragge] the Romishe ragge *1623*.
      deposed] desposed *1623*. lordes, the Emperours] lordes and Emperours *1623*.
      hym, the Byshop] hym the byshops *B, 1623*. manye of the] *B*; meanie of
244   the *A*; many of *1623*. othe of fidelitie] othe and fidelitie *1623*. deprehended]
      apprehended *1623*. being men most] being then most *1623*. and their
      prince] and to their prince *1623*. but some other] *1623*; by some other *A, B*.
245   to the oppressing] to oppressing *1623*. or so troubled] or troubled *1623*. out
      of histories] out of the histories *1623*. of the olde] of olde *1623*. paganitie]
      Paganisme *1623*. begyn with the cleargie] begyn with the romish cleargie *B,
      1623*. the holy temple] the temple *1623*. miserable] *B, 1623*; miser-
247   ale *A*. Thus have you hearde ... pray.] *B, 1623; omitted A*. The prayer as
      before] *omitted A*; The Prayer as in that time it was published *the complete
      prayer, as printed after Part One, follows 1623*. flee] flie *1623*. justlye have]
      have justly *1623*.